CW00338102

DISCOVERING MATHEMATICS

1A

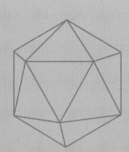

Victor Chow

UK Consultant: Robert Wilne

Singapore Consultant: Berinderjeet Kaur

OXFORD
UNIVERSITY PRESS

OXFORD
UNIVERSITY PRESS

Great Clarendon Street, Oxford, OX2 6DP, United Kingdom

Oxford University Press is a department of the University of Oxford. It furthers the University's objective of excellence in research, scholarship, and education by publishing worldwide. Oxford is a registered trade mark of Oxford University Press in the UK and in certain other countries.

British Library Cataloguing in Publication Data

Data available

978-0-19-842172-6

1 3 5 7 9 10 8 6 4 2

Paper used in the production of this book is a natural, recyclable product made from wood grown in sustainable forests. The manufacturing process conforms to the environmental regulations of the country of origin.

Printed in Great Britain by Bell and Bain Ltd, Glasgow

Acknowledgements

The author and publishers would like to thank the reviewer team of **consultants** – Robert Wilne, Naomi Norman, Simon d'Angelo, Liz Henning, Ann Lui, Berinderjeet Kaur, Ling San – and **teachers** – Pippa Baker, Jill Borcherds, Lana Laidler, Fiona Goddard, Jo Walker, Andrea Wickham and Katie Wood – who have advised on the content of this book. Their contributions have been invaluable.

Editorial team: Dom Holdsworth, Julie Thornton, Sarah Dutton and Matteo Orsini Jones.

With thanks also to Rosie Day, Katherine Bird, Phil Gallagher and Fiona Eadie for their contributions.

The publishers would like to thank the following for permission to use copyright material:

Photos: p3: Predrag Popovski/Shutterstock; **p5:** naipung/Shutterstock; **p9:** Ewelina Wachala/Shutterstock; **p28:** Brian A Jackson/Shutterstock; **p30:** daseaford/Shutterstock; **p32 (T):** gunungkawi/Shutterstock; **p32 (B):** Robert Spriggs/Shutterstock; **p45 (T):** James Kennedy NI/Shutterstock; **p45 (B):** Linda Bestwick/Shutterstock; **p49:** Creatsy/Shutterstock; **p55:** imstock/Shutterstock; **p60:** lkpro/Shutterstock; **p69:** Gameface Media/Virgin sport; **p91:** Daniel Krason/Shutterstock; **p93:** goodluz/Shutterstock; **p99:** Sean Locke Photography/Shutterstock; **p106:** CosminIftode/Shutterstock; **p108:** Peter Gudella/Shutterstock; **p109 (L):** Gregory June/Shutterstock; **109 (R):** Emily Lai/Alamy Stock Photo; **p110:** ALPA PROD/Shutterstock; **p112, p113 (MR) & p121:** Africa Studio/Shutterstock; **p113 (M):** adidas4747/Shutterstock; **p113 (BL):** indigolotos/Shutterstock; **p113 (BR):** cristi180884/Shutterstock; **p114:** Monkey Business Images/Shutterstock; **p31 & p32:** poWAzNiAKi/Shutterstock; **p116:** Adam Gilchrist/Shutterstock; **p116 (TR):** Aquila/Shutterstock; **p116 (M):** Gelpi/Shutterstock; **p116 (B):** mareandmare/Shutterstock; **p119:** Gemenacom/Shutterstock; **p120 (L):** Coprid/Shutterstock; **p120 (R):** Happy monkey/Shutterstock; **p123 (R):** sawaddeebenz/Shutterstock; **p122 & p123 (L):** sawaddeebenz/Shutterstock; **p127:** Moving Moment/Shutterstock; **p127:** akiyoko/Shutterstock; **p138:** Bozena Fulawka/Shutterstock; **p141 (T):** OKAWA PHOTO/Shutterstock; **p141 (B):** Diana Taliun/Shutterstock; **p143 (T):** Sakarin Sawasdinaka/Shutterstock; **p143 (B):** Apl56/Shutterstock; **p143 (B):** Adam Gilchrist/Shutterstock; **p145:** whitemay/iStock; **p147 (T):** Eric Isselee/Shutterstock; **p147 (BL):** Alzay/Shutterstock; **p147 (BR):** Pavel L Photo and Video/Shutterstock; **p148, p150:** Olga Kovalenko/Shutterstock; **p153:** Francesco83/Shutterstock; **p168 (L):** pongsakorn chaina/Shutterstock; **p168 (R):** gst/Shutterstock; **p180:** Dutourdumonde Photography/Shutterstock; **p182 (TR):** Lianella/Shutterstock; **p182 (TL):** Anna Rassadnikova/Shutterstock; **p182 (BL):** Happy monkey/Shutterstock; **p182 (BR):** Africa Studio/Shutterstock; **p183 (ML, R):** ArchMan/Shutterstock; **p183 (L, MR):** Gravicapa/Shutterstock; **p186 (T):** LanKS/Shutterstock; **p186 (B):** clearviewstock/Shutterstock; **p187 (T):** nimon/Shutterstock; **p187 (BL):** hursina Viktoriia/Shutterstock; **p187 (BR):** Chursina Viktoriia/Shutterstock; **p188:** bajinda/Shutterstock; **p192:** Thaiview/Shutterstock; **p195:** Dlart/Shutterstock; **p199 (L):** Vitaly Raduntsev/Shutterstock; **p199 (M):** tristan tan/Shutterstock; **p199 (R):** yuri4u80/Shutterstock; **p201:** Tom K Photo/Shutterstock; **p208 (L):** Vangert/Shutterstock; **p208 (R):** Naparat/Shutterstock; **p209:** Y Photo Studio/Shutterstock;

p1, p218: Losev Artyom/Shutterstock; **p220, p221, p222, p224, p225, p226, p231, p238, p345:** Yulia Glam/Shutterstock; **p223 (B), p231 (BR):** SvitlanaNiko/Shutterstock; **p228:** Peter Gudella/Shutterstock; **p229:** Bobkeenan Photography/Shutterstock; **p231 (TL):** Duda Vasilii/Shutterstock; **p231 (TML):** xpixel/Shutterstock; **p231 (TR):** Jim Barber/Shutterstock; **p231 (TML):** Duda Vasilii/Shutterstock; **p237 (T):** ronstik/Shutterstock; **p237 (M):** Geolilli/Shutterstock; **p237 (B):** Terdsak bundi/Shutterstock; **p219, p239:** Dimedrol68/Shutterstock; **p241 (T):** Leftleg/Shutterstock; **p241 (B):** donatas1205/Shutterstock; **p242:** Nicole Kwiatkowski/Shutterstock; **p244 (T):** Ivan Ponomarev/Shutterstock; **p244 (MR):** chutima kuanamon/Shutterstock; **p244 (ML):** Marco Uliana/Shutterstock; **p244 (BL):** desertfox99/Shutterstock; **p244 (BR):** Max Maier/Shutterstock; **p249 (TL & TM):** art designer/Shutterstock; **p253 (BL), p254 (T):** binik/Shutterstock; **p253 (BM), p254 (M):** MSSA/Shutterstock; **p255 (L):** Alexey Kljatov/Shutterstock; **p255 (R):** Christos Georghiou/Shutterstock; **p256 (L):** Roman Sotola/Shutterstock; **p256 (M):** Becky Stares/Shutterstock; **p256 (R):** notbad/Shutterstock; **p258 (L):** Phatthanit/Shutterstock; **p258 (M):** LiukasArt/Shutterstock; **p258 (R):** Igor Kovalchuk/Shutterstock; **p259 (L):** Pro Symbols/Shutterstock; **p259 (M):** Standard Studio/Shutterstock; **p259 (R):** Martial Red/Shutterstock; **p260:** wavebreakmedia/Shutterstock; **p270 (T):** EFKS/Shutterstock; **p270 (M):** Dream Expander/Shutterstock; **p270 (B):** RadheStudio/Shutterstock; **p288:** NASA; **p290 (a):** Jo Ann Snover/Shutterstock; **p290 (b):** Andrei_M/Shutterstock; **p290 (c):** Fetullah Mercan/Shutterstock; **p290 (d):** avian/Sutterstock; **p290 (e):** pramot/Shutterstock; **p290 (f):** Michael Krumin/Shutterstock; **p295 (a):** paseven/Shutterstock; **p295 (b):** Gts/Shutterstock; **p295 (c):** Zonda/Shutterstock; **p295 (d):** phive/Shutterstock; **p295 (e):** DenisMArt/Shutterstock; **p301 (M):** Mariyana M/Shutterstock; **p301 (R):** graja/Shutterstock; **p301 (L):** CWIS/Shutterstock; **p305:** Gts/Shutterstock; **p309 (L):** optimarc/Shutterstock; **p309 (R):** PeterVrabel/Shutterstock; **p311:** inewsfoto/Shutterstock; **p312 (L):** Corinna Haselmayer/Shutterstock; **p312 (R):** Valentin Agapov/Shutterstock; **p314:** sjenner13/iStock; **p319, p341:** domnitsky/Shutterstock; **p320, p321 (T):** AndriyA/Shutterstock; **p321:** Pixfiction/Shutterstock; **p333:** siamionau pavel/Shutterstock; **p350:** fizkes/Shutterstock; **p351 (TL):** NeMaria/Shutterstock; **p351 (TR):** cherezoff/Shutterstock; **p351 (B):** canon_shooter/Shutterstock; **p352 (T):** cynoclub/Shutterstock; **p352 (B):** Vilor/Shutterstock; **p353:** ArsenLuben/Shutterstock; **p354 (T):** Awe Inspiring Images/Shutterstock; **p354 (M):** Thomson; **p354 (B):** David Ross/BritainExpress.com; **p356 (T):** Predrag Popovski/Shutterstock; **p356 (M):** Minhaj Ahmed Rafi/Shutterstock; **p356 (B):** Chris Curtis/Shutterstock; **p357 (T):** urbanbuzz/Shutterstock; **p357 (B):** Chrislofotos/Shutterstock;

Artworks: Thomson

Cover: Steve Bloom Images/Alamy Stock Photo

Although we have made every effort to trace and contact all copyright holders before publication this has not been possible in all cases. If notified, the publisher will rectify any errors or omissions at the earliest opportunity.

Links to third party websites are provided by Oxford in good faith and for information only. Oxford disclaims any responsibility for the materials contained in any third party website referenced in this work.

CONTENTS

ABOUT THIS BOOK

This book has been written by an experienced author and reviewed by a team of maths consultants and practising teachers. It is based on the top-selling Singaporean maths series and has been adapted carefully to make it suitable for the English National Curriculum, Year 7. It is advisable to use Workbook 1A alongside this book to support your learning. The features and exercises have been designed to help you discover the underlying principles of mathematics and to set you on the road to mastery.

Every chapter starts with an example of how the maths you will learn can be related to real life. This is supported by a **video on the digital book** on Kerboodle.

Flashback is a reminder of what you should already know. Revise this content to prepare to build your knowledge.

Learning objectives at the beginning of the chapter tell you what you will learn.

At the end of every chapter, **Review** summarises the key learning points that have been covered. This can be used for revision.

At the end of every chapter, **Write in Your Journal** sections encourage you to reflect on your learning.

The information and tables in **Number Hacks** at the back of the book are to help you with the calculations in the questions and activities in this book, and when you are doing homework.

You will be told when you should or shouldn't use a calculator. If there is no instruction, you can decide yourself or ask your teacher.

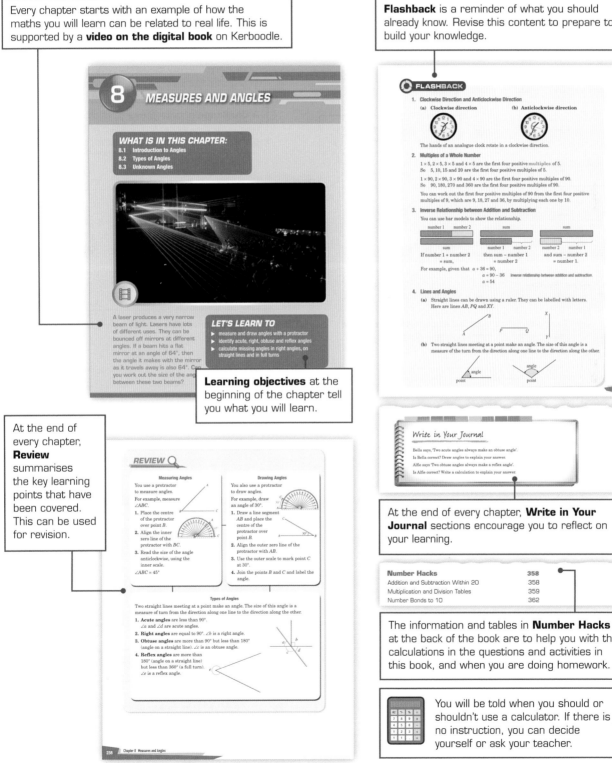

Class activities are led by the teacher and allow the whole class to learn through discovery and exploration.

Worked examples show how ideas and reasoning can be expressed using precise mathematical language. Every worked example is followed by a **Try It!** to practise what you have learnt. Key Try It! questions have a video in the digital book on Kerboodle – these show you step-by-step, narrated model answers.

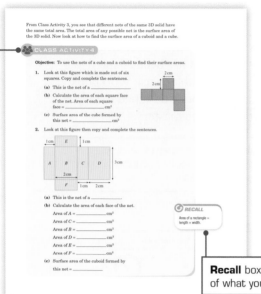

Remark boxes explain common misconceptions and provide extra hints.

Discuss boxes encourage paired and group working.

Recall boxes remind you of what you already know.

A **Challenge** activity in every chapter allows you to develop a deeper understanding of topics. It is also a chance to practise your problem-solving skills.

Assessment occurs regularly to make sure you understand concepts as you go along. Further assessment can be found on Kerboodle.

Problem solving is highlighted in all exercises. Two extra problem-solving sections are also included giving advice on how to approach problem solving, and providing practice of problems in real-life situations.

PROBLEM SOLVING

CHALLENGE 6

In a flowerbed, 0.3 of the flowers are red and $\frac{7}{25}$ are yellow. The rest are pink. Find the percentage of pink flowers in the flowerbed.

Workbook 1A Link
Problem Solving 6

Workbook 1A Links show you when to turn to these extra exercises and activities.

Every chapter section ends with a Practice exercise to assess understanding:

A **Revision Exercise** at the end of every chapter allows revision of concepts:

Questions step up in difficulty from **Level 1** to **2**.

Science and **Finance** contexts are marked.

Open Questions show that more than one answer is possible.

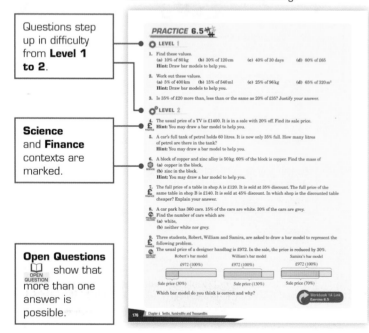

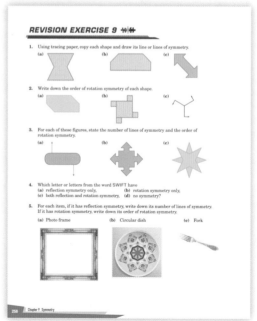

Integrated Examples appear after several chapters to help make connections between different topics. These are each followed by a **Review Exercise** to check on your mastery of concepts.

For additional practice and support on any topic, ask your teacher for the **MyMaths links**, which are provided in the accompanying Teacher Guide.

1 ADDING AND SUBTRACTING WHOLE NUMBERS

WHAT IS IN THIS CHAPTER:

Bethan has £50. She wants to buy a jacket for £37 and a t-shirt for £14. Does she have enough money to buy both items? If she just buys the jacket, how much money will she have left? How do you get your answers?

LET'S LEARN TO

▶ state the place values of the digits in whole numbers
▶ order and compare whole numbers
▶ add and subtract whole numbers, using different methods by hand
▶ recognise and use the inverse relationship between addition and subtraction
▶ use addition and subtraction to solve real-life problems

1. The numbers 0, 1, 2, 3, 4, ... , 99, 100, ... are called **whole numbers**.
   Each whole number is formed by the **digits** 0, 1, 2, 3, 4, 5, 6, 7, 8 and 9.

   The numbers 0, 2, 4, 6, 8, ... are called **even numbers**.
   The numbers 1, 3, 5, 7, 9, ... are called **odd numbers**.

   The value of each digit in a whole number is determined by its **place value**. You can show this on a place value table.

Place value	Thousands 1000	Hundreds 100	Tens 10	Ones 1
Number	7	3	0	8

The number $7308 = 7 \times 1000 \quad + \quad 3 \times 100 \quad + \quad 0 \times 10 \quad + \quad 8 \times 1$
i.e. $\qquad 7308 = \quad 7000 \qquad + \qquad 300 \qquad + \qquad 0 \qquad + \qquad 8$

This is read as seven thousand, three hundred and eight.

Note that zero, 0, is used as a **place holder** for the Tens place. Without it, you would not be able to tell 7308 and 738 apart.

2. Addition

Addition is the process of finding the total (or the **sum**) of two or more numbers.
e.g. $5 + 9 = 14$ means the sum of 5 and 9 is 14. The '+' is called the **addition sign**.

Addition can be carried out using place value counters on a place value table. The ones counters, tens counters and so on are added in order. Take for example the sum $36 + 21$.

Here, $36 = 30 + 6$
$\qquad = 3$ tens $+ 6$ ones.

You place 3 tens counters in the 'Tens' column and 6 ones counters in the 'Ones' column. Do the same for the number 21.

	Tens	Add the tens counters.	Ones	Add the ones counters.
36	10 10 10		1 1 1 1 1 1	
21	10 10		1	
36 + 21	10 10 10 10 10		1 1 1 1 1 1 1	This row shows that the answer is $50 + 7 = 57$.

Using the **column method**, two numbers must be lined up using their place values. Then the digits with the same place value are added.

e.g.
$$\begin{array}{r} 36 \\ + 21 \\ \hline 57 \end{array}$$

In the Ones place, $6 + 1 = 7$.
In the Tens place, $3 + 2 = 5$.
$36 + 21 = 57$

3. Subtraction

Subtraction is the process of taking a number away from another number.

e.g. $13 - 8 = 5$ means the difference between 13 and 8 is 5. The '−' is called the subtraction sign.

Subtraction can also be carried out using place value counters on a place value table. The ones counters, tens counters, and so on, of the second number are taken away from the first number in order. Take for example the subtraction $45 - 13$.

	Tens		Ones	
45	⑩ ⑩ ⑩ ⑩	Take away the tens counter of 13: ⑩	① ① ① ① ①	Take away the ones counters of 13: ① ① ①
45 − 13	⑩ ⑩ ⑩		① ①	

Using the column method, two numbers must be lined up using their place values. Then the digits with the same place value are subtracted.

e.g.
$$\begin{array}{r} 45 \\ -\ 13 \\ \hline 32 \end{array}$$
In the Ones place, $5 - 3 = 2$.
In the Tens place, $4 - 1 = 3$.
$45 - 13 = 32$

1.1   Place Values and Order of Numbers

A   Place Values

What does the digit 7 in the number 75 653 mean?

The place of each digit in a number tells us what the digit represents.

75 653 spectators can fit into Old Trafford stadium.

Ten thousands 10 000	Thousands 1000	Hundreds 100	Tens 10	Ones 1
7	5	6	5	3

From the place value table, you see that
$$75\,653 = 7 \times 10\,000\ +\ 5 \times 1000\ +\ 6 \times 100\ +\ 5 \times 10\ +\ 3 \times 1$$

This is called the expanded form of the number.

The digit 7 is in the Ten thousands place, so the value it represents is 70 000 or seventy thousand (7 ten thousands).

The digit 5 is in two different places. It represents two different values.

The digit 5 in the Thousands place represents the value 5000 (5 thousands).

The digit 5 in the Tens place represents the value 50 (5 tens).

You read 75 653 as seventy-five thousand, six hundred and fifty-three.

RECALL

The equals sign '=' means that the value on the left of the sign is the same as the value on the right of the sign.

DISCUSS

What do the digits 6 and 3 represent in this number?

Example 1

(a) Write the number 30 912 in expanded form.

(b) What is the place value of the digit 9?

(c) What value does the digit 9 represent?

Solution

(a) $30\,912 = 3 \times 10\,000 + 9 \times 100 + 1 \times 10 + 2 \times 1$

(b) The digit 9 is in the Hundreds place.
Its place value is hundreds.

(c) The digit 9 represents the value 900.

DISCUSS

Can you write 30 912 as 3912? What is the purpose of the zero, 0, in the number 30 912?

Try It! 1

(a) Write the number 28 054 in expanded form.

(b) What is the place value of the digit 8?

(c) What value does the digit 8 represent?

Example 2

Look at the number 35 649.

(a) Which digit represents the highest value?
What is this value?

(b) Which digit represents the lowest value?
What is this value?

Solution

(a) The digit 3 is the first digit from the left.
It represents the highest value.
The value of the digit 3 in this number is 30 000.

(b) The digit 9 is the last digit from the left.
It represents the lowest value.
The value of the digit 9 in this number is 9.

REMARK

The value represented by a digit in a number depends on its place value in the number.

Try It! 2

Look at the number 6238.

(a) Which digit represents the highest value?
What is this value?

(b) Which digit represents the lowest value?
What is this value?

B Order of Numbers

Numbers can be represented by points on a **number line**.

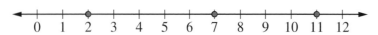

On the number line, a number is less than any number to its right. The signs '<' and '>' are called **inequality signs**. '<' means 'less than' and '>' means 'greater than'.

e.g.   2 is less than 7 and this is written as 2 < 7.

e.g.   7 is less than 11 and this is written as 7 < 11.

REMARK

The other two inequality signs are '≤', which means 'less than or equal to', and '≥', which means 'greater than or equal to'. You'll learn more about these later in this book.

A number is greater than any number to its left.

e.g.   7 is greater than 2 and this is written as 7 > 2.

e.g.   11 is greater than 2 and this is written as 11 > 2.

In this book, you will only use numbers and number lines with positive values. You'll then begin to explore negative numbers in Student Book 2A.

CLASS ACTIVITY 1

Objective: To write an inequality between two numbers and represent it on a number line.

1. **(a)** Copy this number line. Complete the missing numbers.

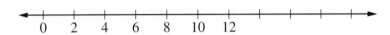

    (b) Which number, 4 or 12, is greater? Explain your answer.

    (c) Name a number on the line that is greater than 10.

2. **(a)** Copy this number line. Complete the missing numbers.

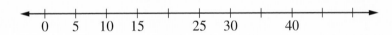

    (b) Which number, 15 or 40, is smaller? Explain your answer.

    (c) Name a number on the line that is smaller than 25.

3. **(a)** In a car boot sale, book A costs 15p and book B costs 48p. Which book has the lower price?

    (b) Copy the number line and plot the points representing the numbers 15 and 48.

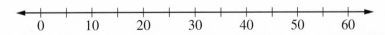

    (c) Copy and complete 15 ▢ 48 using the inequality sign '<' or '>'.

4. **(a)** A bottle of milk is 280 ml. A cup of coffee is 125 ml. Which drink has the larger volume?

    (b) Copy the number line and plot the points representing the numbers 125 and 280.

    (c) Copy and complete 280 ▢ 125 using the inequality sign '<' or '>'.

Instead of a number line, you can compare two numbers using place values.

Example 3

Copy and complete each statement with the inequality sign '<' or '>'. Explain your reasoning in full sentences.

(a) 3271 ⬚ 465

(b) 84 325 ⬚ 84 907

Solution

(a) 3 in 3271 represents the value 3000.
4 in 465 represents the value 400.
As 3000 is greater than 400,
this means 3271 > 465.

Compare the digits representing the highest value in each number.

(b) The digit 8 in both numbers represents 80 000.
You cannot tell which number is smaller by looking at the first digit.
The digit 4 in both numbers represents 4000.
You still cannot tell which number is smaller.
The third highest value digit of 84 325 is 3, which represents 300.
The third digit of 84 907 is 9, which represents 900.
As 300 < 900, this means 84 325 < 84 907.

Try It! 3

Copy and fill in each blank with the inequality sign '<' or '>'. Explain your reasoning in full sentences.

(a) 731 ⬚ 4265

(b) 95 387 ⬚ 95 360

PRACTICE 1.1

LEVEL 1

1. Put these numbers in a place value table using counters. Then write the numbers out in expanded form.
    (a) 328
    (b) 3280
    (c) 32 800
    (d) 30 028

2. Write down the value represented by the digit 3 in each number. Use place value counters to help you.
    (a) 937
    (b) 9703
    (c) 37 900
    (d) 73 090

3. Make and draw these numbers on a place value table. Which of the numbers represents seven thousand and four?

   704   7400   7004   7040

4. Here is a list of numbers:

   6023,   8416,   162,   61 999,   35 679.
   (a) In which number does the digit 6 represent the lowest value? What is this value?
   (b) In which number does the digit 6 represent the highest value? What is this value?

5. Copy and fill in each blank with '<' or '>'. Use a place value table or draw a number line for each part to help you.
   (a) 138 ▨ 38   (b) 7326 ▨ 7845
   (c) 4607 ▨ 4670   (d) 29 731 ▨ 29 751

6. Here is a list of numbers:

   30 007,   38 970,   38 030,   30 907,   30 070,   38 709.
   Write down the numbers that are
   (a) less than 30 709,   (b) less than 37 000,
   (c) greater than 35 000,   (d) greater than 38 500.

⚙ LEVEL 2

7. The floor area of Buckingham Palace is 77 000 m².
   (a) Write 77 000 in expanded form.
   (b) What is the value represented by the first digit 7?

8. The price of a car is £25 639.
   £ (a) State the digit which represents the greatest value.
   FINANCE (b) What is the value of this digit?

9. Isaac is 175 cm tall, Ben is 164 cm tall and Karim is 173 cm tall. Write the names of the boys in order from the shortest to the tallest.
   PROBLEM SOLVING

10. Write down a 5-digit number such that the values of two of its digits represent 80 000 and 20.
   OPEN QUESTION

Workbook 1A Link
Exercise 1.1

1.2 Addition

Anna has a part-time job. She earns £238 in the first week and £167 in the second week. How much does she earn in these two weeks?

The sum she earns in two weeks = £238 + £167.

Let's see how to work out the sum using place value counters. The table below represents the numbers 238 and 167 using place value counters.

	Hundreds	Tens	Ones
238	(100) (100)	10 10 10	1 1 1 1 1 1 1 1
167	(100)	10 10 10 10 10 10	1 1 1 1 1 1 1

First, work out the sum of ones.

$$8 \text{ ones} + 7 \text{ ones} = 15 \text{ ones}$$
$$= 10 \text{ ones} + 5 \text{ ones}$$
$$= 1 \text{ ten} + 5 \text{ ones}$$

The 'Ones' column can only have up to 9 ones. So regroup 10 ones counters to 1 tens counter and put it in the 'Tens' column. Place the 5 ones in an addition row below.

REMARK

You can use the addition table on page 358 to check that 8 + 7 = 15.

	Hundreds	Tens	Ones
238	(100) (100)	10 10 10	1 1 1 1 1 1 1 1
167	(100)	10 10 10 10 10 10	1 1 1 1 1 1 1
238 + 167			1 1 1 1 1
Regroup		10	

Next, work out the sum of tens.

$$3 \text{ tens} + 6 \text{ tens} + 1 \text{ ten} = 10 \text{ tens}$$
$$= 1 \text{ hundred and } 0 \text{ tens}$$

Regroup 10 tens counters to 1 hundreds counter and put it in the 'Hundreds' column.

	Hundreds	Tens	Ones
238	100 100	10 10 10	1 1 1 1 / 1 1 1 1
167	100	10 10 10 10 10 10	1 1 1 1 / 1 1 1
238 + 167			1 1 1 1 1
Regroup	100	10	

Finally work out the sum of hundreds.

2 hundreds + 1 hundred + 1 hundred = 4 hundreds.

Place this in the addition row.

	Hundreds	Tens	Ones
238	100 100	10 10 10	1 1 1 1 / 1 1 1 1
167	100	10 10 10 10 10 10	1 1 1 1 / 1 1 1
238 + 167	100 100 100 100		1 1 1 1 1
Regroup	100	10	

Finally, look at the number of counters in the addition row.

This gives $238 + 167 = 400 + 5$

$= 405.$

Anna earns £405 in the two weeks.

In the **column method**, align the two numbers in columns by their place values. Add the digits in each column from right to left and regroup as shown below.

$$
\begin{array}{r}
238 \\
+\ 167 \\
\hline
405 \\
\hline
{\scriptstyle 1\ 1}
\end{array}
$$

8 ones + 7 ones = 15 ones = 1 ten + 5 ones.

3 tens + 6 tens + 1 ten = 10 tens = 1 hundred.

2 hundreds + 1 hundred + 1 hundred = 4 hundreds.

REMARK

10 tens = 1 hundred + 0 tens. Remember to add 0 as a place holder in the tens column.

Objective: To develop knowledge of addition.

1. Work out the sum $48 + 75$ using

   (a) place value counters,　　(b) the column method.

2. Work out the sum $216 + 397$ using

   (a) place value counters,　　(b) the column method.

3. Which method is easier to understand? What's the same and what's different between the two?

Example 4　　Calculate $934 + 87$.

Solution

$$
\begin{array}{r}
934 \\
+\ \ 87 \\
\hline
1021 \\
\hline
{\scriptstyle 1\ 1\ 1}
\end{array}
$$

4 ones + 7 ones = 11 ones = 1 ten + 1 one.

3 tens + 8 tens + 1 ten = 12 tens = 1 hundred + 2 tens.

9 hundreds + 1 hundred = 10 hundreds = 1 thousand.

$\therefore\ 934 + 87 = 1021$

> **REMARK**
>
> The symbol $\therefore$ stands for 'therefore'.

Try It! 4　　Calculate $86 + 954$.

Example 5　　The mass of an African elephant is 5387 kg. The mass of an Asian elephant is 3641 kg. Find the total mass of these two elephants.

Solution　　You can draw a **bar model** to show how you can find the sum. It lets you see the information in the problem.

5387 kg　　3641 kg

African	Asian

?

Total mass of these two elephants

$= 5387 + 3641$

$= 9028\,\text{kg}$

$$
\begin{array}{r}
5387 \\
+\ 3641 \\
\hline
9028 \\
\hline
{\scriptstyle 1\ 1}
\end{array}
$$

7 ones + 1 one = 8 ones

8 tens + 4 tens = 12 tens

　　　　= 1 hundred + 2 tens

3 hundreds + 6 hundreds + 1 hundred = 10 hundreds

　　　　　　= 1 thousand

5 thousands + 3 thousands + 1 thousand = 9 thousands

Try It! 5 Tom's scores in two computer games are 1387 and 2594. Find his total score for the two games.

Example 6 Lydia had £358 in her savings account. She deposited £216 and then £186 into the account. Find the balance after the deposits.

REMARK

Deposit means putting money into an account.

Solution The bar model for this example is shown.

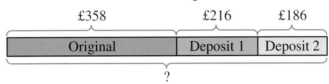

£358   £216   £186

| Original | Deposit 1 | Deposit 2 |

?

Balance after the deposit
= £358 + £216 + £186
= £574 + £186
= £760

After Deposit 1
```
   358
+ 216
─────
   574
     1
```

After Deposit 2
```
   574
+ 186
─────
   760
   1 1
```

DISCUSS

Can the three numbers be placed in columns and added as shown below?

```
   358
   216
+  186
```

Do you still get the same answer?

Try It! 6 A recipe uses 140 g of beef, 165 g of potato and 250 g of tomato. Find the total mass of these ingredients.

PRACTICE 1.2

LEVEL 1

1. Use place value counters to represent these calculations. Then copy and complete them using the column method.

   (a)
   ```
     423
   + 389
   ```
   (b)
   ```
     423
   + 589
   ```
   (c)
   ```
     489
   + 523
   ```
   (d)
   ```
     483
   + 529
   ```

2. Evaluate (that is, work out the values of) these expressions.

   (a) $1432 + 81$ (b) $1432 + 781$ (c) $625 + 2564$ (d) $61438 + 7295$

3. Calculate these sums.

   (a) $23 + 50 + 19$ (b) $47 + 83 + 145$ (c) $328 + 67 + 512$ (d) $426 + 201 + 534$

4. The bar model shows the masses of two fish. Find the total mass of these two fish.

446 g	385 g
Fish 1	Fish 2

 LEVEL 2

5. The capacity of a cup is 250 ml. The capacity of a bowl is 364 ml. Draw a bar model and find the total capacity of the cup and the bowl.

6. Mr Singh earns £3480 a month. Mrs Singh earns £3720 a month. What is their total income in a month?

FINANCE

7. A red ribbon is 187 cm long. A white ribbon is 64 cm long. A blue ribbon is 239 cm long. Draw a bar model and find the total length of
(a) the red ribbon and the white ribbon, **(b)** all three ribbons.

8. **(a)** Create two 4-digit numbers such that their sum is 8888.
(b) Create one 4-digit number and one 3-digit number such that their sum is 8888.
(c) Create one 4-digit number and one 2-digit number such that their sum is 8888.

OPEN QUESTION

9. **(a)** What errors have these students made when adding?

Student A	Student B
19621	19621
+ 379	+ 379
19990	23411

PROBLEM SOLVING

For each student, write a sentence starting with 'Be careful _____'.
Explain what mistake they should avoid when adding.
(b) Calculate the correct answer to the sum of 19 621 and 379.

10. Find the missing digits to complete this addition.

PROBLEM SOLVING

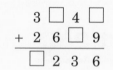

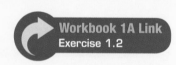

Workbook 1A Link
Exercise 1.2

1.3 Subtraction

A packet contains 524 grams of sugar. 378 grams are poured out. How much sugar is left?

The amount of sugar left = 524 g – 378 g.

Let's see how the subtraction can be done using place value counters. The table represents 524 using place value counters.

	Hundreds	Tens	Ones
524	(100) (100) (100) (100) (100)	(10) (10)	(1) (1) (1) (1)
524 – 378			

Before you start, it's easier to write the number you're subtracting in expanded form.

378 = 300 + 70 + 8

So 378 contains 3 hundreds, 7 tens and 8 ones.

First, subtract the ones. To subtract 8 ones from 4 ones you will need to regroup. Regroup a tens counter from the first number into 10 ones counters.

i.e.   524 = 500 + 10 + 14

	Hundreds	Tens	Ones
Regroup			(1) (1) (1) (1) (1) (1) (1) (1) (1) (1)
524	(100) (100) (100) (100) (100)	(10) (10)	(1) (1) (1) (1)
524 – 378			

> **REMARK**
>
> You can check the answer to subtractions of numbers under twenty with the subtraction table, on page 358.

You now subtract 8 ones from 14 ones. Place the resulting 6 ones in the subtraction row below.

1 ten + 4 ones – 8 ones = 14 ones – 8 ones = 6 ones

	Hundreds	Tens	Ones
Regroup			(1) (1) (1) (1) (1) (1) (X) (X) (X) (X)
524	(100) (100) (100) (100) (100)	(10) (10)	(X) (X) (X) (X)
524 – 378			(1) (1) (1) (1) (1) (1)

Subtract 8 ones from this column.

(1) (1) (1) (1)
(1) (1) (1) (1)

Next, subtract the tens. To subtract 7 tens from 1 ten you need to regroup again. Regroup a hundreds counter from the first number into 10 tens counters.

i.e. $524 = 400 + 110 + 14$

	Hundreds	Tens	Ones
Regroup		10 10 10 10 10 / 10 10 10 10 10	1 1 1 1 1 / 1 X̶ X̶ X̶ X̶
524	100 100 100 100 (100)	10 10	X̶ X̶ X̶ X̶
524 − 378			1 1 1 1 1 1

You now subtract 7 tens from 11 tens.

$$1 \text{ hundred} + 1 \text{ ten} - 7 \text{ tens} = 11 \text{ tens} - 7 \text{ tens}$$
$$= 4 \text{ tens}$$

Place the resulting 4 tens in the subtraction row below.

> **Subtract 7 tens from this column.**
> 10 10 10 10 10
> 10 10

	Hundreds	Tens	Ones
Regroup		10 10 10 10 X̶0̶ / X̶0̶ X̶0̶ X̶0̶ X̶0̶ X̶0̶	1 1 1 X̶ X̶ / 1 1 1 X̶ X̶
524	100 100 100 100 100	X̶0̶ 10	X̶ X̶ X̶ X̶
524 − 378		10 10 10 10	1 1 1 1 1 1

Finally, subtract the hundreds.

$$4 \text{ hundreds} - 3 \text{ hundreds} = 1 \text{ hundred}$$

Place the resulting 1 hundred in the subtraction row below.

	Hundreds	Tens	Ones
Regroup	**Subtract 3 hundreds from this column.** 100 100 100	10 10 10 10 X̶0̶ / X̶0̶ X̶0̶ X̶0̶ X̶0̶ X̶0̶	1 1 1 1 1 / 1 X̶ X̶ X̶ X̶
524	100 1̶0̶0̶ 1̶0̶0̶ 1̶0̶0̶ 100	X̶0̶ 10	X̶ X̶ X̶ X̶
524 − 378	100	10 10 10 10	1 1 1 1 1 1

Look at the final subtraction row to get the final answer.

This gives $524 - 378 = 100 + 40 + 6$

$$= 146$$

There are 146 grams of sugar left.

REMARK

Don't forget to fully answer the question. The final answer isn't just '146' in this case.

In the column method, align the two numbers in columns by their place values. Subtract digits in each column from right to left and regroup as shown below.

```
    4 11 1
    524     To subtract 8 ones from 4 ones, regroup 1 ten as 10 ones.
            14 ones – 8 ones = 6 ones.
  – 378     To subtract 7 tens from 1 ten, regroup 1 hundred as 10 tens.
    ───     11 tens – 7 tens = 4 tens.
    146     4 hundreds – 3 hundreds = 1 hundred.
```

 **CLASS ACTIVITY 3**

Objective: To develop knowledge of subtraction.

1. Calculate $82 - 65$ using

    (a) place value counters, **(b)** the column method.

2. Calculate $435 - 179$ using

    (a) place value counters, **(b)** the column method.

3. Which method is easier to understand? What's the same and what's different about the two methods?

Example 7 Calculate $4063 - 598$.

Solution
```
    3 9 15 1
    4063     To subtract 8 ones from 3 ones, regroup 1 ten as 10 ones.
             13 ones – 8 ones = 5 ones.
   – 598     To subtract 9 tens from 5 tens you regroup 1 hundred to 10 tens.
    ────     The number 4063 has 0 hundreds. You have to regroup 1 thousand as
    3465     10 hundreds. Then regroup 1 hundred as 10 tens, leaving 9 hundreds.
             15 tens – 9 tens = 6 tens.
             9 hundreds – 5 hundreds = 4 hundreds.
             3 thousands – 0 thousands = 3 thousands.
```

$$\therefore \quad 4063 - 598 = 3465$$

Try It! 7 Calculate $7026 - 849$.

Objective: To recognise the inverse relationship between addition and subtraction.

Your teacher will give you resources to work with in this Class Activity.

1. Find the values of these expressions.

   (a) $5 + 8$ (b) $13 - 5$ (c) $13 - 8$

2. Find the values of these expressions.

   (a) $24 + 67$ (b) $91 - 24$ (c) $91 - 67$

3. Find the values of these expressions.

   (a) $147 + 55$ (b) $202 - 147$ (c) $202 - 55$

4. Find the values of these expressions.

   (a) $213 + 546$ (b) $759 - 213$ (c) $759 - 546$

5. By looking at the above results, if number 1 + number 2 = sum, what is

   (a) sum – number 1,   (b) sum – number 2?

Class Activity 4 shows a relationship between addition and subtraction.
You can illustrate this with bar models.

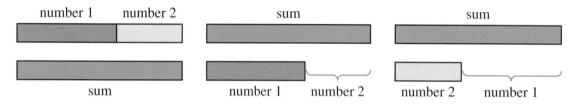

If   number 1 + number 2 = sum,
then   sum – number 1 = number 2   and   sum – number 2 = number 1.
This is called the **inverse relationship** between addition and subtraction.

Example 8   Find the missing number in each expression.

(a) $34 + \boxed{} = 51$ (b) $92 - \boxed{} = 28$

Solution   (a) $34 + \boxed{} = 51$

From the inverse relationship,

the missing number $\boxed{} = 51 - 34$
$$= 17$$

$$\begin{array}{r} {\scriptstyle 4\ 1} \\ 51 \\ -\ 34 \\ \hline 17 \end{array}$$

(b) $92 - \boxed{} = 28$

The missing number $\boxed{} = 92 - 28$
$$= 64$$

$$\begin{array}{r} {\scriptstyle 8\ 1} \\ 92 \\ -\ 28 \\ \hline 64 \end{array}$$

REMARK

The bar models are:

(a)

(b)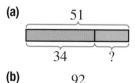

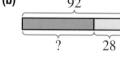

Try It! 8   Find the missing number in each expression.

(a) $56 + \boxed{} = 88$ (b) $75 - \boxed{} = 26$

Example 9

A plot of land is 780 m². The house covers 347 m² and the swimming pool covers 164 m². The rest is a garden. Find the area of the garden.

Solution

The bar model for this example is shown below.

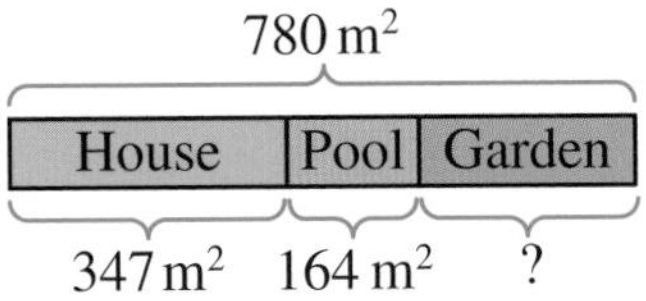

780 m²

| House | Pool | Garden |

347 m²   164 m²   ?

Area of the garden
= land area − house area − swimming pool area
= 780 − 347 − 164
= 433 − 164
= 269 m²

$$\begin{array}{r} {}^{7\,1} \\ 780 \\ -\ 347 \\ \hline 433 \end{array}$$

$$\begin{array}{r} {}^{3\,1\,2\,1} \\ 433 \\ -\ 164 \\ \hline 269 \end{array}$$

Note: Work on calculations like this from left to right. First evaluate 780 − 347 = 433. Then subtract 164 from 433.

Try It! 9

Alyssa has £746 in her savings account. She withdraws £250 from the account. She then pays a bill of £318 using the account. How much is left of her savings?

Example 10

At the start of a science experiment, a cup contains 238 ml of liquid. 154 ml is removed from the cup. It is then topped up with 97 ml of liquid. Find the final volume of liquid in the cup.

Solution

The bar model for this situation is as follows.

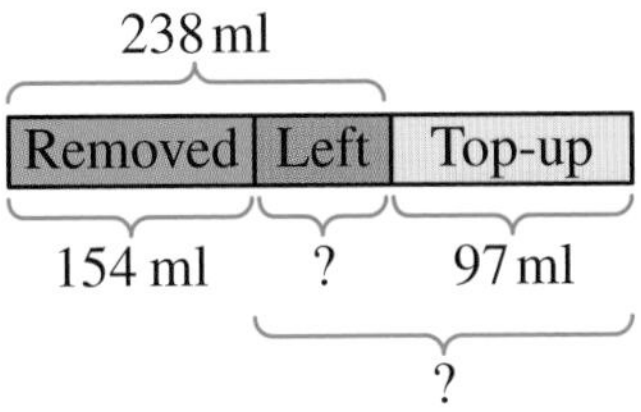

238 ml

| Removed | Left | Top-up |

154 ml   ?   97 ml

?

Final volume of liquid in the cup
= original volume − volume removed
                            + volume topped up
= 238 − 154 + 97
= 84 + 97
= 181 ml

$$\begin{array}{r} {}^{1\,1} \\ 238 \\ -\ 154 \\ \hline 84 \end{array}$$

$$\begin{array}{r} 84 \\ +\ 97 \\ \hline 181 \\ {}^{1\,1} \end{array}$$

Note: Work on calculations like this from left to right. First evaluate 238 − 154 = 84. Then add 97 to 84.

Try It! 10

A lift is 97 m above the ground. It moves up 84 m and then moves down 126 m. How many metres from the ground is the lift in its final position?

PRACTICE 1.3

⚙ LEVEL 1

1. Use place value counters to represent these calculations. Then copy and complete them using the column method.

    (a)   84
        −   35

    (b)   684
        −   35

    (c)   684
        − 235

    (d)   687
        − 238

2. Evaluate these expressions.

    (a) $534 - 310$

    (b) $534 - 390$

    (c) $4382 - 2170$

    (d) $36\,540 - 12\,782$

3. Work out these values.

    (a) $78 - 23 - 18$

    (b) $431 - 86 - 134$

    (c) $342 + 256 - 428$

    (d) $630 - 418 + 253$

4. Find the missing number in each expression using the inverse relationship between addition and subtraction.

    (a) $34 + \boxed{} = 87$

    (b) $\boxed{} + 432 = 710$

    (c) $2689 - \boxed{} = 245$

    (d) $\boxed{} - 4836 = 13\,590$

5. The bar model shows the number of sweets in a full packet and the number of sweets that have been eaten. Find the number of sweets left.

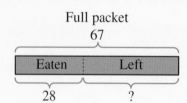

Full packet
67

| Eaten | Left |

28   ?

⚙ LEVEL 2

6. A metal rod is 176 cm long. 89 cm is cut from it. Draw a bar model to represent the information. Find the length of the remaining rod.

7. The longest river in the UK is the Severn. It is 354 km long. The second longest is the Thames. It is 346 km long. Find

    (a) the total length of these two rivers,

    (b) the difference in length between these two rivers.

8. The price of a necklace is £217. The price of a ring is £154.

 (a) Find the total price of the necklace and the ring.

 (b) Jo has £400 and buys both items. How much money is left?

9. **(a)** What errors have these students made when subtracting?

Student A	Student B
83752	83752
− 6104	− 6104
87658	22712

For each student, write a sentence starting with 'Be careful _____'.
Explain what mistake they should avoid when subtracting.

 (b) Calculate the correct answer to 83 752 − 6104.

10. Write an expression with two 4-digit whole numbers where the result is
1500 when the smaller number is subtracted from the larger number.

1.4 Efficient Addition and Subtraction by Hand

Sometimes addition and subtraction can be made more efficient with certain methods.

A Reordering

There are some properties of addition that are simple and useful for carrying out calculations.

Objective: To explore some properties of addition.

1. Find the value of these sums.

    (a) 34 + 18   **(b)** 18 + 34   **(c)** 56 + 79   **(d)** 79 + 56

2. What do you observe from the results in Question **1**? Suggest one property of addition from the results.

3. Work out the sum within the brackets first and then work out the value of the whole calculation.

    (a) (3 + 7) + 8   **(b)** 3 + (7 + 8)   **(c)** (25 + 39) + 41   **(d)** 25 + (39 + 41)

4. What do you observe from the results in Question **3**? Suggest one property of addition from the results.

Question **1** in Class Activity 5 gives examples of this law of addition:

number 1 + number 2 = number 2 + number 1

You can see this by drawing bar models.

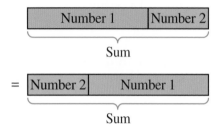

REMARK

This law is called the **commutative law of addition**.

Question **3** in Class Activity 5 shows this law of addition:

(number 1 + number 2) + number 3 = number 1 + (number 2 + number 3)

You can see this by drawing bar models.

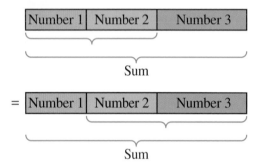

REMARK

This law is called the **associative law of addition**.

These two laws tell you that numbers can be added in any order. Sometimes changing the order of numbers makes addition easier. Spotting pairs of numbers that bond to form a multiple of 10 is one way to make addition more efficient.

REMARK

A pair of numbers add up to a multiple of 10 if the ones digits of the numbers add up to 10.

Example 11   Calculate these sums by reordering the numbers first to make the addition easier.

(a) $34 + 25 + 46$ (b) $128 + 47 + 322 + 253$

REMARK

Look at page 362 for help with finding numbers that bond to form a multiple of 10.

Solution   (a) $34 + 25 + 46 = 34 + 46 + 25$ Reorder to make a pair
$$= 80 + 25$$ that is a multiple of 10.
$$= 105$$

(b) $128 + 47 + 322 + 253$ Reorder to make two pairs
$$= 128 + 322 + 47 + 253$$ that are multiples of 10.
$$= 450 + 300$$
$$= 750$$

Calculate these sums by reordering the numbers first to make the addition easier.

(a) $39 + 42 + 21$

(b) $256 + 145 + 55 + 324$

Example **12**

Calculate these values by reordering the numbers first to make the calculation easier.

(a) $59 + 36 - 29$ (b) $637 - 118 - 437$

Solution

(a) $59 + 36 - 29$

$= 59 - 29 + 36$

$= 30 + 36$

$= 66$

Reorder so that a subtraction gives a multiple of 10.
Notice that the subtraction sign before the 29 needs to move with it.

> **REMARK**
>
> The original calculation is 59 add 36 subtract 29. After reordering, it is 59 subtract 29 add 36. You get the same result.

(b) $637 - 118 - 437$

$= 637 - 437 - 118$

$= 200 - 118$

$= 82$

Reorder so that a subtraction gives a multiple of 100.

$$\begin{array}{r} {}^{1\ 9\ 1} \\ 200 \\ -\ 118 \\ \hline 82 \end{array}$$

Try It! **12**

Calculate these values by reordering the numbers first to make the calculation easier.

(a) $92 - 25 - 62$ (b) $754 - 315 - 254$

DISCUSS

Think about which of the following statements are correct. Use numerical examples to make this easier.

1. number 1 − number 2 = number 2 − number 1
2. number 1 + number 2 − number 3 = number 1 − number 3 + number 2
3. number 1 − number 2 − number 3 = number 1 − number 3 − number 2

B Partitioning

Numbers in addition and subtraction can be partitioned in different ways to make calculations easier.

Example **13**

Calculate the following expressions by first using methods to make them easier.

(a) $83 + 16$

(b) $429 + 175$

(c) $6214 - 5138$

Solution

(a) $83 + 16$

$= 83 + 10 + 6$ Partition 16 into $10 + 6$.

$= 93 + 6$

$= 99$

> **REMARK**
>
> The addition can be shown on a number line.
>
>
>
> +10   +6
>
> 83   93   99

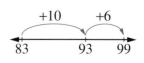

(b) $429 + 175$

$= 429 + 100 + 70 + 5$ Partition 175 into $100 + 70 + 5$.

$= 529 + 70 + 5$

$= 599 + 5$

$= 604$

(c) $6214 - 5138$

$= 6214 - 5000 - 100 - 30 - 8$

$= 1214 - 100 - 30 - 8$

$= 1114 - 30 - 8$

$= 1084 - 8$

$= 1076$

Partition 5138 into thousands, hundreds, tens and ones.

 REMARK

The subtraction can be shown on a number line.

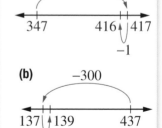

Try It! 13   Calculate the following expressions by first using methods to make them easier.

(a) $74 + 18$

(b) $265 + 346$

(c) $8497 - 2534$

C Use of Near Numbers

When a number is close to a multiple of 10 or 100, you can use that multiple to make the calculation easier.

Example 14   Work out these expressions by first replacing values with near numbers.

(a) $347 + 69$ **(b)** $437 - 298$

Solution   **(a)** $347 + 69$

$= 347 + 70 - 1$ $+69$ is the same as $+70 - 1$.

$= 417 - 1$

$= 416$

(b) $437 - 298$

$= 437 - 300 + 2$ -298 is the same as $-300 + 2$.

$= 137 + 2$

$= 139$

 REMARK

The calculations can be shown on a number line.

(a)

$+70$

347   416   417

-1

(b)

-300

137   139   437

$+2$

Try It! 14   Work out these expressions by first replacing values with near numbers.

(a) $512 + 89$

(b) $625 - 497$

Example 15   Katya has £100. She buys a pair of jeans for £59 and a shirt for £17. How much money does she have left?

Solution

$100 - 59 - 17$

$= 100 - 60 + 1 - 10 - 7$ –59 is the same as –60 + 1.

$= 40 + 1 - 10 - 7$ –17 is the same as –10 – 7.

$= 41 - 10 - 7$

$= 31 - 7$

$= 24$

Katya has £24 left.

Try It! 15   A rope is 150 cm long. A length of 56 cm and a length of 68 cm are cut from the rope. Find the remaining length of the rope.

PRACTICE 1.4

In this exercise, choose the best method for each question to make the calculation easier.

⚙ LEVEL 1

1. Calculate these sums.
   (a) $52 + 28$
   (b) $52 + 31$
   (c) $52 + 47 + 28$
   (d) $31 + 52 + 89$

2. Calculate these expressions.
   (a) $78 - 26 - 18$
   (b) $22 + 15 + 38$
   (c) $362 + 215 - 142$
   (d) $126 + 233 + 134$

3. Work out these values.
   (a) $432 + 199$
   (b) $360 - 238$
   (c) $236 + 317$
   (d) $180 - 139 - 21$

4. Evaluate these expressions.
   (a) $254 + 347$
   (b) $254 + 387$
   (c) $4570 - 2346$
   (d) $4570 - 2386$

5. Work out these expressions.

(a) $34 + 32 + 28 + 46$

(b) $47 + 66 - 37 - 26$

(c) $314 - 205 + 131 - 45$

(d) $625 - 199 - 238 - 147$

⚙ LEVEL 2

6. Find the missing number in each of these calculations using the inverse relationship between addition and subtraction.

(a) $38 + \boxed{} = 67$

(b) $\boxed{} + 59 = 88$

(c) $\boxed{} - 239 = 416$

(d) $381 - \boxed{} = 245$

7. 960 ml of purple paint is made by mixing 346 ml of red paint with 314 ml of blue paint and some white paint. Find the volume of white paint used.

8. The diagram is a 4 by 4 magic square. It is 'magic' because the numbers in each row, each column and each diagonal have the same total. One of the numbers is wrong. Find and correct it.

PROBLEM SOLVING

19	16	13	26
14	25	20	15
24	11	18	21
17	22	24	12

9. Match each calculation to one of the methods A to D.

(a) $678 + 41$

(b) $678 - 39$

(c) $678 - 41$

(d) $678 + 39$

A $+40 - 1$ **B** $+40 + 1$ **C** $-40 - 1$ **D** $-40 + 1$

10. Create a calculation with four whole numbers for a friend. Write your calculation so that your friend will need to reorder the numbers to make it easier to work out. Ask your friend to calculate the answer and then discuss the method used.

OPEN QUESTION

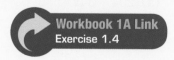

Workbook 1A Link
Exercise 1.4

REVIEW

Place Values

Ten thousands
  Thousands
    Hundreds
      Tens   Expanded form
        Ones

$38\,207 = 3 \times 10000 + 8 \times 1000 + 2 \times 100 + 7$
$ = 30\,000 + 8000 + 200 + 7$

Zero is a place holder.

Order of Numbers

$243 < 518$ means 243 is less than 518.

$1485 > 1467$ means 1485 is greater than 1467.

You can order two numbers by comparing the digits representing the highest value in each number. If they are the same, compare the digits representing the next highest value, and so on.

Whole Numbers

$0, 1, 2, 3, 4, \ldots$

Addition

- Align the place values.
- Add the digits from right to left.
- Regroup if necessary.

e.g.
$$\begin{array}{r} 6075 \\ +\ 4829 \\ \hline 10904 \\ \hline {\scriptstyle 1\ 1} \end{array}$$

Subtraction

- Align the place values.
- Subtract the digits from right to left.
- Regroup if necessary.

e.g.
$$\begin{array}{r} {\scriptstyle 4\ 1\,8\ 1} \\ 5493 \\ -\ 2617 \\ \hline 2876 \end{array}$$

Inverse Relationship between Addition and Subtraction

If number 1 + number 2 = number 3, then number 1 = number 3 − number 2, and number 2 = number 3 − number 1.

Methods for Efficient Calculation by Hand

(a) Reordering

e.g. $36 + 43 + 64$
$= 36 + 64 + 43$
$= 100 + 43$
$= 143$

(b) Partitioning

e.g. $258 + 73$
$= 258 + 70 + 3$
$= 328 + 3$
$= 331$

(c) Use of Near Numbers

e.g. $453 - 298$
$= 453 - 300 + 2$
$= 153 + 2$
$= 155$

CHALLENGE 1

Your classmate Max has a 4-digit combination lock for a bicycle.
You are challenged to work out the number that will unlock it using these statements.

1. The first digit is the hundreds digit of the year of Max's birth.

2. The second digit is the tens digit of the sum of 6789 and 9876.

3. The third digit is the ones digit of the whole number that is greater than 6789 but less than 6791.

4. The fourth digit is the digit representing the highest value in the answer to 9876 − 6789.

What number will unlock Max's bicycle?

Workbook 1A Link
Problem Solving 1

REVISION EXERCISE 1

1. (a) Write the expanded form of the number 30 947.
   (b) State the value of the digit which represents the highest value.

2. The mass of a car is 1478 kg.
   (a) What is the place value of the digit 8?
   (b) What is the value represented by the digit 4?

3. Copy and complete each statement using '<' or '>'.
   (a) 458 [   ] 1309
   (b) 73 256 [   ] 73 265

4. Work out these values.
   (a) 345 + 2679
   (b) 36 709 + 25 418
   (c) 8325 − 2678
   (d) 93 560 − 9356

5. Calculate these expressions, by first using methods to make the calculations easier.
   (a) 53 + 48 + 17 + 52
   (b) 836 + 104 − 236
   (c) 625 + 87
   (d) 1564 − 889

6. The price of a sofa set is £2859 in Shop Budget and £2895 in Shop Value.

   £ FINANCE

    (a) Which shop's price is lower?

    (b) How much cheaper is it?

7. Look at the numbers 8031, 3081, 1038, 8310 and 3180.

    Find the sum of the numbers that are less than 3180.

8. A burger provides 2125 kJ of energy. Four chicken nuggets provide 722 kJ. Three fish fingers

   SCIENCE

    provide 813 kJ. What is the total energy provided by all these food items?

9. Alana scores 7863 marks in a computer game. Oli scores 1295 fewer marks than Alana.

   PROBLEM SOLVING

    What is their total score?

10. Copy and complete the circle diagram with the numbers 212, 213, 214, 215, 216, 217 and 218.

   PROBLEM SOLVING

    You can use each number only once. Each line of numbers should give the same total.

    Hint: You may first consider a simpler problem. Try to fill the diagram with the numbers
          2, 3, 4, 5, 6, 7 and 8.

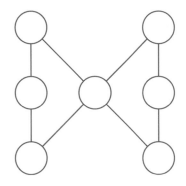

Write in Your Journal

In a Science class, students are asked to measure out liquid from a flask. The flask contains 1438 ml of liquid. Sean measures out 372 ml. Claire measures out 269 ml. Jessica and Huang work out the remaining volume of liquid as shown below.

Jessica: Total amount of liquid measured = 372 + 269

                               = 641 ml

        Remaining volume of liquid = 1438 − 641

                               = 797 ml

Huang: Remaining volume of liquid = 1438 − 372 − 269

                              = 1066 − 269

                              = 797 ml

Are they both correct? Which method do you prefer? Write down your reason.

2 MULTIPLYING AND DIVIDING WHOLE NUMBERS

WHAT IS IN THIS CHAPTER:

2.1 Multiplication

2.2 Division

2.3 Multiplying and Dividing Efficiently Without a Calculator

2.4 Factors, Multiples and Prime Numbers

A group of students decide to hold a cake sale to raise money for charity. They sell 60 cakes at £2 each and they divide the money equally among three charities. How much will each charity receive? Solving this type of problem is covered in this chapter.

LET'S LEARN TO

▶ multiply and divide whole numbers, using different methods and techniques

▶ recognise the inverse relationship between multiplication and division

▶ use multiplication and division to solve real-life problems

▶ calculate square and cube numbers and write these numbers using indices

▶ list factors, common factors and find highest common factors

▶ list multiples, common multiples and find lowest common multiples

▶ list primes and prime factors

1. Addition

You can find the total of two or more numbers using addition.
You can add using the **column method** or place value counters.
Regroup values if necessary.

$$\begin{array}{r} 1360 \\ + 5640 \\ \hline 7000 \\ \hline {\scriptstyle 1\ 1} \end{array}$$

Example The price of car A is £1360. The price of car B is £5640.
       Sum of the two prices = £1360 + £5640
                             = £7000.

2. Subtraction

You can take away one number from another using subtraction.
You can subtract using the **column method** or place value counters.
Regroup values if necessary.

$$\begin{array}{r} {\scriptstyle 6\ 9\ 1} \\ 7000 \\ - 5640 \\ \hline 1360 \end{array}$$

Example A bakery makes 7000 loaves of bread in a week and sells 5640 of them.
       The remaining number of loaves
       = **difference** from 5640 to 7000
       = 7000 − 5640
       = 1360.

3. Inverse Relationship between Addition and Subtraction

If   number 1 + number 2 = sum,
then   number 1 = sum − number 2   and   number 2 = sum − number 1.

Example The total price of car A and car B is £7000. The price of car B is £5640.
       Price of car A + price of car B = total price
       Price of the car A = total price − price of car B
                         = £7000 − £5640
                         = £1360

4. Multiplication

$5 + 5 + 5 = 3 \times 5$ and $7 + 7 + 7 + 7 = 4 \times 7$
You can write repeated addition as **multiplication** with the **multiplication sign** '×'.

3×5 is three lots of 5. You read it as '3 multiplied by 5' or '3 times 5'.

From the above repeated addition, $3 \times 5 = 15$.

Here, three rows of five marbles give a total of 15 marbles.

5. Division

When 15 fish are shared equally among 3 tanks, each tank has 5 fish.
This is a division (dividing 15 by 3). It is written as

$$15 \div 3 = 5.$$

The '÷' is called the **division sign**.

6. Inverse Relationship between Multiplication and Division

If number $1 \times$ number $2 =$ number 3,

then   number $1 =$ number $3 \div$ number 2

and   number $2 =$ number $3 \div$ number 1.

Example If there are three rows and each row has two
marbles, total number of marbles $= 3 \times 2$
$$= 6.$$
If the marbles are divided into two equal groups,
number of marbles in each group $= 6 \div 2$
$$= 3.$$

2.1 Multiplication

A Representing Multiplication

There are 4 rows of chairs. Each row has 5 chairs. How many chairs are there? You can find the number of chairs by **repeated addition**.

Number of chairs $= 5 + 5 + 5 + 5 = 20$.

A simpler way of writing this is to use **multiplication**. You write

$$5 + 5 + 5 + 5 = 4 \times 5.$$

You read this as '4 multiplied by 5' or '4 **times** 5'. The result $4 \times 5 = 20$ is called the **product** of 4 and 5.

You can use **multiplication tables** to check calculations.
Class Activity 1 shows some properties of multiplication.

REMARK

There are multiplication tables up to 20 × 20 on page 359.

Objective: To explore multiplication patterns using a multiplication table and a calculator.

×	1	2	3	4	5	6	7	8	9	10	11	12
1	1	2	3	4	5	6	7	8	9	10	11	12
2	2	4	6	8	10	12	14	16	18	20	22	24
3	3	6	9	12	15	18	21	24	27	30	33	36
4	4	8	12	16	20	24	28	32	36	40	44	48
5	5	10	15	20	25	30	35	40	45	50	55	60
6	6	12	18	24	30	36	42	48	54	60	66	72
7	7	14	21	28	35	42	49	56	63	70	77	84
8	8	16	24	32	40	48	56	64	72	80	88	96
9	9	18	27	36	45	54	63	72	81	90	99	108
10	10	20	30	40	50	60	70	80	90	100	110	120
11	11	22	33	44	55	66	77	88	99	110	121	132
12	12	24	36	48	60	72	84	96	108	120	132	144

This is a multiplication table. It shows the product of any two numbers from 1 to 12. For example, $4 \times 5 = 20$ (the highlighted number). Use this table for this activity.

1. **(a)** State these products.

   (i) 3×8 and 8×3 **(ii)** 6×7 and 7×6
   (iii) 4×11 and 11×4 **(iv)** 9×12 and 12×9

   (b) What do you notice?

2. **(a)** State these products.

   (i) 1×5 and 2×5 **(ii)** 3×7 and 6×7
   (iii) 9×4 and 9×8 **(iv)** 6×4 and 4×12

   (b) What pattern do you notice?

   (c) If $2 \times$ a number $= 32$, what will the value of $4 \times$ the number be? Explain your answer.

3. **(a)** Write down the values in this list.

   $1 \times 10, 2 \times 10, 3 \times 10, 4 \times 10, 5 \times 10, 6 \times 10, 7 \times 10, 8 \times 10, \ldots$

(b) Using place value counters, represent the next four numbers in the list. Copy the table and complete the values.

Number	Place value counters	Value
9×10	10 10 10 10 10 10 10 10 10	
10×10	10 10 10 10 10 10 10 10 10 10	
11×10	10 10 10 10 10 10 10 10 10 10 10	
12×10	10 10 10 10 10 10 10 10 10 10 10 10	

(c) What do you notice?

4. (a) Using place value counters, represent the values of 2×100, 3×100, 4×100, 5×100. Copy the table and complete the values.

Number	Place value counters	Value
2×100	100 100	
3×100	100 100 100	
4×100	100 100 100 100	
5×100	100 100 100 100 100	

(b) What do you notice?

5. (a) Using place value counters, find the values of 4×9, 4×90 and 4×900.
Hint: Use regrouping to explain your answer.

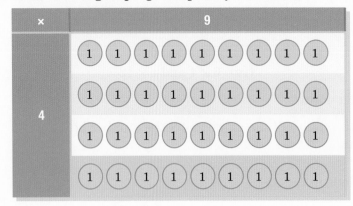

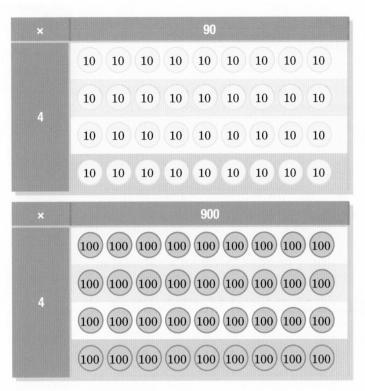

(b) What do you notice?

6. (a) Using the above results, copy and complete this place value table.

Number	Thousands	Hundreds	Tens	Ones
4				4
4 × 10			4	0
4 × 100				
4 × 9				
4 × 90				
4 × 900				

(b) If a number is multiplied by 10, how does the position of its digits in the place value table change?

(c) If a number is multiplied by 100, how does the position of its digit in the place value table change?

Class Activity 1 shows some properties of multiplication.

1. number 1 × number 2 = number 2 × number 1.

2. If number 1 × number 2 = number 3,

   then (twice number 1) × number 2 = twice number 3.

3. When a number is multiplied by 10, each digit moves one place to the left in the place value table.

4. When a number is multiplied by 100, each digit moves two places to the left in the place value table.

 **REMARK**

In mathematics, a property is a rule. The first property opposite is called the commutative law of multiplication.

For example,

1. $27 \times 21 = 21 \times 27 = 567$

2. If you know that $3 \times 37 = 111$, then you know that $6 \times 37 = 222$.

3. $73 \times 10 = 730$ because the 7 moves one place to the left from the tens to the hundreds place value, and the 3 moves one place to the left from the ones to the tens place value. You write 0 as a place holder in the ones place value.

4. $46 \times 100 = 4600$ because the 4 moves two places to the left from the tens to the thousands place value, and the 6 moves two places to the left from the ones to the hundreds place value. You write 0 as a place holder in the ones and tens place values.

These facts are useful when you multiply numbers without a calculator.

B Grid Method and Column Method of Multiplication

If the product of two numbers does not appear in multiplication tables, you can find the product by using the **grid method** or **column method**.

Example 1

Calculate these products.

(a) 54×3 (b) 254×3

Solution (a) *Place Value Counter Method*

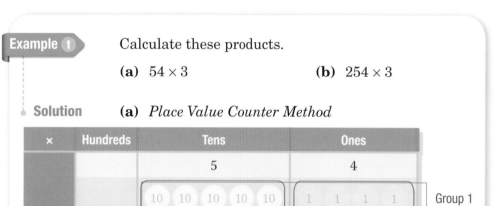

You can represent 54×3 with 3 groups, each of 5 tens and 4 ones.

Place the corresponding number of tens and ones counters as shown.

You see that there is a total of 1 hundreds counter, 6 tens counters and 2 ones counters

$\therefore \quad 54 \times 3 = 100 + 60 + 2$
$= 162$

RECALL

When you have ten of one kind of place value counter, regroup them into one of the place value counters to the left. For example, ten '1's become one '10'. Ten '10's become one '100'. And so on.

Grid Method

Developing the place value counter method, you can draw a grid instead of using the counters.

1. Draw the grid and partition 54 into 5 tens and 4 ones.

×	50	4
3		

2. Multiply 50 by 3 and 4 by 3 and write the answers in the cells below 50 and 4.

×	50	4
3	150	12

5 tens × 3 = 15 tens

4 ones × 3 = 12 ones

3. Find the sum of the two products in Step 2 to get the answer.

$$\begin{array}{r} 150 \\ + \ 12 \\ \hline 162 \end{array}$$

∴ 54 × 3 = 162

Column Method

Align the place values of 54 and 3. Multiply the ones digit 4 by 3 and the tens digit 5 by 3, step by step, as shown. Regroup when necessary.

$$\begin{array}{r} 54 \\ \times \quad 3 \\ \hline 162 \\ \scriptstyle 1 \end{array}$$

4 ones × 3 = 12 ones = **1 ten** + 2 ones

5 tens × 3 = 15 tens

15 tens + **1 ten** = 16 tens = **1 hundred** + 6 tens

∴ 54 × 3 = 162

REMARK

'Align the place values' means line up the ones, tens and hundreds in each number.

(b) *Place Value Counter Method*

	Hundreds	Tens	Ones	
	2	5	4	
3	(100)(100)	10 10 10 10 10	1 1 1 1	Group 1
	(100)(100)	10 10 10 10 10	1 1 1 1	Group 2
	(100)(100)	10 10 10 10 10	1 1 **1 1**	Group 3
254 × 3	(100)(100) (100)(100) (100)(100) (100)	10 10 10 10 10 / 10	1 1	

Continued

You can represent 254×3 with 3 groups, each of 2 hundreds, 5 tens and 4 ones.

Place the corresponding numbers of hundreds, tens and ones counters as shown.

You see that there is a total of 7 hundreds counters, 6 tens counters and 2 ones counters.

$$\therefore \quad 254 \times 3 = 700 + 60 + 2$$
$$= 762$$

Grid Method

254×3

×	200	50	4
3	600	150	12

$$\begin{array}{r} 600 \\ 150 \\ +\ \ 12 \\ \hline 762 \end{array}$$

$$\therefore\ 254 \times 3 = 762$$

Column Method

Multiply 254 by 3, digit by digit, from right to left. Multiply the ones digit 4 by 3, then the tens digit 5 by 3, and then the hundreds digit 2 by 3, step by step as shown. Regroup when necessary.

$$\begin{array}{r} 254 \\ \times\ \ \ 3 \\ \hline 762 \\ \scriptstyle 1\ 1 \end{array}$$

4 ones × 3 = 12 ones = 1 ten + 2 ones

5 tens × 3 = 15 tens

15 tens + 1 ten = 16 tens = 1 hundred + 6 tens

2 hundreds × 3 = 6 hundreds

6 hundreds + 1 hundred = 7 hundreds

$$\therefore\ 254 \times 3 = 762$$

Try It! ① Calculate these products.

(a) 37×4 **(b)** 137×4

DISCUSS

Which method of multiplication do you find easiest to understand and use? Give your reason.

DISCUSS

What do you notice about the products 54×3 and 254×3?

Example 2

Calculate 8135×7.

Solution

Grid Method

8135×7

×	8000	100	30	5
7	56 000	700	210	35

8 thousands $\times$ 7 = 56 thousands

$$
\begin{array}{r}
56000 \\
700 \\
210 \\
+ \quad 35 \\
\hline
56945
\end{array}
$$

$\therefore 8135 \times 7 = 56\,945$

Column Method

$$
\begin{array}{r}
8135 \\
\times \quad 7 \\
\hline
56945 \\
{\scriptstyle 2\,3}
\end{array}
$$

5 ones $\times$ 7 = 35 ones = **3 tens** + 5 ones

3 tens $\times$ 7 = 21 tens

21 tens + **3 tens** = 24 tens = **2 hundreds** + 4 tens

1 hundred $\times$ 7 = 7 hundreds

7 hundreds + **2 hundreds** = 9 hundreds

8 thousands $\times$ 7 = 56 thousands

$\therefore 8135 \times 7 = 56\,945$

Try It! 2

Calculate 5829×6.

REMARK

You can use the multiplication tables on page 359 to check individual parts of the calculation.

Example 3

(a) Use the grid method to work out 36×82.

(b) Use the column method to calculate these products.

   (i) 36×2 (ii) 36×80 (iii) 36×82

Solution

(a) 36×82

×	30	6
80	2400	480
2	60	12

$30 \times 80 = 3 \times 10 \times 8 \times 10$
$= 3 \times 8 \times 10 \times 10$
$= 24 \times 100$
$= 2400$

REMARK

3 groups of 8 tens counters
= 24 tens counters.
30 groups of 8 tens counters
= 240 tens counters
= 24 hundreds counters
= 2400.

Continued

$$\begin{array}{r}
2400 \\
480 \\
60 \\
+\ \ 12 \\
\hline
2952 \\
\end{array}$$
<small>1</small>

$$\therefore\ 36 \times 82 = 2952$$

(b) (i)
$$\begin{array}{r}
36 \\
\times\ \ 2 \\
\hline
72 \\
\end{array}$$
<small>1</small>

$$\therefore\ 36 \times 2 = 72$$

(ii)
$$\begin{array}{r}
36 \\
\times\ \ 80 \\
\hline
2880 \\
\end{array}$$
<small>4</small>

6×8 tens $= 48$ tens
48 tens $= 40$ tens and 8 tens,
           $= $ **4 hundreds** and 8 tens
30×8 tens $= 240$ tens $= 24$ hundreds
24 hundreds $+$ **4 hundreds** $= 28$ hundreds

$$\therefore\ 36 \times 80 = 2880$$

(iii)
$$\begin{array}{r}
36 \\
\times\ \ 82 \\
\hline
72 \\
2880 \\
\hline
2952 \\
\end{array}$$
<small>1</small>

Step 1 $36 \times 2 = 72$ (From **(i)**)
Step 2 $36 \times 80 = 2880$ (From **(ii)**)
Step 3 Add together. $72 + 2880 = 2952$.

$$\therefore\ 36 \times 82 = 2952$$

Try It! ③

(a) Use the grid method to work out 47×65.

(b) Use the column method to calculate these products.

    (i) 47×5 **(ii)** 47×60 **(iii)** 47×65

DISCUSS

Which of these are equal?
Can you explain why?
3×20
30×20
30×2
300×2
3×200
30×200
300×20
3000×2
2000×3

Example ④

Evaluate 518×37 by using

(a) the grid method,

(b) the column method.

Solution

(a) 518×37

×	500	10	8
30	15 000	300	240
7	3500	70	56

Sum of the products in the first row
= 15 000 + 300 + 240
= 15 540
Sum of the products in the second row
= 3500 + 70 + 56
= 3626

```
  15540
+  3626
  19166
     1
```

∴ 518 × 37 = 19 166

(b)
```
       518
  ×     37
      3626   Step 1   518 × 7 = 3626
     15540   Step 2   518 × 30 = 15 540
     19166   Step 3   Add together. 3626 + 15 540 = 19 166.
         1
```

∴ 518 × 37 = 19 166

 Evaluate 219 × 61 using

(a) the grid method,

(b) the column method.

 **DISCUSS**

Can you add together the products in each column (rather than each row) to get the answer?

 **REMARK**

```
      518
  ×     7
     3626
       15
```

```
      518
  ×    30
    15540
        2
```

C Applications

 The price of a dress is £124. The price of a coat is five times as much as the price of the dress. How much does the coat cost?

Solution You can use a bar model to represent the situation.

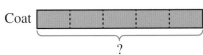

Price of the coat

= £124 × 5

= £620

```
     124
  ×    5
     620
      1 2
```

George has 256 photos on his mobile phone.
Peter has three times as many photos as George.
How many photos does Peter have?

Example 6

A carpenter makes 16 tables. Each table has four legs.
Each leg is 73 cm long. What is the total length of all
the legs?

73 cm

Solution

Total length of the four legs of one table		73		292
$= 4 \times 73$ cm		$\times\ 4$		$\times\ \ 16$
Total length of all the legs of 16 tables		292		1752
$= 4 \times 73 \times 16$ cm				2920
$= 4672$ cm				4672

Try It! 6

A school has 24 classes. Each class has 30 students.
For a fundraising day, each student donates £5.
How much do they donate in total?

D Indices (Square and Cube Numbers)

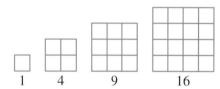

1   4   9   16

You can use square tiles to make the pattern shown. The numbers
of tiles in the squares are 1, 4, 9 and 16. These are called **square
numbers**. You can write these square numbers as

$1^2 = 1 \times 1 = 1,$
$2^2 = 2 \times 2 = 4,$
$3^2 = 3 \times 3 = 9,$
$4^2 = 4 \times 4 = 16.$

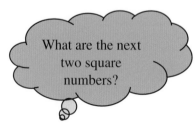

What are the next
two square
numbers?

You read the number 1^2 as '1 squared', 2^2 is '2 squared', 3^2 is '3 squared'
and so on. The small number 2 in the top right corner is called the
index. For instance, in 4^2, 2 is the index of the number 4.

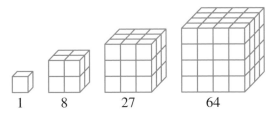

You can use small linking cubes to form the pattern shown. The numbers of small cubes in these solids are 1, 8, 27 and 64. These are called **cube numbers**. You can write these numbers as

$1^3 = 1 \times 1 \times 1 = 1,$
$2^3 = 2 \times 2 \times 2 = 8,$
$3^3 = 3 \times 3 \times 3 = 27,$
$4^3 = 4 \times 4 \times 4 = 64,$ and so on.

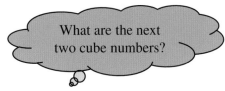
What are the next two cube numbers?

You read the number 1^3 as '1 cubed', 2^3 is '2 cubed', 3^3 is '3 cubed' and so on. The small number 3 in the top right corner is the index. For instance, in 4^3, 3 is the index of the number 4.

Example 7

Calculate these values.

(a) 13^2 **(b)** 7^3

Solution

(a) $13^2 = 13 \times 13$
$= 169$

$$\begin{array}{r} 13 \\ \times\ 13 \\ \hline 39 \\ 130 \\ \hline 169 \end{array}$$

(b) $7^3 = 7 \times 7 \times 7$
$= 49 \times 7$
$= 343$

$$\begin{array}{r} 49 \\ \times\ \ 7 \\ \hline 343 \\ \scriptstyle 6 \end{array}$$

Try It! 7

Calculate these values.

(a) 14^2 **(b)** 8^3

DISCUSS

Is 2^3 equal to 3^2?

Give your reason.

PRACTICE 2.1

 **LEVEL 1**

Take a 12 × 12 grid with numbers 1 to 12 across the top and 1 to 12 down the left side. Complete the table with multiplications without using a calculator. Compare your answers with the table on page 33. See if you can fill in more of the grid correctly, and whether you can do it any faster.

1. Copy and complete these calculations.

   (a) $28 + 28 + 28 = \boxed{} \times 28$

   $= \boxed{}$

   (b) $47 + 47 + 47 + 47 = \boxed{} \times 47$

   $= \boxed{}$

   (c) $51 + 51 + 51 + 51 + 51 = \boxed{} \times \boxed{}$

   (d) $\boxed{} + \boxed{} + \boxed{} = \boxed{} \times 79$

2. **(a)** Copy and complete the grids and calculate these products.

   (i) 53×2

×	50	3
2		

   (ii) 4×53

×	4
50	
3	

   (iii) 218×3

×	200	10	8
3			

   (iv) 218×5

×	200	10	8
5			

   (b) What is the relationship between 53×2 and 4×53?

3. **(a)** Find these values, using the column method.

   (i) 603×8 **(ii)** 6003×8 **(iii)** 235×10 **(iv)** 235×50

   (b) What is the relationship between 235×10 and 235×50?

4. **(a)** Work out these products.

   (i) 16×21 **(ii)** 21×17 **(iii)** 829×13 **(iv)** 25×617

   (b) What is the relationship between 16×21 and 21×17?

   (c) Without calculating it, what do you predict the value of 830×13 to be? Calculate the answer to check your prediction.

5. Find these values.

   (a) 10^2 **(b)** 15^2 **(c)** 6^3 **(d)** 9^3

 **LEVEL 2**

6. Mr Taylor's electricity bill is twice as much as Mr Smith's electricity bill. This information is shown using a bar model. How much is Mr Taylor's electricity bill?

   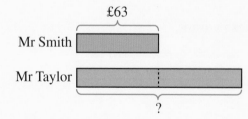

7. Anita is four times as old as her daughter. The information is shown using a bar model. Find Anita's age.

   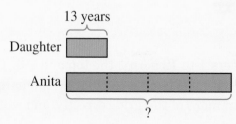

8. The price of a chair is £187. The price of a table is three times as much as the price of the chair. Draw a bar model to represent the information. Find the price of the table.

9. A technician prepares 230 ml of a solution in each of 26 flasks. What is the total volume of the solution?

10. A multi-storey car park has six levels. On each level there are seven rows of 12 spaces. How many spaces are there altogether in the car park?

Workbook 1A Link
Exercise 2.1

2.2 Division

Say you have twelve £1 coins and you want to divide them by three. Or in other words, you want to perform a **division** of 12 by 3.

You write this as $12 \div 3$ or $\frac{12}{3}$, and you read it as 'twelve divided by three'. The '$\div$' is called the **division sign**.

One way of picturing this is sharing the 12 coins equally amongst 3 children. To do this, you could create 3 rows (1 for each child) and arrange the 12 coins evenly in those 3 rows.

The number of coins that each child has is the number of coins in each row.

As shown in the diagram, you have

$$12 \div 3 = 4 \quad \text{or} \quad \frac{12}{3} = 4.$$

Each child has four coins.

Another way of picturing 12 coins divided by three is imagining you are filling purses with 3 coins each until you run out of coins. The number of purses is then the answer to the division.

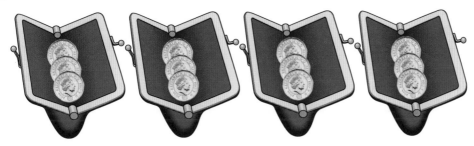

 DISCUSS

Both calculations are written as $12 \div 3 = 4$. What does each number represent in each calculation? Can you think of a situation where it would be easier to share something out, and a situation where it would be easier to fill things up?

Again, as shown in the diagram, you have

$$12 \div 3 = 4 \quad \text{or} \quad \frac{12}{3} = 4.$$

Objective: To explore the relationship between multiplication and division.

1. Calculate these values.

   (a) 2×3 (b) $6 \div 2$ (c) $6 \div 3$

2. Calculate these values.

   (a) 2×5 (b) $10 \div 2$ (c) $10 \div 5$

3. Calculate these values.

   (a) 3×7 (b) $21 \div 3$ (c) $21 \div 7$

4. Calculate these values.

   (a) 4×6 (b) $24 \div 4$ (c) $24 \div 6$

5. Observe the above results. If number 1 × number 2 = number 3, what is

   (a) number 3 ÷ number 1,   (b) number 3 ÷ number 2?

> **REMARK**
>
> You can use number discs if necessary. For example, you can show 2×3 as
>
>

Class Activity 2 shows the following relationship between multiplication and division.

> If   number 1 × number 2 = number 3,
> then   number 3 ÷ number 1 = number 2
> and   number 3 ÷ number 2 = number 1.

This is called the **inverse relationship** between multiplication and division.

For example, knowing that $4 \times 9 = 36$, you also know

$$36 \div 4 = 9 \quad \text{and} \quad 36 \div 9 = 4.$$

Recall that in the division $36 \div 4 = 9$, the number 36 is called the **dividend**. The number 4 is called the **divisor**. The resulting number 9 is called the **quotient**.

This division in column form is

$$
\begin{array}{r}
9 \leftarrow \text{quotient} \\
\text{divisor} \longrightarrow 4\,\overline{)\,36\,} \leftarrow \text{dividend} \\
36 \leftarrow 4 \times 9 = 36 \\
\hline
0 \leftarrow \text{remainder}
\end{array}
$$

The number 0 is called the **remainder**. You can interpret this by saying that when 36 items are divided into 4 groups, each group will have 9 items and there are no remaining items.

> **REMARK**
>
> The relationship between 4, 9 and 36 can be represented by a factor tree.
>
>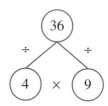
>
> Here, the product of the two lower numbers is the top number. When the top number is divided by one of the lower numbers, the quotient is the other lower number.

Example 8

Calculate these quotients.

(a) $68 \div 2$

(b) $67 \div 4$

Solution **(a)** Use place value counters to demonstrate the division first.

Divisor = 2	Tens					Ones				
Dividend 68	10	10	10	10	10	1	1	1	1	1
	10					1	1	1		
Quotient Group 1	10	10	10			1	1	1	1	
Group 2	10	10	10			1	1	1	1	

The dividend = 68 = 6 tens counters + 8 ones counters.

As the divisor = 2, the 6 tens counters are divided into two equal groups with 3 tens counters in each group. 3 is the tens digit of the quotient.

Then the 8 ones counters are divided into two equal groups with 4 ones counters in each group. 4 is the ones digit of the quotient.

$\therefore$ the quotient = 34

The above steps can be represented as **long division** as follows.

Step 1

$$\begin{array}{r} 3 \\ 2\overline{)68} \\ 6 \\ \hline 8 \end{array}$$

Divide 6 tens by 2.   6 tens $\div$ 2 = 3 tens.

3×2

$6 - 6 = 0$, so the zero is left out. Rewrite the 8.

Step 2

$$\begin{array}{r} 34 \\ 2\overline{)68} \\ 6 \\ \hline 8 \\ 8 \\ \hline 0 \end{array}$$

Divide 8 ones by 2. 8 ones $\div$ 2 = 4 ones.

4×2

$8 - 8 = 0$. 0 indicates no remainder.

$\therefore 68 \div 2 = 34$

Continued

(b) Use the place value counters to demonstrate the division first.

Divisor = 4	Tens	Ones
Dividend 67	10 10 10 10 10 10	1 1 1 1 1 1 1
Regroup		1 1 1 1 1 1 1 1 1 1 1 1 1 1 1 1 1 1 1 1
Quotient Group 1	10	1 1 1 1 1 1
Group 2	10	1 1 1 1 1 1
Group 3	10	1 1 1 1 1 1
Group 4	10 Regroup	1 1 1 1 1 1
Remainder	10 10	1 1 1

The dividend = 67 = 6 tens counters + 7 ones counters.

As the divisor = 4, the 6 tens counters are divided into four equal groups with 1 tens counter in each group. 1 is the tens digit of the quotient. There are 2 remaining tens counters.

The 2 remaining tens counters are regrouped into 20 ones counters.

Then the total 27 ones counters are divided into four equal groups with 6 ones counters in each group. 6 is the ones digit of the quotient. There are 3 remaining ones counters. Thus, the remainder is 3.

∴ the quotient = 16 and the remainder is 3.

The above steps can be represented as **long division** as follows.

Step 1

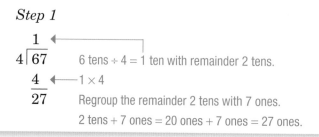

4 | 67   6 tens ÷ 4 = 1 ten with remainder 2 tens.

4 ← 1 × 4

27   Regroup the remainder 2 tens with 7 ones.

2 tens + 7 ones = 20 ones + 7 ones = 27 ones.

Step 2

$$16 \text{ r } 3 \longleftarrow \quad \text{r 3 indicates the remainder is 3.}$$
$$4\overline{)67}$$
$$\underline{4}$$
$$27 \qquad \text{27 ones} \div 4 = 6 \text{ ones with remainder 3 ones.}$$
$$\underline{24} \longleftarrow 6 \times 4$$
$$3 \qquad 27 - 24 = 3$$

$$\therefore \ 67 \div 4 = 16, \text{ r } 3$$

Note: $67 \div 4 = 16$, r 3 means the quotient is 16 and the remainder is 3.

Say, for example, 67 shells are shared equally among 4 children. Each child will have 16 shells and 3 shells will be left over.

Child 1

Child 2

Child 3

Child 4

Number of shells left over

Try It! 8 Calculate these quotients.

(a) $48 \div 2$

(b) $50 \div 3$

Example 9 Find each quotient and remainder.

(a) $\dfrac{635}{5}$

(b) $\dfrac{6035}{7}$

RECALL

$\dfrac{635}{5}$ is another way of writing $635 \div 5$.

Solution (a) Use the place value counters to demonstrate the division first.

Continued

49

Divisor = 5	Hundreds	Tens	Ones
Dividend 635	100 100 100 100 100 100	10 10 10	1 1 1 1 1
Regroup		10 10 10 10 10 10 10 10 10 10	1 1 1 1 1 1 1 1 1 1 1 1 1 1 1 1 1 1 1 1 1 1 1 1 1 1 1 1 1 1
Quotient Group 1	100	10 10	1 1 1 1 1 1 1
Group 2	100	10 10	1 1 1 1 1 1 1
Group 3	100	10 10	1 1 1 1 1 1 1
Group 4	100	10 10	1 1 1 1 1 1 1
Group 5	100	10 10	1 1 1 1 1 1 1
Remainder	100	10 10 10	

The dividend = 635 = 6 hundreds counters + 3 tens counters + 5 ones counters.

As the divisor = 5, the 6 hundreds counters are divided into five equal groups with 1 hundreds counter in each group. 1 is the hundreds digit of the quotient. There is 1 remaining hundreds counter.

The 1 remaining hundreds counter is regrouped into 10 tens counters.

The total 13 tens counters are divided into five equal groups with 2 tens counters in each group. 2 is the tens digit of the quotient. There are 3 remaining tens counters.

The 3 remaining tens counters are regrouped into 30 ones counters.

Then the total 35 ones counters are divided into five equal groups with 7 ones counters in each group. 7 is the ones digit of the quotient. There is no remaining ones counter. Thus, the remainder is 0.

∴ the quotient = 127 and the remainder = 0.

The above steps can be represented as **long division** as follows.

REMARK

You can use the division table on page 359 to check that $35 \div 7 = 5$.

$$\begin{array}{r} 1 \\ 5\overline{)635} \\ 5 \\ \hline 13 \end{array}$$

6 hundreds ÷ 5 = 1 hundred with remainder 1 hundred.

1 × 5

Regroup the remainder 1 hundred with 3 tens to make 13 tens.

$$\begin{array}{r} 12 \\ 5\overline{)635} \\ 5 \\ \hline 13 \\ 10 \\ \hline 35 \end{array}$$

13 tens ÷ 5 = 2 tens with remainder 3 tens.

2 × 5

Regroup the remainder 3 tens with 5 ones to make 35 ones.

$$\begin{array}{r} 127 \\ 5\overline{)635} \\ 5 \\ \hline 13 \\ 10 \\ \hline 35 \\ 35 \\ \hline 0 \end{array}$$

35 ones ÷ 5 = 7 ones with remainder 0.

7 × 5

35 − 35 = 0

Hence, $\frac{635}{5} = 127$.

∴   the quotient = 127 and the remainder = 0.

Note: When the remainder is zero, the dividend is said to be **divisible** by the divisor. Here, 635 is divisible by 5.

(b) $7\overline{)6035}$

$$\begin{array}{r} 8 \\ 7\overline{)6035} \\ 56 \\ \hline 43 \end{array}$$

60 hundreds ÷ 7 = 8 hundreds with remainder 4 hundreds.

8 × 7

Regroup the remainder 4 hundreds with 3 tens to 43 tens.

REMARK

6 is less than 7. Regroup 6 thousands with 0 hundreds to 60 hundreds.

Continued

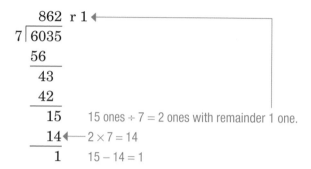

$$
\begin{array}{r}
86 \\
7\overline{)6035} \\
56 \\
\hline
43 \\
42 \\
\hline
15
\end{array}
$$

43 tens ÷ 7 = 6 tens with remainder 1 ten.

6 × 7

Regroup the remainder 1 ten with 5 ones to 15 ones.

DISCUSS

How would you regroup the remainder when 17 thousands are divided by 7?

$$
\begin{array}{r}
862 \;\; r\,1 \\
7\overline{)6035} \\
56 \\
\hline
43 \\
42 \\
\hline
15 \\
14 \\
\hline
1
\end{array}
$$

15 ones ÷ 7 = 2 ones with remainder 1 one.

2 × 7 = 14

15 − 14 = 1

Hence, $\frac{6035}{7} = 862,\ r\ 1.$

∴ the quotient = 862 and the remainder = 1.

Note: When the remainder is NOT zero, the dividend is said to be NOT divisible by the divisor. Here, 6035 is **not divisible** by 7.

 Try It! 9

Find each quotient and remainder.

(a) $\dfrac{534}{3}$

(b) $\dfrac{5034}{8}$

The method of writing the division in Example **9** is called **long division**. You can skip the lower part of the division and simply write:

$$
\begin{array}{r}
1\,2\,7 \\
5\overline{)6^{1}3^{3}5}
\end{array}
$$

or

$$
\begin{array}{r}
8\,6\,2 \;\; r\,1 \\
7\overline{)60^{4}3^{1}5}
\end{array}
$$

This method is called **short division**.

DISCUSS

Work through the long division method and the short division method side by side for the same example. Compare the methods. Which do you prefer, and why?

Example 10

Find the missing numbers.

(a) $96 \div$ ▮ $= 12$

(b) ▮ $\div 11 = 14$

Solution

(a) $96 \div$ ▮ $= 12$ number 3 ÷ number 1 = number 2

▮ $= 96 \div 12$ number 1 = number 3 ÷ number 2

▮ $= 8$

$$\begin{array}{r} 8 \\ 12\overline{)96} \\ 96 \\ \hline 0 \end{array}$$

(b) ▮ $\div 11 = 14$ number 3 ÷ number 1 = number 2

▮ $= 11 \times 14$ number 3 = number 1 × number 2

▮ $= 154$

$$\begin{array}{r} 11 \\ \times\ 14 \\ \hline 44 \\ 110 \\ \hline 154 \end{array}$$

Try It! 10

Find the missing numbers.

(a) $208 \div$ ▮ $= 8$

(b) ▮ $\div 15 = 22$

REMARK

Use a factor tree to help you visualise this problem.

REMARK

Use the division tables on page 359 to check that:

$96 \div 8 = 12$ and

$154 \div 11 = 14$.

Example 11

A scholarship of £2560 is shared equally between four students. How much does each student get?

Solution

The bar model for this situation is shown.

£2560

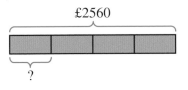

?

$$\begin{array}{r} 640 \\ 4\overline{)2560} \\ 24 \\ \hline 16 \\ 16 \\ \hline 0 \\ 0 \\ \hline 0 \end{array}$$

Scholarship for each student

$= £2560 \div 4$

$= £640$

RECALL

Since $16 - 16 = 0$, the 0 is left out in the division.

Try It! 11

In a woodland, 1080 trees are planted in nine equal rows. How many trees are in each row?

Example 12

Each tray can hold 24 bottles of milk. Find the number of trays needed to carry 367 bottles.

Solution

Number of trays = 367 ÷ 24
= 15, r 7

There are 15 trays with 7 bottles left.
Since the 7 bottles also need a tray,
the number of trays needed is 16.

$$
\begin{array}{r}
15\ \text{r}\ 7 \\
24\overline{)367} \\
\underline{24} \leftarrow 1 \times 24 \\
127 \\
\underline{120} \leftarrow 5 \times 24 \\
7
\end{array}
$$

DISCUSS

What does the remainder 7 represent here? Are there 7 trays remaining, or 7 bottles left over?

Note: You may find it helpful to write down the products of 24 and each of the digits 1 to 9.
$1 \times 24 = 24,$ $2 \times 24 = 48,$ $3 \times 24 = 72,$
$4 \times 24 = 96,$ $5 \times 24 = 120,$ $6 \times 24 = 144,$
$7 \times 24 = 168,$ $8 \times 24 = 192,$ $9 \times 24 = 216.$

For example, the dividend 127 is between 120 and 144, so the digit 5 should be placed in the quotient.

REMARK

Using short division, the working is:
$$
\begin{array}{r}
1\ \ 5\ \text{r}\ 7 \\
24\overline{)36^{12}7}
\end{array}
$$

Try It! 12

There are 200 ml of medicine in a bottle. How many full spoons can be filled and how much is left in the bottle if each spoon can hold 18 ml?

PRACTICE 2.2

⚙ LEVEL 1

1. **(a)** Calculate these quotients. You may use place value counters to help you.
   (i) 75 ÷ 3 　　**(ii)** 75 ÷ 5 　　**(iii)** 896 ÷ 7 　　**(iv)** 896 ÷ 8

   (b) Without working it out, which would be greater, 3696 ÷ 7 or 3696 ÷ 8? Explain your answer.

2. Work out these values.
   (a) 108 ÷ 9 　　**(b)** 1008 ÷ 9 　　**(c)** 143 ÷ 13 　　**(d)** 651 ÷ 21

3. Find these quotients and remainders. You may use place value counters to help you.
   (a) 58 ÷ 4 　　**(b)** 905 ÷ 6 　　**(c)** $\dfrac{123}{10}$ 　　**(d)** $\dfrac{870}{15}$

4. Find the missing numbers. Explain your answers.
   (a) 153 ÷ ▢ = 9 　　　　　　　**(b)** ▢ ÷ 7 = 26

   (c) 23 × ▢ = 414 　　　　　　**(d)** ▢ × 11 = 715

5. The bar model shows jelly beans shared equally among five children. How many jelly beans does each child get?

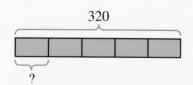

6. Given that $325 \times 79 = 25\,675$, state the value of

    (a) $25\,675 \div 79$,   **(b)** $25\,675 \div 325$,   **(c)** $256\,750 \div 79$.

7. A ribbon is 216 cm long. It is cut into four equal parts. Draw a bar model to show this. Find the length of each part.

8. A farmer has 651 eggs. They are packed into boxes of 12 for sale.

    (a) How many boxes are filled?

    (b) How many eggs are left after all the boxes have been packed?

9. A school hires some buses for a school trip. A total of 428 students and staff go on the trip. Each bus can take 54 passengers and the cost of each bus is £310.

    (a) How many buses are needed?   **(b)** What is the total cost?

10. Find the digits represented by ▲, ● and ▇ in this multiplication.

$$
\begin{array}{r}
5\blacktriangle \\
\times \quad \bullet\,4 \\
\hline
212 \\
\blacksquare\,240 \\
\hline
\blacksquare\,452 \\
\end{array}
$$

Workbook 1A Link
Exercise 2.2

2.3 Multiplying and Dividing Efficiently Without a Calculator

A   Reordering

In Section 2.1, you learnt that

    $3 \times 5 = 5 \times 3$ and $4 \times 9 = 9 \times 4$.

This property allows you to swap the factors in multiplication.

Consider $4 \times 7 \times 3$. If you calculate 4×7 first,

    $4 \times 7 \times 3 = 28 \times 3 = 84$.

What happens if you calculate 7×3 first? It turns out that

    $(4 \times 7) \times 3 = 4 \times (7 \times 3)$,

where you calculate the product within the brackets first.

 **REMARK**

The property that

$(4 \times 7) \times 3 = 4 \times (7 \times 3)$

is called the associative law of multiplication.

The brackets mean that the product inside the brackets has to be calculated first. This is discussed further in Chapter 3.

A property of multiplication is that factors can be multiplied together in any order without changing the value of the product. This means you can multiply efficiently by reordering.

DISCUSS

1. Is $9 \div 3 = 3 \div 9$?
2. Is $(36 \div 6) \div 2$
   $= 36 \div (6 \div 2)$?

Explain your answers.

Example 13

Calculate these products by first reordering to make them easier.

(a) $5 \times 17 \times 2$ (b) $4 \times 39 \times 25$

Solution

(a) $5 \times 17 \times 2$
    $= 5 \times 2 \times 17$
    $= 10 \times 17$
    $= 170$

Reorder so that the first product is 10 or a multiple of 10.

(b) $4 \times 39 \times 25$
    $= 4 \times 25 \times 39$
    $= 100 \times 39$
    $= 3900$

Reorder so that the first product is 100 or a multiple of 100.

REMARK

When a number is multiplied by 10, each digit moves one place to the left in a place value table. When a number is multiplied by 100, each digit moves two places to the left in a place value table.

Try It! 13

Calculate these products by first reordering to make them easier.

(a) $2 \times 47 \times 5$ (b) $50 \times 68 \times 2$

B Doubling and Halving

Doubling and halving can make some multiplication and division calculations easier.

Example 14

Work these out by first halving one of the numbers.

(a) 123×8 (b) $196 \div 4$

Solution

(a) 123×8
    $= 123 \times 2 \times 2 \times 2$
    $= 246 \times 2 \times 2$
    $= 492 \times 2$
    $= 984$

Write 8 as $2 \times 2 \times 2$ (halve it twice)
$123 \times 2 = 246$
$123 \times 4 = 123 \times 2 \times 2$
         $= 246 \times 2$
         $= 492$

(b) $196 \div 4$
    $= 196 \div 2 \div 2$
    $= 98 \div 2$
    $= 49$

$\div 4$ is the same as halving twice.
$196 \div 2 = 98$

REMARK

$\square \times 4 = \square \times 2 \times 2$
$\square \times 8 = \square \times 2 \times 2 \times 2$
$\square \div 4 = \square \div 2 \div 2$
$\square \div 8 = \square \div 2 \div 2 \div 2$

It is easier to multiply by 2 than by 4 or 8.

It is easier to divide by 2 than by 4 or 8.

Try It! 14

Work these out by first doubling or halving one of the numbers.

(a) 152×4 (b) $256 \div 8$

Example 15

Work these out by first doubling or halving one of the numbers.

(a) 624×5 **(b)** 269×20 **(c)** 72×25

(a) 624×5
$= 624 \times 10 \div 2$ Convert $\times 5$ to $\times 10 \div 2$.
$= 6240 \div 2$
$= 3120$

(b) 269×20
$= 269 \times 10 \times 2$ Convert $\times 20$ to $\times 10 \times 2$.
$= 2690 \times 2$
$= 5380$

(c) 72×25
$= 72 \times 100 \div 4$ $25 = 100 \div 4$
$= 72 \times 100 \div 2 \div 2$ Convert $\times 25$ to $\times 100 \div 2 \div 2$.
$= 7200 \div 2 \div 2$
$= 3600 \div 2$
$= 1800$

Work these out using a method to make them easier.

(a) 217×5 **(b)** 148×20 **(c)** 86×25

REMARK

$\square \times 5 = \square \times 10 \div 2$
$\square \times 20 = \square \times 10 \times 2$
$\square \times 25 = \square \times 100 \div 2 \div 2$
$\square \times 50 = \square \times 100 \div 2$

In these calculations, those on the right-hand side are easier.

C Distributive Law and Partitioning

I buy 4 bags of apples. Each bag contains 3 red apples and 5 green apples. How many apples are there in total? There are two ways of calculating this. You can either find

(number of green apples in 1 bag × number of bags)
+ (number of red apples in 1 bag × number of bags)

or

(number of red apples in 1 bag + number of green apples in 1 bag)
× number of bags

$5 \times 4 + 3 \times 4$ or $(3 + 5) \times 4$
$= 20 + 12$ $= 8 \times 4$
$= 32$ $= 32$

As you can see, both methods give the same answer. More generally:

number 1 × (number 2 + number 3) = number 1 × number 2 + number 1 × number 3

This property is called the **distributive law** of multiplication over addition.

This law can be applied to subtraction and division as well. For example,

$$7 \times (23 - 8) = 7 \times 23 - 7 \times 8$$

and

$$
\begin{array}{ll}
(45 - 20) \div 5 & \text{or} \qquad 45 \div 5 - 20 \div 5 \\
= 25 \div 5 & \qquad\qquad = 9 - 4 \\
= 5 & \qquad\qquad = 5
\end{array}
$$

You can apply these properties, together with partitioning, to make calculations without a calculator easier.

Example 16

Calculate these products by partitioning first.

(a) 326×7

(b) 415×11

(c) 267×98

Solution

(a) 326×7

$$
\begin{array}{ll}
= (300 + 20 + 6) \times 7 & \text{Partition 326 to } 300 + 20 + 6. \\
= 300 \times 7 + 20 \times 7 + 6 \times 7 & \text{Use the distributive law.} \\
= 2100 + 140 + 42 & \text{It is easier to multiply 300, 20 and} \\
= 2282 & \text{6 by 7 than 326 by 7.}
\end{array}
$$

(b) 415×11

$$
\begin{array}{ll}
= 415 \times (10 + 1) & \text{Partition 11 to } 10 + 1. \\
= 415 \times 10 + 415 \times 1 & \text{Use the distributive law.} \\
= 4150 + 415 & \text{It is easier to multiply by 10 and 1 than} \\
= 4565 & \text{by 11.}
\end{array}
$$

(c) 125×98

$$
\begin{array}{ll}
= 125 \times (100 - 2) & \text{Partition 98 to } 100 - 2. \\
= 125 \times 100 - 125 \times 2 & \text{Use the distributive law.} \\
= 12\,500 - 250 & \text{It is easier to multiply by 100 and 2} \\
= 12\,250 & \text{than by 98.}
\end{array}
$$

Try It! 16

Calculate these products by partitioning first.

(a) 257×3

(b) 634×9

(c) 185×102

Example 17

Work these out by first applying techniques to make them easier.

(a) $852 \div 6$
(b) $360 \div 15$

Solution

(a) $852 \div 6$
$= (600 + 252) \div 6$ Express 852 as 600 + 252 since 600 ÷ 6 = 100.
$= 600 \div 6 + 252 \div 6$ Use the distributive law.
$= 100 + 42$
$= 142$

(b) $360 \div 15$
$= 360 \div 3 \div 5$
$= 120 \div 5$
$= 24$

Convert ÷ 15 into ÷ 3 ÷ 5.

Dividing by 15 is equivalent to dividing by 3 and then by 5.

Dividing by a single digit is easier than dividing by a 2-digit number.

Note, it might be clearer to see why this works if you look at these images.

The first diagram divides a bar into 15 parts.

The second diagram divides the bar into 3 large parts.

The third diagram divides one large part into 5 parts.

You see that the parts in the first diagram are the same as the parts in the third diagram.

This shows that ÷ 15 is the same as ÷ 3 ÷ 5.

Try It! 17

Work these out by first applying techniques to make them easier.

(a) $553 \div 7$
(b) $432 \div 18$

DISCUSS

Annie and Boris use the following partitions to work out 852 ÷ 6.

Annie:
$852 \div 6$
$= (600 + 240 + 12) \div 6$
$= 600 \div 6 + 240 \div 6$
   $+ 12 \div 6$
$= 100 + 40 + 2$
$= 142$

Boris:
$852 \div 6$
$= (600 + 300 - 48) \div 6$
$= 600 \div 6 + 300 \div 6$
   $- 48 \div 6$
$= 100 + 50 - 8$
$= 142$

Compare their methods with the solution.
Which do you prefer?
Why?

Example 18

Each butterfly has six legs. There are 299 butterflies in a greenhouse. Find the total number of legs on the butterflies.

Solution

Total number of legs on the butterflies
$= 299 \times 6$
$= (300 - 1) \times 6$
$= 300 \times 6 - 1 \times 6$
$= 1800 - 6$
$= 1794$

Try It! 18

Each spider has eight legs. Find the total number of legs on 198 spiders.

PRACTICE 2.3

For each question in this exercise, choose the best method to make the calculation easier.

LEVEL 1

1. Calculate these products.

    (a) $2 \times 78 \times 5$ **(b)** $50 \times 29 \times 2$ **(c)** 2×90 **(d)** 59×4

2. Evaluate these expressions.

    (a) $86 \div 2$ **(b)** $4 \times 31 \times 5$ **(c)** 65×8 **(d)** 237×8

3. Work out these values.

    (a) 132×5 **(b)** $96 \div 4$ **(c)** 568×9 **(d)** $342 \div 18$

4. Work out these values.

    (a) $368 \div 4$ **(b)** $1000 \div 8$ **(c)** 67×25 **(d)** 214×25

5. Compute these expressions. Explain your method.

    (a) 926×20 **(b)** 762×11 **(c)** $680 \div 20$ **(d)** 65×102

6. Evaluate these expressions. Explain your method.

    (a) $936 \div 8$ **(b)** 315×8 **(c)** 875×99 **(d)** $315 \div 21$

LEVEL 2

7. The weekly salary of a clerk in a company is £735. There are nine clerks. What is their total weekly salary?

   £ FINANCE

8. A scholarship of £5096 is shared equally among eight students. How much does each student get?

   £ FINANCE

9. The price of a Big Ben souvenir is £25. A shop sells 234 of these souvenirs. How much does the shop receive from the sales?

   PROBLEM SOLVING

10. Describe a real-life situation where you can use multiplication or division to work out a solution. For this situation, write three examples of a calculation you may have to do without a calculator. Explain your method for calculating the answers efficiently.

    OPEN QUESTION

> **Workbook 1A Link**
> Exercise 2.3

2.4 Factors, Multiples and Prime Numbers

You can express a number as a product of some numbers. You can use this property for further calculations.

A Factors

Which two whole numbers can be multiplied to give an answer of 12?

$1 \times 12 = 12$
$2 \times 6 = 12$
$3 \times 4 = 12$

The numbers 1, 2, 3, 4, 6 and 12 are **factors** of 12.

In general, two whole numbers are the factors of their product. A number can have negative factors too, but in this book you will only consider positive (whole number) factors.

 Example 19   List all the whole number factors of 28.

 Solution
$1 \times 28 = 28$
$2 \times 14 = 28$
$4 \times 7 = 28$
∴ the whole number factors of 28 are 1, 2, 4, 7, 14 and 28.

Try It! 19   List all the whole number factors of 18.

If a whole number is a factor of two numbers, it is called a **common factor** of both of them. The largest such factor is called the **highest common factor** (or **HCF**) of the two numbers.

Example 20   (a) Find the common whole number factors of the numbers 24 and 30.

(b) State the HCF of the numbers 24 and 30.

Solution   (a) Work out the   Work out the
factors of 24.   factors of 30.
$1 \times 24 = 24$ $1 \times 30 = 30$
$2 \times 12 = 24$ $2 \times 15 = 30$
$3 \times 8\ = 24$ $3 \times 10 = 30$
$4 \times 6\ = 24$ $5 \times 6\ = 30$
1, 2, 3, 4, 6, 8, 12 and 24 are factors of 24.
1, 2, 3, 5, 6, 10, 15 and 30 are factors of 30.
Hence, 1, 2, 3 and 6 are common factors of 24 and 30 (as shown in blue).

Continued

 REMARK

The diagram is a factor wall. It shows how a wall of length 12 units can be laid with 1 brick that is 12 units long, 2 bricks each 6 units long, 3 bricks each 4 units long, 4 bricks each 3 units long, 6 bricks each 2 units long or 12 bricks each 1 unit long.

12		
6		6
4		
3		
2		
1		

 REMARK

You can represent factors using square tiles.

28 square tiles can be arranged as 4 rows of 7 tiles each. 4 and 7 are factors of 28.

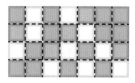

(b) The greatest common factor is 6.
i.e. HCF of 24 and 30 is 6.

Try It! 20 **(a)** Find the common whole number factors of the numbers 20 and 25.

(b) State the HCF of the numbers 20 and 25.

B Multiples

The product of a whole number and another whole number, such as 1, 2, 3 and 4, is called a **multiple** of the original number.
For example, the whole number multiples of 2 are

$$1 \times 2, \ 2 \times 2, \ 3 \times 2, \ 4 \times 2, \ 5 \times 2, \ 6 \times 2, \ 7 \times 2, \ ...$$
giving   2, 4, 6, 8, 10, 12, 14, ...

DISCUSS

How can you tell if a number is divisible by 2? What do you notice about its last digit? What do you call these numbers?

Example 21 List the first six whole number multiples of 5.

Solution The first six multiples of 5 are:
$$1 \times 5, 2 \times 5, 3 \times 5, 4 \times 5, 5 \times 5 \text{ and } 6 \times 5,$$
giving   5, 10, 15, 20, 25 and 30.

Try It! 21 List the first six whole number multiples of 7.

DISCUSS

How can you tell if a number is divisible by 5? What do you notice about its last digit?

When a whole number is a multiple of two numbers, it is called a **common multiple** of both of them. The smallest such number is called the **lowest common multiple** (or **LCM**) of the two original numbers.

REMARK

You can use the multiplication table on page 359 to quickly check multiples of a number. Moving down a column, you will see all the multiples of the number at the start of that column. The smallest number that appears in two different columns is the lowest common multiple for those two columns.

Example 22 **(a)** List the first ten whole number multiples of each of the numbers 6 and 8.

(b) Write down the first two common multiples of 6 and 8.

(c) State the LCM of 6 and 8.

Solution **(a)** The first ten whole number multiples of 6 are:
$$1 \times 6, 2 \times 6, 3 \times 6, 4 \times 6, 5 \times 6, 6 \times 6, 7 \times 6,$$
$$8 \times 6, 9 \times 6 \text{ and } 10 \times 6,$$
giving   6, 12, 18, 24, 30, 36, 42, 48, 54 and 60.

The first ten whole number multiples of 8 are:
$$1 \times 8, 2 \times 8, 3 \times 8, 4 \times 8, 5 \times 8, 6 \times 8, 7 \times 8,$$
$$8 \times 8, 9 \times 8 \text{ and } 10 \times 8,$$
giving   8, 16, 24, 32, 40, 48, 56, 64, 72 and 80.

DISCUSS

What is the third common multiple of 6 and 8?

(b) From part **(a)**, the first two common multiples of 6 and 8 are 24 and 48.

(c) The LCM of 6 and 8 is 24.

Note: The multiples of 6 are the total lengths of some rods of length 6 units laid end-to-end. The multiples of 8 are the total lengths of some rods of length 8 units laid end-to-end. The LCM is the total length (in either row) when the ends of the rods in both rows line up for the first time.

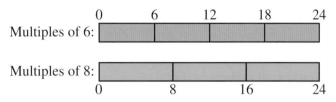

Try It! 22

(a) List the first ten whole number multiples of the numbers 3 and 9.

(b) Write down the first three common whole number multiples of 3 and 9.

(c) State the LCM of 3 and 9.

C Prime Numbers

Prime numbers are whole numbers greater than 1 that have exactly two whole number factors. These two factors are 1 and the number itself.

The whole number factors of 2 are 1 and 2.
The whole number factors of 3 are 1 and 3.
The whole number factors of 4 are 1, 2 and 4.
The whole number factors of 5 are 1 and 5.
The whole number factors of 6 are 1, 2, 3 and 6.
The whole number factors of 7 are 1 and 7.
The whole number factors of 8 are 1, 2, 4 and 8.
The whole number factors of 9 are 1, 3 and 9.
The whole number factors of 10 are 1, 2, 5 and 10.

From this list, the numbers 2, 3, 5 and 7 are therefore prime numbers. This is because each of them has only two whole number factors. The numbers 4, 6, 8, 9 and 10 are not prime numbers.

DISCUSS

Is 1 a prime number? Explain your answer.

REMARK

You can use a factor tree to help you work out factors.

Example 23

Write down the prime number that is more than 24 but less than 30.

Solution

You can draw a table to list the whole number factors of the numbers 25 to 29.

Number	Factors
25	1, 5, 25
26	1, 2, 13, 26
27	1, 3, 9, 27
28	1, 2, 4, 7, 14, 28
29	1, 29

The number with only two factors is 29.

∴ the prime number that is more than 24 but less than 30 is 29.

Try It! 23

List the prime numbers that are more than 15 but less than 20.

↻ RECALL

As $1 \times 26 = 26$ and $2 \times 13 = 26$, the factors of 26 are 1, 2, 13 and 26.

If a factor of a number is prime, it is called a **prime factor** of the number. If a number greater than 1 is not a prime number, it can be expressed as a product of its prime factors.

Example 24

Express 60 as a product of its prime factors.

Solution

$60 = 2 \times 30$
$\quad = 2 \times 2 \times 15$
$\quad = 2 \times 2 \times 3 \times 5$

Note: This means 2, 3 and 5 are the prime factors of 60.

Alternative Method
You can use a factor tree to show the prime factors.

Divide each number on the top rows into two factors until you get all the prime factors.

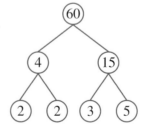

Here, the prime factors are 2, 3 and 5.

Try It! 24

Express 90 as a product of prime factors.

PRACTICE 2.4

LEVEL 1

1. List all the whole number factors of each number.

   (a) 10   **(b)** 27

   (c) 36   **(d)** 40

2. List the first six whole number multiples of each number.

   (a) 3   **(b)** 10

   (c) 11   **(d)** 20

3. Determine which of these numbers are prime numbers.

   (a) 30   **(b)** 31

   (c) 47   **(d)** 53

4. Which of these numbers would you consider the odd one out? Explain your answer.

   OPEN QUESTION   21, 31, 36, 81

LEVEL 2

5. **(a)** List the whole number factors of the numbers 10 and 15.

   (b) List the common whole number factors of 10 and 15.

   (c) State the HCF of 10 and 15.

6. **(a)** List the first 10 whole number multiples of each of the numbers 4 and 6.

   (b) Write down the first three common whole number multiples of the numbers 4 and 6.

   (c) State the LCM of 4 and 6.

7. Express each number as a product of its prime factors.

   PROBLEM SOLVING   **(a)** 42   **(b)** 105

   (c) 24   **(d)** 99

8. A model kit has red rods of length 12 cm and blue rods of length 15 cm.

Some red rods are joined in a straight line to form a long red stick. Some blue rods are joined in a straight line to form a long blue stick. If the red stick and the blue stick have the same length, what is the minimum length of the red stick?

9. **(a)** Pick the multiples of 3 from this list.

42   96   101   135

(b) For each multiple of 3 in part **(a)**, add up the digits. Is the sum of the digits also a multiple of 3? Does this work for any multiple of 3?

Workbook 1A Link
Exercise 2.4

REVIEW

Multiplication

- Repeated addition can be calculated by multiplication.

  $7 + 7 + 7 + 7 = 4 \times 7$

- Multiplication laws

  1. Commutativity: $4 \times 7 = 7 \times 4$
  2. Associativity: $(3 \times 4) \times 7 = 3 \times (4 \times 7)$

- Grid method for 476×8:

×	400	70	6
8	3200	560	48

  $$
  \begin{array}{r}
  3200 \\
  560 \\
  +\ \ 48 \\
  \hline
  3808 \\
  {\scriptstyle 1}
  \end{array}
  $$

  $476 \times 8 = 3808$

- Column method for 476×8:

  $$
  \begin{array}{r}
  476 \\
  \times\ \ \ \ 8 \\
  \hline
  3808 \\
  {\scriptstyle 6\ 4}
  \end{array}
  $$

  $476 \times 8 = 3808$

- Indices

  $5^2 = 5 \times 5 = 25$ (square number)

  $5^3 = 5 \times 5 \times 5 = 125$ (cube number)

Division

- $20 \div 4 = \dfrac{20}{4} = 5$

  When 20 pens are shared equally among 4 students, each student is given 5 pens.
  When 20 pens are used to fill up cases each containing 4 pens, there are 5 cases.

- Inverse relationship between multiplication and division:

  knowing $28 \times 3 = 84$,

  gives $84 \div 28 = 3$

  and $84 \div 3 = 28$.

- Long division:

  $$
  \begin{array}{r}
  165\ \text{r } 2 \\
  5\overline{)827} \\
  5 \\
  \hline
  32 \\
  30 \\
  \hline
  27 \\
  25 \\
  \hline
  2
  \end{array}
  $$

  $827 \div 5 = 165$ r 2

  The quotient = 165 and the remainder = 2.

- Short division:

  $531 \div 4 = 132$ r 3

  $$
  \begin{array}{r}
  1\ 3\ 2\ \text{ r } 3 \\
  4\overline{)5^13^11}
  \end{array}
  $$

Multiplying and Dividing Efficiently Without a Calculator

- Reordering

$$2 \times 47 \times 5 = 47 \times 2 \times 5$$
$$= 47 \times 10$$
$$= 470$$

- Doubling and halving

$$123 \times 8 = 123 \times 2 \times 2 \times 2$$
$$= 246 \times 2 \times 2$$
$$= 492 \times 2$$
$$= 984$$

$$324 \div 4 = 324 \div 2 \div 2$$
$$= 162 \div 2$$
$$= 81$$

- Distributive law and partitioning

$$53 \times 199 = 53 \times (200 - 1)$$
$$= 53 \times 200 - 53 \times 1$$
$$= 10\,600 - 53$$
$$= 10\,547$$

Factors, Multiples and Prime Numbers

- $4 \times 9 = 36$
  4 and 9 are factors of 36.
  36 is a multiple of both 4 and 9.

- 1, 2, 3, 4, 6 and 12 are factors of 12.
  1, 2, 3, 6, 9 and 18 are factors of 18.
  The common whole number factors of 12 and 18 are 1, 2, 3 and 6.
  The HCF of 12 and 18 is 6.

- The first three common whole number multiples of 3 and 5 are 15, 30 and 45.
  The LCM of 3 and 5 is 15.

- The first ten prime numbers are:
  2, 3, 5, 7, 11, 13, 17, 19, 23, 29.

- As $42 = 2 \times 3 \times 7$,
  2, 3 and 7 are called prime factors of 42.

CHALLENGE 2

Here are four digits: 2, 3, 6 and 8. Use these digits to make two whole numbers. You can only use each digit once. What is the greatest possible product of the two whole numbers you can make?

Hint: The products you can make are 23×68, 362×8, etc.

Workbook 1A Link
Problem Solving 2

REVISION EXERCISE 2 ✦✦

1. Calculate these products.
   (a) 235×6 **(b)** 418×7 **(c)** 9×306 **(d)** 5×1209

2. Find these values.
   (a) 34×11 **(b)** 25×64 **(c)** 408×13 **(d)** 38×157

3. **(a)** You are told that $369 \times 258 = 95\,202$. State the value of
   (i) $95\,202 \div 369$,   **(ii)** $95\,202 \div 258$.

   (b) Find the missing number in $518 \div \boxed{} = 14$.

4. Find each quotient and remainder.
   (a) $\dfrac{536}{4}$ **(b)** $\dfrac{1289}{3}$ **(c)** $562 \div 11$ **(d)** $2458 \div 23$

5. Work out these expressions by first using methods to make the calculations easier. Explain your steps.
   (a) $5 \times 167 \times 2$ **(b)** $384 \div 8$ **(c)** 625×101 **(d)** 73×499

6. **(a)** Write down the whole number factors of 36 and 45.
   (b) Find the common whole number factors of 36 and 45.
   (c) State the HCF of 36 and 45.

7. **(a)** Write down the first ten whole number multiples of 10 and 15.
   (b) Write down the first three common whole number multiples of 10 and 15.
   (c) State the LCM of 10 and 15.
   (d) List the factors of the LCM of 10 and 15 that are prime numbers.

8. A bakery has two trays of muffins. Each tray has five rows and each row has 18 muffins. Find the total number of muffins on the two trays.

9. There are 254 guests attending a dinner party. Each table at the party has seats for eight guests. How many tables are needed for the party?

   PROBLEM SOLVING

10. A school has 1086 students. Each student donates £5. The total donation is shared equally among three charities. How much is the donation to each charity?

   PROBLEM SOLVING

Write in Your Journal

Your friend does not understand the methods for multiplying and dividing efficiently without a calculator. Write some examples to teach your friend. Advise them on the mistakes to avoid.

3 CALCULATION

A record 8357 runners took part in the Oxford Half Marathon 2017. Approximately, how many thousands of runners were there? Approximately, how many hundreds of runners were there?

LET'S LEARN TO

▶ round numbers to the nearest 10, 100, 1000 or 10000

▶ estimate answers to calculations

▶ use the order of operations

▶ use a calculator

1. Place Value

The value represented by each digit in a number depends on its place. Take 82 906 as an example.

Ten thousands 10 000	Thousands 1000	Hundreds 100	Tens 10	Ones 1
8	2	9	0	6

From the above **place value table**, you can see that
$$82\,906 = 80\,000 + 2000 + 900 + 0 + 6$$
This is read as eighty-two thousand, nine hundred and six. The zero in the 'Tens' column is a **place holder**.

2. Number Line

A number can be represented by a point on a **number line**. The diagram shows the numbers 3, 45 and 573 on different number lines.

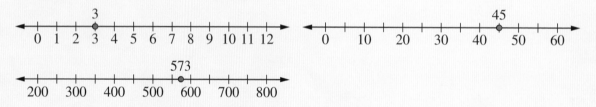

3. Multiplication

573×4

(a) Grid Method

×	500	70	3
4	2000	280	12

$$
\begin{array}{r}
2000 \\
280 \\
+ \quad 12 \\
\hline
2292
\end{array}
$$

(b) Column Method

$$
\begin{array}{r}
573 \\
\times \quad 4 \\
\hline
2292 \\
\scriptstyle 2\,1
\end{array}
$$

$\therefore \quad 573 \times 4 = 2292$ ◄—— 2292 is called the product of 573 and 4.

(c) $\quad 4 \times 67 \times 25 = 67 \times 4 \times 25 \qquad$ Reorder 4 and 67.
$\qquad\qquad\qquad = 67 \times 100 \qquad$ Multiply 4 and 25 first.
$\qquad\qquad\qquad = 6700$

(d) Square Numbers
$\quad$ e.g. $\quad 7^2 = 7 \times 7 \qquad$ (2 is called the **index** of 7.)
$\qquad\qquad = 49$

(e) Cube Numbers
$\quad$ e.g. $\quad 5^3 = 5 \times 5 \times 5 \qquad$ (3 is called the **index** of 5.)
$\qquad\qquad = 125$

4. Division

$2548 \div 8$

(a) Long Division

$$
\begin{array}{r}
318 \ \text{r } 4 \\
8\overline{\smash{)}2548} \\
\underline{24} \\
14 \\
\underline{8} \\
68 \\
\underline{64} \\
4 \leftarrow \text{remainder}
\end{array}
$$

$\therefore \quad 2548 \div 8 = \dfrac{2548}{8}$

$\qquad\qquad\quad = 318 \ \text{r } 4$

(b) Short Division

quotient ⟶ $3\,1\,8$ r 4 ⟵ remainder
divisor ⟶ $8\overline{\smash{)}25^14^68}$ ⟵ dividend

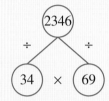

This relationship can be represented as a factor tree.

(c) Inverse Relationship between Multiplication and Division

$34 \times 69 = 2346$ also tells you that
$2346 \div 34 = 69 \qquad$ and $\qquad 2346 \div 69 = 34.$

3.1 Rounding Numbers

David buys a car for £23 765. He tells his friends that the price is about £24 000. The number 24 000 is a **rounded number**. It is an **approximation** of the original number 23 765. You may round a number in different ways, for example to the nearest 10, 100, 1000 or 10 000.

CLASS ACTIVITY 1

Objective: To round numbers to the nearest 10, 100, 1000 and 10 000.

1.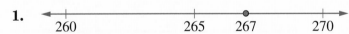

   As you can see from the number line, 267 is between 260 and 270.

   (a) Which is 267 closer to: 260 or 270?
   (b) Which number, 260 or 270, would you use as an approximation of 267? Explain your answer.

2.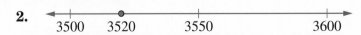

   As you can see from the number line, 3520 is between 3500 and 3600.

   (a) Which is 3520 closer to: 3500 or 3600?
   (b) Which number, 3500 or 3600, would you use as an approximation of 3520? Explain your answer.

3.

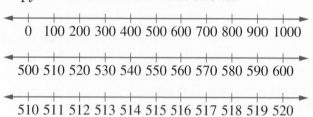

The number line above shows the digits from 0 to 10. If you were rounding to the nearest 10,

    (a) which whole numbers would you round to 0,

    (b) which whole numbers would you round to 10?

4.

The number line above counts up in thousands. 17 500 is between 17 000 and 18 000.

Which number, 17 000 or 18 000, would you use as an approximation of 17 500? Explain your answer.

5.

As you can see from the number line, 17 500 is between 10 000 and 20 000.

    (a) Which is 17 500 closer to: 10 000 or 20 000?

    (b) Which number, 10 000 or 20 000, would you use as an approximation of 17 500? Explain your answer.

6. Copy the three number lines shown.

    (a) Add a circle to each number line to represent the number 513.

    (b) Round 513 to the nearest 10, 100 and 1000.

Class Activity 1 involves rounding a number.

As 267 is closer to 270 than 260, you have

      267 = 270   (to the nearest 10).

This is called **rounding up**.

As 3520 is closer to 3500 than 3600, you have

      3520 = 3500   (to the nearest 100).

This is called **rounding down**.

17 500 is midway between 17 000 and 18 000.

By convention, you round up the number 17 500 and have

      17 500 = 18 000 (to the nearest 1000).

17 500 is closer to 20 000 than 10 000, so you have

      17 500 = 20 000   (to the nearest 10 000).

REMARK

Convention means a general agreement about a matter.

Note that the same number can be rounded to different numbers, depending on the **degree of accuracy** required.

The degree of accuracy indicates the number is rounded to the nearest 10, 100, 1000 or 10 000, etc.

Steps for rounding a number:

1. Locate the desired place value of rounding. For example, if you are rounding a number to the nearest 100, the desired place value is hundreds.

2. Look at the digit in the next place value to the right. For example, if you are rounding a number to the nearest 100, you look at the tens digit. This is sometime called the **check digit**. If it is **4** or less, round **down** the number. If the digit is **5** or more, round **up** the number.

3. Write the rounded number and state the degree of accuracy.

Let's see some examples.

Example ① The mass of a car is 1653 kg. Round the mass to

    (a) the nearest 10 kg,

    (b) the nearest 100 kg.

Solution

                    ↓ desired place value (tens)

    (a) Mass of the car = 1653 kg

                    ↑ The digit in the ones place (the check digit) is 3, which fits the '4 or less' rule. Round down.

        = 1650 kg   (to the nearest 10 kg)
        ↑   ↑
  rounded number   degree of accuracy

                  ↓ desired place value (hundreds)

    (b) Mass of the car = 1653 kg

                  ↑ The digit in the tens place is 5, which fits the '5 or more' rule. Round up.

        = 1700 kg   (to the nearest 100 kg)

Try It! ① The volume of milk in a jug is 1827 ml. Round the volume to

    (a) the nearest 10 ml,

    (b) the nearest 100 ml.

DISCUSS

Round 87 452 to the nearest

(a) 10,

(b) 100,

(c) 1000,

(d) 10 000.

Draw an appropriate number line to help you.

REMARK

These number lines show the rounding situations in **(a)** and **(b)**.

(a)   1653

     1650 1655 1660

(b)   1653

     1600 1650 1700

Example 2

There are 1354 people in a concert audience. The ticket price for the concert is £8. Find the total ticket price, giving your answer to the nearest £1000.

Solution

The total ticket price = £8 × 1354
$$= £10\,832$$
$$= £11\,000 \quad \text{(to the nearest £1000)}$$

Note: You must always round at the end of the actual calculation.

DISCUSS

What is your answer if you round the number of people in the concert audience to the nearest 1000 first, and then find the total ticket price?

Try It! 2

The number of people taking part in a charity run is 2497. Each participant pays a £6 entry fee. Find the total entry fee, giving your answer to the nearest £1000.

PRACTICE 3.1

LEVEL 1

1. The number 1384 is rounded to the nearest 10. Which of these gives the correct answer?
   A 1380   **B** 1390   **C** 1400   **D** 1300

2. **(a)** Draw each number on a number line. Then use that to round the number to the nearest 10.
   (i) 927 (number line between 920 and 930)
   (ii) 451 (number line between 450 and 460)

   (b) Round each number to the nearest 10, explaining your reasoning.
   (i) 1689   **(ii)** 3925

3. **(a)** Draw each number on a number line. Then use that to round each number to the nearest 100.
   (i) 369 (number line between 300 and 400)
   (ii) 447 (number line between 400 and 500)

   (b) Round each number to the nearest 100, explaining your reasoning.
   (i) 2455   **(ii)** 36 308

4. **(a)** Round each number to the nearest 1000.
   (i) 4561   **(ii)** 9963   **(iii)** 26 718   **(iv)** 63 039

   (b) Round each number to the nearest 10 000.
   (i) 30 912   **(ii)** 7123   **(iii)** 844 596   **(iv)** 96 712

5. Which of the following numbers rounds to 4800, when rounding to the nearest 100? (There may be more than one number)
   A 4700   **B** 4750   **C** 4825   **D** 4775

6. The volume of juice in a carton is 405 ml. Round the volume to the nearest 10 ml.

7. The highest mountain in the UK is Ben Nevis. Its height is 1344 m. Round the height to the nearest 100 m.

8. The price of a necklace is £3450. Find the total price of three such necklaces, giving your answer to the nearest £1000.

PROBLEM SOLVING

9. Mrs Thomas's annual income is £53 278. Mr Thomas's annual income is £64 914.

   £ FINANCE

   (a) Find the total annual income of Mr and Mrs Thomas.

   PROBLEM SOLVING

   (b) Round the answer in (a) to the nearest £10 000.

   (c) Find the total annual income of Mr and Mrs Thomas by rounding each of their annual incomes to the nearest £10 000 first. Compare this answer with the answer in (b).

10. Alice thinks of a number and rounds it. She says her number is 38 000 to the nearest 1000. Write a possible value of Alice's number which is

    OPEN QUESTION

    (a) smaller than 38 000,

    (b) greater than 38 000.

Workbook 1A Link
Exercise 3.1

3.2 Estimation

Estimation is often used in real-world situations and to solve mathematical problems. It is used when the exact value is impossible or difficult to find, for example, the size of the UK population. It is also used to check the reasonableness of an answer. One way to estimate is to use approximation by rounding numbers.

£68.90 £31.30

CLASS ACTIVITY 2

Objective: To estimate the total cost of buying two items.

Mrs Roberts wants to buy a vase that costs £68.90 and a teapot that costs £31.30. She has £100 in her purse. Two of her grandchildren, Leanne and William, estimate the total price of the two items for her.

1. Leanne rounds each price to the nearest £10 and then finds the sum of the two rounded numbers. What is her estimate?

2. William rounds **up** each price to the nearest £10 (no matter what the ones digit is) and then finds the sum of the two rounded numbers. What is his estimate?

3. Whose estimate, Leanne's or William's, will guarantee that Mrs Roberts has or hasn't got enough money for these two items? Explain your answer.

DISCUSS

Find the exact total cost of the two items in Class Activity 2. Compare the estimated total cost with the exact total cost. Is the estimation useful? Why are both prices rounded up instead of rounded to the nearest £10?

Class Activity 2 shows that you must choose an appropriate method to estimate a value. Let's see some examples.

Example 3

Estimate these calculations by first rounding the numbers to the nearest 10.

(a) $76 + 98$

(b) $89 - 43$

(c) 128×49

(d) $449 \div 51$

Solution

(a) $76 \approx 80$ Round to the nearest 10.

$98 \approx 100$ Round to the nearest 10.

$76 + 98 \approx 80 + 100$

$= 180$

(b) $89 \approx 90$ Round to the nearest 10.

$43 \approx 40$ Round to the nearest 10.

$89 - 43 \approx 90 - 40$

$= 50$

(c) $128 \approx 130$ Round to the nearest 10.

$49 \approx 50$ Round to the nearest 10.

$128 \times 49 \approx 130 \times 50$

$= 6500$

(d) $449 \approx 450$ Round to the nearest 10.

$51 \approx 50$ Round to the nearest 10.

$449 \div 51 \approx 450 \div 50$

$= 9$

REMARK

The symbol $\approx$ means is approximately equal to.

Try It! 3

Estimate these calculations by first rounding the numbers to the nearest 10.

(a) $58 + 91$

(b) $97 - 34$

(c) 273×92

(d) $416 \div 68$

Example 4

Estimate $245 + 371$ by first rounding each number to

(a) the nearest 100,

(b) the nearest 10.

Solution

(a) $245 + 371 \approx 200 + 400$ Each number is rounded

$= 600$ to the nearest 100.

(b) $245 + 371 \approx 250 + 370$ Each number is rounded

$= 620$ to the nearest 10.

REMARK

The actual answer for $245 + 371$ is 616. Different methods of estimation can result in different estimated values.

Try It! 4

Estimate $395 - 217$ by first rounding each number to

(a) the nearest 100,

(b) the nearest 10.

Example 5

Deva needs to join three computers to the office network using network cables. The lengths of the cables are 23 m, 39 m and 47 m. Estimate the total length of cables that Deva needs. Is this an under-estimation or an over-estimation of the actual length?

Solution

One way to estimate is to round the length of each cable to the nearest 10 m.

23 m ≈ 20 m
39 m ≈ 40 m
47 m ≈ 50 m
20 m + 40 m + 50 m = 110 m

Deva needs about 110 m of network cables.

The actual length needed is 23 + 39 + 47 = 109 m. The estimated value is an over-estimate of the actual length needed.

Try It! 5

Simon wants to paint some of the rooms in his house. He needs 12 litres of paint for the bathrooms, 13 litres for the bedrooms and 9 litres for the hall. Estimate the total amount of paint he needs. Is the estimated amount an under-estimate or an over-estimate of the actual amount needed?

DISCUSS

Should the estimate always be an over-estimation? How can you ensure that the estimate is an over-estimation?

Example 6

Karen wants to buy a dress that costs £178 and twelve shirts that cost £19 each. She estimates that she needs £640 in total. Is this an under-estimate or an over-estimate? Is it reasonable?

Solution

Price of the dress = £178
          = £180   (to the nearest £10)

Price of 12 shirts = 12 × £19
          ≈ 12 × £20   Round £19 to the nearest £10.
          = £240

Total price ≈ £180 + £240 = £420

Price of 12 shirts = 12 × £19 = £228

The actual total price = £178 + £228 = £406

So Karen's estimate of £640 is a large over-estimate. It is not reasonable.

DISCUSS

Why is the number of shirts not rounded?

Try It! 6

Mrs Simpson wants to buy two pots that cost £159 each and 16 plates that cost £12 each. She estimates that she needs £610 in total. Use estimation to check whether her estimate is reasonable.

PRACTICE 3.2

LEVEL 1

1. Four students are asked to estimate the calculation $75 + 291$ by rounding to the nearest 10. Which student has written the correct calculation?

   A $80 + 300$ **B** $70 + 290$ **C** $80 + 290$ **D** $70 + 300$

2. Estimate these calculations by first rounding the numbers to the nearest 10.

   (a) $12 + 68$ **(b)** $569 - 46$ **(c)** 42×31 **(d)** $704 \div 65$

3. Estimate these calculations by first rounding the numbers to the nearest 100.

   (a) $350 + 634$ **(b)** $7413 - 483$ **(c)** 53×9112 **(d)** $2974 \div 503$

4. Estimate these calculations by first rounding the numbers to the nearest 10.

   (a) $67 + 15 - 22$ **(b)** $96 - 78 + 20$ **(c)** $216 + 49 + 113$ **(d)** $398 - 214 - 67$

LEVEL 2

5. Estimate these calculations by first rounding the numbers to the nearest 100.

   (a) $168 - 215 + 23$ **(b)** $5618 + 3480 - 219$ **(c)** $5671 - 206 - 1598$ **(d)** $1192 + 72 + 368$

6. A student estimates a calculation by rounding to the nearest 100. They write $1200 - 800$. Which of these was the original calculation?

   A $1255 - 750$ **B** $1150 - 755$ **C** $1200 - 855$ **D** $1155 - 850$

7. Mr Watkins has £450 in his wallet. He buys three items at £23, £85 and £208. Estimate the amount of money he has left by rounding each amount spent to the nearest £100. Is this an under-estimate or an over-estimate?

   FINANCE

8. A builder requires 123 kg of cement and 277 kg of sand for a job. He estimates that the amount of material needed is 500 kg in total. Use estimation by rounding each given quantity to the nearest 10 kg to check whether the builder's estimate is reasonable. Has he made an under-estimate or an over-estimate?

9. In the stands at a football match there are 9874 fans supporting one team and 7573 fans supporting the other team.

   (a) Estimate the total number of fans attending the match by

       (i) rounding each number to the nearest 1000,

       (ii) rounding each number to the nearest 100.

   (b) Compare the two estimates in **(a)**.

10. Emma and Luke estimate the sum of the volumes of juice in two cartons of drinks. One carton contains 337 ml and one contains 275 ml. Emma estimates the answer by rounding the volumes to the nearest 10 ml. Luke estimates the answer by rounding the volumes to the nearest 100 ml. Whose estimation is closer to the actual value?

    PROBLEM SOLVING

Workbook 1A Link
Exercise 3.2

3.3 Order of Operations

There are three bananas and two bags of oranges, with five oranges in each bag. Carla works out the total number of fruits by first calculating the number of oranges.

$$\text{Number of oranges} = 2 \text{ lots of } 5 = 2 \times 5$$
$$= 10$$

$$\text{Total number of fruits} = \text{number of bananas} + \text{number of oranges}$$
$$= 3 + 10$$
$$= 13$$

Her brother Dan works out $3 + 2 \times 5$ by calculating $3 + 2$ first and gets:

$$3 + 2 \times 5 = 5 \times 5$$
$$= 25$$

Their answers are different, but which of the two is correct?

The order of operations in a calculation, such as $3 + 2 \times 5$, is the order in which you carry out the individual calculations. It's important to get the order right, because it may affect the answer. Let's study and discuss the general principles.

A Four Operations

The four operations discussed here are multiplication, division, addition and subtraction. The order of these is:

> First, work out all multiplication and division.
>
> Next, work out all addition and subtraction from left to right.

 DISCUSS

You usually perform all multiplications and divisions from left to right, but you don't always need to. Take the calculation $45 \times 18 \div 9$. Why might you want to calculate the division first?

In which situations would you have to complete them from left to right?

Example 7

Calculate
(a) $24 \times 3 + 96 \div 8$,
(b) $52 - 75 \div 5 \times 3 + 10$.

Solution

(a) $24 \times 3 + 96 \div 8$
$= 72 + 12$ Work out multiplication and division first.
$= 84$ Work out addition.

(b) $52 - 75 \div 5 \times 3 + 10$
$= 52 - 15 \times 3 + 10$ Work out division and multiplication.
$= 52 - 45 + 10$
$= 7 + 10$ Work out subtraction and addition.
$= 17$

Calculate

(a) $84 \div 7 + 16 \times 3$, (b) $67 + 9 \times 4 \div 3 - 71$.

B Indices

You need to evaluate calculations written with indices before you work out multiplication, division, addition and subtraction.

Example 8 Calculate

(a) $5^3 - 6^2 \times 3$, (b) $8^2 \div 4 \times 5 + 7^2 - 29$.

Solution

(a) $5^3 - 6^2 \times 3$
$= 125 - 36 \times 3$ Evaluate calculations with indices first.
$= 125 - 108$ Work out multiplication.
$= 17$ Work out subtraction.

(b) $8^2 \div 4 \times 5 + 7^2 - 29$
$= 64 \div 4 \times 5 + 49 - 29$ Evaluate calculations with indices first.
$= 16 \times 5 + 49 - 29$ Work out division and multiplication.
$= 80 + 49 - 29$
$= 129 - 29$ Work out addition and subtraction.
$= 100$

REMARK

Indices is the plural of index.

$5^3 = 5 \times 5 \times 5$

$6^2 = 6 \times 6$

Try It! 8 Calculate

(a) $6^3 + 5^2 \times 4$, (b) $4^3 - 3^2 \times 5 + 63 \div 9$.

C Brackets

There are 14 boys and 16 girls in a class. If each student donates £5, how much can be collected?

You can first find the total number of students by adding 14 and 16. The sum of 14 and 16 is 30.

Then you multiply the sum by 5.

In the above scenario, you have to perform addition before multiplication. You indicate this order of operations by using **brackets**.

When a calculation involves brackets, work out the calculations in the brackets before any other calculations. The brackets override the order of multiplication and division before addition and subtraction.

The amount collected $= (14 + 16) \times £5$
$$= 30 \times £5 \qquad \text{Work out the sum in the brackets first.}$$
$$= £150 \qquad \text{Then work out the multiplication.}$$

In general, the order of operations is:

First **brackets**,

Next **indices**,

Followed by **multiplication** and **division**, usually from left to right,

Finally **addition** and **subtraction**, usually from left to right.

 **CLASS ACTIVITY 3**

Objective: To explore the order of operations.

Work in pairs. Using the digits 1, 2, 3 and 4 in that order, in a row, insert some operation signs $(+, -, \times, \div)$ and brackets. Can you create thirteen calculations that have the answers 0 to 12?

For example, $(1 + 2) \times 3 - 4 = 5$,
$$12 \div 3 + 4 = 8,$$
$$1 + 2 + 3 + 4 = 10.$$

Compare your answers with other classmates.

What do you notice about the order you carry out the operations on the numbers?

Example 9 Calculate the following.

(a) $96 - (28 + 37)$

(b) $(96 - 28) + 37$

Solution **(a)** $96 - (28 + 37)$
$$= 96 - 65 \qquad \text{Work out the sum in the brackets first.}$$
$$= 31$$

(b) $(96 - 28) + 37$
$$= 68 + 37 \qquad \text{Work out the subtraction in the brackets first.}$$
$$= 105$$

 DISCUSS

Look at the solutions to **(a)** and **(b)**. Do the brackets change the answer? What if there were no brackets?

Try It! 9 Calculate the following.

(a) $85 - (41 - 23)$

(b) $(85 - 41) - 23$

Example 10

Calculate the following.

(a) $16 \times (12 - 7)$　　　　　**(b)** $(38 + 94) \div 11$

Solution

(a) $16 \times (12 - 7)$

$= 16 \times 5$ 　　　Work out the subtraction in the brackets first.

$= 80$

(b) $(38 + 94) \div 11$

$= 132 \div 11$ 　　　Work out the sum in the brackets first.

$= 12$

Try It! 10

Calculate the following.

(a) $12 \times (9 + 8)$　　　　　**(b)** $(324 - 168) \div 13$

REMARK

You can use the multiplication and division table on page 359 to check some of these calculations.

Example 11

Calculate the following.

(a) $(5 + 40) \div 9 + 11 \times (36 - 28)$

(b) $5 + 40 \div (9 + 11) \times (36 - 28)$

Solution

(a) $(5 + 40) \div 9 + 11 \times (36 - 28)$

$= 45 \div 9 + 11 \times 8$ 　　Work out the calculations in the brackets first.

$= 5 + 88$ 　　Work out the division and multiplication.

$= 93$ 　　Work out the addition.

(b) $5 + 40 \div (9 + 11) \times (36 - 28)$

$= 5 + 40 \div 20 \times 8$ 　　Work out the calculations in the brackets first.

$= 5 + 2 \times 8$ 　　Calculate the division.

$= 5 + 16$ 　　Calculate the multiplication.

$= 21$ 　　Work out the addition.

Try It! 11

Calculate the following.

(a) $(17 - 12) \times 18 - 15 \div (29 - 26)$

(b) $17 - 12 \times (18 - 15) \div (29 - 26)$

Example 12

Work out $5^2 \times (36 - 32) + 6^3 \div 9 - 51$.

Solution

$5^2 \times (36 - 32) + 6^3 \div 9 - 51$

$= 5^2 \times 4 + 6^3 \div 9 - 51$ 　　Carry out the subtraction in the brackets.

$= 25 \times 4 + 216 \div 9 - 51$ 　　Evaluate the calculations with indices.

$= 100 + 24 - 51$ 　　Work out the multiplication and the division.

$= 124 - 51$ 　　Work out the addition and the subtraction.

$= 73$

Try It! 12

Work out $4^3 \div (5 - 3) + 15 \times 5 - 7^2 \times 2$.

Example 13

Olivia's weekly salary is £700. She saves £95 each week and spends the rest. Work out the amount spent in eight weeks.

Solution

Amount spent each week = £700 − £95
Amount spent in eight weeks
= 8 × (700 − 95)
= 8 × 605   Work out the subtraction in the brackets.
= £4840   Work out the multiplication.

Try It! 13

Chocolate bars are delivered in boxes containing 12 bars. In each box three bars have nuts. Find the total number of chocolate bars without nuts in five boxes.

You learned about averages in primary school. Let's recall how to calculate the mean.

$$\text{Mean} = \frac{\text{Sum of all the values}}{\text{Total number of values}}$$

REMARK

Mean is a type of average in statistics. The values are usually collected in a survey or experiment.

Example 14

John's marks in three tests are 67, 89 and 72. Find his mean mark in these three tests.

Solution

The bar model shows the situation.

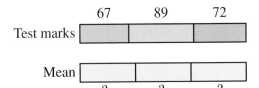

The mean of the three test marks is the sum of the test marks divided into three equal parts.
Mean mark = (67 + 89 + 72) ÷ 3
= 228 ÷ 3
= 76

DISCUSS

Does the expression
67 + 89 + 72 ÷ 3
give the mean mark?

Try It! 14

At a charity event, Sarah walks 8 miles, Akira walks 10 miles, Leah walks 11 miles and Evie walks 7 miles. Find the mean distance that the four girls walk.

PRACTICE 3.3

LEVEL 1

1. Calculate these expressions.

   (a) $6 + 7 \times 3$ **(b)** $20 - 8 \times 2$ **(c)** $19 + 42 \div 6$ **(d)** $88 - 96 \div 8$

2. The value of each of these expressions can be changed by adding brackets. Copy each expression then add brackets so that its value changes. (You don't need to work out the answers.)

   (a) $8 \times 3 + 2 \times 9$ **(b)** $160 \div 40 - 32 \div 8$

   (c) $84 \div 12 - 6 \times 2$ **(d)** $81 \div 3 + 13 + 15 \div 3 \times 4$

3. James buys two 6-packs of juice cartons, then gives 2 cartons to a friend. Which of these calculations represents how many cartons James has left?

   A $2 \times 6 - 2$ **B** $2 \div 6 - 2$ **C** $2 \times (6 - 2)$ **D** $2 \div (6 - 2)$

4. Evaluate these expressions.

   (a) 2×5^2 **(b)** 5×2^3 **(c)** $5 \times 4 + 8^2$ **(d)** $100 - 8^3 \div 16$

5. Work out these values.

   (a) $28 - (17 - 5)$ **(b)** $(23 - 12) \times 8$ **(c)** $26 \div (15 - 2)$ **(d)** $(21 + 3) \times (4 + 6)$

LEVEL 2

6. Calculate these expressions.

   (a) $(20 + 7) \times 4 - 3$ **(b)** $(20 + 7) \times (4 - 3)$

   (c) $(20 + 7 \times 4) - 3$ **(d)** $20 + 7 \times (4 - 3)$

   (e) $(2^3 + 11) \times 3$ **(f)** $2^3 + 11 \times 3$

   (g) $(200 - 5^3) \div 25$ **(h)** $3 \times 3^3 \div (4^2 - 7)$

7. Work out these values.

   (a) $7 \times 5 + (9^2 - 6) \times 3$ **(b)** $7 \times 5 + (9^2 - 6 \times 3)$

   (c) $416 \div (2^3 - 4) + 3 \times 7$ **(d)** $416 \div 2^3 - (4 + 3) \times 7$

8. Calculate each pair of expressions, working from left to right where there are no brackets, and compare the results. Can you describe a pattern or a rule?

   (a) $85 + (47 - 46)$ and $85 + 47 - 46$ **(b)** $263 - (53 + 47)$ and $263 - 53 + 47$

   (c) $9 \times (8 \div 4)$ and $9 \times 8 \div 4$ **(d)** $12 \div (6 \times 2)$ and $12 \div 6 \times 2$

9. In an experiment, $100\,\text{cm}^3$ of water is added to $250\,\text{cm}^3$ of vinegar. The mixture is poured equally into ten test tubes. What is the volume of the mixture in each test tube?

10. Ava donates 470 ml of blood. Ben donates 456 ml. Cathy donates 466 ml. Find the mean volume of their blood donations.

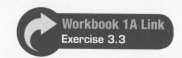
Workbook 1A Link
Exercise 3.3

3.4 Using a Calculator

Most scientific calculators apply the order of operations. However, different calculators may have different special keys and operations. You have to become familiar with how your own calculator works.

Example 15

Calculate the following.

(a) $347 \times 18 + 17^3$

(b) $9235 - 86^2 \div 43$

(c) $176 \times (478 - 251)$

Solution

(a) Calculator key sequence:

$$347 \boxed{\times} 18 \boxed{+} 17 \boxed{x^3} \boxed{=}$$

$$347 \times 18 + 17^3 = 11\,159$$

(b) Calculator key sequence:

$$9235 \boxed{-} 86 \boxed{x^2} \boxed{\div} 43 \boxed{=}$$

$$9235 - 86^2 \div 43 = 9063$$

(c) Calculator key sequence:

$$176 \boxed{\times} \boxed{(} 478 \boxed{-} 251 \boxed{)} \boxed{=}$$

$$176 \times (478 - 251) = 39\,952$$

Note: Calculators will not give you a correct answer if your key entry is wrong. It is good practice to check your answer using estimation.
For instance, rounding each given number to the nearest 10,

$$347 \times 18 + 17^3 \approx 350 \times 20 + 20^3$$
$$= 7000 + 8000$$
$$= 15\,000$$

As the answer in **(a)** and the estimate are both 5-digit numbers, the answer is in a reasonable range.
On the other hand, if your answer from a calculator was $111\,590$ while your estimate was $15\,000$, your answer would probably be wrong. You would need to re-enter the sequence in your calculator.

Try It! 15

Calculate the following.

(a) $8395 \div 23 - 18^2$

(b) $476 + 21^3 \times 59$

(c) $(3851 - 2701) \div 25$

You should check your answers using estimation.

✏️ **REMARK**

$5 \boxed{x^2} \boxed{=}$ gives 5^2.

$7 \boxed{x^3} \boxed{=}$ gives 7^3.

💬 **DISCUSS**

How could you work out 350×20 without a calculator? And how could you work out 20^3 without a calculator?

Example 16

Find the quotient and remainder when 356 is divided by 11.

Solution

The calculator key sequence for 356 ÷ 11 is:

356 ÷ 11 =

The answer display is $\frac{356}{11}$.

Change it to decimal display by pressing the key S↔D.
The answer display becomes the decimal $32.\overset{\cdot}{3}\overset{\cdot}{6}$.
This means

$$356 ÷ 11 = 32.36363636…$$

where the quotient is 32 and the decimal part 36 is recurring (repeating).
To obtain the remainder, subtract the quotient 32 from this result to get

$$0.36363636…$$

Then multiply by the divisor, 11.
The display 4 is then the remainder.

∴ $356 ÷ 11 = 32 \text{ r } 4$

Try It! 16

Find the quotient and remainder when
(a) 17 is divided by 3,   **(b)** 473 is divided by 12.

REMARK

You can use the multiplication and division tables on page 359 to find quotients and remainders.

REMARK

Alternatively, you could calculate $11 × 32 = 352$.
The remainder is then $356 − 352 = 4$.

Example 17

314 students and 16 teachers are going on a day trip in coaches. Each coach has 44 seats. How many coaches are required?

Solution

Total number of passengers = 314 + 16
$(314 + 16) ÷ 44 = 7.5$
You have to make sure there are enough coaches for everyone to go on the trip.

∴   you must round up because the remaining passengers need a coach.

∴   the number of coaches required = 8.

Note: Calculator key sequence:

(314 + 16) ÷ 44 =

The answer display is $\frac{15}{2}$.
You may change to decimal display by pressing the key S↔D.

The answer display becomes 7.5.

REMARK

Remember that different calculators may have different presentations.

A lab technician mixes 8432 ml of one chemical with 7243 ml of another chemical to form a substance that will be used by students in a chemistry experiment. If each student requires 190 ml of the substance, how many students will be able to perform this experiment?

Example 18

The mean monthly salary of four people in a company is £3095. The monthly salaries of three of them are £2535, £3264 and £3625. Find the monthly salary of the fourth person.

Solution

Use bar models to help you visualise this situation. The total salary of the four people is the same as 4 × the mean salary.

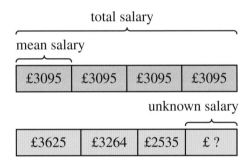

As mean monthly salary = $\dfrac{\text{total salary of the 4 people}}{4}$,

total salary of the 4 people = mean monthly salary × 4.
Monthly salary of the fourth person
= total salary of the 4 people − total salary of the first 3 people
= 3095 × 4 − (2535 + 3264 + 3625)
= £2956

Note: The key sequence is:
3095 × 4 − (2535 + 3264
+ 3625) =

Try It! 18

The mean sales in a shop for three days is £1830. The sales on the first two days are £2061 and £1647. Find the value of the sales on the third day.

PRACTICE 3.4

Use a calculator for this exercise.

⚙ LEVEL 1

You should check your answers using estimation.

1. Calculate these expressions.

   (a) $3156 + 478$

   (b) $98\,370 - 56\,142$

   (c) 937×56

   (d) $31\,590 \div 78$

   (e) 451^2

   (f) 47^3

2. Find the quotient and the remainder in each case.

   (a) $451 \div 7$

   (b) $4398 \div 23$

   (c) $3840 \div 15$

   (d) $52\,639 \div 624$

3. Work out these expressions.

   (a) $3872 - 1298 + 4561$

   (b) $145 \times 324 \div 36$

   (c) $987 + 56 \times 4^3$

   (d) $67^2 - 14\,445 \div 45$

4. Evaluate these expressions.

   (a) $987 \times (675 - 301)$

   (b) $(2875 + 5189) \div 12^2$

   (c) $43 + (9871 - 16^3) \div 55$

   (d) $4717 \div 53 + 5^3 \times (264 - 189)$

⚙ LEVEL 2

5. Georgia goes to a gym 19 times in a month. She pays £5 each time. How much does she
   PROBLEM SOLVING spend on the gym in a year?

6. A train has 578 passengers. At the next station, 124 people get off and 236 people get on
   the train. Find the number of passengers on the train now.

7. The heights of five basketball players are 209 cm, 198 cm, 187 cm, 205 cm and 196 cm. Find
   the mean height of these players.

8. There are some boxes each containing 750 grams of cornflakes. Each serving of cornflakes
   PROBLEM SOLVING is 30 grams. A family has four members. Each member has one serving of cornflakes every
   morning. How many boxes of cornflakes should be bought for 30 days?

9. Ava, Ben, Chloe and David do the same assignment. The mean time taken by them to
   PROBLEM SOLVING complete the assignment is 43 minutes. Ava takes 45 minutes. Ben takes 38 minutes.
   Chloe takes 40 minutes. What is the time taken by David?

> **Workbook 1A Link**
> Exercise 3.4

REVIEW

Rounding Numbers

- Use a number line to help with rounding.
- If the check digit is 4 or less, round down.
- If the check digit is 5 or more, round up.

e.g. $43516 = 43520$ (to the nearest 10)

$43516 = 43500$ (to the nearest 100)

$43516 = 44000$ (to the nearest 1000)

$43516 = 40000$ (to the nearest 10000)

Estimation

Estimation is the use of approximation to find a value close to the actual value.

e.g. $348 + 273$

$\approx 350 + 270$ Round each number
$= 620$ to the nearest 10.

$348 + 273 = 621$

620 is an estimation of the actual value 621.

Order of Operations

The order is usually:

First **brackets**,

Next **indices**,

Followed by **multiplication** and **division**, usually from left to right,

Finally **addition** and **subtraction**, usually from left to right.

e.g. $135 \div 5 + (43 - 17) \times 2^3$

$= 135 \div 5 + 26 \times 2^3$ Brackets

$= 135 \div 5 + 26 \times 8$ Indices

$= 27 + 208$ Division and multiplication

$= 235$ Addition

Using a Calculator

A scientific calculator uses the order of operations, but you need to key in sequences correctly.

e.g. $36 \times 7 - (45 + 18) \div 3^2$

Calculator key sequence:

36 ×　7 −　(　45 +

18)　÷　3 x^2 =

$36 \times 7 - (45 + 18) \div 3^2 = 245$

CHALLENGE 3

Write a calculation using all the digits 5, 6, 7 and 8 once only with some of the operators +, −, ×, ÷ and brackets.

   (a) What is the smallest non-zero whole number result you can get?

   (b) What is the greatest whole number result you can get?

Hint: Here are a few examples of calculations:

    5×678 $85 \times 76(8 - 6) + 5 - 7$ $8 - 5 \div (7 - 6)$

Workbook 1A Link
Problem Solving 3

1. Round these numbers to the given degree of accuracy.
    (a) 328, to the nearest 10
    (b) 3125, to the nearest 100
    (c) 9504, to the nearest 1000
    (d) 51 978, to the nearest 10 000

2. Which of these numbers can be rounded to 61 700 to the nearest 100?

    61 734   61 783   61 649   61 659   61 650

3. Estimate the values of these expressions by first rounding each number to the nearest 100.
    (a) $328 + 1745 - 34$
    (b) $6178 - 2319 + 4753$
    (c) $69 325 - 417 \times 97$
    (d) $249 + 35 350 \div 202$

4. Use a calculator to work out these expressions.
    (a) $89 + 12 \times 11$
    (b) $84 - 162 \div 3^2$
    (c) $16 + (98 - 56) \times 12$
    (d) $4^2 \times (70 - 57) - 5^3$

5. Use a calculator to work out these expressions.
    (a) $8713 - (2566 + 1704)$
    (b) $45 \times 96 - 15^2 \div 45$
    (c) $7326 + 13^3 \times (242 - 239)$
    (d) $801 - (47 + 12) \times 7 + 19^2$

6. The mass of a can of pineapple is 453 grams.
    (a) Find the total mass of three cans of pineapple.
    (b) Round your answer in (a) to the nearest 100 grams.

7. A garden has an area of 345 m^2. Trees cover 109 m^2, and flowers cover 137 m^2. The rest is lawn.
    (a) Find the area of the garden that is lawn.
    (b) Round your answer in (a) to the nearest 10 m^2.

8. **PROBLEM SOLVING** The Emirates Air Line is a cable car link across the River Thames in London. The maximum capacity of each cabin is ten people. 2374 people want to take a ride on the cable car.
    (a) What is the smallest number of cabins required?
    (b) Round your answer in (a) to the nearest 10 cabins.

9. **PROBLEM SOLVING** A metal wire is 125 cm long. Four pieces each of length 20 cm are cut from the wire to form a square frame. The remaining length of the wire is cut into three equal pieces to form an equilateral triangle (all sides the same length). What is the length of a side of the triangle?

10. The mass of a basketball is 623 grams. The mass of a football is 431 grams. The mass of a volleyball is 272 grams. Find the mean mass of these three balls.

Write in Your Journal

Write a calculation that includes brackets but has the same result if the brackets are removed.
Write a calculation without brackets and change its result by inserting brackets.

4 USE OF LETTERS

WHAT IS IN THIS CHAPTER:
4.1 Using Letters to Represent Numbers
4.2 Substitution of Numbers for Letters

In 2017, Spotify reported that it had approximately twice the number of paid subscribers as Apple Music. If x represents the number of Apple subscribers, can you represent the number of Spotify subscribers in terms of x?

LET'S LEARN TO
▶ use letters to represent numbers
▶ substitute numbers for letters

1. Addition

Add 497 to 126

126 + 497

126 **plus** 497

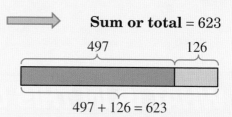

$$\begin{array}{r} 126 \\ + 497 \\ \hline 623 \\ \scriptstyle 1\ 1 \end{array}$$

Sum or total = 623

$$497 + 126 = 623$$

2. Subtraction

Subtract 497 from 623

623 − 497

623 **take away** 497

or

the **difference between** 497 and 623

$$\begin{array}{r} \scriptstyle 5\ 111 \\ 623 \\ - 497 \\ \hline 126 \end{array}$$

Result = 126

623

$$623 - 497 = 126$$

3. Multiplication

Multiply 56 by 28

56 × 28

56 **times** 28

$$\begin{array}{r} 56 \\ \times\ \ 28 \\ \hline 448 \\ 1120 \\ \hline 1568 \end{array}$$

Product = 1568

4. Division

Divide 379 by 4

379 ÷ 4

4 is **divided into** 379

you can also write this

as $\frac{379}{4}$

$$\begin{array}{r} 94\ \ \mathrm{r}\ 3 \\ 4\overline{)379} \\ 36 \\ \hline 19 \\ 16 \\ \hline 3 \end{array}$$

Quotient = 94

Remainder = 3

5. Order of Operations

First evaluate calculations inside brackets

Next evaluate calculations written with indices

Then evaluate multiplications and divisions, usually (but not always) from left to right

Finally, evaluate additions and subtractions, usually (but not always) from left to right

Example

$18 - \boxed{(5 + 10 \times 12)} \div 5^2$ The multiplication before the addition for the calculation within the brackets.

$= 18 - \boxed{(5 + 120)} \div 5^2$ The addition calculation before the division, because the addition is within the brackets.

$= 18 - 125 \div \boxed{5^2}$ The calculation written with index notation.

$= 18 - \boxed{125 \div 25}$ The division calculation before the subtraction

$= 18 \boxed{- 5}$ The subtraction

$= 13$

4.1 Using Letters to Represent Numbers

Did you know you can use maths to express the relationship between your age and your mother's age? How do you think you could express this relationship?

 **CLASS ACTIVITY 1**

Objective: To use letters to represent numbers and the relationship between numerical quantities.

Anne is 28 years older than her son Lucas. The relationship between their ages can be shown in a table.

There are some blanks where information is missing.

1. Copy the table and fill in the blanks in the 4th row.

2. Explain what the relationship is between the numbers on the same row but in different columns.

3. If Lucas's age is x years, how can you represent Anne's age in terms of x?

4. If Anne's age is y years, how can you represent Lucas's age in terms of y?

5. Now, represent your reasoning from questions **3** and **4** to fill in the bottom two rows.

 **REMARK**

"In terms of x" means "describe using x".

Lucas's age (years)	Anne's age (years)
0	28
1	$28 + 1 = 29$
11	$28 + 11 = 39$
16	$28 + \ldots = \ldots$
x	
	y

 **DISCUSS**

Is there more than one way of representing Anne's age when Lucas's age is represented by x? Is there more than one way of representing Lucas's age when Anne's age is represented by y?

In Class Activity 1, you used letters to represent numbers that can change in value.

In **algebra**, letters are used to represent numbers whose values you don't yet know. The letters x and y are called **variables**. This is because their values can vary. For instance, as time goes by, Lucas's and Anne's ages change. Variables are used to show relationships between the quantities they represent.

Expressions that involve numbers and letters, such as $28 + x$ and $y - 28$, are called **algebraic expressions**.

CLASS ACTIVITY 2

Objective: To match algebraic expressions with the correct statements.

1. Match the statements on the left with the algebraic expressions on the right. An algebraic expression may be matched by more than one statement.

    Hint: Remember x represents a value. If you are not sure about which statement matches which expression, give x a value (a number) and see if this helps you decide which are the matching pairs.

Product of x and 5.	$5 + x$
Sum of 5 and x.	
	$x \times 5$
Subtract x from 5.	
x groups of 5.	$5 - x$
x more than 5.	
	$x - 5$
x less than 5.	
Divide 5 by x.	$\dfrac{5}{x}$

2. Can you write a statement that would match the unmatched expression, and compare with your classmates?

Example 1 Write two possible statements, in words, for each algebraic expression.

    (a) $a + 5$ **(b)** $12 - b$

    (c) $6 \times c$ **(d)** $d \div 7$

Solution   **(a)** $a + 5$ is 'add 5 to a' or 'a plus 5'.

    (b) $12 - b$ is 'subtract b from 12' or '12 take away b'.

    (c) $6 \times c$ is '6 is multiplied by c' or '6 times c'.

    (d) $d \div 7$ is 'd is divided by 7' or '7 divided into d'.

DISCUSS

Can you use these words: sum, difference, product?

Try It! 1 Write two possible statements, in words, for each algebraic expression.

    (a) $4 + p$ **(b)** $q - 8$

    (c) $r \times 13$ **(d)** $20 \div s$

Example 2

Ava and Mia work on the same assignment. Ava takes ten minutes less than Mia. Find the time taken by Ava if Mia takes

(a) 28 minutes,　**(b)** 46 minutes,　**(c)** t minutes.

Solution

You should draw and label a bar model to represent the relationship between the variables.

Time taken by Ava ⬚ 10 mins
Time taken by Mia ⬚

You can summarise this by writing that "Ava's time is Mia's time – 10 minutes".

(a) If Mia takes 28 minutes,
　　Ava's time = 28 – 10
　　　　　　= 18 minutes.

(b) If Mia takes 46 minutes,
　　Ava's time = 46 – 10
　　　　　　= 36 minutes.

(c) If Mia takes t minutes,
　　Ava's time = $(t - 10)$ minutes.

Note: In **(c)**, Ava's time taken is expressed in terms of t.

REMARK

A variable on its own has no units. The brackets in '$(t - 10)$ minutes' indicate that the unit 'minutes' is applied to the whole expression 't subtract 10'.

Try It! 2

Aiden and Mason take the same test. Aiden scores seven marks more than Mason. Draw a bar model. Find Aiden's score if Mason's score is

(a) 62 marks,　**(b)** 89 marks,　**(c)** p marks.

Example 3

The price of a watch is three times the price of a calculator. Find the price of the watch if the price of the calculator is

(a) £8,　　　**(b)** £11,　　　**(c)** £n.

Solution

The bar model that represents the relationship between the variables is:

Price of watch ⬚
Price of calculator ⬚

Continued

We know that "the price of the watch = 3 times the price of the calculator ".

(a) If the price of the calculator is £8,
the price of the watch = 3×8
= £24

(b) If the price of the calculator is £11,
the price of the watch = 3×11
= £33

(c) If the price of the calculator is £n,
the price of the watch = $3 \times n$
= £$3n$

Note:
- $3 \times n$ or $n \times 3$ is written as $3n$, without the $\times$ sign.
- The number is always written before the letter.
- $1 \times n$ or $n \times 1$ is written as n, not $1n$.
- In **(c)**, the price of the watch is expressed in terms of n.

Try It! ③ The length of a nail is twice the length of a screw. Draw and label a bar model to represent the relationship between the variables. Find the length of the nail if the length of the screw is

(a) 25 mm, **(b)** 37 mm, **(c)** d mm.

DISCUSS

What's the same and what's different about
$3n$
$3 + n$
n^3
Are the three expressions always, sometimes or never equal?

Example ④ 144 pens are distributed equally among some children. Find the number of pens that each child gets if there are

(a) 9 children, **(b)** 18 children, **(c)** N children.

Solution **(a)**
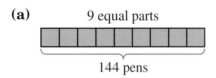
9 equal parts

144 pens

Number of pens that each child gets = $144 \div 9$
= 16

(b)
18 equal parts

144 pens

Number of pens that each child gets = $144 \div 18$
= 8

REMARK
A variable can be a lowercase or an uppercase letter. However, N and n might have different values so it is important that you use the same case as the question.

RECALL

You can use the table on page 359 to help you calculate these divisions.

(c)

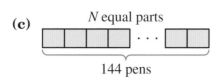

N equal parts

144 pens

Number of pens each child gets $= 144 \div N$

$$= \frac{144}{N}$$

Note: In algebra, you usually express $144 \div N$ as $\frac{144}{N}$.

Try It! ④ A prize of £750 is shared equally among some winners. Draw bar models and find the amount that each winner gets if there are

(a) 5 winners,

(b) 15 winners,

(c) W winners.

PRACTICE 4.1

⚙ LEVEL 1

1. Write two possible statements, in words, for each algebraic expression.
   (a) $a + 9$ **(b)** $10 - b$ **(c)** $8 \times c$ **(d)** $d \div 12$

2. In the diagram, m represents the value of B. Express the value of A in terms of m.

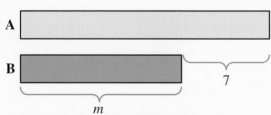

A

B

7

m

3. In the diagram, C is p units less than D. Express the value of C in terms of p.

C

p

D

36

4. In the bar model, the value of F is q. Express the value of E in terms of q.

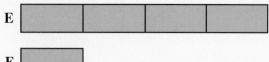

5. In the bar model, the value of H is W. Express the value of G in terms of W.

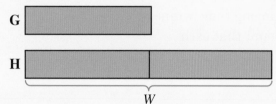

 **LEVEL 2**

Draw and label bar models to help you with these questions if necessary.

6. A tank contains seven fish. Find the total number of fish in the tank after

    (a) three fish are added to the tank,

    (b) eight fish are added to the tank,

    (c) n fish are added to the tank.

7. Emma is 5 cm shorter than John. Find Emma's height if John's height is

    (a) 176 cm,

    (b) 184 cm,

    (c) h cm.

8. One ant has six legs. Find the total number of legs on

    (a) five ants,

    (b) nine ants,

    (c) p ants.

9. 90 apples are shared equally among some families. How many apples does each family get if there are

    (a) 10 families,

    (b) 18 families,

    (c) M families?

10. A class is usually made up of x students. On a particular day, there are $(x - 1)$ students present. Describe what has happened.

OPEN
QUESTION

Workbook 1A Link
Exercise 4.1

4.2 Substitution of Numbers for Letters

Anne is 28 years older than her son Lucas. When Lucas is x years old,

Anne's age $= (28 + x)$ years.

When Lucas is 22 years old and graduating from university, **substituting** $x = 22$ gives

Anne's age $= 28 + 22$

$= 50$ years.

This is called **substitution** of numbers for letters. You can use it to find the value of an expression.

Example 5

Find the value of $120 - h$ when

(a) $h = 20$, **(b)** $h = 23$.

Solution

(a) When $h = 20$,

$120 - h = 120 - 20$ Substitute $h = 20$.

$= 100$

(b) When $h = 23$,

$120 - h = 120 - 23$ Substitute $h = 23$.

$= 97$

REMARK
Different values of a variable may be substituted into the same expression. This may give different results.

Try It! 5

Find the value of $t - 18$ when

(a) $t = 29$, **(b)** $t = 35$.

Example 6

(a) Work out the value of $4n$ when $n = 7$.

(b) Work out the value of $\dfrac{63}{n}$ when $n = 7$.

Solution

(a) When $n = 7$,

$4n = 4 \times 7$ Substitute $n = 7$.

$= 28$

(b) When $n = 7$,

$\dfrac{63}{n} = \dfrac{63}{7}$ Substitute $n = 7$.

$= 9$

REMARK
The same value of a variable may be substituted into different expressions. This may give different results.

REMARK
You can use the multiplication and division table on page 359 to check these calculations.

Try It! 6

(a) Work out the value of $5q$ when $q = 6$.

(b) Work out the value of $\dfrac{q}{2}$ when $q = 6$.

Example 7

The mass of a box containing x dumbbells is $(2x + 1)\,\text{kg}$. Find the mass when there are

(a) no dumbbells,

(b) five dumbbells.

Solution

(a) Mass = $(2x + 1)\,\text{kg}$

When $x = 0$,

mass = $2 \times 0 + 1$ Substitute $x = 0$.

     = $1\,\text{kg}$

(b) When $x = 5$,

mass = $2 \times 5 + 1$ Substitute $x = 5$.

     = $11\,\text{kg}$

DISCUSS

What does the answer in **(a)** tell you?

Try It! 7

The number of fish oil pills in a bottle after y days is $54 - 3y$. Find the number of pills after

(a) 0 days,

(b) eight days.

CLASS ACTIVITY 3

Objective: To match expressions with values.

1. In this question, $m = 2$ and $n = 5$. Copy and evaluate each expression below, using the numbers in the circle. You may use each number more than once.

(a) $m + 10 =$

(b) $7 - m =$

(c) $3m =$

(d) $18 \div m =$

(e) $2n + 2 =$

(f) $4n - 13 =$

(g) $\dfrac{6n}{10} =$

(h) $m + n =$

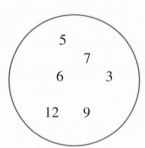

2. Create an expression in x such that the expression has the value 14 when $x = 4$.

3. Create an expression in y such that the expression has the value 7 when $y = 3$, and the expression has the value 13 when $y = 6$. Discuss this with your classmates and compare your expressions with theirs. **Hint:** Your expression can contain more than one operation, like examples **(e)**, **(f)** and **(g)** in question **1**.

PRACTICE 4.2

LEVEL 1

1. Find the value of $a + 8$ when
   (a) $a = 3$,   (b) $a = 7$.

2. Find the value of $10 - b$ when
   (a) $b = 2$,   (b) $b = 9$.

3. Find the value of $5c$ when
   (a) $c = 4$,   (b) $c = 11$.

4. Work out the value of $\frac{d}{3}$ when
   (a) $d = 12$,   (b) $d = 21$.

LEVEL 2

Where necessary, draw and label bar models for each of these questions to represent the relationship between the variables.

5. Mason's age in m years' time will be $(11 + m)$ years.

   (a) Find his age eight years from now.

   (b) Find his age 12 years from now.

   (c) How old is Mason now?

6. The length of a rod is L cm. After a length of 10 cm is cut from it, the length of the rod remaining is $(L - 10)$ cm. Find the length of the rod remaining when

   (a) $L = 85$,   (b) $L = 102$.

7. The number of days in n weeks is $7n$. Find the number of days in

   (a) four weeks,   (b) nine weeks.

8. A ribbon of length 120 cm is cut into p equal parts. The length of each part is $\frac{120}{p}$ cm. Find the length of each part when there are

   (a) five parts,   (b) eight parts.

   (c) How many parts are there if the length of each part is 10 cm?

9. Water is being poured into a beaker. After t seconds, the volume of water in the beaker is $(5t + 18)$ cm^3.

   SCIENCE

   PROBLEM SOLVING

   (a) Find the volume of water when $t = 7$.

   (b) What is the initial volume of water in the beaker?

10. Create more than one algebraic expression in x such that the value of each expression is 7 when $x = 3$.

    OPEN QUESTION

Workbook 1A Link
Exercise 4.2

Use of Letters to Represent Numbers

A letter represents a number in an expression. It is called a variable.

These are some examples of algebraic expressions in variables a, b, c and d.

$\quad a + 3$ (the sum of a and 3, or a plus 3)

$\quad 5 - b$ (5 subtract b, or b less than 5)

$\quad 4c \quad$ (the product of 4 and c, or 4 groups of c)

$\quad \dfrac{d}{6} \quad$ (divide d by 6)

Substitution of Numbers for Letters

The value of an expression can be found by substituting each variable with a numerical value.

When $a = 7$,

$$a + 3 = 7 + 3$$
$$= 10$$

When $b = 4$,

$$5 - b = 5 - 4$$
$$= 1$$

When $c = 8$,

$$4c = 4 \times 8$$
$$= 32$$

When $d = 30$,

$$\frac{d}{6} = \frac{30}{6}$$
$$= 5$$

CHALLENGE 4 💡

There are 500 sheets in a ream of paper. To print a booklet, 30 sheets are needed.

(a) Find the number of sheets remaining if

    (i) 16 booklets are printed,

    (ii) n booklets are printed, giving your answer in terms of n.

(b) Can 18 booklets be printed from the ream of paper?

    Explain your answer.

Workbook 1A Link
Problem Solving 4

REVISION EXERCISE 4

Where necessary, draw and label bar models to help you represent the relationship between the variables.

1. The capacity of a bowl is 240 ml more than that of a cup. Find the capacity of the bowl when the capacity of the cup is

   (a) 250 ml, **(b)** 280 ml, **(c)** x ml.

2. In a basketball match, Sophia's score is nine less than Aria's score. Find Sophia's score if Aria's score is

   (a) 13, **(b)** 26, **(c)** a.

3. **£** The monthly salary of a manager is four times the monthly salary of a clerk. Find the monthly salary of the manager if the monthly salary of the clerk is

   FINANCE

   (a) £2000, **(b)** £2350, **(c)** £y.

4. Sulfur powder is divided equally into five portions for an experiment. Find the mass of each portion if the total mass of the sulfur powder is

   SCIENCE

   (a) 120 grams, **(b)** 325 grams, **(c)** m grams.

5. Find the value of $56 + p$ when

   (a) $p = 12$, **(b)** $p = 39$.

6. Find the value of $q - 15$ when

   (a) $q = 17$, **(b)** $q = 24$.

7. Work out the value of $3r$ when

   (a) $r = 7$, **(b)** $r = 14$.

8. Evaluate the value of $\frac{s}{9}$ when

   (a) $s = 18$, **(b)** $s = 45$.

9. The temperature of water in a sauce pan is $(13 + 5t)\,°C$, after being heated on the stove for t minutes.

   PROBLEM SOLVING

   (a) Find the temperature when $t = 11$.

   (b) What is the initial temperature of the water?

10. The amount of money left on a travel card after x journeys is £$(73 - 5x)$.

    PROBLEM SOLVING

    (a) Find the amount left after 12 journeys.

    (b) Can you use the expression to work out the amount left after 15 journeys? Explain your answer.

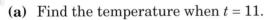

Write in Your Journal

Charlie reads that "the number of days in n weeks is $7n$".
Charlie writes in his maths book "the number of days in 6 weeks is 76".
Is this correct? If not, what should Charlie have written? Explain your answer.

Integrated Examples

Example ①

(a) Calculate 23×38.

(b) Work out $2338 \div 7$.

(c) Is the missing number ▮ in

$$23 \times 38 - ▮ = 2338 \div 7$$

a prime number?

Solution

(a)
$$
\begin{array}{r}
23 \\
\times\ 38 \\
\hline
184 \\
690 \\
\hline
874
\end{array}
$$

$23 \times 38 = 874$

Alternatively, you can use the grid method.

×	20	3
30	600	90
8	160	24

$23 \times 38 = 600 + 90 + 160 + 24$
$\qquad\quad = 874$

(b)
$$
\begin{array}{r}
334 \\
7\,\overline{\smash{)}\,2338} \\
21 \\
\hline
23 \\
21 \\
\hline
28 \\
28 \\
\hline
0
\end{array}
$$

$2338 \div 7 = 334$

(c) $23 \times 38 - ▮ = 2338 \div 7$

$\qquad 874 - ▮ = 334$

$\qquad\qquad ▮ = 874 - 334$ — Inverse relationship between addition and subtraction.

$\qquad\qquad ▮ = 540$

The missing number is 540.

> **REMARK**
>
> You can use the tables on page 359 to check the steps of these calculations.

$$540 = 54 \times 10$$

540 has factors other than 1 and 540.

$\therefore$ the missing number 540 is not a prime number.

Try It! ①

(a) Calculate the product of 23 and 22.

(b) Work out the answer when 4920 is divided by 8.

(c) Is the missing number [ ] in

$$4920 \div 8 - \boxed{} = 23 \times 22$$

a prime number?

Example ②

(a) Consider the expression $868 - 52 \times 9$.

    (i) Estimate the value of the expression by rounding each number to the nearest 10.

    (ii) Use efficient calculation methods to work out the value of the expression.

(b) Using the result in **(a)(ii)**, calculate $(868 - 52 \times 9) \times 2^2 \div 5$.

(c) Is the result in **(b)** a multiple of 3? Explain your answer.

Solution

(a) (i) $868 - 52 \times 9$

      $\approx 870 - 50 \times 10$ Round each number to the nearest 10.

      $= 870 - 500$

      $= 370$

    (ii) 52×9

       $= (50 + 2) \times 9$

       $= (50 \times 9) + (2 \times 9)$ Using the distributive law of

       $= 450 + 18$ multiplication over addition.

       $= 468$

       $868 - 52 \times 9$ Calculate the multiplication

       $= 868 - 468$ before the subtraction.

       $= 868 - 400 - 68$ Partition 468 as 400 and 68.

       $= 468 - 68$

       $= 400$

(b) $(868 - 52 \times 9) \times 2^2 \div 5$ Evaluate the calculation within the

    $= 400 \times 2^2 \div 5$ brackets.

    $= 400 \times 4 \div 5$ Calculate the index expression.

    $= 1600 \div 5$ You can calculate the multiplication,

                    then the division from left to right.

    $= 1600 \div 10 \times 2$ Convert $\div 5$ to $\div 10 \times 2$.

    $= 160 \times 2$ Calculate the division then the

                    multiplication from left to right.

    $= 320$

Continued

(c)

$$\begin{array}{r} 106 \ \ \text{r } 2 \\ 3\overline{)320} \\ \underline{3} \\ 20 \\ \underline{18} \\ 2 \end{array}$$

$320 \div 3 = 106$ r 2

Since the remainder is non-zero,
320 is not divisible by 3.
Hence, 320 is not a multiple of 3.

$320 = 300 + 20$
$ = 300 + 18 + 2$
How does this partitioning show you that 320 is not a multiple of 3?

 Try It! 2

(a) Consider the expression $228 + 12 \times 31$.

   (i) Estimate the value of the expression by rounding each number to the nearest 10.

   (ii) Use efficient calculation methods to work out the value of the expression.

(b) Using the result in **(a)(ii)**, calculate $(228 + 12 \times 31) \div 12 \times 3^2$.

(c) Is the result in **(b)** a multiple of 7? Explain your answer.

Example 3

The number of spectators at a match is $29\,753$.

(a) What is the place value of the digit 2?

(b) Round the number of spectators to the nearest 1000. Use a number line to explain your reasoning.

(c) The number of spectators at the next match is p more than the number of spectators at this match.

   (i) Express the number of spectators at the next match in terms of p.

   (ii) Find the number of spectators at the next match if $p = 1064$.

Solution

(a) In the number 29 753, the place value of the digit 2 is ten thousands.

(b)

29 753

```
←——+————————+————●————+——→
  29 000      29 500      30 000
```

29 753 is closer to 30 000 than 29 000.
Number of spectators = 29 753
$$= 30\,000 \quad \text{(to nearest 10\,000)}$$

(c) **(i)** Number of spectators at the next match
$$= 29\,753 + p$$

(ii) If $p = 1064$,
number of spectators at the
next match
$$= 29\,753 + 1064 \quad \text{Substitute } p = 1064.$$
$$= 30\,817$$

$$\begin{array}{r} 29753 \\ + \ 1064 \\ \hline 30817 \\ \tiny 1 \ \ \ 1 \end{array}$$

REMARK

The digit 2 represents 20 000.

Try It! **3**

The score for completing a computer game, without hitting any obstacles, is 43 285.

(a) What is the place value of the digit 2?

(b) Round the score to the nearest 10 000. Use a number line to explain your reasoning.

(c) Sam loses x points for each obstacle she hits. In the next game, she completes it but hit 2 obstacles.

(i) Express her score in the next game in terms of x.

(ii) Find her score in the next game if $x = 300$.

REVIEW EXERCISE 1

1. The price of a car is £23 085.

FINANCE

(a) Write the price in expanded form.

(b) What is the value of the digit 3 in £23 085?

(c) Round the price to the nearest £100. Use a number line to explain your reasoning.

2. **(a)** Work out these values.

(i) $5417 + 2638$

(ii) $9458 - 1247 + 619$

(b) Which answer in **(a)** is smaller?

3. Find the missing number in each statement.

(a) $356 + \boxed{} = 873$

(b) $\boxed{} - 852 = 479$

4. **(a)** **(i)** Use place value counters to work out 25×6.
    (ii) Use the grid method to work out 25×30.
    (iii) Use your answers to parts **(i)** and **(ii)** to work out 25×36.
    (b) Work out 64×23.

5. A lottery chooses 15 winners to share a prize pot of £7170 between them.
    (a) How much money will each winner receive?
    (b) How does your answer to part **(a)** change if the prizes are paid in cash, in £10 notes?

6. Find the missing number in each statement.
    (a) $\boxed{} \times 11 = 9097$
    (b) $952 \div \boxed{} = 17$

7. **(a)** Write down the first ten non-zero whole number multiples of 6.
    (b) Write down the first ten non-zero whole number multiples of 9.
    (c) What is the lowest common whole number multiple of 6 and 9?
    (d) Work out the lowest common whole number multiple of 6 and 10.

8. Calculate these expressions efficiently by hand, showing each step of your reasoning.
    (a) $847 - 169 - 347$
    (b) $38 + 47 + 52 + 63$
    (c) 65×99

9. Work out the values of these expressions efficiently by hand.
    (a) $56 \times 4 - 76 \div 4$
    (b) $(73 + 17) \times 11 - 5^2 \times 4$
    (c) $138 - (456 - 69) \div 9$

10. A spider has eight legs.
    Find the number of legs that
    (a) three spiders,
    (b) nine spiders,
    (c) n spiders have.

11. **(a)** Find the value of $28 + a$ when $a = 13$.
    (b) Find the value of $6b - 23$ when $b = 11$.
    (c) Work out the value of $\frac{150}{c}$ when $c = 30$.
    (d) Copy and fill in each blank with '<' or '>', assuming the values of a, b and c are the same as in parts **(a)** to **(c)**.
        (i) $28 + a \boxed{} 6b - 23$
        (ii) $6b - 23 \boxed{} \frac{150}{c}$

12. (a) Find the value of each of these square numbers.

    (i) 4^2 **(ii)** 5^2 **(iii)** 6^2

(b) Which of these numbers are prime numbers? Explain your decision.

    $4^2 + 1$, $5^2 + 1$, $6^2 + 1$

(c) Find the highest common whole number factor of 4^2 and 6^2.

13. A bakery makes 1375 cookies. Cookies are packed in boxes. Each box contains eight cookies.

(a) How many boxes are packed?

(b) What is the number of cookies remaining after packing as many full boxes as possible?

(c) The cost of each box of cookies is £3. What is the total cost of all the boxes?

14. The price of a necklace is £x more than the price of a bracelet.
The price of the bracelet is £128.

(a) Express the price of the necklace in terms of x and represent the relationship using a bar model.

(b) If $x = 70$, find

    (i) the price of the necklace,

    (ii) the mean price of the necklace and the bracelet.

15. A dishwasher uses four times as much power as a food blender.
The power of the food blender is y watts.

(a) Express the power of the dishwasher in terms of y and represent the relationship using a bar model.

(b) If $y = 325$, find

    (i) the power of the dishwasher,

    (ii) the difference between the power of the dishwasher and the power of the food blender.

16. A cinema gives members a discount of £4 on their own ticket for each non-member they bring to see a film. Tickets usually cost £15 each.

(a) Write an expression for the cost of a member's ticket in terms of n, where n is the number of non-members brought.

(b) Work out how much a ticket costs for a member who brings two non-members.

(c) The terms and conditions state that this deal only applies for up to 3 non-members. Explain why.

5 UNDERSTANDING FRACTIONS

Jasmine is baking bread rolls. The recipe needs 500 grams of flour to make 10 rolls, but Jasmine only wants to make six rolls. How much flour will she need?

LET'S LEARN TO

▶ understand and use fraction notation
▶ convert between improper fractions and mixed numbers
▶ identify equivalent fractions
▶ compare fractions with the same numerator or denominator
▶ calculate fractions of quantities

1. Number Line

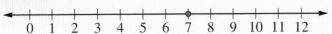

A number can be represented by a point on a number line. In the above number line, the red dot represents the number 7.

2. Multiplication of Whole Numbers

A repeated addition can be calculated with multiplication. For example,

$$7 + 7 + 7 + 7 = 4 \times 7$$
$$= 28$$

Multiplication can be set out using the grid method or the column method.
For example, consider 253×7.

Grid Method

×	200	50	3
7	1400	350	21

```
  1400
   350
 +  21
 ─────
  1771
```
$253 \times 7 = 1771$

Column Method

```
   253
 ×   7
 ─────
  1771
   3 2
```

3. Division of Whole Numbers

Splitting a quantity into equal shares, or making equal-sized groups out of the quantity, can be calculated with division.

Division can be set out using long division or short division. For example, consider $1771 \div 7$.

Long Division

```
      253
   7 │1771
      14
     ───
      37
      35
     ───
      21
      21
     ───
       0
```

Short Division

```
    2 5 3
  7 │17 ³7 ²1
```

REMARK

Alternatively, this means that 1771 items can be divided into groups each containing 7 items and there will be 253 groups.

$1771 \div 7 = 253$ remainder 0. This means that 1771 items can be shared between 7 equal groups, and each group will have 253 items.

Multiplication and division have an inverse relationship.
Knowing $253 \times 7 = 1771$ means you also know $1771 \div 7 = 253$ and $1771 \div 253 = 7$.

4. Factors

(a) If a number can be written as a product of two whole numbers, the whole numbers are called the **factors** of that number.

e.g. $14 = 1 \times 14$
$\qquad = 2 \times 7$

1, 2, 7 and 14 are factors of 14.

$\qquad 35 = 1 \times 35$
$\qquad\quad = 5 \times 7$

1, 5, 7 and 35 are factors of 35.

(b) List the factors of two whole numbers. The factors that appear on both lists are the **common factors**.

e.g. 1 and 7 are common factors of 14 and 35 (from **(a)**).

1 is the common whole number factor of all the non-zero whole numbers.

(c) The **highest common factor (HCF)** of the two numbers you have chosen is the largest factor that appears on both lists.

e.g. 1, 2, 7 and 14 are factors of 14 and 1, 5, 7 and 35 are factors of 35, so 7 is the largest factor on both lists. The HCF of 14 and 35 is 7.

5. Multiples

(a) The product of a whole number and another whole number is called a **multiple** of the original number.

e.g. Some of the multiples of 3 are

$1 \times 3, 2 \times 3, 3 \times 3, 4 \times 3, 5 \times 3, 6 \times 3, 7 \times 3, 8 \times 3, 9 \times 3, \ldots$

i.e. 3, 6, 9, 12, 15, 18, 21, 24, 27, ...

Some of the multiples of 4 are

$1 \times 4, 2 \times 4, 3 \times 4, 4 \times 4, 5 \times 4, 6 \times 4, 7 \times 4, 8 \times 4, 9 \times 4, \ldots$

i.e. 4, 8, 12, 16, 20, 24, 28, 32, 36, ...

(b) List multiples of two whole numbers. The multiples that appear on both lists are the **common multiple**.

e.g. 12 and 24 are common multiples of 3 and 4 (read from the above lists).

(c) The **lowest common multiple (LCM)** of the two numbers you have chosen is the smallest (whole number) multiple that appears on both lists.

e.g. The LCM of 3 and 4 is 12.

REMARK

0 is also a common multiple of 3 and 4, because $0 \times 3 = 0$ and $0 \times 4 = 0$. 0 is a common multiple of all numbers.

However, when calculating the LCM of two numbers, you should always ignore 0.

This chapter covers positive numbers. You will learn about negative numbers in Student Book 2A.

5.1 Idea of Fractions

Plain
$\frac{1}{2}$

Mushroom
$\frac{3}{4}$

Pepperoni
$\frac{5}{8}$

Look at the portion enclosed by the dashed lines on each pizza.
The plain pizza portion is 1 slice out of 2 equal slices in the whole pizza. This shows $\frac{1}{2}$ of the plain pizza.
The mushroom pizza portion is 3 equal slices out of 4 equal slices in the whole pizza. This shows $\frac{3}{4}$ of the mushroom pizza.

The pepperoni portion is 5 equal slices out of 8 equal slices in the whole pizza. This shows $\frac{5}{8}$ of the pepperoni pizza.

You can also have a fraction of a group. In this pizza, there are 9 toppings (3 olives, 4 pieces of tomato and 2 basil leaves). You can say that the pieces of tomato make up $\frac{4}{9}$ of the toppings.

In general, a fraction represents a part of a whole: the whole can be a single item, like a pizza, or a group of items like the pizza toppings. The bottom number is the number of **equal** parts that the whole has been divided into. It is called the **denominator**. The top number is the number of parts of the portion, or some items in the group. This is called the **numerator**. The horizontal line between the numerator and denominator is called the **vinculum**.

$$\frac{5}{8} \begin{array}{l} \leftarrow \text{Numerator} \\ \leftarrow \text{Vinculum} \\ \leftarrow \text{Denominator} \end{array}$$

Any shape can be divided into equal parts to show fractions. Here are the shares of two chocolate bars. The dark chocolate bar has 10 equal parts. Four equal parts out of 10 equal parts are circled. This shows four-tenths of the dark chocolate bar.
The white chocolate bar has 18 equal parts. Seven equal parts out of 18 equal parts are circled. This shows seven-eighteenths of the white chocolate bar.

Circled share = $\frac{4}{10}$

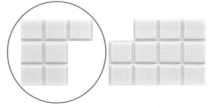

Circled share = $\frac{7}{18}$

REMARK

$\frac{1}{2}$ is read as 'one-half'.

$\frac{3}{4}$ is read as 'three-quarters'.

$\frac{5}{8}$ is read as 'five-eighths'.

REMARK

It is important that slices or parts are of **equal size**. This pizza is not cut into equal slices. Three out of four slices are enclosed by the dashed line **but** this is **not** three-quarters.

113

Objective: To create representations of fractions.

Work with a partner. Take a number of identical shapes such as squares, rectangles, triangles, or different colour linking cubes, and put them together to form a shape that is your 'whole' on top of a piece of paper. Draw around the outline of your whole. One of you may need to hold the shapes while the other draws around them.

1. How many parts make up your whole?

2. Do you have an odd or even number of parts?

3. Can you fill the outline with half of your shapes?

Make another 'whole' from identical shapes on a different sheet of paper. This should have a different number of parts to the first one. You can use the same type of shape as before or try a new set of identical shapes. Take turns to fill the whole with a number of your shapes, each of you saying the fraction that the other has filled in.

4. What fractions did you make?

5. Why do you think all the parts of each 'whole' need to be identical?

6. Make two or more examples where the same fraction is represented with different arrangements of the shapes.

> **REMARK**
>
> Sketch 5 triangles and shade 3 of them red.
>
> In the diagram, the whole consists of a group of 5 triangles. 3 of the triangles are red. You can say that the fraction of red triangles is $\frac{3}{5}$.
>
> Here, the fraction is considered as a fraction of a group.

CLASS ACTIVITY 2

Objective: To describe parts of wholes using fractions.

1. What fraction of each shape is shaded?

   (a)   **(b)**   **(c)**   **(d)**   **(e)**

2.

   (a) What fraction of this group of children are wearing jeans?

   (b) What fraction of this group of children have blonde hair?

3. **(a)** Copy each diagram. Shade some parts to show the given fraction.

(b) Represent each fraction as a fraction of a group.
Hint: Draw the whole group and circle the section that represents the fraction of the whole group. Draw a different group each time.

(i) $\frac{2}{7}$ **(ii)** $\frac{3}{4}$ **(iii)** $\frac{5}{6}$

4. Ali says all these shapes show $\frac{1}{3}$ shaded. Is this correct? Explain your answer.

(a) **(b)** **(c)**

If Ali is incorrect about any of the shapes, redraw them to show $\frac{1}{3}$ shaded.

5. In which diagram is the shaded portion $\frac{7}{8}$ of the whole diagram? Explain your answer.

(a) **(b)**

6. If you considered your class to be a whole, write down some fractions of that whole. For example, what fraction of your class wear glasses?

From Class Activity 2, you see that shaded portions of different wholes, or items chosen in different groups, may represent the same fraction. Remember that the whole must always be divided into EQUAL parts. Now let's look at how you can represent fractions on a number line.

Example 1 Mark the fraction $\frac{3}{4}$ on the given number line.

Solution The length between 0 and 1 can be considered as a whole.
Divide the whole into 4 equal parts.
The total length of 3 equal parts represents $\frac{3}{4}$.
This is shown below.

Note: The first dot represents $\frac{1}{4}$. The second dot represents $\frac{2}{4}$.

Try It! **1** Draw this number line and mark the fraction $\frac{2}{3}$ on your number line.

Fractions also occur in daily life.

CLASS ACTIVITY 3

Objective: To explore fractions in daily life.

1. What fraction of this 50p coin is shaded?

2. Write down the fraction of shaded panes in this window frame.

3. **(a)** The whole is all of these counters together. How many counters are shown?

  (b) Write down the fraction of purple counters.

  (c) Write down the fraction of green counters.

4. Use some counters or shapes to show $\frac{2}{5}$ and $\frac{6}{9}$.

Example **2** The photo shows a group of students. What fraction of the group have their arms crossed?

Solution Number of students in the whole group = 5
Number of students with arms crossed = 2

Fraction with arms crossed = $\frac{2}{5}$

$$\frac{\text{number with arms crossed}}{\text{number of students in the whole group}}$$

Try It! **2** The photo shows a collection of balloons. What fraction of the balloons are blue?

Example 3

A string of bunting consists of four red triangles, five blue triangles and two yellow triangles.
- **(a)** Draw a possible design for the string of bunting.
- **(b)** Find the fraction of red triangles on the bunting.

Solution

(a)

The above diagram shows a possible design. There are many other possible designs.

(b) Total number of triangles = 4 + 5 + 2
$$= 11$$

Number of red triangles = 4

Fraction of red triangles = $\frac{4}{11}$

Try It! 3

(a) Draw an arrangement of four green tiles, six purple tiles and three orange tiles.

(b) What fraction of the tiles are purple?

DISCUSS

Did you arrange the coloured tiles differently to others in your class? Does the arrangement change the answer to **(b)**?

Example 4

(a) Draw a rectangular bar and use it to show $\frac{3}{7}$.

(b) What fraction added to $\frac{3}{7}$ makes 1?

Solution

(a)

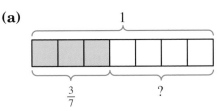

The bar is 1 whole. It is divided into 7 equal parts. 3 equal parts out of 7 equal parts are shaded. The shaded portion is $\frac{3}{7}$.

(b) The number of unshaded parts = 7 − 3
$$= 4 \text{ parts}$$

Therefore the unshaded portion is $\frac{4}{7}$ of the whole bar. The shaded portion and the unshaded portion make up the whole, i.e. 1.

∴ the required fraction is $\frac{4}{7}$.

REMARK

In **(a)**, $\frac{7}{7}$ is one whole, i.e. 1.

In **(b)**,

$$\frac{3}{7} + \frac{4}{7} = \frac{7}{7}$$
$$= 1$$

What fraction added to $\frac{5}{7}$ makes 1?

Try It! 4

(a) Draw a rectangular bar and use it to show $\frac{5}{9}$.

(b) What fraction added to $\frac{5}{9}$ makes 1? Explain your answer.

Example 5

(a) Draw a rectangular bar and use it to show $\frac{5}{11}$.

(b) Work out $1 - \frac{5}{11}$.

Solution **(a)**

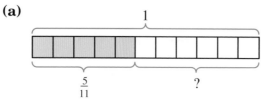

1

$\frac{5}{11}$?

The bar is 1 whole. It is divided into 11 equal parts.

5 equal parts out of 11 equal parts are shaded.

The shaded portion is $\frac{5}{11}$.

(b) You can see that there are 6 equal parts in the unshaded portion, so this is $\frac{6}{11}$ of the whole bar.

$1 - \frac{5}{11}$ = the unshaded portion

$= \frac{11}{11} - \frac{5}{11}$ One whole $= 1 = \frac{11}{11}$

$= \frac{6}{11}$

Try It! 5 **(a)** Draw a rectangular bar and use it to show $\frac{3}{8}$.

(b) Work out $1 - \frac{3}{8}$. Explain your answer.

REMARK

A rectangular bar made up of sections (either of equal size like this one, or different sizes) is sometimes called a **bar model**.

DISCUSS

(a) What other fractions can be represented by this bar?

(b) What is $1 - \frac{8}{11}$ equal to?

Example 6 A ribbon is divided into nine equal parts. Four of the equal parts are used to wrap a gift. What fraction of the original length of the ribbon is left?

Solution You can draw a bar model to show this.

$1 = \frac{9}{9}$

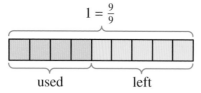

used   left

Number of parts left $= 9 - 4$

$= 5$

Fraction of the ribbon left $= \frac{5}{9}$

Try It! 6 The acid in a beaker is divided into 12 equal cups. Seven cups are used for experiments. What fraction of the original amount of acid is left? Use a bar model to explain your answer.

Example ⑦   **(a)** Express 23 minutes as a fraction of an hour.
            (b) Express 7 hours as a fraction of a day.

Solution   **(a)** An hour has 60 minutes.
            Fraction of 23 minutes in

            an hour $= \dfrac{23}{60}$

            (b) A day has 24 hours.
            Fraction of 7 hours in

            a day $= \dfrac{7}{24}$

Note: In a fraction of a measurement, the numerator and the denominator must have the same unit.

$$\therefore \quad \frac{23 \text{ minutes}}{1 \text{ hour}} = \frac{23 \text{ minutes}}{60 \text{ minutes}}$$

$$= \frac{23}{60}$$

Try It! ⑦   **(a)** Express 49 minutes as a fraction of an hour.
            (b) Express 5 hours as a fraction of a day.

REMARK

When you are asked to 'express', it simply means 'write'. For example, 'Express 23 minutes as a fraction of an hour' means 'Write 23 minutes as a fraction of an hour'.

DISCUSS

The whole must be divided into equal parts in fractions. In **(a)** has the hour been divided into equal parts? In **(b)** has the day been divided into equal parts?

PRACTICE 5.1

⚙ LEVEL 1

1. What fraction of each whole is shaded?

   (a)    **(b)** 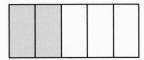   **(c)**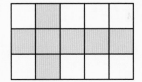

2. Copy each diagram. Shade some parts to show the given fraction.

   (a) $\dfrac{1}{4}$ **(b)** $\dfrac{6}{12}$

3. If these blue circles represent a quarter, copy and add to the drawing to create the whole.

4. (a) Write down the fraction of red beads out of all the beads shown.

(b) Write down the fraction of cats out of all the animals shown.

5. In which diagram is the shaded portion $\frac{1}{5}$ of the whole diagram? Explain your answer.

(a)

(b)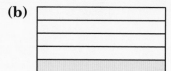

6. (a) Copy the number line and mark $\frac{3}{6}, \frac{4}{6}$ and $\frac{5}{6}$ on it.

(b) Saira has shown $\frac{2}{6}$ on the number line below. What has she done wrong?

LEVEL 2

7. Find the fraction which makes 1 when added to the given fraction.

(a) $\frac{1}{3}$ (b) $\frac{2}{5}$

8. (a) Express 43 seconds as a fraction of a minute.
(b) Express 19 minutes as a fraction of an hour.
(c) Express 11 hours as a fraction of a day.

9. A fence has eight equal sections. Seven sections are painted. Express the number of unpainted sections as a fraction of the whole fence.

PROBLEM SOLVING

10. (a) Draw two or more wholes and represent the fraction $\frac{9}{16}$ of each whole.

OPEN QUESTION (b) Draw one of your wholes again and represent the fraction $\frac{3}{4}$ of the whole.

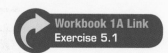

Workbook 1A Link
Exercise 5.1

5.2 Improper Fractions and Mixed Numbers

You have learnt that a fraction is a part of a whole. This pizza is divided into 8 equal slices.

> The portion of 3 equal slices out of 8 equal slices in the whole pizza $= \frac{3}{8}$.
>
> The portion of 5 equal slices out of 8 equal slices in the whole pizza $= \frac{5}{8}$.
>
> The portion of 8 equal slices out of 8 equal slices in the whole pizza $= \frac{8}{8}$.

As 8 slices is the whole pizza, this gives $\frac{8}{8} = 1$.

In general, when a pizza is divided into n equal slices, the portion of all n slices is the whole. This gives:

If n is a non-zero whole number,
$\frac{n}{n} = 1$

This means $\frac{1}{1} = \frac{2}{2} = \frac{3}{3} = \frac{4}{4} = \ldots = \frac{8}{8} = \ldots = 1$.

Look at these pizzas. Each whole pizza has 8 equal slices. Each slice is $\frac{1}{8}$ of a whole pizza.

If you have a portion of 9 slices, it is 1 slice more than 1 whole pizza.

The portion $= \frac{9}{8}$ or $1\frac{1}{8}$ which means $1 + \frac{1}{8}$.

If you have a portion of 16 slices, there are 2 whole pizzas.

The portion $= \frac{16}{8}$ or 2.

If you have a portion of 19 slices, there are two whole pizzas and also three slices.

The portion $= \frac{19}{8}$ or $2\frac{3}{8}$ which means $2 + \frac{3}{8}$.

A fraction where the numerator is less than the denominator is called a **proper fraction**.

A fraction where the numerator is greater than or equal to the denominator is called an **improper fraction**.

A number which consists of a whole number and a proper fraction is called a **mixed number**.

$\frac{2}{3}, \frac{4}{5}$ and $\frac{1}{7}$ are proper fractions.

$\frac{5}{3}, \frac{5}{5}$ and $\frac{11}{7}$ are improper fractions.

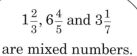
$1\frac{2}{3}, 6\frac{4}{5}$ and $3\frac{1}{7}$ are mixed numbers.

CLASS ACTIVITY 4

Objective: To write improper fractions and mixed numbers.

1. **(a)** Write down the improper fraction and the whole number represented by the shaded portion in each diagram. Part **(i)** has been done for you.

   (i)

   whole   whole   whole   whole

   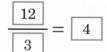
   $\dfrac{\boxed{12}}{\boxed{3}} = \boxed{4}$

   (ii)

   whole   whole   whole

   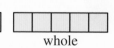
   $\dfrac{\boxed{}}{\boxed{}} = \boxed{}$

   (b) Write down the improper fraction and the whole number represented by the eggs. One whole box of eggs contains six eggs.

   whole   whole

   $\dfrac{\boxed{}}{\boxed{}} = \boxed{}$

2. (a) Write down the improper fraction and the mixed number represented by the shaded portion in each diagram. Part **(i)** has been done for you.

(i)

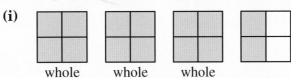

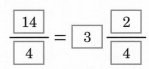

whole   whole   whole

$$\frac{14}{4} = 3\,\frac{2}{4}$$

(ii)

whole   whole

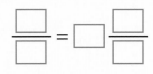

$$\frac{\Box}{\Box} = \Box\,\frac{\Box}{\Box}$$

(b) Write down the improper fraction and the mixed number represented by the eggs. One whole box of eggs contains six eggs.

whole

$$\frac{\Box}{\Box} = \Box\,\frac{\Box}{\Box}$$

3. Make up two improper fractions of your own and represent them in two or more different ways.

4. Make up two mixed numbers of your own and represent them in two or more different ways.

In Class Activity 4, question 1 shows you that

$\frac{12}{3} = 4$ (wholes), $\frac{16}{8} = 2$ (wholes)

and $\frac{15}{5} = 3$ (wholes).

You already know that

$12 \div 3 = 4$, $8 \div 4 = 2$ and $18 \div 6 = 3$.

Therefore it makes sense to say that

$\frac{12}{3} = 12 \div 3$, $\frac{16}{8} = 16 \div 8$ and $\frac{15}{5} = 15 \div 5$.

When you have a proper fraction, for example $\frac{1}{5}$, you take 1 whole and divide it into 5 equal parts. Then $\frac{1}{5}$ is represented by one part out of the five equal parts. Therefore it makes sense to say that $\frac{1}{5} = 1 \div 5$.

Using this information, and Class Activity 4, you can see that you can convert an improper fraction to a whole number or a mixed number. Here are some examples.

$\frac{1}{5}$ is 1 section of a whole when the whole is divided into 5 equal sections.

Example 8

Express each improper fraction as a whole number or a mixed number.

(a) $\dfrac{12}{3}$ (b) $\dfrac{7}{4}$

Solution

(a) $\dfrac{12}{3}$ is 12 thirds.

Draw shapes with 3 equal parts for each whole to show 3 thirds.

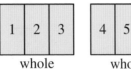

| 1 | 2 | 3 | | 4 | 5 | 6 | | 7 | 8 | 9 | | 10 | 11 | 12 |

whole   whole   whole   whole

There are exactly 4 wholes.

$\therefore \quad \dfrac{12}{3} = 4$

Note: This can also be done using repeated addition.

$\dfrac{12}{3} = \dfrac{3}{3} + \dfrac{3}{3} + \dfrac{3}{3} + \dfrac{3}{3}$ 3 thirds + 3 thirds + 3 thirds + 3 thirds

$\quad = 1 + 1 + 1 + 1$ 1 whole + 1 whole + 1 whole + 1 whole

$\quad = 4$

(b) $\dfrac{7}{4}$ is 7 quarters.

Draw shapes or groups with 4 equal parts for each whole to show 4 quarters.

whole

$\dfrac{7}{4} = 4 \text{ quarters} + 3 \text{ quarters}$

$\quad = 1 \text{ whole and 3 quarters}$

$\quad = 1 + \dfrac{3}{4}$

$\quad = 1\dfrac{3}{4}$

Note: $\dfrac{7}{4} = \dfrac{4}{4} + \dfrac{3}{4}$

$\quad\quad = 1 + \dfrac{3}{4}$

$\quad\quad = 1\dfrac{3}{4}$

Try It! 8

Express each improper fraction as a whole number or a mixed number. Use diagrams to show your reasoning.

(a) $\dfrac{8}{4}$ (b) $\dfrac{4}{3}$

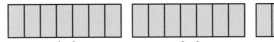

Example 9

Convert each mixed number to an improper fraction.

(a) $2\frac{5}{7}$ **(b)** $5\frac{1}{3}$

Solution

(a) *Method 1*

From the diagram,

$2\frac{5}{7} = 1 + 1 + \frac{5}{7}$

$= \frac{7}{7} + \frac{7}{7} + \frac{5}{7}$ 7 sevenths + 7 sevenths + 5 sevenths

$= \frac{19}{7}$ 19 sevenths

Method 2

1 whole = 7 sevenths

$2\frac{5}{7}$ = 2 wholes + 5 sevenths

    = 2 × 7 sevenths + 5 sevenths

    = 14 sevenths + 5 sevenths

    = 19 sevenths

    $= \frac{19}{7}$

(b) *Method 1*

From the diagram,

$5\frac{1}{3} = 5 + \frac{1}{3}$ 5 wholes + 1 third

$= \frac{3}{3} + \frac{3}{3} + \frac{3}{3} + \frac{3}{3} + \frac{3}{3} + \frac{1}{3}$ = 3 thirds + 3 thirds + 3 thirds + 3 thirds + 3 thirds + 1 third

$= \frac{16}{3}$ = 16 thirds

Method 2

$5\frac{1}{3} = 5$ wholes $+ \frac{1}{3}$

$= 5 \times \frac{3}{3} + \frac{1}{3}$ 5 × 3 thirds + 1 third

$= \frac{5 \times 3}{3} + \frac{1}{3}$

$= \frac{15}{3} + \frac{1}{3}$ 15 thirds + 1 third

$= \frac{16}{3}$ 16 thirds

Try It! 9

Convert each mixed number to an improper fraction, using diagrams to show your reasoning.

(a) $1\frac{5}{6}$ **(b)** $4\frac{7}{8}$

REMARK

In the diagram there are 19 parts shaded. Each part is $\frac{1}{7}$ of the whole, so there are $\frac{19}{7}$ altogether.

DISCUSS

Can you write the whole number 5 as an improper fraction?

DISCUSS

Here are several methods for converting a mixed number to an improper fraction. Which one suits you? Why?

Example 10

Represent the numbers $\frac{9}{5}$ and $3\frac{1}{4}$ on a number line.

Solution

$\frac{9}{5} = \frac{5}{5} + \frac{4}{5}$ 9 fifths = 5 fifths + 4 fifths

$= 1\frac{4}{5}$ = 1 whole + 4 fifths

Thus, $\frac{9}{5}$ lies between 1 and 2.

Divide the length between 1 and 2 into 5 equal parts to locate the point for $\frac{9}{5}$.

$3\frac{1}{4}$ lies between 3 and 4.

Divide the length between 3 and 4 into 4 equal parts to locate the point for $3\frac{1}{4}$.

The number line below shows the given numbers.

Try It! 10

Represent the numbers $\frac{14}{3}$ and $2\frac{1}{2}$ on a number line.

Example 11

23 kg of flour are divided equally among four families. How many kg does each family get?

Solution

Split 23 kg into the biggest number you know that can be divided by 4 (from your 4 times table) and another number:

20 kg			
5 kg	5 kg	5 kg	5 kg

3 kg			
$\frac{3}{4}$ kg	$\frac{3}{4}$ kg	$\frac{3}{4}$ kg	$\frac{3}{4}$ kg

$\frac{20}{4} = 5\,\text{kg}$ $\frac{3}{4} = \frac{3}{4}\,\text{kg}$

You can see that the amount each family gets is 5 kg and $\frac{3}{4}$ kg, which is $5\frac{3}{4}$ kg in total. You can also work this out using improper fractions:

The amount each family gets $= 23 \div 4$

$= \frac{23}{4}$

$= 5\frac{3}{4}\,\text{kg}$

Try It! 11

A rod of length 5 m is divided into three pieces. How long is each piece?

> **REMARK**
>
> You can use the multiplication table on page 359 to check the 4 times table.

> **REMARK**
>
> For fraction problems, it can help to draw a diagram.

PRACTICE 5.2

LEVEL 1

1. Sort these numbers into groups. Explain your choices.

   $\frac{7}{3}$, $\frac{3}{4}$, $\frac{4}{4}$, $3\frac{1}{5}$, $\frac{2}{9}$, $5\frac{2}{9}$, $\frac{9}{7}$, $\frac{4}{6}$

2. **(a)** Write down the improper fraction and the mixed number or whole number that is represented by the shaded parts in each diagram.

   (i)

   whole   whole

   (ii)

    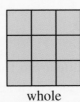

   whole   whole   whole

   (b) Write down the improper fraction and the mixed number that is represented by the cookies in the diagram. One whole tray of cookies contains six cookies.

   whole

3. Write each improper fraction as a mixed number or a whole number.

   (a) $\frac{13}{5}$ **(b)** $\frac{13}{8}$

   (c) $\frac{16}{8}$ **(d)** $\frac{16}{7}$

   Hint: Draw diagrams to explain your reasoning.

4. Convert each mixed number to an improper fraction.

   (a) $1\frac{3}{7}$ **(b)** $2\frac{1}{5}$

   (c) $3\frac{7}{8}$ **(d)** $4\frac{7}{10}$

   Hint: Draw diagrams to explain your reasoning.

5. Find the missing values, using diagrams to explain your reasoning.

   (a) $2 = \frac{\square}{5}$ **(b)** $3 = \frac{\square}{7}$ **(c)** $8 = \frac{\square}{1}$

6. Represent each pair of numbers on a number line.

    (a) $\frac{5}{4}, 3\frac{4}{5}$ (b) $\frac{15}{6}, 4\frac{2}{3}$

7. 17 pizzas are shared equally among six groups of students. What fraction of the pizzas does each group get?

8. Susie wants to give all the people at her birthday party a slice of cake. She has 29 guests at the party. If she divides each cake into eight slices, how many whole cakes will she need?

PROBLEM SOLVING

9. Write two improper fractions between 3 and 4 with different denominators. Draw diagrams or use number lines to represent your fractions.

OPEN QUESTION

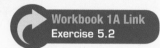 **Workbook 1A Link** Exercise 5.2

5.3 Equivalent Fractions

Equivalent fractions have the same value, even though they have different numerators and denominators. Let's do a simple activity.

 **CLASS ACTIVITY 5**

Objective: To identify equivalent fractions.

1. Fold a rectangular piece of paper into two halves.

   Shade half of the piece of paper.

   One part out of two equal parts,

   i.e. $\frac{1}{2}$, is shaded.

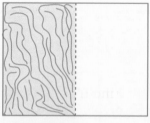

2. Fold the same paper in half again.

   Two equal parts out of four equal parts,

   i.e. $\frac{\square}{\square}$, are shaded.

3. Fold the same paper in half again.

   _____ equal parts out of eight equal parts,

   i.e. $\frac{\square}{\square}$, are shaded.

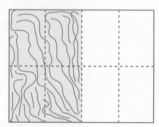

4. Fold the same paper in half again.

   Eight equal parts out of _____ equal parts,

   i.e. $\frac{\square}{\square}$, are shaded.

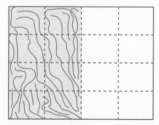

5. **(a)** Take a new piece of paper. Divide it into three equal parts and shade two of them. Write down how much is shaded as a fraction of the whole page.

(b) Fold the paper in half again and write down the fraction that is shaded now.

(c) Fold the paper in half again and write down the fraction that is shaded now.

Notice that in questions **1–4** in Class Activity 5, the four different fractions represent the same area on the paper. You can say that $\frac{1}{2} = \frac{2}{4} = \frac{4}{8} = \frac{8}{16}$.

$\frac{1}{2}, \frac{2}{4}, \frac{4}{8}$ and $\frac{8}{16}$ are equivalent fractions.

Are the fractions below equivalent to $\frac{1}{2}$ too? Why?

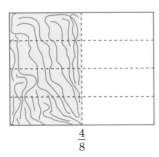

$\frac{4}{8}$

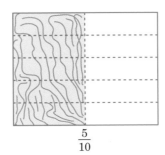

$\frac{5}{10}$

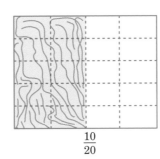

$\frac{10}{20}$

DISCUSS

Can you describe how to transform the fraction $\frac{1}{2}$ into each of these equivalent fractions?

Example 12

Find five equivalent fractions for each of these fractions.

(a) $\frac{1}{2}$ **(b)** $\frac{2}{6}$

Solution

(a) If you multiply the numerator and denominator of $\frac{1}{2}$ by the same non-zero whole number, you will get an equivalent fraction.

$\frac{1 \times 2}{2 \times 2} = \frac{2}{4}$ $\frac{1 \times 3}{2 \times 3} = \frac{3}{6}$ $\frac{1 \times 4}{2 \times 4} = \frac{4}{8}$

$\frac{1 \times 5}{2 \times 5} = \frac{5}{10}$ $\frac{1 \times 6}{2 \times 6} = \frac{6}{12}$

$\therefore$ five equivalent fractions are $\frac{2}{4}, \frac{3}{6}, \frac{4}{8}, \frac{5}{10}$ and $\frac{6}{12}$.

You could have other equivalent fractions than the above, for example $\frac{50}{100}$.

REMARK

There's more help with identifying equivalent fractions on page 361.

DISCUSS

How are the parts in Example 12 (a) and (b) different?

Continued

(b) If you multiply or divide the numerator and denominator of $\frac{2}{6}$ by the same non-zero whole number, you will get an equivalent fraction.

$$\frac{2 \div 2}{6 \div 2} = \frac{1}{3} \qquad \frac{2 \times 2}{6 \times 2} = \frac{4}{12} \qquad \frac{2 \times 3}{6 \times 3} = \frac{6}{18}$$

$$\frac{2 \times 4}{6 \times 4} = \frac{8}{24} \qquad \frac{2 \times 5}{6 \times 5} = \frac{10}{30}$$

$\therefore$ five equivalent fractions are $\frac{1}{3}, \frac{4}{12}, \frac{6}{18}, \frac{8}{24}$ and $\frac{10}{30}$.

Try It! 12 Find five equivalent fractions for each of these fractions.

(a) $\frac{1}{4}$ **(b)** $\frac{2}{3}$

Example 13 Find the missing values to make the fractions in each pair equivalent.

(a) $\frac{1}{20} = \frac{\square}{100}$ **(b)** $\frac{3}{11} = \frac{21}{\square}$

(c) $\frac{\square}{7} = \frac{24}{28}$ **(d)** $\frac{8}{\square} = \frac{64}{104}$

Solution **(a)** You have to find which number multiplied by 20 gives 100.

$100 \div 20 = 5$

$\frac{1}{20} = \frac{1 \times 5}{20 \times 5}$ Multiply the numerator and denominator of $\frac{1}{20}$ by the same number, 5.

$\quad\ = \frac{5}{100}$

$\therefore$ the missing value is 5.

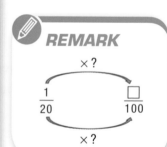

REMARK

(b) You have to find which number multiplied by 3 gives 21.

$21 \div 3 = 7$

$\frac{3}{11} = \frac{3 \times 7}{11 \times 7}$ Multiply the numerator and denominator of $\frac{3}{11}$ by the same number, 7.

$\quad\ = \frac{21}{77}$

$\therefore$ the missing value is 77.

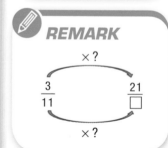

REMARK

(c) $28 \div 7 = 4$

$\frac{24}{28} = \frac{24 \div 4}{28 \div 4}$ Divide the numerator and denominator of $\frac{24}{28}$ by the same number, 4.

$\quad\ = \frac{6}{7}$

$\therefore$ the missing value is 6.

REMARK

(d) $64 \div 8 = 8$

$$\frac{64}{104} = \frac{64 \div 8}{104 \div 8}$$

Divide the numerator and denominator of $\frac{64}{104}$ by the same number, 8.

$$= \frac{8}{13}$$

∴ the missing value is 13.

Try It! 13 Find the missing values to make the fractions in each pair equivalent.

(a) $\frac{2}{9} = \frac{\square}{36}$ **(b)** $\frac{4}{13} = \frac{20}{\square}$ **(c)** $\frac{\square}{5} = \frac{18}{45}$ **(d)** $\frac{6}{\square} = \frac{54}{99}$

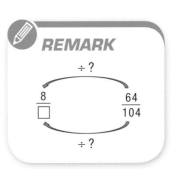

REMARK

$$\div\ ? $$
$$\frac{8}{\square} \qquad \frac{64}{104}$$
$$\div\ ?$$

A fraction is in its **simplest form** when its numerator and denominator have no common whole number factor other than 1. A fraction in its simplest form is also known as the fraction in its **lowest terms**.

Example 14 Reduce each fraction to its lowest terms.

(a) $\frac{18}{27} = \frac{\square}{3}$ **(b)** $\frac{32}{40} = \frac{4}{\square}$

Solution

(a) $27 \div 3 = 9$

$$\frac{18}{27} = \frac{18 \div 9}{27 \div 9}$$

$$= \frac{2}{3}$$

Whole number factors of 2 are 1 and 2. Whole number factors of 3 are 1 and 3. There is no common whole number factor other than 1. $\frac{2}{3}$ is in its lowest terms.

(b) $32 \div 4 = 8$

$$\frac{32}{40} = \frac{32 \div 8}{40 \div 8}$$

$$= \frac{4}{5}$$

Whole number factors of 4 are 1, 2 and 4. Whole number factors of 5 are 1 and 5. There is no common whole number factor other than 1. $\frac{4}{5}$ is in its lowest terms.

Try It! 14 Reduce each fraction to its lowest terms by completing the missing parts.

(a) $\frac{24}{48} = \frac{\square}{2}$ **(b)** $\frac{18}{72} = \frac{1}{\square}$

Example 15

Simplify each fraction to its lowest terms.

(a) $\dfrac{12}{16}$ **(b)** $\dfrac{54}{66}$

Solution

(a) $\dfrac{12}{16} = \dfrac{12 \div 4}{16 \div 4}$ Divide both the numerator and the denominator by 4.

$= \dfrac{3}{4}$

(b) $\dfrac{54}{66} = \dfrac{54 \div 6}{66 \div 6}$ 54 and 66 have a common factor 6.

$= \dfrac{9}{11}$

Try It! 15

Reduce each fraction to its lowest terms.

(a) $\dfrac{24}{28}$ **(b)** $\dfrac{63}{72}$

DISCUSS

David simplifies $\dfrac{54}{66}$ as follows:

$\dfrac{54}{66} = \dfrac{54 \div 2}{66 \div 2}$

$= \dfrac{27}{33}$

$= \dfrac{27 \div 3}{33 \div 3}$

$= \dfrac{9}{11}$

Is he correct? What is the relationship between the numbers 54, 66, 2, 3 and 6?

Example 16

Which of these pairs are equivalent fractions?

(a) $\dfrac{2}{5}, \dfrac{6}{15}$ **(b)** $\dfrac{4}{12}, \dfrac{5}{10}$ **(c)** $\dfrac{56}{96}, \dfrac{84}{144}$

Solution

(a) Equivalent fractions reduce to the same fraction in their lowest terms.

$\dfrac{2}{5}$ is already in its lowest terms.

3 is a common factor of 6 and 15.

$\dfrac{6}{15} = \dfrac{6 \div 3}{15 \div 3}$

$= \dfrac{2}{5}$

Both fractions reduce to $\dfrac{2}{5}$ in their lowest terms.

$\therefore \dfrac{2}{5}$ and $\dfrac{6}{15}$ are equivalent fractions.

(b) 4 is a common factor of 4 and 12.

$\dfrac{4}{12} = \dfrac{4 \div 4}{12 \div 4}$

$= \dfrac{1}{3}$

5 is a common factor of 5 and 10.

$\dfrac{5}{10} = \dfrac{5 \div 5}{10 \div 5}$

$= \dfrac{1}{2}$

The fractions do not reduce to the same fraction in their lowest terms.

$\therefore \dfrac{4}{12}$ and $\dfrac{5}{10}$ are not equivalent fractions.

REMARK

$\dfrac{2}{5}$

$\dfrac{6}{15}$

As you can see from the diagrams, if the whole is the same, shading $\dfrac{2}{5}$ of the whole is the same as shading $\dfrac{6}{15}$. Therefore they are equivalent fractions.

(c) 8 is a common factor of 56 and 96.

$$\frac{56}{96} = \frac{56 \div 8}{96 \div 8}$$

$$= \frac{7}{12}$$

12 is a common factor of 84 and 144.

$$\frac{84}{144} = \frac{84 \div 12}{144 \div 12}$$

$$= \frac{7}{12}$$

Both fractions reduce to the same fraction $\frac{7}{12}$ in their lowest terms.

$\therefore \frac{56}{96}$ and $\frac{84}{144}$ are equivalent fractions.

Try It! 16 Which of these pairs are equivalent fractions?

(a) $\frac{3}{4}, \frac{15}{20}$ **(b)** $\frac{4}{5}, \frac{28}{40}$ **(c)** $\frac{7}{15}, \frac{21}{45}$

 **DISCUSS**

Eddie simplifies $\frac{56}{96}$ as follows:

$$\frac{56}{96} = \frac{56 \div 2}{96 \div 2}$$

$$= \frac{28}{48}$$

$$= \frac{28 \div 4}{48 \div 4}$$

$$= \frac{7}{12}$$

Aengus simplifies $\frac{56}{96}$ as follows:

$$\frac{56}{96} = \frac{56 \div 4}{96 \div 4}$$

$$= \frac{14}{24}$$

$$= \frac{14 \div 2}{24 \div 2}$$

$$= \frac{7}{12}$$

Discuss what is the same and what is different about their reasoning.

PRACTICE 5.3

LEVEL 1

1. Find an equivalent fraction for each of these fractions.

 (a) $\frac{1}{5}$ **(b)** $\frac{1}{6}$ **(c)** $\frac{4}{10}$

2. Find five equivalent fractions for each of these fractions.

 (a) $\frac{2}{5}$ **(b)** $\frac{4}{7}$ **(c)** $\frac{12}{20}$

3. Reduce each fraction to its simplest form.

 (a) $\frac{30}{100}$ **(b)** $\frac{5}{50}$ **(c)** $\frac{16}{64}$ **(d)** $\frac{33}{121}$

 (e) $\frac{72}{96}$ **(f)** $\frac{56}{112}$ **(g)** $\frac{48}{120}$ **(h)** $\frac{104}{130}$

4. Which might be the odd one out of $\frac{8}{12}$, $\frac{18}{27}$ and $\frac{28}{35}$?

LEVEL 2

5. Find the missing values to make the fractions in each pair equivalent.

 (a) $\frac{7}{10} = \frac{\square}{100}$ **(b)** $\frac{3}{4} = \frac{\square}{36}$ **(c)** $\frac{5}{12} = \frac{20}{\square}$

 (d) $\frac{\square}{5} = \frac{36}{60}$ **(e)** $\frac{7}{9} = \frac{42}{\square}$ **(f)** $\frac{8}{\square} = \frac{64}{88}$

6. Which of these pairs are equivalent fractions?

(a) $\dfrac{2}{3}, \dfrac{14}{28}$ (b) $\dfrac{5}{6}, \dfrac{30}{36}$ (c) $\dfrac{7}{12}, \dfrac{77}{132}$

(d) $\dfrac{11}{44}, \dfrac{22}{84}$ (e) $\dfrac{7}{9}, \dfrac{63}{81}$ (f) $\dfrac{56}{84}, \dfrac{8}{12}$

7. Siti has $\dfrac{6}{8}$ kg of white rice and Jane has $\dfrac{9}{12}$ kg of brown rice. Do they have the same amount of rice? Explain your answer.

PROBLEM SOLVING

8. (a) $\dfrac{\square}{5}$ and $\dfrac{8}{20}$ are equivalent fractions. Find the missing value $\square$.

PROBLEM SOLVING

    (b) $\dfrac{12}{\bigcirc}$ and $\dfrac{8}{20}$ are equivalent fractions. Find the missing value $\bigcirc$.

Workbook 1A Link
Exercise 5.3

5.4 Comparing Fractions

Not all fractions are equivalent. A fraction may be greater than or smaller than another fraction.

 CLASS ACTIVITY 6

Objective: To compare fractions.

1. The diagram is a fraction wall. Each row is a bar model that divides a whole into equal parts.

$\frac{1}{2}$					$\frac{1}{2}$				
$\frac{1}{3}$			$\frac{1}{3}$			$\frac{1}{3}$			
$\frac{1}{4}$		$\frac{1}{4}$		$\frac{1}{4}$		$\frac{1}{4}$			
$\frac{1}{5}$		$\frac{1}{5}$		$\frac{1}{5}$		$\frac{1}{5}$		$\frac{1}{5}$	
$\frac{1}{6}$		$\frac{1}{6}$		$\frac{1}{6}$		$\frac{1}{6}$		$\frac{1}{6}$	$\frac{1}{6}$
$\frac{1}{7}$	$\frac{1}{7}$	$\frac{1}{7}$	$\frac{1}{7}$	$\frac{1}{7}$	$\frac{1}{7}$	$\frac{1}{7}$			
$\frac{1}{8}$	$\frac{1}{8}$	$\frac{1}{8}$	$\frac{1}{8}$	$\frac{1}{8}$	$\frac{1}{8}$	$\frac{1}{8}$	$\frac{1}{8}$		
$\frac{1}{9}$	$\frac{1}{9}$	$\frac{1}{9}$	$\frac{1}{9}$	$\frac{1}{9}$	$\frac{1}{9}$	$\frac{1}{9}$	$\frac{1}{9}$	$\frac{1}{9}$	
$\frac{1}{10}$	$\frac{1}{10}$	$\frac{1}{10}$	$\frac{1}{10}$	$\frac{1}{10}$	$\frac{1}{10}$	$\frac{1}{10}$	$\frac{1}{10}$	$\frac{1}{10}$	$\frac{1}{10}$

0   1

> **REMARK**
>
> The fractions $\dfrac{1}{2}, \dfrac{1}{3},$ $\dfrac{1}{4}, \dfrac{1}{5}, \dfrac{1}{6}, \dfrac{1}{7}, \dfrac{1}{8}, \dfrac{1}{9}, \dfrac{1}{10}$ all have numerators equal to 1, and are called **unit fractions**. A unit fraction is one part of the whole.

(a) Use the fraction wall to arrange the fractions $\dfrac{1}{2}, \dfrac{1}{3}, \dfrac{1}{4}, \dfrac{1}{5}, \dfrac{1}{6}, \dfrac{1}{7}, \dfrac{1}{8}, \dfrac{1}{9}, \dfrac{1}{10}$ from the smallest to the greatest. Explain your answer.

(b) From the fraction wall, you can see $\dfrac{1}{2} = \dfrac{2}{4}$. That is, $\dfrac{1}{2}$ and $\dfrac{2}{4}$ are equivalent fractions. Use the wall to write down four other pairs of equivalent fractions.

2. Use the fraction wall to decide which fraction is greater in each pair. Explain your answer.

(a) $\frac{2}{3}, \frac{2}{7}$

Hint: You may copy the rows with denominators 3 and 7 from the fraction wall on the previous page and shade these fraction to compare.

(b) $\frac{4}{5}, \frac{4}{9}$

Hint: You may copy the rows with denominators 5 and 9 from the fraction wall on the previous page and shade these fractions to compare.

3. Which fraction is greater, $\frac{11}{5}$ or $\frac{27}{5}$? Explain your answer.

4. Choose values that make these true:

(a) $\frac{2}{5} < \frac{2}{\square}$

(b) $\frac{2}{5} < \frac{\square}{5}$

5. Choose values that make these true:

(a) $\frac{4}{7} > \frac{4}{\square}$

(b) $\frac{3}{7} > \frac{\square}{7}$

RECALL

The symbol '>' means greater than.

The symbol '<' means less than.

Class Activity 6 reveals the following properties.

> When two fractions have the same numerator, the one with the smaller denominator is greater.
>
> When two fractions have the same denominator, the one with the bigger numerator is greater.

Let's have a look at comparing some fractions.

Which fraction is smaller, $\frac{5}{11}$ or $\frac{7}{11}$? Use a bar model to explain your answer.

Solution

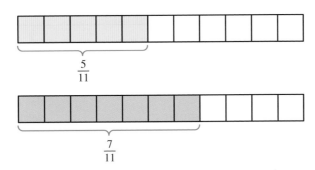

$\frac{5}{11}$

$\frac{7}{11}$

Both fractions have the same denominator, 11.
Comparing their numerators, 5 < 7.

Continued

The bar model shows that there is a greater number of equal parts represented by the fraction $\frac{7}{11}$ than are represented by the fraction $\frac{5}{11}$.

Hence, $\frac{5}{11} < \frac{7}{11}$,

i.e. $\frac{5}{11}$ is smaller.

Try It! 17 Which fraction is smaller, $\frac{8}{9}$ or $\frac{5}{9}$? Use a bar model to explain your answer.

If two fractions have **the same denominator**, they represent two identical wholes that have been divided into the same number of equal parts, as in Example 17.

The **different numerators** represent choosing different numbers of those parts.

The fraction with the bigger numerator represents choosing more of those parts so the fraction with the bigger numerator is the greater of the fractions.

Example 18 Which fraction is greater, $\frac{3}{8}$ or $\frac{3}{10}$? Use a bar model to explain your answer.

Solution

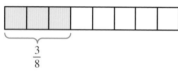

$$\frac{3}{8}$$

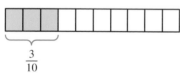

$$\frac{3}{10}$$

Both fractions have the same numerator, 3. Comparing their denominators, 8 < 10.

The bar model shows that the whole is divided into fewer equal parts when representing the fraction $\frac{3}{8}$ than it is when representing $\frac{3}{10}$. This means that each of the 3 equal parts representing $\frac{3}{8}$ is greater in size than each of the 3 equal parts representing $\frac{3}{10}$.

Therefore, the 3 parts representing $\frac{3}{8}$ are greater in size than the 3 parts representing $\frac{3}{10}$.

i.e. $\frac{3}{8}$ is greater.

Try It! 18 Which fraction is greater, $\frac{2}{7}$ or $\frac{2}{13}$? Use a bar model to explain your answer.

 DISCUSS

Write down any two fractions with the same denominator and say which one is greater.

Write down any two fractions with the same numerator and say which one is greater.

Two fractions with **different denominators** represent dividing two identical wholes into different numbers of equal parts as in Example 18.

The bigger denominator represents dividing the whole into more parts than the smaller denominator does.

If there are are more parts in total, each part must be smaller in size.

When the **numerators** are the **same**, this represents choosing the **same** number of parts of each whole. However, the parts represented by the fraction with the smaller denominator are greater in size than the parts represented by the fraction with the bigger denominator.

So the fraction with the smaller denominator is the greater of the two fractions.

Example 19 Which number is smaller, $3\frac{1}{4}$ or $\frac{23}{4}$?

Solution

$3\frac{1}{4} = 3 + \frac{1}{4}$ Convert $3\frac{1}{4}$ to an improper fraction.

$= \frac{4}{4} + \frac{4}{4} + \frac{4}{4} + \frac{1}{4}$ 4 quarters + 4 quarters + 4 quarters + 1 quarter

$= \frac{13}{4}$ = 13 quarters

The fractions $\frac{13}{4}$ and $\frac{23}{4}$ have the same denominator, 4. Comparing their numerators, 13 < 23. Hence, $\frac{13}{4} < \frac{23}{4}$, i.e. $3\frac{1}{4}$ is smaller.

Note: $\frac{13}{4} = 3\frac{1}{4}$ and $\frac{23}{4} = 5\frac{3}{4}$. On a number line $3\frac{1}{4}$ is on the left of $5\frac{3}{4}$, showing that $3\frac{1}{4} < 5\frac{3}{4}$.

Try It! 19 Which number is smaller, $\frac{37}{6}$ or $4\frac{5}{6}$?

PRACTICE 5.4

⚙ LEVEL 1

1. Write down the fractions represented by the shaded portions of the shapes. Connect the two fractions using an inequality sign '<' or '>'.

   (a)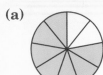

   (b)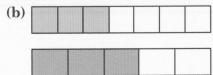

2. Copy and fill in the blank with an inequality sign '<' or '>'.

(a) $\dfrac{1}{5}$ ____ $\dfrac{1}{8}$ (b) $\dfrac{2}{3}$ ____ $\dfrac{2}{5}$

(c) $\dfrac{3}{7}$ ____ $\dfrac{3}{4}$ (d) $\dfrac{19}{100}$ ____ $\dfrac{19}{1000}$

3. Which fraction in each pair is smaller? Use bar models to explain your answers.

(a) $\dfrac{3}{6}, \dfrac{5}{6}$ (b) $\dfrac{7}{10}, \dfrac{2}{10}$ (c) $\dfrac{2}{11}, \dfrac{5}{11}$ (d) $\dfrac{13}{15}, \dfrac{9}{15}$

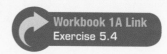 **LEVEL 2**

4. Which number in each pair is greater? Use bar models to explain your answers.

(a) $1\dfrac{2}{9}, \dfrac{5}{9}$ (b) $\dfrac{16}{5}, 1\dfrac{4}{5}$

5. Arrange the fractions $\dfrac{5}{7}, \dfrac{5}{4}$ and $\dfrac{5}{9}$ from the smallest to the greatest.

6. Arrange the numbers $\dfrac{5}{7}, 1\dfrac{3}{7}$ and $\dfrac{3}{7}$ from the greatest to the smallest.

7. Arrange the fractions $\dfrac{5}{7}, \dfrac{5}{8}$ and $\dfrac{13}{7}$ from the smallest to the greatest.

8. A pole is $2\dfrac{3}{8}$ m long. A mast is $\dfrac{21}{8}$ m long. Which one is longer? Explain your answer.

PROBLEM SOLVING

9. Write a fraction that lies between $\dfrac{3}{4}$ and $\dfrac{13}{4}$. Explain your answer.

OPEN QUESTION

Workbook 1A Link Exercise 5.4

5.5 Fractions of Quantities

What are the values of $\dfrac{1}{3}$ of 6 and $\dfrac{1}{3} \times 6$? How are they related?

$\dfrac{1}{3}$ of 6 can be considered as dividing the whole, which is 6, into three equal parts and getting one part.

Here is the bar model.

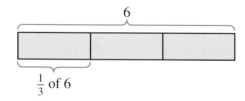

$\dfrac{1}{3}$ of 6

Hence, $\dfrac{1}{3}$ of 6 = 6 ÷ 3
$\phantom{Hence, \dfrac{1}{3} of 6}$ = 2

> **DISCUSS**
>
> If you had six apples, and you ate $\dfrac{1}{3}$ of them, how many apples did you eat? Use the bar model to explain your answer.
>
>

$\frac{1}{3} \times 6 = \frac{1}{3} + \frac{1}{3} + \frac{1}{3} + \frac{1}{3} + \frac{1}{3} + \frac{1}{3}$ Repeated addition of six $\frac{1}{3}$.

$\qquad = 6 \text{ thirds}$

$\qquad = 3 \text{ thirds} + 3 \text{ thirds}$

$\qquad = 1 \text{ whole} + 1 \text{ whole}$

$\qquad = 2$

This can be modelled as six $\frac{1}{3}$ slices, which form two wholes.

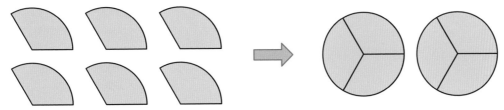

You can see that $\frac{1}{3}$ of 6 and $\frac{1}{3} \times 6$ and $6 \div 3$ are the same.

There is a short way to work out $\frac{1}{3} \times 6$. The method is called **cancelling common factors**.

$\frac{1}{3} \times 6 = \frac{1}{\cancel{3}_1} \times \cancel{6}^2$ Simplify by dividing both 3 and 6 by their common factor 3.
Write the quotients next to the dividends.

$\qquad = \frac{1}{1} \times 2 \qquad \frac{1}{1} = 1$

$\qquad = 2$

Example 20

Find $\frac{3}{5}$ of £20.

Solution

Method 1

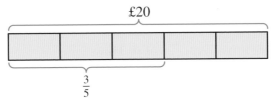

From the bar model,

$\frac{1}{5}$ of £20 = 20 ÷ 5

$\qquad\qquad = £4$

$\frac{3}{5}$ of £20 = 3 × 4

$\qquad\qquad = £12$

Method 2

$\frac{3}{5}$ of £20 = $\frac{3}{\cancel{5}_1} \times \cancel{20}^4$ Divide 5 and 20 by their common factor 5.

$\qquad\qquad = \frac{3}{1} \times 4$

$\qquad\qquad = 3 \times 4$

$\qquad\qquad = £12$

REMARK

You can use the multiplication and division table on page 359 to check the calculations in these examples.

Try It! 20

Find $\frac{3}{4}$ of 24 kg. Justify your answer in two different ways.

Example **21** There are 60 apples. A class has eaten $\frac{7}{10}$ of them. How many apples are left?

Solution

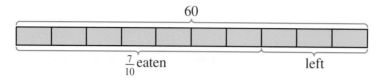

$$\underbrace{}_{\frac{7}{10}\text{ eaten}} \quad \underbrace{}_{\text{left}}$$

Method 1

$\frac{1}{10}$ of $60 = 60 \div 10$

$\qquad\qquad = 6$

Number of apples eaten $= \frac{7}{10}$ of 60

$\qquad\qquad\qquad\qquad = 7 \times 6$

$\qquad\qquad\qquad\qquad = 42$

Number of apples left $= 60 - 42$

$\qquad\qquad\qquad\qquad = 18$

Method 2

Fraction of apples left $= 1 - \frac{7}{10}$ 10 tenths – 7 tenths

$\qquad\qquad\qquad\qquad\qquad\qquad = 3$ tenths

$\qquad\qquad\qquad\qquad = \frac{3}{10}$

Number of apples left $= \frac{3}{10}$ of 60

$\qquad\qquad\qquad\qquad = \frac{3}{10_{1}} \times 60^{6}$ Divide 10 and 60 by their common factor 10.

$\qquad\qquad\qquad\qquad = \frac{3}{1} \times 6$

$\qquad\qquad\qquad\qquad = 18$

Try It! **21** A novel has 200 pages. You have read $\frac{65}{100}$ of it. How many pages do you have left to read?

REMARK

Here, there is a group of 60 apples. The fraction $\frac{7}{10}$ is a fraction of this group. Each part of the bar model represents six apples.

Example **22** Find the number of minutes in one-fifth of an hour.

Solution One-fifth of an hour $= \frac{1}{5}$ of an hour

$\qquad\qquad\qquad\qquad = \frac{1}{5}$ of 60 minutes   1 hour = 60 minutes

$\qquad\qquad\qquad\qquad = \frac{1}{5_{1}} \times 60^{12}$ minutes

$\qquad\qquad\qquad\qquad = 12$ minutes

Try It! **22** Find the number of minutes in two-thirds of an hour.

REMARK

You can also use a bar model:

1 hour = 60 minutes

$\frac{1}{5}$

PRACTICE 5.5

1. There are 9 fish in a pond. Find

   (a) $\frac{1}{3}$ of the 9 fish,

   (b) $\frac{2}{3}$ of the 9 fish.

2. There are 15 beads on a table. Find

   (a) $\frac{1}{5}$ of the 15 beads,

   (b) $\frac{4}{5}$ of the 15 beads.

3. Calculate these values.

   (a) $\frac{2}{7}$ of 28 kg   (b) $\frac{4}{9}$ of £108   (c) $\frac{3}{10}$ of 480 ml   (d) $\frac{80}{100}$ of 400 m

⚙ **LEVEL 2**

4. The price of an adult ticket for a show is £18. The price of a child ticket is $\frac{1}{2}$ of the price of an adult ticket. Find the price of a child ticket.

   £ FINANCE

5. There are 40 marks available in a test. David gets $\frac{5}{8}$ of the full marks. How many marks does David get?

6. (a) Find the number of minutes in three-quarters of an hour. Show your reasoning.

   PROBLEM SOLVING (b) Find the number of hours in $\frac{1}{6}$ of a day.

7. There are 50 households in a small town. $\frac{3}{10}$ of the households have pets.

   (a) How many households have pets?
   (b) How many households do not have pets?

8. A pack has 36 jelly beans and $\frac{2}{9}$ of the jelly beans are red. Find the number of jelly beans that are not red.

   PROBLEM SOLVING

9. A box has 54 apples. You can take $\frac{5}{9}$ or $\frac{11}{18}$ of the total number of apples. Which fraction would you choose to get more apples? Explain your answer.

   PROBLEM SOLVING

Workbook 1A Link
Exercise 5.5

Idea of Fractions

A fraction is a part of a whole.

If a whole is divided into 7 **equal** parts, the fraction that represents 3 equal parts is $\frac{3}{7}$.

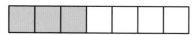

$$\frac{3}{7} \quad \begin{array}{l} \leftarrow \text{Numerator} \\ \leftarrow \text{Vinculum} \\ \leftarrow \text{Denominator} \end{array}$$

When the numerator is less than the denominator, the fraction is called a proper fraction.

Equivalent Fractions

Equivalent fractions represent equal values.

e.g. $\frac{2}{3} = \frac{4}{6} = \frac{10}{15} = \frac{18}{27}$

$\therefore \frac{2}{3}, \frac{4}{6}, \frac{10}{15}, \frac{18}{27}$ are equivalent fractions.

They can be obtained by multiplying or dividing the numerator and denominator by the same non-zero whole number.

e.g. $\frac{2}{3} = \frac{2 \times 5}{3 \times 5}$ $\qquad \frac{18}{27} = \frac{18 \div 9}{27 \div 9}$

$\quad = \frac{10}{15}$ $\qquad\qquad\quad = \frac{2}{3}$

Improper Fractions

The numerator is greater than or equal to the denominator in an improper fraction, e.g. $\frac{17}{5}$.

Converting to a mixed number:

$\frac{17}{5} = 3 \times 5$ fifths $+ 2$ fifths

$\quad = 3 + \frac{2}{5}$

$\quad = 3\frac{2}{5}$

Mixed Numbers

A mixed number is made up of a whole number and a proper fraction,

e.g. $3\frac{2}{5}$.

Converting to an improper fraction:

$3\frac{2}{5} = \frac{5}{5} + \frac{5}{5} + \frac{5}{5} + \frac{2}{5}$

$\quad = \frac{17}{5}$

or

3 wholes and 2 fifths

$= 3 \times 5$ fifths $+ 2$ fifths

$= 15$ fifths $+ 2$ fifths

$= 17$ fifths

Comparing Fractions

If two fractions have the same numerator, the fraction with the smaller denominator is the greater of the two,

e.g. $\frac{1}{3} > \frac{1}{10}$.

If two fractions have the same denominator, the fraction with the greater numerator is the greater of the two,

e.g. $\frac{29}{100} > \frac{14}{100}$.

Fractions of Quantities

e.g. $\frac{3}{10}$ of $150\,\text{m}$

$= \frac{3}{10_1} \times 150^{15}\,\text{m}$

$= 3 \times 15\,\text{m}$

$= 45\,\text{m}$

CHALLENGE 5 💡

Mr Miller has a monthly income of £3600. He spends $\frac{1}{4}$ of it on a home loan and $\frac{3}{24}$ of it on food. What fraction of the income is remaining?

Workbook 1A Link
Problem Solving 5

REVISION EXERCISE 5 ✤✤

1. What fraction is the shaded portion in each diagram?

   (a)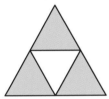

   (b)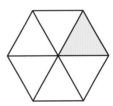

   (c)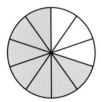

   (d)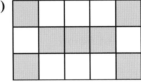

2. What fraction of the eggs are white?

3. Write the shaded portion as an improper fraction and a mixed number.

   whole   whole

4. Four cans in a box form a whole. Write the portion of 13 cans as a mixed number and as an improper fraction.

   whole   whole   whole

5. Write each improper fraction as a mixed number or a whole number.

    (a) $\frac{11}{3}$
    (b) $\frac{15}{4}$
    (c) $\frac{15}{5}$
    (d) $\frac{30}{7}$

6. Convert each mixed number to an improper fraction.

    (a) $1\frac{2}{3}$
    (b) $2\frac{3}{5}$
    (c) $3\frac{5}{6}$
    (d) $4\frac{1}{8}$

7. Find the missing numbers if the given fractions are equivalent.

    (a) $\frac{2}{5}, \frac{\square}{20}$
    (b) $\frac{10}{\square}, \frac{28}{42}$

    Hint: Start by expressing $\frac{28}{42}$ in its simplest form.

8. Which one is smaller in each pair? Explain your answer.

    (a) $\frac{1}{10}, \frac{1}{20}$
    (b) $\frac{19}{100}, \frac{59}{100}$

9. Reduce each fraction to its simplest form.

    (a) $\frac{16}{20}$
    (b) $\frac{8}{48}$
    (c) $\frac{81}{90}$
    (d) $\frac{14}{56}$

10. Find these quantities.

    (a) $\frac{3}{8}$ of £32
    (b) $\frac{5}{6}$ of 54 cm

    (c) $\frac{4}{9}$ of 18 grams
    (d) $\frac{7}{6}$ of 120 minutes

11. There are 132 ml of a mixture. One-third of it is vinegar and the rest is water. Calculate

    (a) the volume of vinegar,

SCIENCE

    (b) the volume of water in the mixture.

12. Sophia takes $\frac{3}{4}$ of an hour to do an assignment. Donna takes $\frac{3}{5}$ of an hour to do the same task.

PROBLEM SOLVING

    (a) Who is faster? Explain your answer.

    (b) How many minutes does the faster person take?

Write in Your Journal

Anouk wants to compare the fractions $\frac{5}{6}$ and $\frac{4}{5}$. She says "I can't work out which is bigger because they don't have either the same denominator or the same numerator". Can you help Anouk decide? Can you explain your answer in more than one way?

6 TENTHS, HUNDREDTHS AND THOUSANDTHS

WHAT IS IN THIS CHAPTER:

6.1 Decimal Place Values

6.2 Conversion between Fractions and Decimals

6.3 Multiplying and Dividing by 10, 100 and 1000

6.4 Introducing Percentages

6.5 Percentages of Quantities

You see price tags on items everywhere. Here they are on some flowers. The prices are £1.50, £2.50, £2.00 and £2.99. Numbers in this form are called decimal numbers. You will learn more about decimals in this chapter.

LET'S LEARN TO

▶ identify the tenths, hundredths and thousandths in decimals

▶ order decimals up to three decimal places

▶ convert fractions to decimals

▶ convert decimals up to three decimal places to fractions

▶ multiply and divide by 10, 100 and 1000

▶ convert money and measures

▶ define percentages

▶ express percentages

▶ relate fractions, decimals and percentages

▶ find percentages of quantities

1. Place Value of a Whole Number

Place value	Ten thousands	Thousands	Hundreds	Tens	Ones
Number	2	3	8	5	7

The number 23 857 represents twenty-three thousand, eight hundred and fifty-seven.

The number in expanded form is:

$$23\,857 = 2 \times 10\,000 + 3 \times 1000 + 8 \times 100 + 5 \times 10 + 7 \times 1.$$

The value represented by each digit in the number depends on its place value.

The place value of the digit 2 is ten thousands, and so the digit 2 represents 20 000.

The place value of the digit 8 is hundreds, and so the digit 8 represents 800.

2. Four Operations of Whole Numbers

To add and subtract, you have to align numbers by place value. This ensures that ones are added to ones, tens are added to tens, hundreds are added to hundreds, and so on. Sometimes, regrouping is necessary.

(a) Addition

```
    473
+   829
-------
   1302
    11
```

(b) Subtraction

```
   4 15 1
    562
-   384
-------
    178
```

(c) Multiplication

```
     47
×    59
-------
    423
   2350
-------
   2773
```

$$47 \times 59 = 2773$$

(d) Division

```
        46 r 6
    7 ) 328
        28
        --
         48
         42
         --
          6
```

$$328 \div 7 = 46 \text{ r } 6$$

3. Fractions

(a) A fraction is a part of a whole. The whole = 1.

The shares represented by the shaded parts of these diagrams are the fractions $\frac{1}{2}$, $\frac{7}{10}$ and $\frac{43}{100}$.

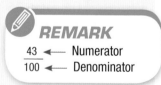

REMARK

$$\frac{43}{100}$$ ← Numerator
← Denominator

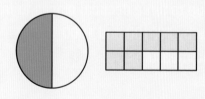

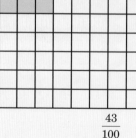

$$\frac{1}{2} \qquad \frac{7}{10} \qquad \frac{43}{100}$$

You can also have fractions of groups. For example, there are three dogs out of a total of five pets.

$\frac{3}{5}$ of the pets are dogs.

(b) Proper fractions are fractions whose numerator is less than the denominator.

e.g. $\frac{1}{3}$, $\frac{7}{9}$ and $\frac{85}{100}$ are proper fractions.

Improper fractions are fractions with a numerator greater than or equal to the denominator.

e.g. $\frac{3}{3}$, $\frac{29}{10}$ and $\frac{185}{100}$ are improper fractions.

Mixed numbers are the sum of whole numbers and proper fractions.

e.g. $2\frac{1}{3}$, $5\frac{3}{10}$ are $1\frac{71}{100}$ are mixed numbers.

Note that $2\frac{1}{3}$ means $2 + \frac{1}{3}$.

(c) Improper fractions and mixed numbers can be converted from one to the other.

e.g.
$$\frac{13}{5} = \frac{10}{5} + \frac{3}{5}$$ 13 fifths = 10 fifths + 3 fifths

$$= 2 + \frac{3}{5}$$ $\frac{10}{5} = \frac{5}{5} + \frac{5}{5} = 1 + 1$

$$= 2\frac{3}{5}$$

whole   whole

$$1\frac{2}{3} = 1 + \frac{2}{3}$$

$$= \frac{3}{3} + \frac{2}{3}$$

$$= \frac{5}{3}$$ 3 thirds + 2 thirds = 5 thirds

whole

6.1 Decimal Place Values

A Representation of Decimal Numbers

You use a measuring tape or a ruler to measure the length or height or width of an object. You know that

$$1\,m = 100\,cm \qquad \text{and} \qquad 1\,cm = 10\,mm.$$

∴ $$1\,m = 100 \times 10\,mm = 1000\,mm.$$

Hence, $$1\,cm = \frac{1}{100}\,m \qquad \text{and} \qquad 1\,mm = \frac{1}{10}\,cm = \frac{1}{1000}\,m.$$

RECALL

The symbol ∴ means 'therefore'.

If the height of a boy is 143 cm. This can be expressed as

$$143 \text{ cm} = 100 \text{ cm} + 43 \text{ cm}$$
$$= 1 \text{ m} + \frac{43}{100} \text{ m}$$
$$= 1\frac{43}{100} \text{ m}$$

On the ruler, every cm is divided into 10 equal parts and each equal part represents 1 mm.

The length of the red bar = 6 cm + 7 mm

$$= \frac{6}{100} \text{ m} + \frac{7}{1000} \text{ m}$$
$$= \frac{60}{1000} \text{ m} + \frac{7}{1000} \text{ m}$$
$$= \frac{67}{1000} \text{ m}$$

The numbers $1\frac{43}{100}$ and $\frac{67}{1000}$ can be represented as 1.43 and 0.067. These numbers 1.43 and 0.067 are called **decimal numbers**.

They can be represented in a place value table.

Metres 1 m	10 Centimetres $\frac{1}{10}$ m	Centimetres $\frac{1}{100}$ m	Millimetres $\frac{1}{1000}$ m
Ones 1	Tenths $\frac{1}{10}$	Hundredths $\frac{1}{100}$	Thousandths $\frac{1}{1000}$
1	4	3	
0	0	6	7

That is, $1.43 = 1 + 4 \times \frac{1}{10} + 3 \times \frac{1}{100}$

and $0.067 = 6 \times \frac{1}{100} + 7 \times \frac{1}{1000}$.

> **REMARK**
>
> You read 1.43 as 'one and four tenths and three hundredths'.
> You read 0.067 as '6 hundredths and 7 thousandths'.

The expressions on the right-hand side are called the **expanded forms** of these two decimal numbers.

Here is the expanded form of another two decimal numbers.

Tens 10	Ones 1	Tenths $\frac{1}{10}$	Hundredths $\frac{1}{100}$
2	3	5	7

$$23.57 = 2 \times 10 + 3 \times 1 + 5 \times \frac{1}{10} + 7 \times \frac{1}{100}$$

Ones 1	Tenths $\frac{1}{10}$	Hundredths $\frac{1}{100}$	Thousandths $\frac{1}{1000}$
8	9	0	4

$$8.904 = 8 \times 1 + 9 \times \frac{1}{10} + 4 \times \frac{1}{1000}$$

> **DISCUSS**
>
> Is 8.904 the same as 8.94 and 8.9004? What is the purpose of the zero in 8.904?

In a decimal number, the whole number part and the part that is less than one are separated by a **decimal point**.

Let's look at another decimal number.

Place value	Ten thousands 10000	Thousands 1000	Hundreds 100	Tens 10	Ones 1	Tenths $\frac{1}{10}$	Hundredths $\frac{1}{100}$	Thousandths $\frac{1}{1000}$
Number	2	3	8	5	7	4	9	6

23857.496

whole number part · decimal point · part less than one

The number 23857.496 can be read as twenty-three thousand, eight hundred, fifty-seven and four tenths, nine hundredths and six thousandths.

The number of digits after the decimal point is called the **number of decimal places**. The number 1.4 has one decimal place. The number 23.57 has two decimal places. The numbers 8.904 and 23857.496 both have three decimal places.

REMARK

Note that
ten = 10,
ten**th** = $\frac{1}{10}$;
hundred = 100,
hundred**th** = $\frac{1}{100}$;
thousand = 1000,
thousand**th** = $\frac{1}{1000}$.

Example 1

(a) Write the number 19.87 in expanded form and in words.

(b) Show that $19.87 = 19\frac{87}{100}$.

Solution

(a) $19.87 = 1 \times 10 + 9 \times 1 + 8 \times \frac{1}{10} + 7 \times \frac{1}{100}$

The number is nineteen, eight tenths and seven hundredths.

(b) $19.87 = 19 + \frac{8}{10} + \frac{7}{100}$

$= 19 + \frac{8 \times 10}{10 \times 10} + \frac{7}{100}$ Express $\frac{8}{10}$ as the

$= 19 + \frac{80}{100} + \frac{7}{100}$ equivalent fraction $\frac{80}{100}$.

$= 19\frac{87}{100}$ 80 hundredths + 7 hundredths = 87 hundredths

Try It! 1

(a) Write the number 5.093 in expanded form and in words.

(b) Show that $5.093 = 5\frac{93}{1000}$.

Example 2

Write down the value represented by the digit 7 in each of these numbers.

(a) 32.075   (b) 4.197

Solution

(a) In the number 32.075, the digit 7 is in the hundredths place.

∴ the digit 7 represents $\frac{7}{100}$.

Continued

(b) In the number 4.197, the digit 7 is in the thousandths place.

∴ the digit 7 represents $\dfrac{7}{1000}$.

Try It! ② Write down the value represented by the digit 4 in each of these numbers.

(a) 50.413 **(b)** 2.948

You have seen that the same number can be written as a decimal and as a mixed number.

$$8.634 = 8 + \dfrac{6}{10} + \dfrac{3}{100} + \dfrac{4}{1000}$$

This can be read as eight and six tenths, three hundredths and four thousandths.

You can also use equivalent fractions.

$$8.634 = 8 + \dfrac{6 \times 100}{10 \times 100} + \dfrac{3 \times 10}{100 \times 10} + \dfrac{4}{1000}$$

Express $\dfrac{6}{10}$ as the equivalent fraction $\dfrac{600}{1000}$, and express $\dfrac{3}{100}$ as the equivalent fraction $\dfrac{30}{1000}$.

$$= 8 + \dfrac{600}{1000} + \dfrac{30}{1000} + \dfrac{4}{1000}$$

600 thousandths + 30 thousandths + 4 thousandths
= 634 thousandths

$$= 8 \dfrac{634}{1000}$$

B Ordering of Decimal Numbers

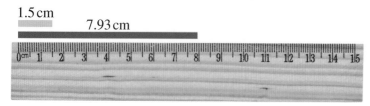

Here are two bars of lengths 1.5 cm and 7.93 cm. To read these two lengths more accurately, the ruler has to be magnified. You can also represent decimal numbers, such as 1.5 and 7.93, on a number line.

As $1.5 \left(= 1 + \dfrac{5}{10}\right)$ is between 1 and 2, you divide the section between 1 and 2 on the number line into 10 equal parts. Then you locate the point representing 1.5 as shown below.

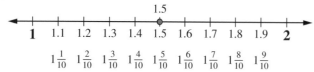

7.93 is between 7 and 8. First divide the section between 7 and 8 on the number line into 10 equal parts. Because 7.93 = 7 and 9 tenths and 3 hundredths, it is greater than 7 and 9 tenths but less than 8, so 7.93 lies between 7.9 and 8.

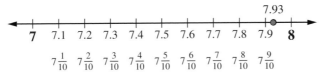

If you divide the section between 7.9 and 8 into 10 equal parts, 7.93 is the third mark after 7.9.

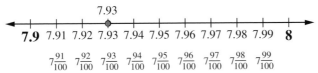

A number is less than any other number to its right when they are marked on a standard number line.

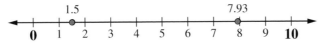

The above number line shows that 1.5 < 7.93.

Example 3

The prices of two packs of chicken breast are £3.75 and £3.72. Which pack costs less?

Solution

Method 1
The price of the first pack = £3.75
= £3 and 75 pence

The price of the second pack = £3.72
= £3 and 72 pence

72 pence is 3 pence less than 75 pence.
Hence, the pack with price £3.72 costs less.

Method 2
You may draw the numbers 3.75 and 3.72 on a magnified number line between 3.7 and 3.8.

3.75 is on the right of 3.72.
∴   3.72 is smaller.   i.e. 3.72 < 3.75
Hence, the pack with price £3.72 costs less.

Method 3
Write the numbers in expanded form.

$$3.75 = 3 + \frac{7}{10} + \frac{5}{100} \qquad 3.75 = 3 + 7 \times \frac{1}{10} + 5 \times \frac{1}{100}$$

$$3.72 = 3 + \frac{7}{10} + \frac{2}{100} \qquad 3.72 = 3 + 7 \times \frac{1}{10} + 2 \times \frac{1}{100}$$

These two numbers both contain the same number of ones and the same number of tenths.

However, $\frac{2}{100}$ is smaller than $\frac{5}{100}$,

so, overall, 3.72 is smaller.

Hence, the pack with price £3.72 costs less.

REMARK

Just like lengths can be compared using a measuring tape, numbers can be compared on a number line.

RECALL

The symbol < means 'less than'.
The symbol > means 'greater than'.

The prices of two packs of steak are £8.67 and £8.64. Which pack costs less? Explain your reasoning.

Example ④

The mass of pumpkin A is 5.246 kg. The mass of pumpkin B is 5.283 kg. Which pumpkin is heavier?

Solution

Method 1

Draw a magnified number line as shown.

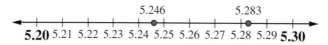

5.283 is on the right of 5.246.

∴ $5.283 > 5.246$

Pumpkin B is heavier.

Method 2

Compare the numbers 5.246 and 5.283 digit by digit from left to right.

Ones	Tenths	Hundredths	Thousandths
5	2	4	6
5	2	8	3

From the place value table, the two numbers have the same number of ones and tenths. However, 8 hundredths > 4 hundredths, so 5.283 is greater.

Pumpkin B is heavier.

Try It! ④

The mass of melon C is 3.147 kg. The mass of melon D is 3.145 kg. Which melon is heavier? Explain your reasoning.

REMARK

Method 2 here is closely linked to Method 3 in Example 3.

The digit 4 represents $\frac{4}{100}$.

The digit 8 represents $\frac{8}{100}$.

Since 8 > 4, you know $\frac{8}{100} > \frac{4}{100}$.

Hence, 5.283 is greater than 5.246.

DISCUSS

Lennox says that $5.246 > 5.283$ because 6 is greater than 3. Do you agree with Lennox's reasoning?

Example ⑤

Joe took 4.527 seconds to work out a sum and Eva took 4.52 seconds to work out the same sum. Who was faster?

Solution

Ones	Tenths	Hundredths	Thousandths
4	5	2	7
4	5	2	0

First compare the ones. Both numbers, having 4 ones, are the same so far.

Next compare the tenths. Both numbers, having 5 tenths, are the same so far.

Then compare the hundredths. Both numbers, having 2 hundredths, are still the same so far.

Finally compare the thousandths digit of these two numbers.

0 thousandths < 7 thousandths.

So 4.52 < 4.527.

Therefore, Eva was faster.   The faster time is the shorter time.

 **REMARK**

$4.52 = 4.520$

$4.52 = 4 + \frac{5}{10} + \frac{2}{100}$

$4.520 = 4 + \frac{5}{10} + \frac{2}{100} + \frac{0}{1000}$

$\therefore 4.52 = 4.520$

The value of a number does not change when zeros are written at the end of the decimal part of the number.

Try It! 5   James took 2.73 seconds to work out a sum and Gloria took 2.736 seconds to work out the same sum. Who was slower?

PRACTICE 6.1

 **LEVEL 1**

1. Write each decimal number in expanded form. Then write the expanded form in words.
   (a) 12.3   (b) 9.34   (c) 9.034   (d) 0.934

2. Write each expression as a decimal.
   (a) $1 + \frac{4}{10} + \frac{7}{100}$ (b) $\frac{1}{10} + \frac{4}{100} + \frac{7}{1000}$ (c) $30 + \frac{5}{10} + \frac{8}{1000}$ (d) $3 + \frac{8}{100} + \frac{1}{1000} + \frac{5}{10}$

3. Write down the value represented by the digit 5 in each number.
   (a) 2.567   (b) 0.258   (c) 5.67   (d) 9.105

4. Copy and fill in the blank with '<' or '>'.
   (a) 3.24 _____ 5.17   (b) 2.48 _____ 3.46
   (c) 1.924 _____ 1.93   (d) 15.037 _____ 15.032
   Explain your reasoning using a number line or a place value table to help you.

5. Which is the smaller number in each pair? Explain your reasoning.
   (a) 0.273, 0.28   (b) 3.507, 3.50
   (c) 16.98, 16.91   (d) 1.698, 1.699

LEVEL 2

6.

Shop A
£1.99 a kg

Shop B
£1.95 a kg

In which shop are tomatoes cheaper?

7. In a 100 m race, Alice's time was 11.32 seconds and Sophia's time was 11.38 seconds. Who was faster?

8. The mass of diamond A is 0.237 grams. The mass of diamond B is 0.23 grams.
   (a) Write down the number of decimal places in
      (i) 0.237,   **(ii)** 0.23.
   (b) Which diamond is heavier?

9. The number 7.8☐1 is greater than 7.865. What are the possible values of the missing digit ☐?

PROBLEM
SOLVING

10. Write down a decimal number which is between $\frac{3}{10}$ and 0.5.

OPEN
QUESTION

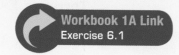

Workbook 1A Link
Exercise 6.1

6.2 Conversion between Fractions and Decimals

A   Converting Decimals to Fractions

A decimal can be converted to a fraction by considering its expanded form.

Example 6

Convert each decimal to a fraction in its simplest form.
   (a) 0.6   **(b)** 0.75

Solution

(a) $0.6 = \dfrac{6}{10}$ The digit 6 represents 6 tenths.

      $= \dfrac{6 \div 2}{10 \div 2}$ Simplify the fraction.

      $= \dfrac{3}{5}$

(b) $0.75 = \dfrac{7}{10} + \dfrac{5}{100}$ Express in expanded form.

        $= \dfrac{70}{100} + \dfrac{5}{100}$ 7 tenths = 70 hundredths

        $= \dfrac{75}{100}$ 70 hundredths + 5 hundredths = 75 hundredths

        $= \dfrac{75 \div 25}{100 \div 25}$ Simplify the fraction.

        $= \dfrac{3}{4}$

RECALL

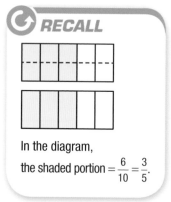

In the diagram,
the shaded portion $= \dfrac{6}{10} = \dfrac{3}{5}$.

REMARK

A decimal with up to three decimal places can be expressed directly as a fraction with 10, 100 or 1000 as the denominator.

e.g. $0.6 = \dfrac{6}{10}$

       $0.28 = \dfrac{28}{100}$

       $0.625 = \dfrac{625}{1000}$

Note: You can use a hundred square to convert 0.75 to a fraction.

75 out of 100 little squares are shaded in the hundred square.

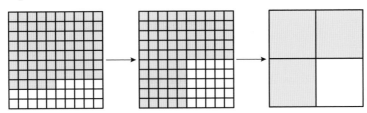

You can shift the shaded squares around into 5×5 sections because $5 \times 5 = 25$ and $3 \times 25 = 75$.

Then merge each section of 25 squares.

Now 3 out of 4 larger squares are shaded.

Try It! **6**　Convert each decimal to a fraction in its simplest form.

(a) 0.4　　　　　　　　　　(b) 0.028

Example **7**　Convert each decimal to a mixed number in its simplest form.

(a) 13.28　　　　　　　　(b) 9.625

Solution

(a) $13.28 = 13 + \dfrac{28}{100}$　　$13.28 = 13 + 0.28$

$= 13 + \dfrac{28 \div 4}{100 \div 4}$　Simplify the fraction.

$= 13 + \dfrac{7}{25}$

$= 13\dfrac{7}{25}$　Express as a mixed number.

(b) $9.625 = 9 + \dfrac{625}{1000}$　$9.625 = 9 + 0.625$

$= 9 + \dfrac{625 \div 125}{1000 \div 125}$　Simplify the fraction.

$= 9 + \dfrac{5}{8}$

$= 9\dfrac{5}{8}$　Express as a mixed number.

Try It! **7**　Convert each decimal to a mixed number in its simplest form.

(a) 71.25　　　　　　　　(b) 7.125

 REMARK

You can use the multiplication table on page 359 to check these calculations.

 DISCUSS

How can you show that $0.605 = \dfrac{605}{1000}$?

 **REMARK**

$\dfrac{625}{1000}$ can be simplified in three stages.

$\dfrac{625}{1000} = \dfrac{625 \div 5}{1000 \div 5}$

$= \dfrac{125}{200}$

$= \dfrac{125 \div 5}{200 \div 5}$

$= \dfrac{25}{40}$

$= \dfrac{25 \div 5}{40 \div 5}$

$= \dfrac{5}{8}$

B Converting Fractions to Decimals

A fraction can be easily converted to a decimal if its denominator is 10, 100 or 1000, e.g. $\frac{3}{10}, \frac{75}{100}, \frac{283}{1000}$.

As you have seen from the place value tables, the place values of a decimal number in the part that is less than one are shown as tenths, hundredths and thousandths.

So, for example, $4\frac{3}{10}$ can be converted, using a place value table, to 4.3.

$6\frac{75}{100}$ can be converted to 6.75.

$9\frac{283}{1000}$ can be converted to 9.283.

Ones	Tenths	Hundredths	Thousandths
4	3		
6	7	5	
9	2	8	3

Example 8

Write each fraction as a decimal.

(a) $\frac{1}{5}$

(b) $\frac{7}{20}$

Solution

(a) $\frac{1}{5} = \frac{1 \times 2}{5 \times 2}$ Change to an equivalent fraction with denominator 10.

$= \frac{2}{10}$

$= 0.2$

In the bar model below, 1 part out of 5 equal parts is shaded.
Split each part into two smaller equal parts.

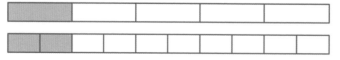

2 equal parts out of 10 equal parts are shaded, i.e. 2 tenths.
To change 1 part into 2 smaller parts and 5 parts into 10 smaller parts, you halve the **size** of each part and therefore multiply the **number** of parts by 2.

(b) $\dfrac{7}{20} = \dfrac{7 \times 5}{20 \times 5}$ Change to an equivalent fraction with denominator 100.

$$= \dfrac{35}{100}$$

$$= 0.35$$

In the diagram below, 7 equal parts out of 20 equal parts are shaded.

Split each part into five smaller equal parts.

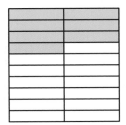 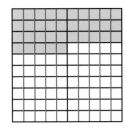

Now, 35 equal parts out of 100 equal parts are shaded, i.e. 35 hundredths.

To change 7 parts into 35 smaller parts and 20 parts into 100 smaller parts, you make the **size** of each part five times smaller, so you multiply the **number** of parts by 5.

Try It! 8

Write each fraction as a decimal.

(a) $\dfrac{3}{5}$ **(b)** $\dfrac{11}{50}$

Example 9

Write each mixed number as a decimal.

(a) $3\dfrac{6}{25}$ **(b)** $29\dfrac{7}{8}$

Solution

(a) $3\dfrac{6}{25} = 3 + \dfrac{6 \times 4}{25 \times 4}$ Change to an equivalent fraction with denominator 100.

$$= 3 + \dfrac{24}{100}$$

$$= 3.24$$

(b) $29\dfrac{7}{8} = 29 + \dfrac{7 \times 125}{8 \times 125}$ Change to an equivalent fraction with denominator 1000.

$$= 29 + \dfrac{875}{1000}$$

$$= 29.875$$

Try It! 9

Write each mixed number as a decimal.

(a) $2\dfrac{4}{25}$ **(b)** $16\dfrac{9}{200}$

PRACTICE 6.2

⚙ LEVEL 1

1. Express each decimal as a fraction in its simplest form.
   (a) 0.3   (b) 0.8   (c) 0.12   (d) 0.08

2. Express each decimal as a mixed number in its simplest form.
   (a) 3.5   (b) 3.6   (c) 4.32   (d) 5.06

3. Write each fraction as a decimal.
   (a) $\frac{1}{2}$ (b) $\frac{3}{5}$ (c) $\frac{9}{20}$ (d) $\frac{2}{25}$

4. Write each mixed number as a decimal.
   (a) $1\frac{1}{4}$ (b) $2\frac{4}{5}$ (c) $3\frac{1}{20}$ (d) $4\frac{7}{25}$

⚙ LEVEL 2

5. The number line shows the scale in tenths between 0 and 1.

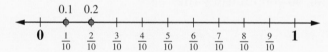

   (a) Copy and complete the number line by marking 0.3, 0.4, 0.5, …, 0.9 on it.
   (b) What is the relationship between the scale in tenths and the scale in decimals 0.1, 0.2, 0.3, … , 0.9?
   (c) Use the number line to copy and complete these number sentences.

   0.3 ___ 0.4
   ___ > 0.6
   ___ < ___

6. Express each decimal as a fraction in its simplest form.
   (a) 0.004   (b) 0.125

7. Express each decimal as a mixed number in its simplest form.
   (a) 2.016   (b) 2.106

8. Write each fraction as a decimal.
   (a) $\frac{5}{8}$ (b) $\frac{6}{250}$

9. Write each mixed number as a decimal.
   (a) $5\frac{33}{200}$ (b) $6\frac{9}{500}$

10. The mass of a fish is $1\frac{13}{25}$ kg. The mass of a crab is 1.62 kg.
    Which one is heavier?

6.3 Multiplying and Dividing by 10, 100 and 1000

A Multiplying by 10, 100 and 1000

A bunch of roses costs £2.50. How much is the total price of 100 bunches?

The total price of 100 bunches = £2.50 × 100.

You are going to learn a quick way to work out the answer.

CLASS ACTIVITY 1

Objective: To explore the rules for multiplying a decimal by 10, 100 and 1000.

The number $3.75 = 3 + \dfrac{7}{10} + \dfrac{5}{100}$.

1. Work out these products.

   (a) 3×10 **(b)** 3×100 **(c)** 3×1000

2. **(a)** Copy and complete this place value table.

Number	Hundreds	Tens	Ones	Tenths
$\dfrac{7}{10}$				•
$\dfrac{7}{10} \times 10$				•
$\dfrac{7}{10} \times 100$				•
$\dfrac{7}{10} \times 1000$				•

(b) Copy and fill in the blanks.

(i) $\dfrac{7}{10} \times 10 = 7$ tenths $\times 10$

         $= \underline{\hspace{1.5cm}}$ tenths

         $= \underline{\hspace{1.5cm}}$ (a whole number)

(ii) $\dfrac{7}{10} \times 100 = 7$ tenths $\times 100$

         $= \underline{\hspace{1.5cm}}$ tenths

         $= \underline{\hspace{1.5cm}}$ (a whole number)

(iii) $\dfrac{7}{10} \times 1000 = 7$ tenths $\times 1000$

         $= \underline{\hspace{1.5cm}}$ tenths

         $= \underline{\hspace{1.5cm}}$ (a whole number)

REMARK

7 tenths $= \dfrac{7}{10}$

70 tenths $= \dfrac{70}{10}$

700 tenths $= \dfrac{700}{10}$

3. **(a)** Copy and complete this place value table.

Number	Tens	Ones	Tenths	Hundredths
$\frac{5}{100}$				
$\frac{5}{100} \times 10$				
$\frac{5}{100} \times 100$				
$\frac{5}{100} \times 1000$				

(b) Copy and fill in the blanks.

(i) $\frac{5}{100} \times 10 = 5 \text{ hundredths} \times 10$

$= \underline{\hspace{1cm}}$ hundredths

$= \underline{\hspace{1cm}}$ tenths

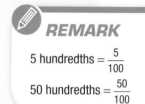

REMARK

5 hundredths $= \frac{5}{100}$

50 hundredths $= \frac{50}{100}$

(ii) $\frac{5}{100} \times 100 = 5 \text{ hundredths} \times 100$

$= \underline{\hspace{1cm}}$ hundredths

$= \underline{\hspace{1cm}}$ (a whole number)

(iii) $\frac{5}{100} \times 1000 = 5 \text{ hundredths} \times 1000$

$= \underline{\hspace{1cm}}$ hundredths

$= \underline{\hspace{1cm}}$ (a whole number)

4. Using the answers in Questions **1** to **3**, copy and complete this place value table.

Number	Thousands	Hundreds	Tens	Ones	Tenths	Hundredths
3.75				3	7	5
3.75 × 10						
3.75 × 100						
3.75 × 1000						

5. When a decimal number is multiplied by 10, 100 and 1000, how does the position of each of its digits change in the place value table?

From Class Activity 1, you can observe the following rules.

When a decimal number is multiplied by

1. 10, each digit moves one place to the left in the place value table,

2. 100, each digit moves two places to the left in the place value table,

3. 1000, each digit moves three places to the left in the place value table.

Example 10 ▶ Work out these products using place value tables.

(a) 12.8×10 (b) 3.128×100 (c) 3.128×1000

Solution   (a)

Number	Hundreds	Tens	Ones	Tenths
12.8		1	2	8
12.8 × 10	1	2	8	

$12.8 \times 10 = 128$ Each digit moves one place to the left in the place value table.

(b)

Number	Thousands	Hundreds	Tens	Ones	Tenths	Hundredths	Thousandths
3.128				3	1	2	8
3.128 × 100		3	1	2	8		
3.128 × 1000	3	1	2	8			

$3.128 \times 100 = 312.8$ Each digit moves two places to the left in the place value table.

(c) $3.128 \times 1000 = 3128$ Each digit moves three places to the left in the place value table.

Try It! 10 ▶ Work out these multiplications using place value tables.

(a) 39.6×10 (b) 3.965×100 (c) 3.965×1000

Example 11 ▶ A bunch of roses costs £2.50. How much is the total price of

(a) 10 bunches,

(b) 100 bunches?

Solution   (a) Total price of 10 bunches = £2.50 × 10

                = £25.0

                = £25

(b) Total price of 100 bunches = £2.50 × 100

                = £250

 DISCUSS

Why is £25.0 the same as £25? Why is £25.0 incorrect as a final answer in this context? Why do you sometimes see prices like £25.00?

Try It! 11 ▶ The price of a pen is £1.40. How much is the total price of

(a) 10 pens,

(b) 1000 pens?

Example 12

Brittany and Jackson are asked to calculate 76.4×100. Brittany says the answer is 764. Jackson says the answer is 7640. Who is correct?

Solution

Number	Thousands	Hundreds	Tens	Ones	Tenths
76.4			7	6	4
76.4 × 100	7	6	4	0	

As 76.4 is multiplied by 100, each digit moves two places to the left in the place value table. This leaves the 'Ones' column without a digit, so you need to use 0 as a place holder.

Therefore, $76.4 \times 100 = 7640$. Jackson is correct.

Try It! 12

Frances and Isobel are asked to calculate 5.8×1000. Frances says the answer is 5800. Isobel says the answer is 58000. Who is correct? Explain your answer.

B Dividing by 10, 100 and 1000

There are 38.9 grams of sulfur powder. The powder is equally divided into 10 dishes for an experiment. What is the mass of the powder in each dish? The mass in each dish = $38.9 \div 10$ grams.

You are going to learn a quick way to work out the answer.

 CLASS ACTIVITY 2

Objective: To find the rules for dividing a decimal by 10, 100 and 1000.

The number 476 in expanded form is $4 \times 100 + 7 \times 10 + 6 \times 1$.

1. **(a)** Copy and complete this place value table.

Number	Hundreds	Tens	Ones	Tenths
400				
400 ÷ 10				
400 ÷ 100				
400 ÷ 1000				

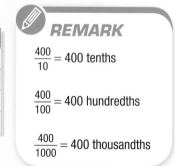

REMARK

$\dfrac{400}{10} = 400$ tenths

$\dfrac{400}{100} = 400$ hundredths

$\dfrac{400}{1000} = 400$ thousandths

(b) Copy and fill in the blanks.

(i) $400 \div 10 = \dfrac{400}{10}$

$\dfrac{400}{10} = \dfrac{400 \div 10}{10 \div 10} = \dfrac{40}{1}$

$= \underline{\hspace{2cm}}$

(ii) $400 \div 100 = \dfrac{400}{100}$

$= \underline{\hspace{2cm}}$

(iii) $400 \div 1000 = \dfrac{400}{1000}$

$$= \dfrac{4}{10}$$

$$= \underline{\hspace{3cm}} \text{ tenths}$$

2. **(a)** Copy and complete this place value table.

Number	Tens	Ones	Tenths	Hundredths
70				
70 ÷ 10				
70 ÷ 100				
70 ÷ 1000				

(b) Working in a similar way to Question **1**, copy and fill in the blanks.

(i) $70 \div 10 = \underline{\hspace{2.5cm}}$

(ii) $70 \div 100 = \underline{\hspace{2.5cm}}$ tenths

(iii) $70 \div 1000 = \underline{\hspace{2.5cm}}$ hundredths

3. **(a)** Copy and complete this place value table.

Number	Ones	Tenths	Hundredths	Thousandths
6				
6 ÷ 10				
6 ÷ 100				
6 ÷ 1000				

(b) Working in a similar way to Question **1**, copy and fill in the blanks.

(i) $6 \div 10 = \underline{\hspace{2.5cm}}$ tenths

(ii) $6 \div 100 = \underline{\hspace{2.5cm}}$ hundredths

(iii) $6 \div 1000 = \underline{\hspace{2.5cm}}$ thousandths

4. Using the results in Questions **1** to **3**, copy and complete the place value table.

Number	Hundreds	Tens	Ones	Tenths	Hundredths	Thousandths
476	4	7	6			
476 ÷ 10						
476 ÷ 100						
476 ÷ 1000						

5. When a decimal number is divided by 10, 100 and 1000, how does the position of each of its digits change in the place value table?

From Class Activity 2, you can observe the following rules.

When a decimal number is divided by
1. 10, each digit moves one place to the right in the place value table,
2. 100, each digit moves two places to the right in the place value table,
3. 1000, each digit moves three places to the right in the place value table.

Example 13

Work out these quotients using place value tables.
(a) $76.9 \div 10$ **(b)** $76.9 \div 100$ **(c)** $5769 \div 1000$

Solution

Number	Tens	Ones	Tenths	Hundredths	Thousandths
76.9	7	6 .	9		
76.9 ÷ 10		7 .	6	9	
76.9 ÷ 100		0 .	7	6	9

(a) $76.9 \div 10$
$= 7.69$

Each digit moves one place to the right in the place value table.

(b) $76.9 \div 100$
$= 0.769$

Each digit moves two places to the right in the place value table.

(c)

Number	Thousands	Hundreds	Tens	Ones	Tenths	Hundredths	Thousandths
5769	5	7	6	9 .			
5769 ÷ 1000				5 .	7	6	9

$5769 \div 1000$
$= 5.769$

Each digit moves three places to the right in the place value table.

REMARK

When you calculate $76.9 \div 100$, you need to write a 0 in the Ones column and write .769 as 0.769.

Try It! 13

Work out these divisions using place value tables.
(a) $5.21 \div 10$ **(b)** $52.1 \div 100$ **(c)** $8521 \div 1000$

Example 14

Stacey and Ellie calculate $1.3 \div 100$.
Stacey says the answer is 0.013. Ellie says the answer is 0.13. Who is correct?

Solution

Number	Ones	Tenths	Hundredths	Thousandths
1.3	1 .	3		
1.3 ÷ 100	0 .	0	1	3

As 1.3 is divided by 100, each digit moves two places to the right in the place value table. This leaves the 'Tenths' column without a digit, so you need to use 0 as a place holder.
Therefore, $1.3 \div 100 = 0.013$. Stacey is correct.

Alice and Gillian are asked to calculate 54 ÷ 1000. Alice says the answer is 0.54. Gillian says the answer is 0.054. Who is correct? Explain your answer.

Example 15

A rope of length 38.9 m is cut into pieces of equal length. Find the length of each piece if there are

(a) 10 pieces, **(b)** 100 pieces.

Solution **(a)** Length of each piece = 38.9 ÷ 10
$$= 3.89\,\text{m}$$

(b) Length of each piece = 38.9 ÷ 100
$$= 0.389\,\text{m}$$

Try It! 15

A manufacturer pours 350 litres of juice equally into containers. Find the volume of juice in each container if there are

(a) 100 containers, **(b)** 1000 containers.

C Conversion between Units

Here are some conversions of units.

Length:	1 km = 1000 m, 1 m = 100 cm, 1 cm = 10 mm
Mass:	1 tonne = 1000 kg, 1 kg = 1000 g
Capacity:	1 litre = 1000 ml
Time:	1 hour = 60 minutes, 1 minute = 60 seconds
Money:	£1 = 100p

REMARK

The standard units are metre, gram and litre.

'Milli' means 'one thousandth of'. 'Centi' means 'one hundredth of'. 'Kilo' means 'one thousand of'. So kilometre, for example, means one thousand metres.

Example 16

(a) Express 2.8 km in m.
(b) Express 576 grams in kg.

Solution **(a)**

Number	Thousands	Hundreds	Tens	Ones	Tenths
2.8				2	8
2.8 × 1000	2	8	0	0	

$$2.8\,\text{km} = 2.8 \times 1000\,\text{m}$$
$$= 2800\,\text{m}$$

1 km = 1000 m
× 1000

(b)

Number	Hundreds	Tens	Ones	Tenths	Hundredths	Thousandths
576	5	7	6			
576 ÷ 1000			0	5	7	6

$$576\,\text{g} = 576 \div 1000\,\text{kg}$$
$$= 0.576\,\text{kg}$$

1 kg = 1000 g
÷ 1000

DISCUSS

Millie says '0.9 metres equals 90 centimetres'. Why is she correct? Ethan says '0.9 hours equals 90 seconds'. Why is he incorrect?

REMARK

In conversion of units, you must write the unit on each line. For instance, it is not correct to write 2.8 = 2.8 × 1000, without stating the units on both sides.

Try It! 16

(a) Express 375 ml in litres.

(b) Express 4.2 kg in grams.

Hint: You could use place value tables to help explain your reasoning.

Example 17

(a) The length of a queen-size bed is 190 cm. Express the length in

(i) mm, **(ii)** metres.

(b) The time taken to go to school is 0.3 hours.

Express the time taken in minutes.

(c) The price of a bag of sweets is 95p. Find the price of 20 bags of sweets in £.

Solution

(a) (i) Length of the bed = 190 cm

$= 190 \times 10$ mm

$= 1900$ mm

1 cm = 10 mm
$\times 10$

(ii) Length of the bed = 190 cm

$= 190 \div 100$ m

$= 1.9$ m

1 m = 100 cm
$\div 100$

(b) Time taken = 0.3 hours

$= 0.3 \times 60$ minutes

$= 0.3 \times 10 \times 6$ minutes

$= 3 \times 6$ minutes

$= 18$ minutes

1 hour = 60 min
$\times 60$

(c) Price of 20 bags = 95×20p

$= 95 \times 2 \times 10$p

$= 190 \times 10$p

$= 1900$p

$= £1900 \div 100$

$= £19.00$

$= £19$

£1 = 100p
$\div 100$

Try It! 17

(a) The width of a king-size bed is 150 cm. Express the width in

(i) mm, **(ii)** metres.

(b) The time taken to solve a problem is 0.4 hours. Express the time taken in minutes.

(c) The price for 1 kg of prawns is £23. Find the price of 1 gram of prawns in pence.

DISCUSS

When converting from a bigger unit to a smaller unit (e.g. m to cm or kg to g), do you use multiplication or division? Explain why.

When converting from a smaller unit to a bigger unit (e.g. ml to litre or minutes to hours), do you use multiplication or division? Explain why.

DISCUSS

0.3 hours = 18 minutes. Why isn't 0.3 hours the same as 30 minutes? What decimal of an hour is 30 minutes?

PRACTICE 6.3

LEVEL 1

Use place value tables in Questions **1** to **3** to help you.

1. Work out these products.
   (a) 24.8×10
   (b) 2.48×10
   (c) 0.236×100
   (d) 23.006×100
   (e) 93.8×1000
   (f) 9.38×1000

2. Find the values of these quotients.
   (a) $41.9 \div 10$
   (b) $40.19 \div 10$
   (c) $908.1 \div 100$
   (d) $9081 \div 100$
   (e) $53\,904 \div 1000$
   (f) $5394 \div 1000$

3. Which is bigger: 0.374×10 or 0.0375×100? Explain your answer.

4. Express the given measurements in the specified units.
   (a) 267 cm in metres
   (b) 3.6 litres in ml
   (c) 1590 grams in kg
   (d) £3 in pence
   (e) 0.25 hours in minutes
   (f) 4.8 km in metres

   Hint: When you express 267 cm in metres, do you expect the number of metres to be bigger or smaller than the number of cm, which is 267?

LEVEL 2

5. The price of a book is £4.95. Find the total price of
   (a) 10 books,
   (b) 100 books.

6. Which is the odd one out of 2.3×100, 0.23×1000 and 20.3×10?
   Explain your answer.

7. Ross says 'to multiply a decimal number by 10, you just add a 0'. Do you agree with Ross?
   Explain your answer.

8. The mass of a heap of sand is 237 kg.
   (a) Find the mass of
      (i) $\frac{1}{100}$ of the heap,
      (ii) $\frac{1}{1000}$ of the heap.
   (b) What is the number of decimal places in answer **(a)(ii)**?

9. A car completes a journey of 36 km in 0.4 hours.

   PROBLEM SOLVING
   (a) Express the length of the journey in metres.
   (b) Express the time of travel in minutes.
   (c) How many metres does the car travel in one minute?

Workbook 1A Link
Exercise 6.3

6.4 Introducing Percentages

A Meaning of Percentage

Nutrition Facts
Serving Size 100 g

Amount Per Serving	
Calories 250	Calories from fat 10

	% Daily Value*
Total Fat 4%	4%
Saturated Fat 1.5%	4%
Trans Fat	
Cholesterol 50mg	28%
Sodium 150mg	15%
Total Carbohydrate 10g	3%
Dietary Fiber 5g	
Sugars 3g	
Protein 16%	

Vitamin A 1%	•	**Vitamin C** 3%
Calcium 2%	•	**Iron** 2%

*Percent Daily Values are based on a 2,000 calorie diet. Your daily values may be higher or lower depending on your calorie needs.

You sometimes see the **percentage sign** '%' in shop windows and in nutrition information on food packaging. The percentage sign means 'out of a hundred'.

In the hundred square below, 37 small squares out of 100 squares are shaded.

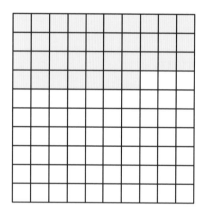

The fraction of shaded squares $= \frac{37}{100}$.

This can be expressed as

the **percentage** of shaded squares $= 37\%$.

That means $\frac{37}{100} = 37\%$.

Note that $\frac{100}{100} = 100\%$.
Hence,

$$100\% = 1$$

DISCUSS

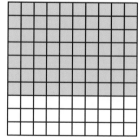

Here, the percentage of shaded squares = 70%.
If each square represents £1, then all 100 squares represent £100.
The usual price of a coat is £100. If it is reduced in the sale by 70%, how much is its sale price? How is this represented in the hundred square?

Example 18

A company has 28 male staff and 72 female staff. Find the percentage of female staff.

Solution

Total number of staff = 28 + 72

$$= 100$$

Fraction of female staff $= \dfrac{72}{100}$

∴ percentage of female staff = 72%

The number of staff could be represented using a hundred square.

You can see that the total number of staff is 100.

Try It! 18

A flower shop has 61 red roses and 39 yellow roses. Find the percentage of red roses.

B Conversion between Fractions and Percentages

As % means 'out of a hundred', a fraction of a quantity can be expressed as a percentage of the same quantity by changing it to an equivalent fraction with 100 as the denominator.

The fraction of shaded bars out of all the bars $= \dfrac{7}{10}$.

Divide each bar into 10 parts.

Example 19

Express these fractions as percentages.

(a) $\dfrac{7}{10}$ **(b)** $\dfrac{3}{4}$ **(c)** $\dfrac{9}{20}$

Solution

(a) *Method 1*

$$\dfrac{7}{10} = \dfrac{7 \times 10}{10 \times 10}$$

Change to an equivalent fraction with denominator 100.

$$= \dfrac{70}{100}$$

$$= 70\%$$

Write as a percentage.

Method 2

$$\dfrac{7}{10} = \dfrac{7}{10} \times 100\%$$

Multiply by 100%.

$$= \dfrac{7}{\cancel{10}_1} \times \cancel{100}^{10}\ \%$$

Divide 10 and 100 by 10.

$$= 70\%$$

(b) *Method 1*

$$\dfrac{3}{4} = \dfrac{3 \times 25}{4 \times 25}$$

Change to an equivalent fraction with denominator 100.

$$= \dfrac{75}{100}$$

$$= 75\%$$

Write as a percentage.

The fraction of shaded squares out of all the squares $= \dfrac{70}{100}$ $= 70\%$.

REMARK

Multiplying by 100% is the same as multiplying by 1. It does not change the original value.

DISCUSS

How could you represent these calculations using hundred squares or other diagrams?

Continued

Method 2

$$\frac{3}{4} = \frac{3}{4} \times 100\%$$

Multiply by 100%.

$$= \frac{3}{\cancel{4}_1} \times \cancel{100}^{25}\%$$

Divide 4 and 100 by 4.

$$= 75\%$$

(c) *Method 1*

$$\frac{9}{20} = \frac{9 \times 5}{20 \times 5}$$

Change to an equivalent fraction with denominator 100.

$$= \frac{45}{100}$$

$$= 45\%$$

Write as a percentage.

Method 2

$$\frac{9}{20} = \frac{9}{20} \times 100\%$$

Multiply by 100%.

$$= \frac{9}{\cancel{20}_1} \times \cancel{100}^5\%$$

Divide 20 and 100 by 20.

$$= 45\%$$

Try It! 19 Express these fractions as percentages.

(a) $\dfrac{1}{10}$ **(b)** $\dfrac{2}{5}$ **(c)** $\dfrac{9}{25}$

Example 20 Express these percentages as fractions in their simplest form.

(a) 50% **(b)** 40% **(c)** 36%

Solution

(a) $50\% = \dfrac{50}{100}$

Change to an equivalent fraction with denominator 100.

$$= \frac{50 \div 50}{100 \div 50}$$

50 is the HCF of 50 and 100.

$$= \frac{1}{2}$$

(b) $40\% = \dfrac{40}{100}$

Change to an equivalent fraction with denominator 100.

$$= \frac{40 \div 20}{100 \div 20}$$

20 is the HCF of 40 and 100.

$$= \frac{2}{5}$$

(c) $36\% = \dfrac{36}{100}$

Change to an equivalent fraction with denominator 100.

$$= \frac{36 \div 4}{100 \div 4}$$

4 is the HCF of 36 and 100.

$$= \frac{9}{25}$$

Try It! 20 Express these percentages as fractions in their simplest form.

(a) 30% **(b)** 35% **(c)** 68%

C Conversion between Decimals and Percentages

A decimal proportion of a quantity can be converted to a fractional proportion of the same quantity. Hence, it can also be converted to a percentage of the same quantity.

Example 21

Express these decimals as percentages.

(a) 0.39   **(b)** 0.06   **(c)** 0.6

Solution

(a) *Method 1*

$$0.39 = \frac{39}{100}$$ Express as a fraction with 100 as the denominator.

$$= 39\%$$ Write as a percentage.

Method 2

$$0.39 = 0.39 \times 100\%$$ Multiply by 100%.

$$= 39\%$$ Move each digit two places to the left in the place value table.

(b) *Method 1*

$$0.06 = \frac{6}{100}$$ Express as a fraction with 100 as the denominator.

$$= 6\%$$ Write as a percentage.

Method 2

$$0.06 = 0.06 \times 100\%$$ Multiply by 100%.

$$= 6\%$$ Move each digit two places to the left in the place value table.

(c) *Method 1*

$$0.6 = \frac{6}{10}$$ Express as a fraction.

$$= \frac{60}{100}$$ Express as an equivalent fraction with 100 as the denominator.

$$= 60\%$$ Write as a percentage.

Method 2

$$0.6 = 0.6 \times 100\%$$ Multiply by 100%.

$$= 60\%$$ Move each digit two places to the left in the place value table.

Try It! 21

Express these decimals as percentages.

(a) 0.67   **(b)** 0.04   **(c)** 0.4

RECALL

You can draw place value tables to check these calculations.

DISCUSS

What are 0.02 and 0.2 as percentages?

171

Example 22

Express these percentages as decimals.

(a) 32%   (b) 20%   (c) 7%

Solution

(a) $32\% = \dfrac{32}{100}$

       $= 0.32$ Move each digit two places to the right in the place value table.

(b) $20\% = \dfrac{20}{100}$

       $= 0.20$ Move each digit two places to the right in the place value table.

       $= 0.2$

(c) $7\% = \dfrac{7}{100}$

       $= 0.07$ Move each digit two places to the right in the place value table.

Try It! 22

Express these percentages as decimals.

(a) 47%   (b) 60%   (c) 6%

Example 23

A scientist conducts an experiment. She succeeds 18 times and fails 7 times. Find her percentage of success in the experiment.

Solution

In calculating the percentage of success, you should compare the number of successes with the total number of times the experiment is conducted.

Total number of times the experiment is conducted
$= 18 + 7$
$= 25$

Percentage of success $= \dfrac{18}{25} \times 100\%$

                   $= \dfrac{18}{25_{1}} \times 100^{4}\%$ Divide 25 and 100 by 25.

                   $= 72\%$

Try It! 23

A basket has 14 good apples and 6 rotten apples.

(a) How many apples are there altogether?

(b) Find the percentage of good apples in the basket.

Hint: Draw a bar model to help you.

REMARK

You could draw a bar model to represent the number of experiments conducted.

Experiments conducted

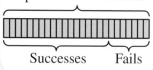

Successes   Fails

DISCUSS

Can you find the percentage of success using another method? If so, write down your solution.

PRACTICE 6.4

LEVEL 1

1. (a) Write down the percentage of shaded squares in Diagram 1.
   (b) Do the shaded squares in Diagram 2 represent the same percentage? How do you know?

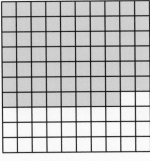

Diagram 1

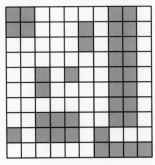

Diagram 2

2. At a school party, there are 64 students and 36 parents. Find the percentage of students at the party.

3. Express these fractions as percentages.
   (a) $\frac{3}{10}$ (b) $\frac{1}{4}$ (c) $\frac{3}{5}$ (d) $\frac{17}{25}$

4. Write each percentage as a fraction in its simplest form.
   (a) 80%   (b) 48%   (c) 8%   (d) 45%

5. Express these decimals as percentages.
   (a) 0.09   (b) 0.9   (c) 0.21   (d) 0.56

6. Express these percentages as decimals.
   (a) 40%   (b) 4%   (c) 38%   (d) 59%

7. Group together the fractions, decimals and percentages that represent an equal proportion, assuming they are all of the same quantity.

0.88	4%	$\frac{2}{5}$	$\frac{22}{25}$
$\frac{6}{20}$	40%	0.04	88%
0.4	$\frac{8}{200}$	30%	0.3

LEVEL 2

8. A shelf has 29 mathematics books and 21 science books. Find
   (a) the fraction of mathematics books on the shelf,
   (b) the percentage of mathematics books on the shelf.

9. A class has 25 students. There are 14 boys in the class. Find

PROBLEM SOLVING
   (a) the percentage of boys in the class,
   (b) the percentage of girls in the class.

Workbook 1A Link
Exercise 6.4

6.5 Percentages of Quantities

A percentage is a special fraction with 100 as the denominator. The percentage of a quantity can be worked out like the fraction of a quantity.

Example 24

Find 20% of 300 cm.

Solution

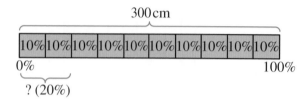

300 cm

0% 10%|10%|10%|10%|10%|10%|10%|10%|10%|10% 100%

? (20%)

Method 1
The bar model shows that 300 cm is 100%.
i.e.

$$100\% \longrightarrow 300 \text{ cm}$$
$$10\% \longrightarrow 300 \div 10 = 30 \text{ cm}$$
$$20\% \longrightarrow 30 \times 2 = 60 \text{ cm}$$
$$\therefore \quad 20\% \text{ of } 300 \text{ cm is } 60 \text{ cm.}$$

Method 2
$$10\% \text{ of } 300 \text{ cm} = \frac{1}{10} \text{ of } 300 \text{ cm}$$
$$= \frac{1}{10_1} \times \overset{30}{300} \text{ cm} \qquad \text{Divide 10 and 300 by 10.}$$
$$= 30 \text{ cm}$$
$$20\% \text{ of } 300 \text{ cm} = 2 \times (10\% \text{ of } 300 \text{ cm})$$
$$= 2 \times 30 \text{ cm}$$
$$= 60 \text{ cm}$$

Method 3
$$20\% \text{ of } 300 \text{ cm} = 20\% \times 300 \text{ cm}$$
$$= \frac{20}{100} \times 300 \text{ cm}$$
$$= \frac{20}{100_1} \times \overset{3}{300} \text{ cm} \qquad \text{Divide 100 and 300 by 100.}$$
$$= 20 \times 3 \text{ cm}$$
$$= 60 \text{ cm}$$

Try It! 24

Find 30% of 80 kg.

REMARK

The first blue arrow shows that 100% of the quantity is the same as the full amount of the given quantity. In this example, this is 300 cm.

DISCUSS

Jane works out the solution like this.
100% → 300 cm
50% → 300 ÷ 2 = 150 cm
5% → 150 ÷ 10 = 15 cm
20% → 15 × 4 = 60 cm

Harry works out the solution like this.
100% → 300 cm
2% → 300 ÷ 50 = 6 cm
20% → 6 × 10 = 60 cm

Compare their methods with the given solution.

Example 25

The usual price of a table is £240. The sale price of the table is 75% of its usual price. Calculate the sale price of the table.

Solution

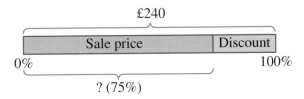

£240

Sale price | Discount

0%   100%

? (75%)

Method 1
The bar model shows that £240 is 100%.

i.e. $100\% \longrightarrow £240$

        $10\% \longrightarrow 240 \div 10 = £24$

        $70\% \longrightarrow 24 \times 7 = £168$

        $5\% \longrightarrow 24 \div 2 = £12$

        $75\% \longrightarrow 168 + 12 = £180$

$\therefore$ the sale price of the table is £180.

Method 2
$$\begin{aligned} \text{Sale price of the table} &= 75\% \text{ of } £240 \\ &= 75\% \times £240 \\ &= £\frac{75}{100} \times 240 \\ &= £\frac{75^{3}}{100_{£1}} \times 240^{60} \quad \text{Divide 75 and 100 by 25.} \\ &= £180 \quad\quad\quad\quad \text{Divide 4 and 240 by 4.} \end{aligned}$$

DISCUSS

How else could you work out 75% of £240? Which method do you prefer and why?

The usual price of a sofa is £3500. The sale price of the sofa is 65% of its usual price. Calculate the sale price of the sofa.

Hint: Read one sentence of the question at a time. Draw a bar model. Add the information to your bar model.

PRACTICE 6.5

LEVEL 1

1. Find these values.
   (a) 10% of 80 kg **(b)** 30% of 120 cm **(c)** 40% of 30 days **(d)** 80% of £65
   Hint: Draw bar models to help you.

2. Work out these values.
   (a) 5% of 400 km **(b)** 15% of 540 ml **(c)** 25% of 96 kg **(d)** 65% of 320 m²
   Hint: Draw bar models to help you.

3. Is 35% of £20 more than, less than or the same as 20% of £35? Justify your answer.

LEVEL 2

4. The usual price of a TV is £1400. It is in a sale with 20% off. Find its sale price.
   £ FINANCE **Hint:** You may draw a bar model to help you.

5. A car's full tank of petrol holds 60 litres. It is now only 35% full. How many litres of petrol are there in the tank?
   Hint: You may draw a bar model to help you.

6. A block of copper and zinc alloy is 50 kg. 60% of the block is copper. Find the mass of
   SCIENCE **(a)** copper in the block,
   (b) zinc in the block.
   Hint: You may draw a bar model to help you.

7. The full price of a table in shop A is £120. It is sold at 35% discount. The full price of the
   £ FINANCE same table in shop B is £140. It is sold at 45% discount. In which shop is the discounted table cheaper? Explain your answer.

8. A car park has 360 cars. 15% of the cars are white. 30% of the cars are grey.
   PROBLEM SOLVING Find the number of cars which are
   (a) white,
   (b) neither white nor grey.

9. Three students, Robert, William and Samira, are asked to draw a bar model to represent the
   £ FINANCE following problem.
   PROBLEM SOLVING The usual price of a designer handbag is £972. In the sale, the price is reduced by 30%.

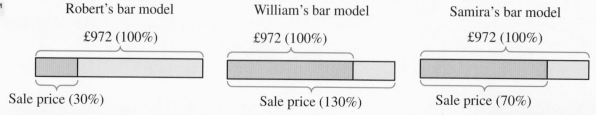

Robert's bar model   William's bar model   Samira's bar model

£972 (100%)   £972 (100%)   £972 (100%)

Sale price (30%)   Sale price (130%)   Sale price (70%)

Which bar model do you think is correct and why?

Workbook 1A Link
Exercise 6.5

REVIEW

Comparing Decimal Numbers

1. Draw the points representing the numbers on a number line.

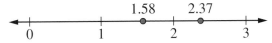

2.37 is on the right of 1.58.

∴ 1.58 < 2.37

2. Compare digit by digit with the same place value from left to right.

   e.g. For 2.834 and 2.81,

   since 3 hundredths > 1 hundredths,

   2.834 > 2.81.

Representation of Decimal Numbers

$$8.437 = 8 + \frac{4}{10} + \frac{3}{100} + \frac{7}{1000}$$

thousandths

hundredths

tenths

decimal point

ones

Introducing Percentages

1. $1\% = \frac{1}{100}, 10\% = \frac{1}{10}$ and $100\% = 1.$

2. Fraction ⟶ Percentage

   e.g. $\frac{7}{50} = \frac{7 \times 2}{50 \times 2} = \frac{14}{100} = 14\%$

3. Percentage ⟶ Fraction

   e.g. $36\% = \frac{36}{100} = \frac{36 \times 5}{100 \times 5} = \frac{9}{25}$

4. Decimal ⟶ Percentage

   e.g. $0.2 = \frac{2}{10} = \frac{2 \times 10}{10 \times 10} = \frac{20}{100} = 20\%$

5. Percentage ⟶ Decimal

   e.g. $6\% = \frac{6}{100} = 0.06$

Conversion between Fractions and Decimals

1. Decimal ⟶ Fraction

   e.g. $0.48 = \frac{48}{100}$

   $= \frac{48 \div 4}{100 \div 4}$

   $= \frac{12}{25}$

2. Fraction ⟶ Decimal

   First write the fraction with 10, 100 or 1000 as the denominator.

   e.g. $\frac{13}{20} = \frac{13 \times 5}{20 \times 5}$

   $= \frac{65}{100}$

   $= 0.65$

Multiplying and Dividing by 10, 100 and 1000

1. *Multiply by*   *Move each digit*

10	1 place to the left
100	2 places to the left
1000	3 places to the left

   e.g. $4.87 \times 10 = 48.7$

   $4.87 \times 100 = 487$

   $4.87 \times 1000 = 4870$

2. *Divide by*   *Move each digit*

10	1 place to the right
100	2 places to the right
1000	3 places to the right

   e.g. $92.6 \div 10 = 9.26$

   $92.6 \div 100 = 0.926$

   $926 \div 1000 = 0.926$

Percentages of Quantities

e.g. 25% of 48 m

$= \frac{25}{100} \times 48\,\text{m}$

$= \frac{25^1}{100_1} \times 48^{12}\,\text{m}$

$= 12\,\text{m}$

? (25%)

CHALLENGE 6

In a flowerbed, 0.3 of the flowers are red and $\frac{7}{25}$ are yellow. The rest are pink. Find the percentage of pink flowers in the flowerbed.

Workbook 1A Link
Problem Solving 6

REVISION EXERCISE 6

1. Stick insect A is 29.57 cm long. Stick insect B is 29.6 cm long.
   (a) Express 29.57 in expanded form.
   (b) Write down the place value of the digit 6 in 29.6.
   (c) Which stick insect is longer? Explain your answer.

2. Express these numbers as fractions or mixed numbers in their simplest form.
   (a) 0.84   (b) 1.25   (c) 3.08

3. Express these numbers as decimals.
   (a) $\frac{8}{25}$ (b) $3\frac{1}{2}$ (c) $4\frac{3}{50}$

4. Copy and complete the table, converting each number into a decimal, fraction and percentage. Write the fractions in their simplest form. Note that these are all decimals, fractions and percentages of the same quantity.

Decimal	Fraction	Percentage
0.05		
0.24		
	$\frac{39}{50}$	
	$\frac{17}{20}$	
		35%
		80%

5. Work out these values.
   (a) 38.16×10
   (b) 5.893×1000
   (c) $9.68 \div 10$
   (d) $67.4 \div 100$
   (e) 5.301×100
   (f) $9065 \div 1000$

6. **(a)** Express $9.36\,\text{m}$ in cm.
   (b) Express 0.6 hours in minutes.
   (c) Express 6503 grams in kg.
   (d) Express $287\,\text{ml}$ in litres.

$1\,\text{m} = 100\,\text{cm}$
1 hour $= 60$ minutes
$1\,\text{kg} = 1000\,\text{g}$
1 litre $= 1000\,\text{ml}$

7. A cake has a mass of 400 grams. 30% of the cake is flour. Find the mass of
   (a) flour in the cake,
   (b) the other ingredients in the cake.

8. John obtains 2000 calories of energy from food in a day. 25% of the energy is from his breakfast.
   SCIENCE
   How many calories of energy are provided by
   (a) his breakfast,
   (b) his other food?

9. **(a)** Ava earns £2500 a month. She saves £375 and spends the rest. What percentage of her income does she save?
   £ FINANCE
   (b) Ben earns £3000 a month. He saves 12% of his income. Does he save more money than Ava in a month? Explain your answer.

10. Cindy wins a prize. She is offered 30% of £1600 (Option A) or $\frac{2}{5}$ of £1300 (Option B). Which option should she take to get the most money? Explain your answer.
   £ FINANCE

Write in Your Journal

Choose a decimal with two decimal places. Write the steps you would take to
(a) convert it to a fraction,
(b) convert it to a percentage.

Check whether your steps work for a decimal with one decimal place and three decimal places.

RECALL

'Two decimal places' means that there are two digits after the decimal point.

7 INTRODUCTION TO RATIO

WHAT IS IN THIS CHAPTER:

7.1   Idea of Ratios
7.2   Relationship between Ratios and Fractions
7.3   Equivalent Ratios and Simplest Form

There is a fixed relationship between the length and the width of the Union Jack. If the length is 108 cm, what should the width be? You will learn how to answer this by using ratios in this chapter.

LET'S LEARN TO

▶ write a ratio between two quantities
▶ relate ratios and fractions
▶ identify equivalent ratios
▶ solve simple problems involving ratios

1. Factors

(a) If a number can be written as a product of two whole numbers, the whole numbers are called **factors** of that number.

For example,

$1 \times 24 = 24$	$1 \times 36 = 36$
$2 \times 12 = 24$	$2 \times 18 = 36$
$3 \times 8 = 24$	$3 \times 12 = 36$
$4 \times 6 = 24$	$4 \times 9 = 36$
	$6 \times 6 = 36$

Hence, 1, 2, 3, 4, 6, 8, 12 and 24 are factors of 24.

1, 2, 3, 4, 6, 9, 12, 18 and 36 are factors of 36.

(b) List the factors of two whole numbers. The factors that appear on both lists are the **common factors**.

For example, as you can see in **(a)** above, the common factors of 24 and 36 are 1, 2, 3, 4, 6 and 12.

(c) The largest common factor that appears in the factor lists of two numbers is called the **highest common factor (HCF)**.

For example, as you can see in **(b)** above, 12 is the HCF of 24 and 36.

2. Fractions

(a) A part of a whole can be represented by a fraction.

$$\frac{2}{3} \begin{array}{l} \longleftarrow \text{Numerator (number of equal parts)} \\ \longleftarrow \text{Vinculum} \\ \longleftarrow \text{Denominator (total number of equal parts in the whole)} \end{array}$$

For example, in these whole circles, the fractions represented by the shaded parts are $\frac{2}{3}$, $\frac{4}{6}$ and $\frac{6}{9}$.

$\frac{2}{3}$ is equal to $2 \div 3$.

$$\frac{2}{3} \qquad \frac{4}{6} \qquad \frac{6}{9}$$

(b) Two different fractions are **equivalent fractions** if they represent the same value.

For example, $\frac{2}{3}$, $\frac{4}{6}$ and $\frac{6}{9}$ are equivalent fractions. This is represented in the three circles above, because the shaded region is the same proportion of each whole identical circle.

A fraction can be converted to an equivalent fraction by multiplying or dividing both its numerator and denominator by the same non-zero whole number.

For example, $\quad \frac{2}{3} = \frac{2 \times 2}{3 \times 2} = \frac{4}{6}, \frac{6}{9} = \frac{6 \div 3}{9 \div 3} = \frac{2}{3}$.

(c) $\frac{2}{3}$ of $45 = \frac{2}{\cancel{3}_1} \times \cancel{45}^{15}$

$\qquad = 30$

7.1 Idea of Ratios

There are three diamonds and five rubies. This information can be represented by using a **ratio**. You say that the ratio of the number of diamonds to the number of rubies is 3 to 5. It is written as

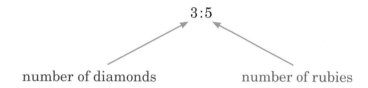

$$3:5$$

number of diamonds   number of rubies

Note that the order of the numbers in a ratio is important. For the ratio of diamonds to rubies, you must represent the number of diamonds first and the number of rubies second.

CLASS ACTIVITY 1

Objective: To represent information using ratios.

1.

Diagram 1   Diagram 2

(a) What is the ratio of the number of cats to the number of dogs in
   (i)   Diagram 1,
   (ii) Diagram 2?

(b) Are the ratios in (a)(i) and (a)(ii) the same? Explain your answer.

2.

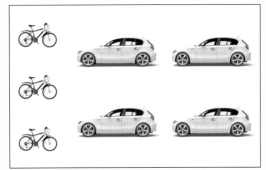

Diagram 3   Diagram 4

(a) Write down the ratio of the number of bicycles to the number of cars in
   (i) Diagram 3,
   (ii) Diagram 4.

(b) Are the ratios in (a)(i) and (a)(ii) the same? Explain your answer.

3. Make up your own pair of examples to show that $2 : 3 \neq 3 : 2$.

From Class Activity 1, you see that the order of the two numbers in a ratio is important.

$$2:1 \neq 1:2 \quad \text{and} \quad 4:3 \neq 3:4.$$

> **REMARK**
>
> $\neq$ means 'is not equal to'.

Example 1

There are two flasks and five beakers on a laboratory table.
(a) Draw a bar model to represent this information.
(b) Write the ratio of the number of flasks to the number of beakers.
(c) Write the ratio of the number of beakers to the number of flasks.

Solution

(a) The bar model is shown below.

(b) Ratio of the number of flasks to the number of beakers $= 2:5$

   number of flasks   number of beakers

(c) Ratio of the number of beakers to the number of flasks $= 5:2$

   number of beakers   number of flasks

Ryan borrows four science books and one history book from the library.

(a) Draw a bar model to represent this information.

(b) Write the ratio of the number of science books to the number of history books.

(c) Write the ratio of the number of history books to the number of science books.

 **DISCUSS**

Tyrese says that the answer to **(b)** is 4:5. Do you agree with Tyrese? Explain your reasoning.

Example ❷

There are eight chickens, 17 ducks and five dogs on a farm.

(a) Draw a bar model to represent this information.

(b) Write the ratio of the number of chickens to the number of dogs.

(c) Write the ratio of the number of dogs to the number of ducks.

(d) Write the ratio of the number of ducks to the total number of chickens, ducks and dogs on the farm.

Solution

(a) The bar model is shown below.

chickens	ducks	dogs
8	17	5

(b) Ratio of the number of chickens to the number of dogs = 8:5

    number of chickens   number of dogs

(c) Ratio of the number of dogs to the number of ducks = 5:17

    number of dogs   number of ducks

 DISCUSS

What is represented by the ratio 25:30?

What is represented by the ratio 16:20? (Think about the feet of the animals.)

(d) Total number of chickens, ducks and dogs on the farm = 8 + 17 + 5

            = 30

Ratio of the number of ducks to the total number of chickens, ducks and dogs on the farm = 17:30

There are four butterflies, seven bees and six birds in a garden.
(a) Draw a bar model to represent this information.
(b) Write the ratio of the number of bees to the number of birds.
(c) Write the ratio of the number of birds to the number of butterflies.
(d) Write the ratio of the number of butterflies to the total number of butterflies, bees and birds in the garden.

Example 3

In a class there are 11 boys and 14 girls.
(a) Draw a bar model to represent this information.
(b) Calin says that the ratio of the number of boys to the number of girls is 14:11. Is Calin correct? Explain your reasoning.
(c) Naomi says that the ratio of the number of boys to the number of boys and girls in the class is 11:14. Is Naomi correct? Explain your reasoning.

Solution

(a) The bar model is shown below.

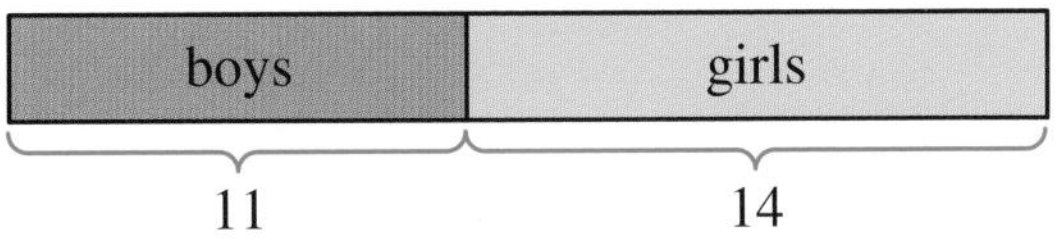

boys	girls
11	14

(b) Calin's statement is not correct. The ratio is in the wrong order.

The ratio of the number of boys to the number of girls = 11:14.

(c) Naomi's statement is not correct. She has not found the number of boys and girls in the class.
The number of boys and girls in the class = 11 + 14
= 25.

So the ratio of the number of boys to the number of boys and girls in the class = 11:25.

Try It! 3

There are five adults and seven children in a doctor's waiting room.
(a) Draw a bar model to represent this information.
(b) Alix says the ratio of the number of children to the number of adults is 7 : 5. Is Alix correct? Explain your answer.
(c) Becky says the ratio of the number of adults to the total number of people in the waiting room is 12:5. Is Becky correct? Explain your answer.

Example 4

The price of a pen is £2. The price of a book is £3.
(a) Write down the ratio of the price of the pen to the price of the book.
(b) Explain what the ratio 2:5 means in this context.

Solution

(a) Ratio of the price of the pen to the price of the book
= £2:£3
= 2:3   You don't need to write the units.

Note: A ratio has no unit.

(b) The ratio 2:5 is the ratio of the price of the pen to the total price of the pen and the book together.

Try It! 4

The length of a red ribbon is 4 m. The length of a blue ribbon is 3 m.
(a) Write down the ratio of the length of the red ribbon to the length of the blue ribbon.
(b) Explain what the ratio 3 : 7 means in this context.
Hint: Draw a bar model to represent this information.

REMARK

You can draw a bar model to represent this information.

pen   book

2   :   3

DISCUSS

Could you also write the ratio in (a) as 200:300?

PRACTICE 7.1

LEVEL 1

1. Write the ratio of the number of red roses to the number of yellow roses in the bunch. Draw a bar model to represent this information.

2. What is the ratio of the number of dogs to the number of sheep? Draw a bar model to represent this information.

3. Find the ratio of the price of a calculator to the price of a watch from the bar model.

£
FINANCE

price of   price of
calculator   watch

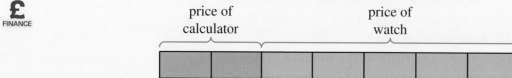

4. State the ratio of the length of a table to the width of a table from the bar model.

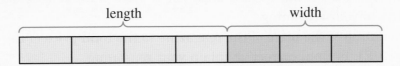

LEVEL 2

5. The image shows some old telephone boxes and post boxes. Write the ratio of the number of telephone boxes to the number of post boxes.

6. Write down the ratio of

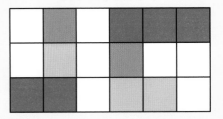

   (a) the number of blue squares to the number of red squares,
   (b) the number of orange squares to the number of white squares,
   (c) the number of red squares to the number of orange squares,
   (d) the number of white squares to the number of red squares.

7. The image shows ten macarons. Find the ratio of
   (a) the number of purple macarons to the number of green macarons,
   (b) the number of green macarons to the number of red macarons,
   (c) the number of orange macarons to the total number of macarons.

8. The price of a book is £7. The price of a magazine is £3.

£ **(a)** Jack says the ratio of the price of the book to the price of the magazine is £7:£3. Is Jack
FINANCE correct? Explain your reasoning.

(b) Dani says the ratio of the price of the magazine to the total price of the book and the
magazine is 3:21. Is Dani correct? Explain your reasoning.

9. The ratio of the number of male contestants to the number of female contestants in a game
show is 4:7.

PROBLEM
SOLVING **(a)** What is the meaning of the ratio 7:4 in this context?

(b) What is the meaning of the ratio 11:4 in this context?

10. Make up your own question, using a real-life context where the
OPEN quantities are in the ratio of 2:3.
QUESTION

Workbook 1A Link
Exercise 7.1

7.2 Relationship between Ratios and Fractions

There are two oranges and three apples in the picture. There are five
pieces of fruit in total.

A bar model representing this information is shown below.

oranges   apples

You can say that

the ratio of the number of oranges to the total number
of fruits in the diagram = 2:5

and   the fraction of oranges = $\dfrac{\text{number of oranges}}{\text{total number of fruits}} = \dfrac{2}{5}$.

The ratio 2:5 and the fraction $\dfrac{2}{5}$ in this example both describe a
relationship between the number of oranges and the total number of
fruits.

REMARK

You can say that the
number of oranges is $\dfrac{2}{5}$
of the total number of
fruits.

Likewise

the ratio of the number of apples to the total number of fruits in the diagram = $3:5$

and the fraction of apples = $\dfrac{\text{number of apples}}{\text{total number of fruits}} = \dfrac{3}{5}$.

The ratio $3:5$ and the fraction $\dfrac{3}{5}$ both represent a relationship between the number of apples and the total number of fruits.

Further,

the ratio of the number of apples to the number of oranges is $3:2$

and the fraction $\dfrac{\text{number of apples}}{\text{number of oranges}} = \dfrac{3}{2}$.

Similarly

the ratio of the number of oranges to the number of apples is $2:3$.

and the fraction $\dfrac{\text{number of oranges}}{\text{number of apples}} = \dfrac{2}{3}$.

REMARK

Here, the number of apples is $\dfrac{3}{2}$ of the number of oranges, **not** $\dfrac{3}{2}$ of the total number of fruits.

Objective: To understand the relationship between ratios and fractions.

The fraction of boys in Year 7 is $\dfrac{5}{11}$.

1. Draw a bar model to represent the information.

2. What is the ratio of the number of boys to the number of girls in Year 7?
   Note: The fraction $\dfrac{5}{11}$ means that the ratio of the number of boys to the number of boys and girls in Year 7 is $5:11$.

REMARK

The ratio $5:11$ does not mean there are only 11 students in Year 7.

3. What is the fraction of girls in Year 7?
   Hint: Use your bar model to explain your reasoning.

4. Explain what the ratio $6:11$ represents.
   Write your answer as a complete sentence beginning '6:11 is the ratio of'.

5. There are 99 boys and girls in Year 7. Use your bar model to work out the number of boys and the number of girls in Year 7.

From Class Activity 2, you see that the ratio of the number of boys to the number of girls is $5:6$. However, the number of boys is 45 and the number of girls is 54.

In general, the two numbers in a ratio of two quantities are not necessarily the actual amounts of each quantity.

Example 5

The ratio of the number of silver earrings to the number of gold earrings in a jewellery box is $7:5$.

(a) Write the number of silver earrings as a fraction of the number of gold earrings.

(b) Use a bar model to find the number of silver earrings as a fraction of the total number of earrings.

Solution

(a) The number of silver earrings as a fraction of the number of gold earrings $= \frac{7}{5}$.

(b) A bar model representing this information is shown below.

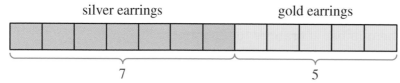

silver earrings   gold earrings

        7   5

The total number of parts in the bar model $= 7 + 5$
$$= 12.$$

The number of silver earrings as a fraction of the total number of earrings $= \frac{7}{12}$.

 DISCUSS

Does this bar model mean that there are two more silver earrings than gold earrings?

Try It! 5

The ratio of the mass of copper to the mass of zinc in an alloy is $9:2$.

(a) Express the mass of copper as a fraction of the mass of zinc.

(b) Use a bar model to find the mass of copper as a fraction of the total mass of the alloy.

Example 6

The fraction of Year 7 students in a school is $\frac{1}{6}$.

(a) Write the ratio of the number of Year 7 students to the total number of students in the school.

(b) Use a bar model to find the ratio of the number of Year 7 students to the number of older students in the school.

Solution

(a) The ratio of the number of Year 7 students to the total number of students $= 1:6$.

(b) A bar model representing this information is shown below.

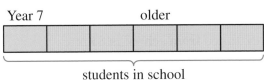

The ratio of the number of Year 7 students to the number of older students in the school = 1:5.

DISCUSS

Tom looks at the bar model and says that there is the same number of students in every year. Why does he think this, and do you agree with him?

Try It! 6 The fraction of lemon juice in a drink is $\frac{3}{14}$.

(a) Write the ratio of the volume of the lemon juice to the volume of the drink.

(b) Use a bar model to find the ratio of the volume of lemon juice to the volume of other liquids in the drink.

Example 7 The ratio of Alice's distance from school to Sophia's distance from school is 3:4.

(a) Express Sophia's distance from school as a fraction of Alice's distance from school.

(b) If Alice's distance from school is 6 km, find Sophia's distance from school.

Solution **(a)** A bar model representing this information is shown below.

Sophia's distance from school as a fraction of Alice's distance from school

$= \frac{4}{3}$.

(b) The bar model below shows the situation.

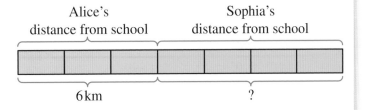

Continued

3 parts   represent   6 km
1 part   represents   6 ÷ 3 = 2 km
4 parts   represent   4 × 2 = 8 km

Hence, Sophia's distance from school is 8 km.

Try It! ⑦ Ben has a bottle of milk and a carton of juice. The ratio of the volume of milk to the volume of juice is $5:3$.

(a) Express the volume of juice as a fraction of the volume of milk.

(b) If the volume of juice is 270 ml, find the volume of milk.

Hint: Draw a bar model to help you.

Example ⑧ In a yellow and blue artwork, the fraction of the area that is yellow is $\frac{2}{9}$.

(a) Find the ratio of the yellow area to the blue area.

(b) If the blue area is 84 cm², find the size of the yellow area.

Solution **(a)** This bar model represents the information.

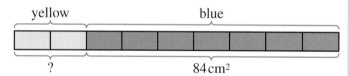

yellow   blue

?   84 cm²

$$\frac{\text{yellow area}}{\text{whole area}} = \frac{2}{9}$$

Consider there are 9 equal parts in the whole area.
Number of parts of yellow area = 2 parts.
Number of parts of blue area = 9 − 2
                              = 7 parts.
Ratio of the yellow area to the blue area = $2:7$.

(b) If the blue area is 84 cm²,
7 parts   represent   84 cm²
1 part   represents   84 ÷ 7 = 12 cm²
2 parts   represent   2 × 12 = 24 cm²

Hence, the yellow area is 24 cm².

REMARK

You can use the multiplication and division tables on page 359 to check the value of 84 ÷ 7.

In a compound formed from iron and sulfur, the fraction of iron in the total mass of the compound is $\frac{7}{11}$.

(a) Find the ratio of the mass of iron to the mass of sulfur in the compound.

(b) If there are 64 grams of sulfur in a sample of the compound, calculate the mass of iron in the same sample.

PRACTICE 7.2

LEVEL 1

1. First draw a bar model to represent the information. Then express the first part of each ratio as a fraction of the two parts together (i.e. the whole), writing your answer as a full sentence.
   (a) In a rectangle, the ratio of the width to the length = 1:3.
   (b) In a zoo, the ratio of the number of lions to the number of zebras = 2:5.
   (c) In a sauce, the ratio of the volume of water to the volume of vinegar = 7:4.
   (d) At a concert, the ratio of the number of adult tickets sold to the number of child tickets sold = 11:6.

2. First draw a bar model to represent the information in each context. Then express each fraction as a ratio of the given part to the whole, writing your answer as a full sentence.
   (a) The fraction of boys in a group of newborn babies = $\frac{1}{2}$.
   (b) The fraction of red roses in a bunch of roses = $\frac{3}{10}$.
   (c) The area of a living room as a fraction of the area of a bedroom = $\frac{12}{5}$.
   (d) The mass of a dog as a fraction of the mass of a cat = $\frac{15}{8}$.

3. (a) In the bar model, a represents the price of a spoon and b represents the price of a fork. Find the ratio $a:b$.

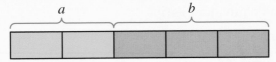

   (b) In the bar model, p is the maximum temperature on a day and q is the minimum temperature on the same day.
      (i) Find the ratio $p:q$.
      (ii) Adam says the bar model shows that the maximum temperature was $5\,°\mathrm{C}$ and the minimum temperature was $4\,°\mathrm{C}$. Is Adam correct? Explain your answer.

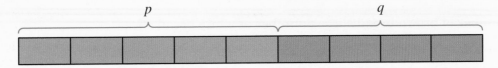

4. The fraction of adults in a cinema is $\frac{7}{9}$. What is the ratio of the number of adults to the number of children in the cinema?

5. The ratio of the length to the width of the Union Jack is 2:1. If the length of the flag is 108 cm, find the width of the flag.

6. The ratio of the area of the garden to the area of the house of a home is 3:7. The area of the house is 350 m². What is the area of the garden?

7. The ratio of the price of a shirt to the price of a jacket is 3:8.

    £
    FINANCE
    (a) Draw a bar model to represent this information.
    (b) Express the price of the jacket as a fraction of the price of the shirt.
    (c) If the price of the shirt is £21, find the price of the jacket.

8. In a class, the ratio of the number of boys to the total number of boys and girls is 5:12.
    (a) Find the ratio of the number of girls to the number of boys.
    (b) If there are 14 girls in the class, find the number of boys.

9. A wallet contains only £10 notes and £50 notes. The ratio of the number of £10 notes to the total number of notes is 4:13.

    PROBLEM
    SOLVING
    (a) Find the ratio of the number of £50 notes to the number of £10 notes.
    (b) There are eight £10 notes. Find the total value of the money in the wallet.

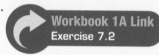
Workbook 1A Link
Exercise 7.2

7.3 Equivalent Ratios and Simplest Form

In Chapter 5, you learned about equivalent fractions. Two fractions are equivalent when they look different but actually represent the same value. Similarly, you can have equivalent ratios.

 CLASS ACTIVITY 3

Objective: To understand equivalent ratios.

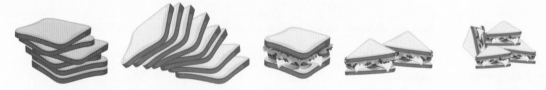

Some students prepare sandwiches for a picnic. They use six slices of brown bread and eight slices of white bread.

Copy and fill in the blanks for Questions **1** to **4**.

1. Number of brown bread slices : number of white bread slices = ___ : ___.

2. Two slices of bread of the same kind are used to form a sandwich.
   Number of brown bread sandwiches : number of white bread sandwiches
   = ___ : ___.

3. Each rectangular sandwich is cut into two large triangular sandwiches. Number of large brown bread triangular sandwiches : number of large white bread triangular sandwiches = ___ : ___.

4. Each triangular sandwich is cut into two small triangular sandwiches. Number of small brown bread triangular sandwiches : number of small white bread triangular sandwiches = ___ : ___.

5. What's the same and what's different about the ratios in Questions **1** to **4**?

Number of bicycles and wheels	Express the number of bicycles as a fraction of the number of wheels in the simplest form	Ratio of the number of bicycles to the number of wheels
1 bicycle, 2 wheels	$\dfrac{1}{2}$	$1:2$
2 bicycles, 4 wheels	$\dfrac{2}{4} = \dfrac{2 \div 2}{4 \div 2}$ $= \dfrac{1}{2}$	$2:4$
3 bicycles, 6 wheels	$\dfrac{3}{6} = \dfrac{3 \div 3}{6 \div 3}$ $= \dfrac{1}{2}$	$3:6$

The numbers 1 and 2 in the ratio $1:2$ do not necessarily represent the actual quantities. The ratio $1:2$ can mean that there are 5 bikes and 10 wheels.

From Class Activity 3, you see that

$6:8 = 3:4 = 12:16.$

From the bike example, you see that

$1:2 = 2:4 = 3:6.$

When two different ratios can be simplified to the same ratio, they are called **equivalent ratios**. In Class Activity 3, $6:8$ and $3:4$ are equivalent ratios.

Example 9

Write down two equivalent ratios for each ratio.

(a) 2:5   (b) 24:18

Solution   (a)

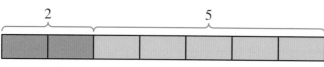

Split each part into two equal parts.

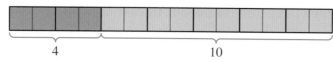

$2:5 = 2 \times 2 : 5 \times 2$
$\quad = \quad\; 4 : 10$

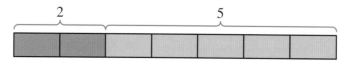

Split each part into three equal parts.

$2:5 = 2 \times 3 : 5 \times 3$
$\quad = \quad\; 6 : 15$

(b)

Group every three parts into one.

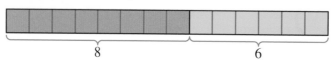

$24:18 = 24 \div 3 : 18 \div 3$
$\quad\quad = \quad\;\; 8 : 6$

Group every six parts into one.

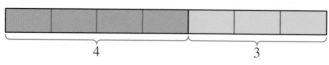

$24:18 = 24 \div 6 : 18 \div 6$
$\quad\quad = \quad\;\; 4 : 3$

Try It! 9

Write down two equivalent ratios for each ratio.
Use bar models to explain your reasoning.

(a) 1:4   (b) 60:30

What other ratios are equivalent to 2:5?

Similar to the way you find equivalent fractions, you can find an equivalent ratio by multiplying or dividing each quantity in the ratio by the same number.

A ratio is in its **simplest form** when all quantities in the ratio are whole numbers and they do not have any common factor other than 1. For example, 2:5 is a ratio in its simplest form while 24:18 is not because 24 and 18 have a common factor of 6.

> Did you know that the ratio of the length to the breadth of the Singapore flag is 5:3? Is this ratio in its simplest form?
>
>

Example 10

Reduce each ratio to its simplest form.
- **(a)** 3:18
- **(b)** 6:8
- **(c)** 21:14
- **(d)** 12:9

Solution

(a)

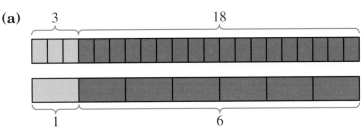

$3:18 = 3 \div 3 : 18 \div 3$
$= 1:6$

3 is the highest common factor of 3 and 18.

(b)

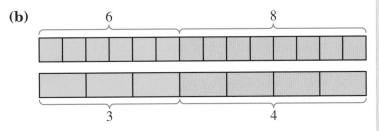

$6:8 = 6 \div 2 : 8 \div 2$
$= 3:4$

2 is the highest common factor of 6 and 8.

(c) $21:14 = 21 \div 7 : 14 \div 7$
$= 3:2$

7 is the highest common factor of 21 and 14.

(d) $12:9 = 12 \div 3 : 9 \div 3$
$= 4:3$

3 is the highest common factor of 12 and 9.

> **DISCUSS**
>
> How would you use bar models to represent the reasoning in **(c)** and **(d)**?

Try It! 10

Reduce each ratio to its simplest form.
- **(a)** 9:36
- **(b)** 12:26
- **(c)** 32:16
- **(d)** 39:24

> **REMARK**
>
> You can draw or imagine bar models to explain your reasoning if required.

Example The ratio of the price of a school bag to the price of a school tie is 60:24.
(a) Write the ratio in its simplest form.
(b) If the price of the tie is £8, find the total price of the bag and the tie.

Solution

(a) The ratio = 60:24
  = 60 ÷ 6 :24 ÷ 6
  = 10:4
  = 10 ÷ 2 :4 ÷ 2
  = 5:2

> **REMARK**
>
> You can simplify a ratio by dividing the parts of the ratio by one common factor at a time.

(b) The bar model represents the information.

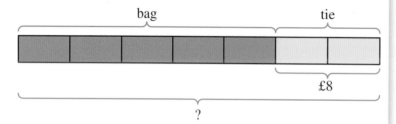

If the price of the tie is £8,

2 parts	represent	£8
1 part	represents	£8 ÷ 2 = £4
7 parts	represent	£4 × 7 = £28

Hence, the total price of the bag and the tie is £28.

Try It! In a recipe, the ratio of the mass of chicken to the mass of tomato is 60:36.
(a) Write the ratio in its simplest form.
(b) If the mass of chicken is 150 g, what is the total mass of chicken and tomato?

> **DISCUSS**
>
> Compare your answer to (a) with a partner. Did you get the same answer? Did you follow the same steps to get it?

PRACTICE 7.3

LEVEL 1

1. Write down an equivalent ratio for each of these ratios. Use bar models to explain your reasoning.

   (a) 3:5 **(b)** 4:3 **(c)** 18:27 **(d)** 14:8

2. Reduce each ratio to its simplest form. Use bar models to explain your reasoning.

   (a) 5:10 **(b)** 15:21 **(c)** 48:16 **(d)** 36:32

3. Which of these pairs of ratios are equivalent?

   (a) 2:3 and 8:12 **(b)** 1:2 and 3:8 **(c)** 7:10 and 28:40
   (d) 8:7 and 40:35 **(e)** 9:4 and 27:12 **(f)** 8:2 and 12:3

   Hint: A bar model might help you explain your reasoning.

4. Which might be the odd one out of 3:6, 3:9 and 6:12? Explain your choice.

LEVEL 2

5. There are 120 boys and 95 girls in a room. Find the ratio of the number of boys to the number of girls in its simplest form.

6. Mark has 64 stamps, John has 16 stamps and Peter has 4 stamps.
   (a) Find the following ratios and express them in their simplest form.
   - **(i)** The number of John's stamps to the number of Mark's stamps
   - **(ii)** The number of Peter's stamps to the number of Mark's stamps
   - **(iii)** The number of Peter's stamps to the number of John's stamps
   (b) Which two ratios in **(a)** are equal?

7. The ratio of the number of children to the number of adults in a room is 42:48.
   (a) Simplify the ratio.
   (b) If there are 70 children, find the number of adults.

8. The ratio of Isla's pocket money to Heather's pocket money is 84:154.
   (a) Simplify the ratio.
   (b) If Isla has £18 a month, find the total amount of both their pocket money in a month.

9. The ratio of Beth's height to Zac's height is 12:25 and the ratio of Beth's height to Asha's height is 24:50. Are Zac and Asha the same height? Explain your answer.

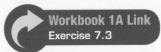

Workbook 1A Link
Exercise 7.3

Relationship between Ratios and Fractions

There are five apples. Two are red and three are green. The ratio of red apples to green apples is $2:3$. $\frac{2}{5}$ of all the apples are red and $\frac{3}{5}$ of all the apples are green. The number of red apples is $\frac{2}{3}$ of the number of green apples. The number of green apples is $\frac{3}{2}$ of the number of red apples.

Ratio

- Two similar quantities A and B can be compared using ratio.
- If A has four units and B has seven units,

  the ratio of A to B is $4:7$,

  the ratio of B to A is $7:4$.
- The order of the numbers in a ratio is important.

  $4:7 \neq 7:4$
- A ratio is not written with units.

Calculating a Quantity in a Ratio

In the bar model,
the ratio of A to B $= 2:3$
and A $= 16$.

2 parts	represent	16
1 part	represents	$16 \div 2 = 8$
3 parts	represent	$3 \times 8 = 24$

So B $= 24$.

Equivalent Ratios

Two different ratios are equivalent if they can be simplified to the same ratio.

A ratio can be changed to an equivalent ratio by multiplying or dividing its parts by the same number.

So $4:7 = 4 \times 5:7 \times 5$

$\quad\quad = 20:35$

$96:72 = 96 \div 24:72 \div 24$

$\quad\quad = 4:3$

If there are eight red balls, 12 green balls, 10 blue balls and 15 yellow balls,

the ratio of red balls to green balls is $8:12$.

$8:12 = 8 \div 4:12 \div 4 = 2:3$.

The ratio of blue balls to yellow balls is $10:15$.

$10:15 = 10 \div 5:15 \div 5 = 2:3$.

So $8:12 = 10:15 = 2:3$.

$8:12$ and $10:15$ are equivalent ratios.

The ratio of the number of boys to the number of girls in a drama club is 2:3. There are 18 boys. For a particular performance, another three boys join the club. Find the ratio of the number of boys to the number of girls now.

Workbook 1A Link
Problem Solving 7

REVISION EXERCISE 7 🧩🧩🧩

1. Mr Taylor buys five adult tickets and four child tickets to watch a show with his family. Find the ratio of
    (a) the number of adult tickets to the number of child tickets,
    (b) the number of child tickets to the total number of tickets.

2. Write down the following ratios.

    (a) The number of oranges to the number of apples.
    (b) The number of apples to the number of bananas.
    (c) The number of bananas to the total number of fruits.

3. **(a)** The ratio of basketballs to footballs in a store is 4:3. Express the number of basketballs as a fraction of the number of footballs.
    (b) The ratio of occupied seats to the total number of seats in an aircraft is 5:8. Write down the number of occupied seats as a fraction of the total number of seats.

4. Find these ratios and express them in the simplest form.
    (a) 45 cm to 200 cm
    (b) £3 to £12
    (c) 30 minutes to 45 minutes
    (d) 125 g to 75 g

5. Reduce each ratio to its simplest form. Show your reasoning.
    (a) 4:12
    (b) 18:24
    (c) 55:45
    (d) 35:21

6. Which of these pairs are equivalent ratios? Explain your answers.
   (a) 3:4 and 15:20
   (b) 24:30 and 4:5
   (c) 9:2 and 18:6
   (d) 30:20 and 21:14

7. A reaction uses 45 grams of chemical A, 60 grams of chemical B and 27 grams of chemical C.
   Find the ratio of
   (a) the mass of chemical C to the mass of chemical B,
   (b) the mass of chemical B to the mass of chemical A.
   Give your answers in the simplest form.
   Hint: Draw a bar model to help you.

8. In a gas formed by nitrogen and oxygen, the ratio of the mass of nitrogen to the mass of oxygen is 7:16.
   (a) Express the mass of oxygen as a fraction of the mass of nitrogen.
   (b) If the mass of nitrogen is 21 grams, find the mass of oxygen.

9. Megan spends $\frac{9}{11}$ of her income and saves the rest.
   (a) Find the ratio of her spending to her income.
   (b) Find the ratio of her spending to her savings.
   (c) If Megan spends £540 a week, what are her savings in a week?

10. In a flat, the area of the bedroom is $10\,m^2$. The ratio of the area of the living room to the area of the bedroom is 3:1. The ratio of the area of the bedroom to the area of the kitchen is 5:4. Calculate
    (a) the area of the living room,
    (b) the area of the kitchen,
    (c) the ratio of the area of the kitchen to the area of the living room, giving your answer in the simplest form.

Write in Your Journal

In the drama club at a school, the ratio of the number of boys to the number of girls is 6:5.
In the swimming club at the school, the ratio of the number of boys to the number of girls is 4:7.
Therefore, the number of boys in the drama club must be more than that in the swimming club because 6 > 4.
Do you agree? Justify your answer.

Integrated Examples

Example 1

In a box of 12 balls, three balls are red. Find

(a) the fraction of red balls in the box,

(b) the percentage of red balls in the box,

(c) the percentage of balls in the box that are not red,

(d) the ratio of the number of red balls to the number of balls in the box that are not red, giving your answer in its simplest form.

Solution

Note: You could use a bar model to represent the number of balls in the box.

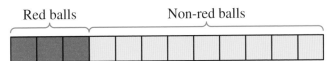

Red balls   Non-red balls

(a) Fraction of red balls $= \dfrac{3}{12}$

$$= \dfrac{3 \div 3}{12 \div 3}$$

$$= \dfrac{1}{4}$$

(b) *Method 1*

Percentage of red balls $= \dfrac{1}{4}$ Rewrite as an equivalent fraction with a denominator equal to 100.

$$= \dfrac{1 \times 25}{4 \times 25}$$

$$= \dfrac{25}{100}$$

$$= 25\%$$

Method 2

Percentage of red balls $= \dfrac{1}{\cancel{4}_1} \times \cancel{100}^{25}\%$

$$= 25\%$$

REMARK

The portion of shaded squares $= \dfrac{1}{4}$ of the whole square.

Divide each large square into 25 smaller squares.

The portion of shaded smaller squares

$$= \dfrac{25}{100} \text{ of the whole}$$

$$= 25\%.$$

Continued

203

(c) The whole is represented by 100%.

Percentage of balls that are not red = 100% − 25%

$$= 75\%$$

(d) Number of balls that are not red = 12 − 3

$$= 9$$

Ratio of the number of red balls to the number of balls that are not red

$$= 3:9$$

$$= 1:3 \quad \text{Divide both 3 and 9 by 3.}$$

REMARK

Two quantities can be compared using fractions, percentages or ratios.

Try It! ❶ There are 10 bars of chocolate. Four bars are dark chocolate and the rest are white chocolate. Find

(a) the fraction of the bars that are dark chocolate,

(b) the percentage of the bars that are dark chocolate,

(c) the percentage of the bars that are white chocolate,

(d) the ratio of the number of bars of dark chocolate to the number of bars of white chocolate, giving your answer in its simplest form.

Hint: Use diagrams to explain your reasoning.

Example ❷ A bottle contains 0.375 litres of juice. Another bottle contains 500 ml of water.

(a) Write 0.375 in expanded form.

(b) What value does the digit 5 represent in

   (i) 0.375, **(ii)** 500?

(c) Express 0.375 litres in ml.

(d) Find the ratio of the volume of water to the volume of juice.

Solution **(a)** $0.375 = 3 \times \dfrac{1}{10} + 7 \times \dfrac{1}{100} + 5 \times \dfrac{1}{1000}$

(b) **(i)** The digit 5 in 0.375 represents $\dfrac{5}{1000}$ or 5 thousandths.

   (ii) The digit 5 in 500 represents 500 or 5 hundreds.

REMARK

You can also express 0.375 as "3 tenths and 7 hundredths and 5 thousandths".

(c) 0.375 litres = 0.375 × 1000 ml

               = 375 ml

(d) Ratio of the volume of water to the volume of juice

= 500 ml : 375 ml	Write the volumes of water first.
= 500 : 375	You don't need to write the units in a ratio if they are the same.
= 100 : 75	Divide both 500 and 375 by 5.
= 4 : 3	Divide both 100 and 75 by 25.

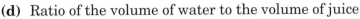
 Try It! **2**

The mass of a fish is 0.918 kg. The mass of a turtle is 612 grams.

(a) Write 0.918 in expanded form.

(b) What value does the digit 1 represent in

    (i) 0.918,   **(ii)** 612?

(c) Express 0.918 kg in grams.

(d) Find the ratio of the mass of the turtle to the mass of the fish.

Example **3**

A straight rod is cut into three parts, A, B and C. The length of part A is $\frac{8}{25}$ of the length of the rod. The length of part B is 0.38 of the length of the rod.

(a) Which part, A or B, is longer?

(b) Copy and complete the bar model for the lengths of the three parts.

A	B	C

0%   100%

$\frac{8}{25}$ = ?%   0.38 = ?%

Express the length of part C as a percentage of the length of the rod.

(c) Find the length of part A if the length of part C is 45 cm.

Solution

(a) Express the length of part A as a decimal in order to compare it with part B.

Length of part A = $\frac{8}{25}$ of the length of the whole rod

                     = $\frac{8 \times 4}{25 \times 4}$ of the length of the rod

                     = $\frac{32}{100}$ of the length of the rod

                     = 0.32 of the length of the rod

 DISCUSS

Why do you multiply the numerator and the denominator by 4?

Continued

Since 8 > 2, 0.38 > 0.32.　　　Compare decimals.

Hence, part B is longer than part A.

(b) $\dfrac{8}{25} = \dfrac{8 \times 4}{25 \times 4}$

$= \dfrac{32}{100}$

$= 32\%$

$0.38 = 0.38 \times 100\%$

$= 38\%$

Hence, the bar model is shown below.

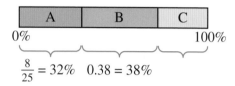

$\dfrac{8}{25} = 32\%$　$0.38 = 38\%$

The length of the whole rod = 100%.

$$32\% + 38\% = 70\%$$

Length of part C as a percentage of the length of the whole rod

$= 100\% - 70\%$

$= 30\%$

(c) Ratio of the length of part A to the length of part C = 32% : 30%

$= 32 : 30$

$= 16 : 15$　　　Divide both 32 and 30 by 2

15 parts　　represent　　45 cm

1 part　　　represents　　$45 \div 15 = 3$ cm

16 parts　　represent　　$3 \times 16 = 48$ cm

∴　the length of part A is 48 cm.

 Try It! ❸

A bag of flour is divided into three portions, P, Q and R. Portion P is $\dfrac{7}{20}$ of the bag. Portion Q is 0.34 of the bag.

(a) Which portion, P or Q, is smaller? Use a number line to represent your reasoning.

(b) Copy and complete the bar model for the three portions.

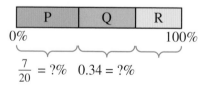

$\dfrac{7}{20} = ?\%$　$0.34 = ?\%$

What percentage of the whole bag is portion R?

(c) If the mass of portion P is 140 grams, find the mass of portion R.

You can represent this on a number line.

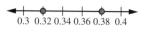

0.3　0.32　0.34　0.36　0.38　0.4

Is there another way to compare the lengths of A and B?

 DISCUSS

Abi says that 32% + 38% = 74%. Explain how you know immediately that her answer is wrong.

 REMARK

You can use the multiplication table on page 359 to check these calculations.

1. (a) What fraction of the whole rectangle is shaded?
   (b) Express this fraction as a decimal.
   (c) Express this fraction as a percentage.

2. Calculate these values.

   (a) $\frac{3}{8}$ of £56

   (b) $\frac{11}{12}$ of 72 kg

   Use a bar model to explain your reasoning.

3. In a competition, Jane gets $\frac{4}{9}$ of the total prize. Zoe gets $\frac{2}{9}$ of the total prize.

   £
   FINANCE

   (a) Who gets a greater prize? Explain your answer using a bar model.
   (b) If the total prize is £10 800, find the amount of money that Jane wins.

4. Cake A has a mass of $1\frac{4}{5}$ kg. Cake B has a mass of $1\frac{2}{7}$ kg.

   (a) Express $1\frac{4}{5}$ and $1\frac{2}{7}$ as improper fractions.

   (b) Which cake is heavier? Explain your answer.

5. David runs 200 m in 25.37 seconds. Annabel runs the same race in 25.34 seconds.

   (a) Write 25.37 in expanded form.
   (b) What value does the digit 7 represent?
   (c) Who is faster in the race?
   Hint: Will the fastest person in a race take the shortest time or the longest time?

6. Express

   (a) 0.76 as a fraction,
   (b) 0.03 as a percentage,
   (c) $3\frac{13}{20}$ as a decimal,
   (d) 49% as a decimal.

7. Convert

   (a) 0.25 kg to grams,
   (b) 1390 ml to litres,
   (c) 465p to £,
   (d) 36.5 m to cm.

207

8. 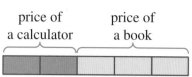 **(a)** Write down the ratio of the price of the calculator to the price of the book, as represented by this bar model.

(b) The price of the book is £15. Find the price of the calculator.

9. An aquarium tank has nine long-tailed goldfish and six short-tailed goldfish.

long-tailed goldfish   short-tailed goldfish

Find the ratio, in the simplest form, of

(a) the number of long-tailed goldfish to the number of short-tailed goldfish,

(b) the number of short-tailed goldfish to the number of long-tailed goldfish,

(c) the number of short-tailed goldfish to the total number of goldfish.

10. (a) Find the value of the missing number if $\frac{16}{9}$ and $\frac{\square}{45}$ are equivalent fractions.

(b) The ratio of the width to the height of a TV is $16 : 9$. The width of the TV is $112\,\text{cm}$. Work out the height of the TV.

11. (a) Copy the number line and plot the points representing 1.3 and $2\frac{1}{4}$ on it.

(b) Which of the two numbers is greater? Explain your answer.

(c) Express 1.3 as an improper fraction.

(d) Hence, write 1.3 as a sum of two proper fractions. Can you do so in more than one way?

OPEN QUESTION **Hint:** You may use a diagram of the improper fraction to explain your choices.

Use bar models to explain your reasoning in the following questions where appropriate.

12. The price of a jacket is £150. The price of a skirt is $\frac{2}{3}$ of the price of the jacket. The price of a handbag is 30% of the price of the jacket.

£ **FINANCE**

Work out

    (a) the price of the skirt,
    (b) the price of the handbag,
    (c) the ratio of the price of the skirt to the price of the handbag, giving your answer in its simplest form.

13. (a) The height of a tulip is $\frac{3}{7}$ of 56 cm. Find the tulip's height.

    (b) The height of a rose is 75% of 60 cm. Find the rose's height.

    (c) Find the ratio of the tulip's height to the rose's height, giving your answer in the simplest form.

14. The ratio of the number of juniors to the number of seniors in a school choir is 10:15.

PROBLEM SOLVING

    (a) Find the ratio of the number of seniors to the number of juniors in the simplest form.

    (b) Find the percentage of seniors in the choir.

    (c) If the choir has 60 students, find the number of seniors in the choir.

15. In a gym, the ratio of the number of 3 kg dumbbells to the number of 5 kg dumbbells is 9:4. The number of 5 kg dumbbells is 12. Find

PROBLEM SOLVING

    (a) the number of 3 kg dumbbells,
    (b) the total mass of all the dumbbells.

PROBLEM-SOLVING PROCESSES AND HEURISTICS

A contemporary mathematician, George Pólya (1887–1985), developed a classic four-step problem-solving process to help students become good problem solvers. A summary of the steps from his book *How to Solve It* is given below.

STEP ①   Understanding the Problem

    (a) Can you restate the problem in your own words?

    (b) What are you going to do or what is the goal?

    (c) What are the given pieces of information and unknowns?

    (d) Is there sufficient information or redundant information?

STEP ②   Devising a Plan

    (a) Find the connection between the given information, the unknowns and the goal.

    (b) Consider some possible actions or heuristics.

Heuristics are simple and efficient strategies that people use to solve problems. Here is a list of some useful heuristics.

- Use guess and check
- Draw a diagram
- Use a variable
- Think of a related problem
- Work backwards
- Look for a pattern
- Make a table
- Write an equation
- Examine a simpler problem
- Identify subgoals

STEP ③   Carrying Out the Plan

    (a) Implement the strategy or strategies that you have chosen.

    (b) Carry out the necessary actions or computations.

    (c) Modify your plan and choose a new strategy if necessary until the problem is solved.

STEP ④   Looking Back

    (a) Check that the solution is reasonable and satisfies the original problem.

    (b) Examine whether there is an easier method to find the solution.

    (c) Extend the solution to solve other problems or more general problems.

Some of the problem-solving strategies are illustrated in these examples.

Example 1

(Make a Table)

A school fete runs a lucky dip in which you win a voucher every time you draw from it. Each voucher is worth £2, £5 or £10. Sophia draws two vouchers. Work out how many different possible total values there are of her two vouchers?

Solution

STEP 1 **Understanding the Problem**

Sophia draws two vouchers. Each voucher may be £2, £5 or £10. You are required to find the number of different possible total sums of her vouchers.

STEP 2 **Devising a Plan**

You can make a table of the possible ways of drawing the vouchers. Then work out the total value for each way. You can then count the different total values this gives.

When you make a table, list the possible ways systematically. This method will be easier to check and help to make sure you don't miss out a possible way.

> **DISCUSS**
>
> Why is making a table helpful? Why is it better to list the ways systematically?

STEP 3 **Carrying Out the Plan**

First Voucher (£)	Second Voucher (£)	Total Value (£)
2	2	4
2	5	7
2	10	12
5	2	7
5	5	10
5	10	15
10	2	12
10	5	15
10	10	20

> **DISCUSS**
>
> Are the rows "2, 10" and "10, 2" the same? Why do we list these as two different rows?

From the table, the possible total values are:

£4, £7, £10, £12, £15, £20.

Hence, Sophia can get 6 different possible total values.

Continued

Looking Back

It can be useful to make a summary table. This table shows the number of vouchers of the different types that Sophia can get.

Number of			Total value (£)
£2 vouchers	£5 vouchers	£10 vouchers	
2	0	0	4
0	2	0	10
0	0	2	20
1	1	0	7
1	0	1	12
0	1	1	15

DISCUSS

What patterns can you see in this table? Do the patterns assure you that you have covered all the possible cases?

Hence, Sophia can get 6 different possible total values.

From the solution, you see that making tables is an effective way of listing all the possible ways of doing certain tasks.

Example 2

(Draw a Diagram)

Freya bought three pizzas and two drinks for her family for £36. Ahsan bought three pizzas and four drinks for his family for £42. If Ellie wants to buy one pizza and two drinks, how much would she have to pay?

Solution

STEP ① **Understanding the Problem**

It is given that

3 pizzas + 2 drinks → £36,

and   3 pizzas + 4 drinks → £42.

To find: 1 pizza + 2 drinks → ?

DISCUSS

We should write "the price of..." before each item on the left hand side: why don't we?

STEP ② **Devising a Plan**

Bar models can be used to solve the problem. Use a rectangle to represent the price of a pizza. Use another rectangle of different length to represent the price of a drink. Draw a bar by joining some of these rectangles to show the given information. This may help you find the prices represented by the rectangles. Then you can find the solution.

STEP 3 **Carrying Out the Plan**

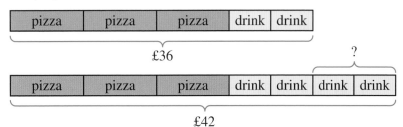

From the bar model,

3 pizzas + 2 drinks ➔ £36,

and 3 pizzas + 4 drinks ➔ £42.

The difference between the total lengths of the two bars represents the price of two extra drinks.

∴ 2 drinks ➔ £42 − £36 = £6.

Thus, 1 drink ➔ £6 ÷ 2 = £3.

As 3 pizzas + 2 drinks ➔ £36,

3 pizzas ➔ £36 − 2 × £3 = £30.

Thus, 1 pizza ➔ £30 ÷ 3 = £10.

∴ the price of 1 pizza and 2 drinks = £10 + 2 × £3

= £16.

Ellie pays £16 for one pizza and two drinks.

STEP 4 **Looking Back**

You can use these results to check that your answers satisfy the original information.

3 × £10 + 2 × £3 = £36,

and 3 × £10 + 4 × £3 = £42.

> **DISCUSS**
>
> Can you represent the bar model in other ways? How does this representation explain how you can find the price of two drinks?

> **DISCUSS**
>
> Why is a bar model useful? Can you represent the problem using icons of pizza and drinks? What other representations could you use? What are the advantages and disadvantages of different representations?

Example 3

(Use Guess and Check, and Use a Variable)

David joins a gym. He has to pay a £10 monthly fee and £3 per visit. His budget for the gym is £50 a month. What is the maximum number of visits that he can make in a month?

Solution

STEP 1 **Understanding the Problem**

A gym charges a monthly fee of £10 and a visit fee of £3. David intends to spend a maximum of £50 per month on the gym. You are required to find the maximum number of visits that David can make in a month.

STEP 2 **Devising a Plan**

You can attempt this problem using 'Guess and Check'. Find the total cost for a guessed number of visits in a month. If the total cost is less than the budget, try a greater number next.

Continued

If the total cost is greater than the budget, try a smaller number next. Continue the process until you find the number that gives a total less than or equal to the budget, while the next number up gives a total greater than the budget.

STEP ❸ **Carrying Out the Plan**

The working can be presented in a table,
where   visit charge = £3 × number of visits
and   total cost = monthly fee + visit charge
                        = £10 + visit charge.

DISCUSS

If your first two guesses are 10 visits and 13 visits, what could your third guess be? Explain your answer.
If your first two guesses are 20 visits and 15 visits, what could your third guess be? Explain your answer.

Number of visits	Visit charge	Total cost	Result
10	£30	£40	< £50
20	£60	£70	> £50
15	£45	£55	> £50
13	£39	£49	< £50
14	£42	£52	> £50

Since 13 visits give a total cost (£49) less than the budget (£50) and 14 visits give a total cost (£52) greater than the budget (£50), the maximum number of visits he can make in a month is 13.

STEP ❹ **Looking Back**

When you use the 'Guess and Check' method, you have to master the skill of narrowing down the possible range of guesses.

After calculating that 10 visits give a total value less than £50 and 20 visits give a total value greater than £50, you know the solution is between 10 and 20 visits.

Then a value between 10 and 20 is tried, which is 15.

As the total value of 15 visits is greater than £50, a value between 10 and 15 is tried, which is 13, and so on.

This systematic way of testing is usually much faster than making wild guesses.

DISCUSS

What other ways can you suggest for choosing the number of visits?
What are the advantages of this way of choosing the number of visits to try?

You can solve the problem by using a variable.
Let n be the number of visits.

$$\text{Visit charge} = £3n \quad \text{This is £3 × n.}$$
$$\text{Total cost in a month} = £(10 + 3n).$$

Then you can use a spreadsheet program to find the value of $10 + 3n$ for different values of n.

	A	B
1	n	$10 + 3n$
2	10	40
3	11	43
4	12	46
5	13	49
6	14	52
7	15	55
8	16	58
9	17	61
10	18	64

REMARK

The formula for cell B2 is
'=10 + 3*A2'.
You can copy this formula
to cells B3 to B10.

From the spreadsheet, you see that for David to keep within the budget of £50 per month, the maximum number of visits to the gym is 13.

As an alternative, you can subtract the £10 monthly fee from the £50 budget and find how many visits David can make.

$$\text{Amount for making visits} = \text{budget} - \text{monthly fee}$$
$$= £50 - £10$$
$$= £40$$
$$\text{Number of visits} = £40 \div £3$$
$$= 13\frac{1}{3}$$

Since the number of possible visits must be a whole number, the maximum number of visits to the gym is 13.

DISCUSS

Explain in your own words to a classmate why this method works.
Could you use a bar model to represent the problem? Show how your bar model is related to this numerical solution method.

Example 4 **(Work Backwards and Use a Diagram)**

Jenny's lunch break starts at 12:30 and ends at 1:30. She needs to do at least 30 minutes of piano practice during her lunch break. It takes 5 minutes to get to and from the music department from the main school building. If she eats lunch first, how much time will she have to eat and what's the latest time she can leave the main school building?

Solution

STEP ❶ **Understanding the Problem**

Jenny needs to do at least 30 minutes of piano practice in her 1 hour lunch break.

It takes 5 minutes to get to the music department and it will take her 5 minutes to get back to the main school building afterwards. She needs to eat her lunch before going to the music department.

You are required to work out how long she has to eat her lunch and what is the latest time she can leave the main school building.

STEP ❷ **Devising a Plan**

By working backwards, you can find the time that she must leave the music department after her piano practice. Then you can find the time she must have arrived at the music department. Continuing to work backwards, you can then find out the time she must have left the main school building and how long she had to eat lunch.

 **DISCUSS**

What kind of diagrams do you think would be useful when answering this question?

STEP ❸ **Carrying Out the Plan**

Start by drawing a timeline that shows Jenny's lunch break, marking in 5-minute intervals. Then draw a bar model for her entire lunch break, and work backwards from the end of her lunch break at 1:30. Then you will find the time when Jenny will have to leave the music department to get back to school.

 **DISCUSS**

Why is it easier to draw the bars going 'backwards in time' rather than 'forwards in time' in this question?

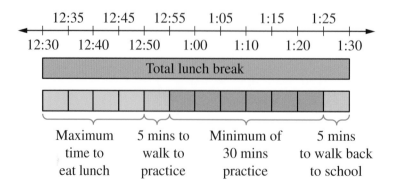

Look at the bars.
Start with the end of lunch break, 1:30. Before she starts walking back to the main school building, it will be 1:25.

If Jenny spends the minimum amount of time, 30 minutes, practising the piano before 1:25, she will need to start her practice at 12:55.
It takes Jenny 5 minutes to walk to the music department from the main school, so she will have to leave the main school at 12:50.
Hence, the latest time Jenny can leave the main school building will be 12:50.
That means she will have between 12:30 and 12:50 to eat her lunch.
50 − 30 = 20 minutes
So Jenny will have 20 minutes to eat her lunch.

STEP ❹ **Looking Back**
You can check your answers by working through the timeline in the opposite direction (from the start).
If she takes 20 minutes to eat her lunch, starting at 12:30, she'll leave for the music department at 12:50.
If it takes her 5 minutes to walk to the music department, she will arrive at 12:55.
If she practises for 30 minutes, she will finish her practice at 1:25.
It will take her 5 minutes to walk back to the main school building. She will arrive at 1:30, which is when the lunch break ends. Therefore her plan works.

8 MEASURES AND ANGLES

WHAT IS IN THIS CHAPTER:

A laser produces a very narrow beam of light. Lasers have lots of different uses. They can be bounced off mirrors at different angles. If a beam hits a flat mirror at an angle of 64°, then the angle it makes with the mirror as it travels away is also 64°. Can you work out the size of the angle between these two beams?

LET'S LEARN TO

▶ measure and draw angles with a protractor
▶ identify acute, right, obtuse and reflex angles
▶ calculate missing angles in right angles, on straight lines and in full turns

1. Clockwise Direction and Anticlockwise Direction

(a) Clockwise direction

(b) Anticlockwise direction

The hands of an analogue clock rotate in a clockwise direction.

2. Multiples of a Whole Number

$1 \times 5, 2 \times 5, 3 \times 5$ and 4×5 are the first four whole number **multiples** of 5.
So   5, 10, 15 and 20 are the first four whole number multiples of 5.

$1 \times 90, 2 \times 90, 3 \times 90$ and 4×90 are the first four whole number multiples of 90.
So   90, 180, 270 and 360 are the first four whole number multiples of 90.

You can work out the first four whole number multiples of 90 from the first four whole number multiples of 9, which are 9, 18, 27 and 36, by multiplying each one by 10.

3. Inverse Relationship between Addition and Subtraction

You can use bar models to show the relationship.

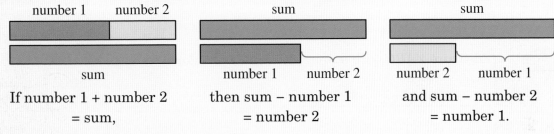

If number 1 + number 2
   = sum,

then sum – number 1
   = number 2

and sum – number 2
   = number 1.

For example, given that $a + 36 = 90$,
$a = 90 - 36$ Inverse relationship between addition and subtraction.
$a = 54$

4. Lines and Angles

(a) Straight lines can be drawn using a ruler. They can be labelled with letters. Here are lines AB, PQ and XY.

(b) Two straight lines meeting at a point make an angle. The size of this angle is a measure of the turn from the direction along one line to the direction along the other.

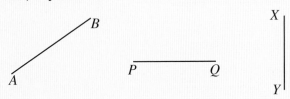

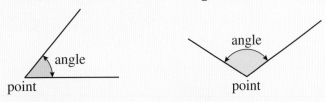

8.1 Introduction to Angles

Let's have a look at identifying and measuring different types of angles.

An angle is measured using a protractor.

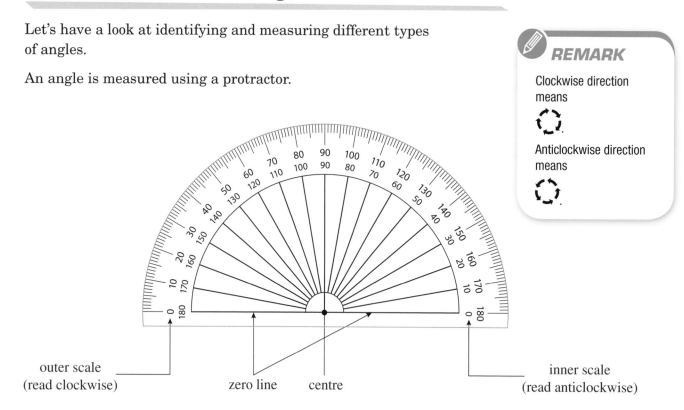

outer scale
(read clockwise)

zero line   centre

inner scale
(read anticlockwise)

REMARK

Clockwise direction means

Anticlockwise direction means

Example 1   Measure $\angle ABC$ with a protractor and write down its size.

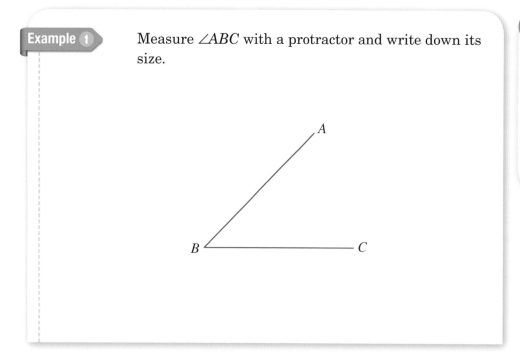

REMARK

You use the symbol $\angle$ to represent an angle. If the angle is at *B*, where the lines *AB* and *BC* meet, the name of the angle is $\angle ABC$ or $\angle CBA$. Notice the angle is always at the middle letter, in this case *B*.

Solution

Step 1

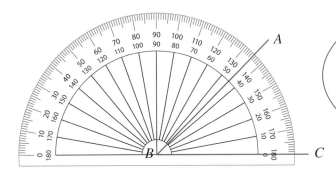

Place the centre of the protractor on point B.
Align the inner zero line of the protractor with the
line segment BC.

You use the inner
scale to measure the angle
because line segment BC lies
on the zero line for the inner
scale.

Step 2

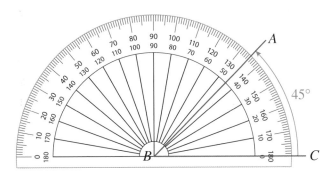

Read the size of the angle anticlockwise using the
inner scale.
$\angle ABC$ is 45°.

REMARK

A line segment is a
continuous part of a
straight line with two end
points.

Try It! ① Measure $\angle ABC$ with a protractor and write down its
size.
Hint: You will need to rotate the protractor or the
page in order to measure the angle.

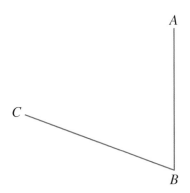

DISCUSS

Can you use curved
lines to draw an angle?
Discuss your answer with
a partner.

Example 2

Measure ∠*PQR* with a protractor and write down its size.

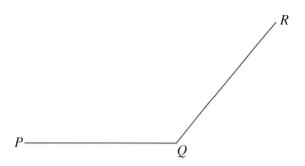

Solution

Since line segment *PQ* lies on the zero line for the outer scale, you read the size of the angle clockwise using the outer scale.

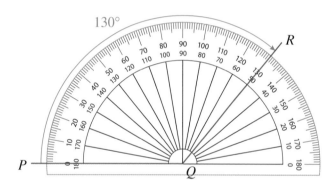

∠*PQR* is 130°.

Try It! 2

Measure ∠*PQR* with a protractor and write down its size.

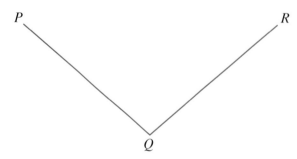

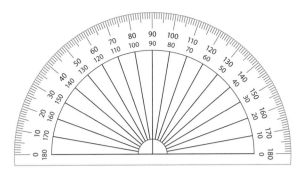

You can see from the protractor above that 180° make a straight line.

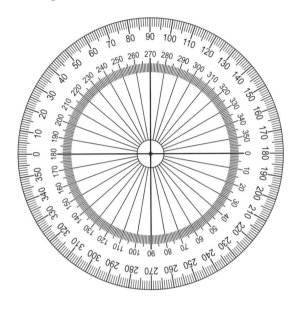

You can see from the circular protractor above that 360° make a full turn.

MATHS

Some ancient calendars used 360 days for a year.

Example 3   Find the size of the marked angle *XYZ*.

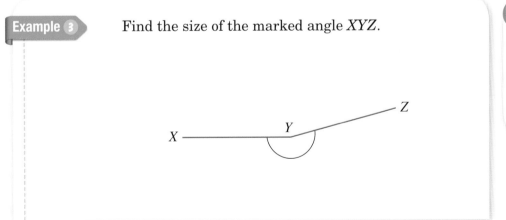

DISCUSS

Is ∠*XYZ* bigger or smaller than ∠*AOB* formed on a straight line below?

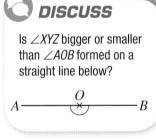

Continued

223

Solution

To work out the value of the marked angle *XYZ* which is 'on the outside', first measure the small angle which is 'on the inside'.

Since line segment *XY* lies on the zero line for the outer scale, use the outer scale to measure the size of the 'inside' angle.

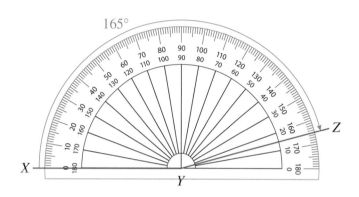

165°

The 'inside' angle is 165°.

There are 360° in a full turn. So, to find the 'outside' angle *XYZ*, subtract the 'inside' angle from 360°.

$$360° - 165° = 360° - 160° - 5°$$
$$= 200° - 5°$$
$$= 195°$$

Hence, ∠*XYZ* is 195°.

Try It! 3   Find the size of the marked angle *PQR*.

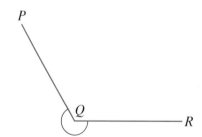

REMARK

In the diagram below, the symbol ∠*XTZ* refers to two angles. You will learn how to identify them in a later section.

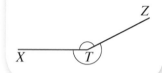

REMARK

The same symbol ∠ is used for angles whatever their size. You shouldn't try to make the symbol look like the size of the angle you are describing.

Example 4

Use a protractor to draw an angle of 65°.

Solution

Step 1

$$A \text{———————} B$$

Draw the line segment AB first.

Step 2

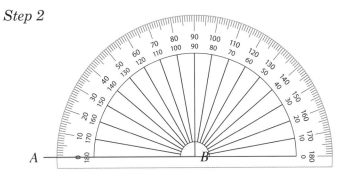

Place the centre of the protractor over point B. Align the zero line of the outer scale of the protractor with the line segment AB.

Step 3

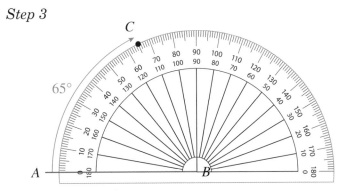

Using the outer scale, mark point C at 65°.

Step 4

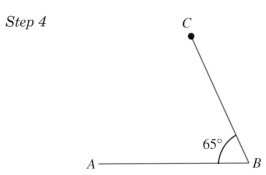

Join the points B and C with a line segment. Label $\angle ABC$ as 65°.

Try It! 4

Use a protractor to draw an angle of 126°.

You use the outer scale to measure the angle because the line segment AB lies on the zero line of the outer scale of the protractor.

DISCUSS

If you put your protractor on the line segment AB with its centre over point A, how would you draw the angle? What is the same and what is different about the two ways of drawing the angle?

DISCUSS

How would you draw an angle of 295°?

Objective: To check understanding of how to draw and measure angles.

1. Lauren is asked to measure ∠ABC. Her steps are shown below.

   Step 1   *Step 2*

    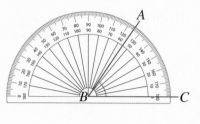

   ∠ABC = 125°

   Is Lauren's answer right? What feedback would you give her?

2. Toby is asked to measure ∠DEF. His steps are shown below.

   Step 1   *Step 2*

   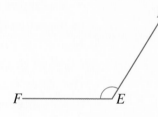 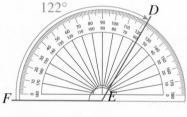

   ∠DEF = 122°

   Is Toby's answer right? What feedback would you give him?

3. Ethan is asked to draw ∠TUV = 190°. His steps are shown below.

   Step 1   *Step 2*

   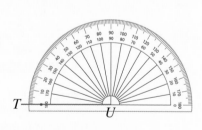 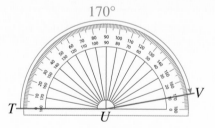

   Step 3

   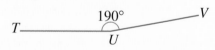

   Is Ethan's answer right? What feedback would you give him?

PRACTICE 8.1

1. Use a protractor to measure each angle and state its size.

(a)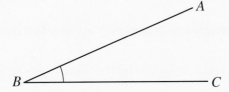

(b)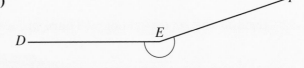

(c)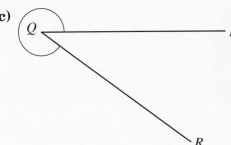

(d)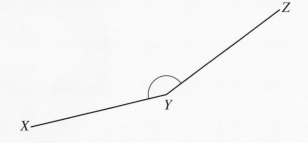

2. Using a ruler and a protractor, draw these angles on separate diagrams.
   (a) 56°   (b) 90°
   (c) 164°   (d) 175°

LEVEL 2

3. Use a protractor to measure the size of each angle indicated in the diagram.
   Hint: You can turn the book to help you measure the angles comfortably.

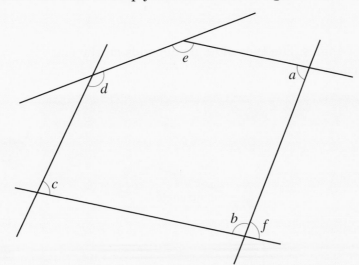

4. Using a ruler and protractor, draw these angles on separate diagrams.
   (a) 190°   (b) 220°
   (c) 318°   (d) 347°

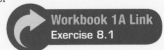

Workbook 1A Link
Exercise 8.1

227

8.2 Types of Angles

CLASS ACTIVITY 2

Objective: To identify angles of different sizes.

Look at the road sign below. There are a number of angles in the sign.

Tasks

1. Copy the arrow and label each of its corners with a letter.

2. Sort the corners into different groups, using your labels to help show you which corners are in the same group.

3. Compare your results with those of a classmate. Did you use the same method of grouping? Can you think of other ways to group the corners?

There are various types of angles. The type of angle depends on the size of the angle, measured in degrees.

Type of angle	Size of angle	Example
Acute angle	Less than 90°	acute angle
Right angle	90°	 right angle

REMARK

Note that the marking for a right angle is different from other angles. When two lines form a right angle they are said to be **perpendicular** to each other. The right angle is marked with a square, as shown in the table.

Type of angle	Size of angle	Example
Obtuse angle	More than 90° but less than 180°	obtuse angle
Reflex angle	More than 180° but less than 360°	reflex angle

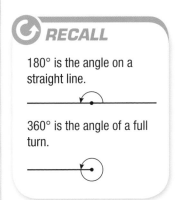

RECALL

180° is the angle on a straight line.

360° is the angle of a full turn.

Now identify an acute angle and an obtuse angle in the yellow shape shown?

Example 5

Identify the types of angles labelled in the diagram.

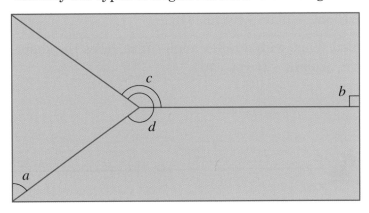

Solution

(a) ∠a is less than a right angle, so it is an acute angle.

(b) ∠b is equal to 90°, so it is a right angle.

(c) ∠c is more than a right angle but less than an angle on a straight line, so it is an obtuse angle.

(d) ∠d is more than an angle on a straight line but less than a full turn, so it is a reflex angle.

Identify the types of angles labelled in the diagram.

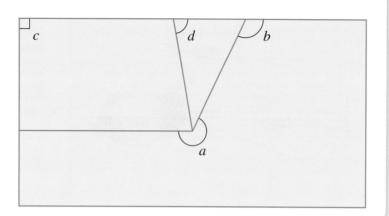

 CLASS ACTIVITY 3

Objective: To explore angles in shapes.

Work in pairs to answer these questions.

1. Can you draw a 3-sided shape with two acute angles? If so, draw the shape and label the angles. If not, explain why you can't.

2. Can you draw a 3-sided shape with two obtuse angles? If so, draw the shape and label the angles. If not, explain why you can't.

3. Can you draw a 4-sided shape with two obtuse angles? If so, draw the shape and label the angles. If not, explain why you can't.

4. Can you draw a 4-sided shape with a reflex angle? If so, draw the shape and label the angles. If not, explain why you can't.

PRACTICE 8.2

 LEVEL 1

1. Copy and complete the table by stating whether the given angles are acute, obtuse or reflex.

Size of angle	36°	72°	95°	107°	182°	242°
Type of angle						

2. Robert says that 'every angle is either acute, obtuse or reflex'. Do you agree with Robert? Explain your answer.

3. Identify the stated type of angle in each of these objects by tracing or sketching the object and marking the angle.

(a)

Acute angle

(b)

Right angle

(c)

Obtuse angle

(d)

Reflex angle

4. Using a ruler and a protractor, draw an example of each of these types of angles. State the size of each angle you have drawn.

OPEN QUESTION

(a) Acute angle   (b) Right angle   (c) Obtuse angle   (d) Reflex angle

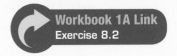
Workbook 1A Link
Exercise 8.2

8.3 Unknown Angles

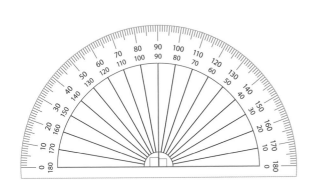

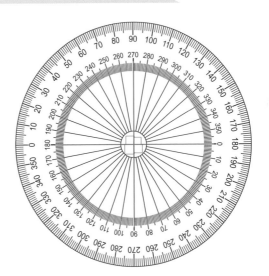

You can see from the protractor that there are two right angles on a straight line.

i.e.   a straight angle is $2 \times 90° = 180°$.

You can see from the circular protractor that there are four right angles in a full turn.

i.e.   a full turn is $4 \times 90° = 360°$.

The following activity explores the properties of angles that combine to form a right angle, a straight line and a full turn.

Objective: To find the relationship between angles that form a right angle, a straight line or a full turn.

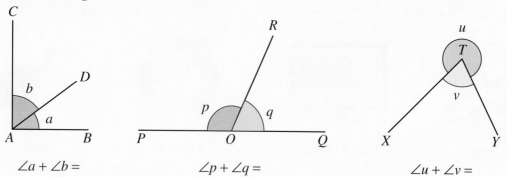

$\angle a + \angle b =$ $\angle p + \angle q =$ $\angle u + \angle v =$

1. **(a)** Use geometry software to create a right angle *BAC*.
   (b) Draw a line *AD* to split the right angle into two angles *a* and *b*.
   (c) Measure angle *a* and angle *b*. Work out their sum.
   (d) Drag the point *D* around and observe the change in the values in **(c)**.
   (e) What can you say about $\angle a + \angle b$?

2. **(a)** Use geometry software to create a straight line *POQ*.
   (b) Draw a line *OR* to form two angles *p* and *q* as shown.
   (c) Measure angle *p* and angle *q*. Work out their sum.
   (d) Drag the point *R* around and observe the change in the values in **(c)**.
   (e) What can you say about $\angle p + \angle q$?

3. **(a)** Use geometry software to draw two lines *TX* and *TY* to create two angles *u* and *v* as shown.
   (b) Measure angle *u* and angle *v*. Work out their sum.
   (c) Drag the point *X* or *Y* around and observe the change in the values in **(b)**.
   (d) What can you say about $\angle u + \angle v$?

From Class Activity 4, you can observe some properties of angles.

> Angles in a right angle add up to 90°.

In the diagram, $\angle BAC = 90°$.
Hence, $\angle a + \angle b = 90°$.   (Angles in a right angle add up to 90°.)
You can represent this relationship using a bar model.

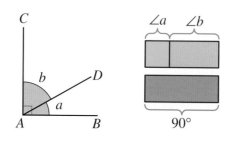

REMARK

Geometrical reasoning for a step in your working is a statement that shows the geometry property that you used to explain that step. You write the reasoning in brackets after the step. It shows you know the geometry-based reason that the step is true.

Example 6

Given that ∠PQR is a right angle and ∠PQS = 34°, find the size of ∠SQR.

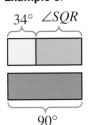
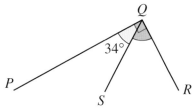

Solution

∠SQR + 34° = 90°   (Angles in a right angle add up to 90°.)

∠SQR = 90° − 34°   Inverse relationship between

= 90° − 30° − 4°   addition and subtraction.

= 60° − 4°

= 56°

Note: When solving a geometry problem, you should write down the geometrical reasoning for the steps.

In questions like this, you should not use a protractor to measure the angle. This is because the diagram may not be drawn accurately.

Try It! 6

Given that ∠ABC is a right angle and ∠DBC = 52°, find the size of ∠ABD.

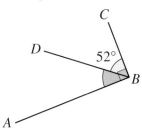

Hint: Look at your diagram. Which angles are known? Which unknown angle are you going to find? What is the relationship between the unknown angle and the known angles?

Draw a bar model to help you.

Angles on a straight line add up to 180°.

In the diagram, AOB is a straight line.

Hence, ∠a + ∠b = 180°.   (Angles on a straight line add up to 180°.)

You can represent this relationship using a bar model.

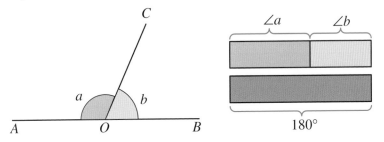

Example 7

DEF is a straight line and ∠*GEF* = 47°.
Calculate ∠*DEG*.

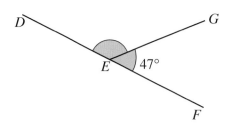

REMARK

Here is the bar model for
Example 7.

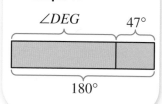

• **Solution**

∠*DEG* + 47° = 180°   (Angles on a straight
∠*DEG* = 180° − 47°   line add up to 180°.)
        = 180° − 40° − 7°
        = 140° − 7°
        = 133°

Try It! 7

KLM is a straight line and ∠*NLM* = 115°.
Calculate ∠*KLN*.

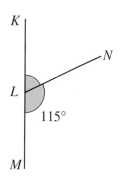

Hint: Identify the angles in the diagram as you read
the question.

DISCUSS

Is your answer going to
be an acute, obtuse or
reflex angle? What does
this tell you about the
possible size of the angle?
Knowing this allows you
to check that the answer
is sensible.

When the angles you are looking at form a full turn you can also call
that situation **angles at a point**.

Angles at a point add up to 360°.

In the diagram, ∠*x* + ∠*y* = 360°.   (Angles at a point add up to 360°.)
You can represent this relationship using a bar model.

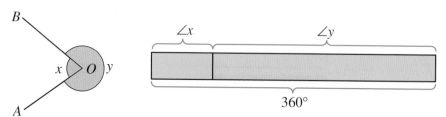

Note that both ∠x and ∠y have the same name, ∠AOB.

To identify which is which, you name the angle that is bigger than 180° 'reflex ∠AOB'. Then the angle on the side smaller than 180° is just ∠AOB.

Therefore,   ∠AOB = ∠x   and   reflex ∠AOB = ∠y.

Depending on how big a reflex angle is, the smaller angle could be acute, right angle or obtuse, but you don't usually have to say which.

Example 8

In the diagram, reflex ∠POQ = 244°. Work out the size of ∠x.

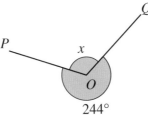

REMARK

Look at the diagram in **Example 8**. Point at the acute angle *POQ*. Point at the reflex angle *POQ*.

Solution

$$∠x + 244° = 360° \quad \text{(Angles at a point add up to 360°.)}$$
$$∠x = 360° - 244°$$
$$= 360° - 240° - 4°$$
$$= 120° - 4°$$
$$= 116°$$

Try It! 8

In the diagram, ∠COD = 43°. Work out the size of ∠y.

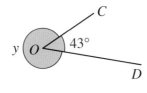

REMARK

Here is the bar model for **Example 8**.

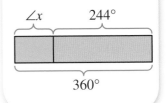

Example 9

(a) How many degrees are there in a three-quarter turn? Draw a bar model to help you.

(b) How many right angles are in a three-quarter turn?

Solution

(a) In the diagram, reflex ∠AOB is a three-quarter turn.

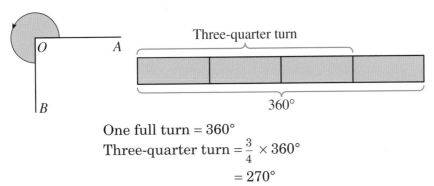

One full turn = 360°

Three-quarter turn = $\frac{3}{4} × 360°$

$= 270°$

REMARK

A quarter turn, such as ∠AOB, is 90°. So a three-quarter turn is 3 × 90° = 270°.

A three-quarter turn is also called three quarters of a turn.

Continued

(b) Number of right angles in a three-quarter turn

$$= \frac{270°}{90°}$$

$$= 3$$

Try It! **9** **(a)** How many degrees are there in a half turn?
Draw a bar model to help you.
(b) How many 45° angles are in a half turn?

PRACTICE 8.3

State the geometrical reasoning in your working.

LEVEL 1

1. Work out the size of the angle x in each diagram.
   Hint: You may draw bar models to help you.

   (a)

   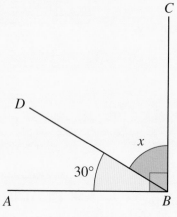

   (b)

   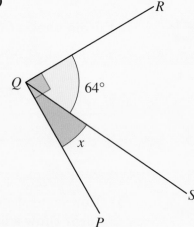

2. Work out the size of the angle y in each diagram, where AOB is a straight line.
   Hint: You may draw bar models to help you.

   (a)

   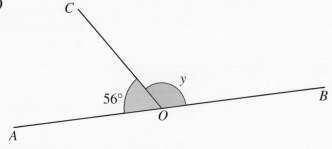

   (b)

   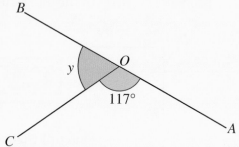

3. Work out the size of angle *z* in each diagram.
   Hint: You may draw bar models to help you.

   (a)

   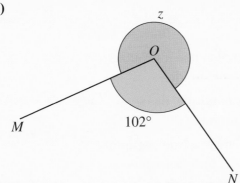

   (b)

   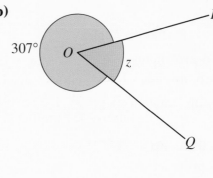

LEVEL 2

4. Find the number of 60° angles in a half turn. Draw a bar model to help you.

5. The diagram shows a right-angle tool, in which
   $\angle ABC = 90°$ and $\angle ABD = 45°$. Find $\angle CBD$.

   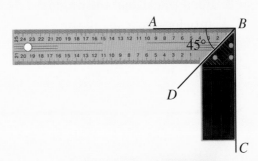

6. The diagram shows some dovetail joints in a drawer.
   ABC is a straight line and $\angle ABD = 78°$. Find $\angle CBD$.

   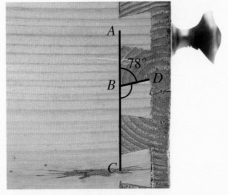

7. The diagram shows a roof top, in which
   $\angle PTQ = 129°$. Calculate reflex $\angle PTQ$.

   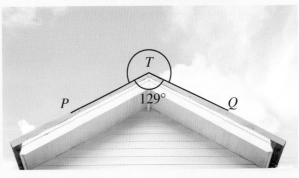

8. Fred is thinking of an angle. It is acute. It is also a multiple of 20°. Twice the angle is an
   obtuse angle. What angles could Fred be thinking of?

   PROBLEM SOLVING

   Workbook 1A Link
   Exercise 8.3

REVIEW

Measuring Angles

You use a protractor to measure angles.

For example, measure ∠*ABC*.

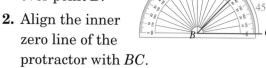

1. Place the centre of the protractor over point *B*.

2. Align the inner zero line of the protractor with *BC*.

3. Read the size of the angle anticlockwise, using the inner scale.

∠*ABC* = 45°

Drawing Angles

You also use a protractor to draw angles.

For example, draw an angle of 30°.

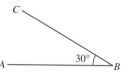

1. Draw a line segment *AB* and place the centre of the protractor over point *B*.

2. Align the outer zero line of the protractor with *AB*.

3. Use the outer scale to mark point *C* at 30°.

4. Join the points *B* and *C* and label the angle.

Types of Angles

Two straight lines meeting at a point make an angle. The size of this angle is a measure of turn from the direction along one line to the direction along the other.

1. **Acute angles** are less than 90°(a right angle). ∠*a* and ∠*d* are acute angles.

2. **Right angles** are equal to 90°. ∠*b* is a right angle.

3. **Obtuse angles** are more than 90° (a right angle) but less than 180° (angle on a straight line). ∠*c* is an obtuse angle.

4. **Reflex angles** are more than 180° (angle on a straight line) but less than 360° (a full turn). ∠*e* is a reflex angle.

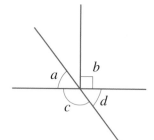

Finding Missing Angles

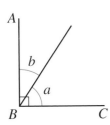

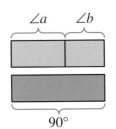

$\angle ABC = 90°$
$\angle a + \angle b = 90°$
(Angles in a right angle add up to 90°.)

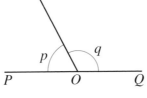

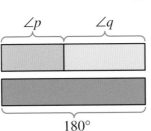

POQ is a straight line.
$\angle p + \angle q = 180°$
(Angles on a straight line add up to 180°.)

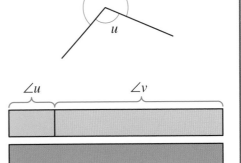

$\angle u + \angle v = 360°$
(Angles at a point add up to 360°.)

CHALLENGE 8

Find the angle that
(a) the minute hand of a clock rotates in
    (i) 1 hour,
    (ii) 25 minutes.
(b) the second hand of a clock rotates in 1 second.

Workbook 1A Link
Problem Solving 8

REVISION EXERCISE 8

1. Measure the sizes of these angles.
   (a)

   (b)

   (c)

   (d)

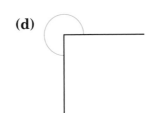

2. Using a ruler and a protractor, draw a separate diagram for each angle.
    (a) 108°
    (b) 29°
    (c) 341°
    (d) 275°

3. Identify the type of each angle.

    (a)

    (b)

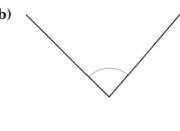

    (c)

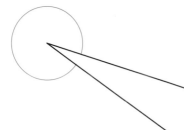

    (d)

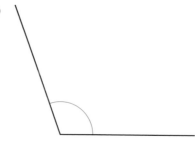

4. In each of these diagrams, work out the size of the missing angle. Give geometrical reasoning for your steps.

    (a)

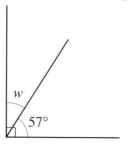

    (b)

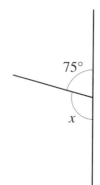

    (c)

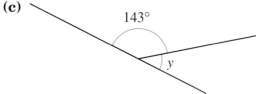

    (d)

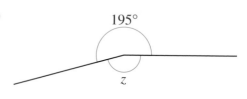

5. Are the following statements true or false? Explain your answers.
    (a) 3° is an example of an acute angle.
    (b) 182° is an example of an obtuse angle.
    (c) A reflex angle is more than 270° and less than 360°.

6. $\angle x$ is more than 100° but less than 360°. Do you have enough information to identify the type of this angle? Explain your answer.

7. The two fingers form an angle *AVB* of 30°. What is the size of reflex ∠*AVB*?

8. A wooden plank is cut along the lines *BE* and *CE*. *ABC* is a straight line, ∠*ACD* = 90°, ∠*EBC* = 40° and ∠*BCE* = 49°.

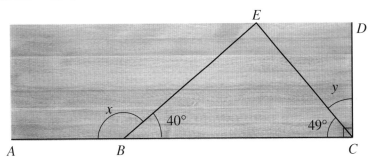

Calculate

(a) ∠*x*,

(b) ∠*y*.

9. Which multiples of 35° are reflex angles?

PROBLEM SOLVING

Write in Your Journal

Bella says, 'The sum of two acute angles is always an obtuse angle.'

Is Bella correct? Explain your answer in full sentences.

Alfie says, 'The sum of two obtuse angles is always a reflex angle.'

Is Alfie correct? Explain your answer in full sentences.

9 SYMMETRY

WHAT IS IN THIS CHAPTER:

9.1 Reflection Symmetry of Plane Figures

9.2 Rotation Symmetry of Plane Figures

You can find symmetry in nature and in a lot of objects made by humans. This is the Taj Mahal. What can you say about the design of the building?

LET'S LEARN TO

▶ identify reflection symmetry and lines of symmetry
▶ create symmetrical figures and patterns
▶ identify rotation symmetry
▶ state the order of rotation symmetry

1. **Key Properties of Shapes**

   (a) A **rectangle** has two pairs of equal sides and four equal angles. The equal sides are opposite each other. They are parallel.

   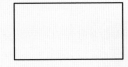

   (b) An **equilateral triangle** has three equal sides and three equal angles.

   (c) A **square** has four equal sides and four equal angles.

   (d) A **regular pentagon** has five equal sides and five equal angles.

   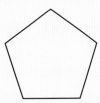

   (e) A **regular hexagon** has six equal sides and six equal angles.

   A regular polygon is a shape with all sides of equal length and all angles of equal size. The shapes in **(b)** to **(e)** are all examples of regular polygons.

2. **Angles**

   (a) Full turn

   360°

   (b) Half turn

   180°

   (c) Quarter turn

    90°

9.1 Reflection Symmetry of Plane Figures

Each half of this photo of a crown looks the same in shape and size and you can say it is symmetrical. In this chapter, you will learn more about two types of symmetry — reflection symmetry and rotation symmetry.

REMARK

A plane figure is a two-dimensional drawing that can be shown on a flat surface such as paper.

Line of symmetry

The photo of a crown can be divided into two identical halves by a straight line. Each half is the mirror image of the other in the line. The line is called a **line of symmetry** or a **mirror line**. This figure is said to have **reflection symmetry**. An object can have more than one line of symmetry. Can you find the other line of symmetry in the figure below?

If you place a mirror along the line of symmetry, you will observe that the image in the mirror is exactly the same as the other half of the figure.

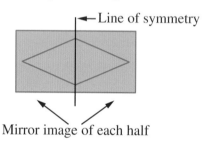

Line of symmetry

Mirror image of each half

 CLASS ACTIVITY 1

Objective: To identify objects that have reflection symmetry.

1. Look at these objects. Which objects have reflection symmetry? If an object has reflection symmetry, sketch it and draw its line or lines of symmetry.

    (a) Butterfly

    (b) Domino

    (c) Propeller

    (d) Cracker

2. Look around your classroom and identify two plane figures that have reflection symmetry. Sketch each shape with its line or lines of symmetry.

Objective: To explore reflection symmetry.
Resources: Geometry software, tracing paper.

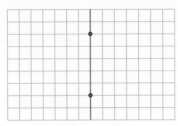

Diagram 1

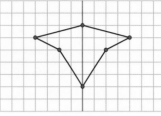

Diagram 2

Diagram 3

1. **(a)** Use geometry software to draw a vertical line in the centre of the screen. This line will be a line of symmetry. See Diagram 1.

   (b) Use line tools to draw a simple design on the right of the line. See Diagram 2.

   (c) Use the reflection symmetry tool to reflect the design in the line to get its image on the left. See Diagram 3.

   (d) Create another design by repeating Steps **(a)** to **(c)**.

   (e) What is different about your two designs? What is the same?

2.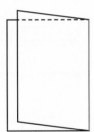

   Diagram 4   Diagram 5   Diagram 6

   (a) Fold the tracing paper into two halves. See Diagram 4.

   (b) Draw your own design on one half. An example is shown in Diagram 5.

   (c) Flip over the paper and copy your design on to the other half. This is called the **image** of your design.

   (d) Open the paper and lie it flat. See Diagram 6.

   (e) What do you notice about your design and its image?

Example 1

How many lines of symmetry does each of these regular polygons have?

(a)

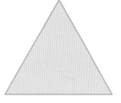

Equilateral triangle

(b)

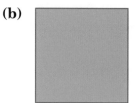

Square

Solution

(a)

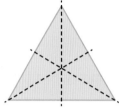

An equilateral triangle has 3 lines of symmetry.

(b)

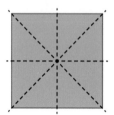

A square has 4 lines of symmetry.

When you fold the shape in half along its line of symmetry, the two halves will match each other.

Try It! 1

How many lines of symmetry does each of these regular polygons have?

(a)

Regular pentagon

(b)

Regular hexagon

Example 2 What is the name of each of these figures? How many lines of symmetry does each one have?

(a)

(b)

(c)

Solution **(a)**

The parallelogram has 0 lines of symmetry.

(b)

The hexagon has 2 lines of symmetry.

(c)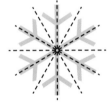

The snowflake has 6 lines of symmetry.

DISCUSS

Cut a parallelogram from a piece of paper. Fold the parallelogram along a diagonal. Do the two halves divided by the diagonal overlap each other?

What happens if you do the same with a rhombus? Explain your observation.

Try It! 2 How many lines of symmetry does each of these figures have?

(a)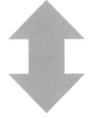

(b)

(c)

REMARK

You may use tracing and folding to check reflection symmetry.

Example 3

Copy and complete these drawings so that they are symmetrical about the dotted line. Do your new shapes have any other lines of symmetry?

(a) 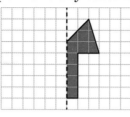 **(b)**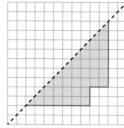

Solution **(a)** 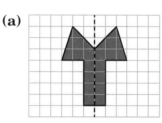 **(b)**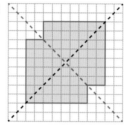

Shape **(a)** has no other lines of symmetry. Shape **(b)** has 1 more line of symmetry, as shown in red.

Try It! 3

Copy and complete these drawings so that they are symmetrical about the dotted line. Do your new shapes have any other lines of symmetry?

(a) 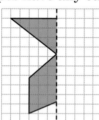 **(b)**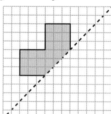

✏️ **REMARK**

You can rotate your paper to help you complete the shape.

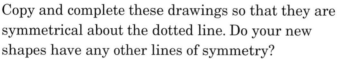

PRACTICE 9.1 🧩

⚙️ **LEVEL 1**

1. Copy each figure and draw its line or lines of symmetry. You may use tracing paper. State how many lines of symmetry each figure has.

   (a)  **(b)** **(c)**

2. Write each letter and draw its line(s) of symmetry.

   (a) H **(b)** A **(c)** X

3. How many letters of the alphabet have at least one line of symmetry?

4. State the number of lines of symmetry of each road sign.

(a)   (b)   (c)

5. Copy each figure and draw its line(s) of symmetry. State how many lines of symmetry each figure has.

(a)  (b)   (c)

6. Write a three-letter word using capital letters. The word should have one line of symmetry.
   Hint: For example, BOX.

7. What is the largest number you can write in digits which has one line of symmetry and in which every digit is different?

8. Copy and complete these drawings so that they are symmetrical about the dotted line.

(a) 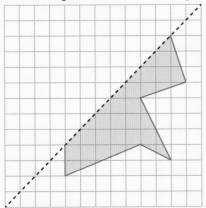 (b)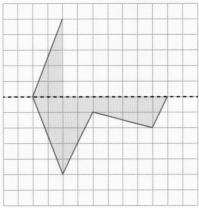

9. Copy each figure and shade one small square so that the figure will have only one line of symmetry. Draw the line of symmetry. Is there more than one choice of square?

(a) 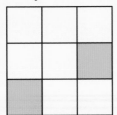 (b)

10. Can you draw a four-sided shape with the following numbers of lines of symmetry?
    (a) 0, (b) 1, (c) 2, (d) 3, (e) 4.

Workbook 1A Link
Exercise 9.1

249

9.2 Rotation Symmetry of Plane Figures

Some shapes can be rotated through an angle less than 360° and map onto themselves. The point around which you rotate the shape is called the **centre of rotation**. Let's look at a rectangle where the chosen centre of rotation is the intersection of its diagonals.

The green rectangle has two blue dots marked on it. Trace the outline of the rectangle in red colouring pencil onto tracing paper and also trace the blue dot in the top right and bottom left corners, as shown below. Hold down the tracing paper with a pencil at the centre of rotation and turn the paper.

By how many degrees does the paper need to be rotated for the rectangle to map onto itself?

REMARK

You can choose any point as the centre of rotation, but rotational symmetry only works around a specific point. For flat (2D) shapes, you can usually say this is at the centre of the shape.

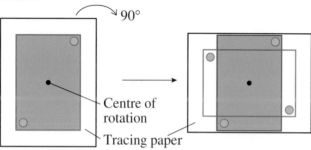

If you turn the tracing paper 90° clockwise about the centre of rotation, the traced rectangle does not overlap with the green rectangle.

REMARK

A 90° rotation is also called a **quarter turn**. A 180° rotation is a **half turn**, and a 360° rotation is a **full turn**.

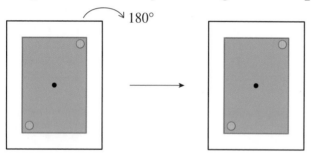

If you turn the tracing paper 180° clockwise, the traced rectangle overlaps with the original rectangle. You can see that the blue dots are in the same positions. The rectangle is said to **map onto itself**. When a shape can be mapped onto itself by a rotation of less than 360°, you say that it has **rotation symmetry**. Hence, the rectangle has rotation symmetry. All rectangles have rotation symmetry. This is because they have two pairs of sides of equal length.

DISCUSS

Imagine that the top left corner is labelled as '1'. Discuss with your classmates where the labelled corner would be after each rotation.

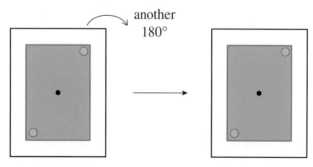

Now turn the tracing paper another 180° clockwise. The rectangle maps onto itself again.

DISCUSS

Would you see the same result if you rotate the rectangle anticlockwise?

The number of times a shape maps onto itself in a 360° rotation is called the **order of rotation symmetry**. The order of rotation symmetry of a rectangle is 2.

When a shape maps onto itself only once after a full turn (that is, not until the full turn is complete), it has **no rotation symmetry**.

 **CLASS ACTIVITY 3**

Objective: To determine the order of rotation symmetry.

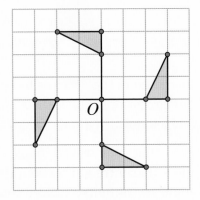

1. Draw the diagram consisting of four flags using geometry software.

2. Does the diagram have reflection symmetry?

3. Copy the table and complete it by using the rotation tool to rotate the diagram about a centre of rotation at point O.

Angle of rotation	Does the image map onto the original? (Yes/No)
30° anticlockwise about point O	
45° anticlockwise about point O	
90° anticlockwise about point O	

4. Using trial and error, find all angles up to rotation 360° about the point O, where the image maps onto itself. Continue the table above to show what you have found.

5. What is the order of rotation symmetry of the diagram about point O?

6. Can you draw a diagram with flags that has rotation symmetry of order 2 and no reflection symmetry? Mark the centre of rotation on your diagram.

7. Can you draw a diagram with flags that has rotation symmetry of order 3 and no reflection symmetry? Mark the centre of rotation on your diagram.

8. Can you draw a diagram with flags that has rotation symmetry of order 4 and 4 lines of symmetry? Mark the centre of rotation on your diagram.

Example ④

What is the order of rotation symmetry of each of these shapes?

(a)

Equilateral triangle

(b)

Regular pentagon

(c)

Regular hexagon

(d)

Solution

(a) Trace the triangle and label the vertices to help you keep track of the rotations. Mark the centre of rotation with a black dot.

You can see from rotating your traced image that in one full turn about its centre of rotation, the equilateral triangle maps onto itself three times.

The equilateral triangle has rotation symmetry of order 3. Therefore, the angle of rotation to map the equilateral triangle onto itself is $360° \div 3 = 120°$.

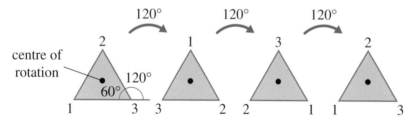

(b) Draw the shape onto tracing paper, mark the centre of rotation, and rotate it about this point. You can see that in one full turn, the regular pentagon maps onto itself five times.

The regular pentagon has rotation symmetry of order 5. Therefore, the angle of rotation to map the regular pentagon onto itself is $360° \div 5 = 72°$.

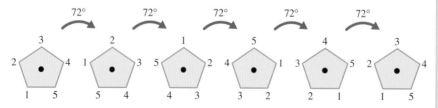

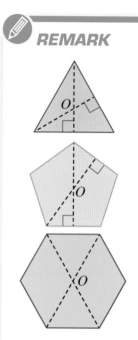
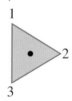

(c) In one full turn about the chosen centre of rotation, the regular hexagon maps onto itself six times.

The regular hexagon has rotation symmetry of order 6. Therefore, the angle of rotation to map the regular hexagon onto itself is $360° ÷ 6 = 60°$.

DISCUSS

Would the regular hexagon map onto itself if you rotated it 45° or 90°? Why not?

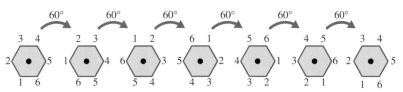

(d)

The shape maps onto itself only once in one full turn. It has no rotation symmetry.

Try It! 4

What is the order of rotation symmetry of each of these shapes?

(a)

Four-arrow shape

(b)

Single arrow

REMARK

If the image is simple to trace, you can copy it onto tracing paper and rotate the image to help you work out the order of rotation symmetry.

(c)

Car logo

(d)

Regular octagon

Example 5

For each of these figures, state the number of lines of symmetry and the order of rotation symmetry.

(a)

(b)

(c)

Continued

Solution

(a) The road-sign has no lines of symmetry.

The road-sign maps onto itself twice in one full turn about the centre of rotation shown.

It has rotation symmetry of order 2. Therefore, the angle of rotation to map this road-sign onto itself is 360° ÷ 2 = 180°.

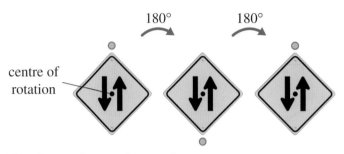

(b) The figure has no lines of symmetry.

The figure maps onto itself three times in one full turn about the centre of rotation shown.

It has rotation symmetry of order 3. Therefore, the angle of rotation to map this figure onto itself is 360° ÷ 3 = 120°.

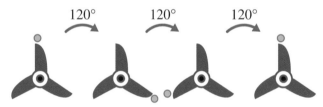

(c) The figure has 5 lines of symmetry.

The figure maps onto itself five times in one full turn about the centre of rotation shown.

It has rotation symmetry of order 5. Therefore, the angle of rotation to map this figure onto itself is 360° ÷ 5 = 72°.

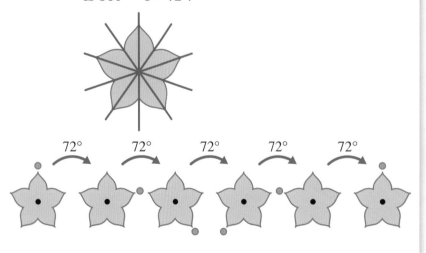

For each of these figures, state the number of lines of symmetry and the order of rotation symmetry.

(a)

(b)

(c)

B

DISCUSS

What should the centre of rotation be for each of these images? For each image, discuss whether it matters where you place the centre of rotation.

PRACTICE 9.2

LEVEL 1

Use tracing paper to help you work out the order of rotation symmetry of each figure.

1. For each of these figures, state the order of rotation symmetry.

   Hint: Remember that dashes at the centre of each side of a shape mean that the sides are equal length.

   (a)

   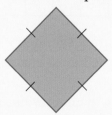

   (b)

   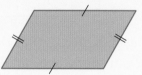

   (c)

2. For each of these figures, state the order of rotation symmetry.

   (a)

   (b)

   (c)

3. State the number of lines of symmetry and the order of rotation symmetry for each figure.

   (a)

   (b)

   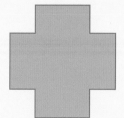

   (c)

   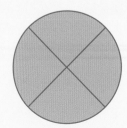

4. State the order of rotation symmetry of each letter.

(a)

(b)

(c)

5. State the number of lines of symmetry and the order of rotation symmetry of each logo.

(a) Recycle

(b) Railway

(c) Radioactive

6. Copy each figure twice.

(i)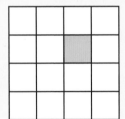

(ii)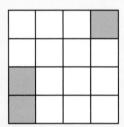

(iii)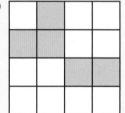

(a) Shade one small square on each figure so that the figure has rotation symmetry.

(b) On which of the figures can you shade one small square so that the figure has rotation symmetry but not reflection symmetry?

(c) Shade two small squares on each figure so that there is reflection symmetry but no rotation symmetry.

7. Use some arrows ⟶ to create a shape which has

OPEN QUESTION

(a) rotation symmetry of order 3 but not reflection symmetry,

(b) rotation symmetry and reflection symmetry,

(c) neither reflection symmetry nor rotation symmetry.

8. Use drawing software to create a logo which has rotation symmetry of order

OPEN QUESTION

(a) 2,

(b) 3,

(c) 4.

Workbook 1A Link
Exercise 9.2

Reflection Symmetry

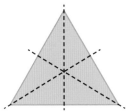

- This equilateral triangle can be divided into two identical halves by a straight line. Each half is the mirror image of the other in the line. This figure is said to have **reflection symmetry**.

- The line is called a **line of symmetry** or a **mirror line**.

- This equilateral triangle has 3 lines of symmetry.

Symmetry

Rotation Symmetry

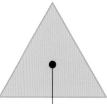

Centre of rotation

- A shape has **rotation symmetry** if it maps onto itself more than once in a full turn about a given centre of rotation.

- The **order of rotation symmetry** is the number of times it maps onto itself in a 360° rotation.

- This equilateral triangle has rotation symmetry of order 3.

CHALLENGE 9

The figure shows a regular hexagon with six identical triangles. Each triangle has equal sides and angles.

Use tracing paper to copy this figure four times. On each figure, shade exactly two triangles so that the resulting figure will have

(a) one line of symmetry,

(b) two lines of symmetry,

(c) rotation symmetry of order 3,

(d) reflection symmetry but no rotation symmetry.

Workbook 1A Link
Problem Solving 9

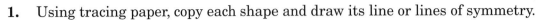

1. Using tracing paper, copy each shape and draw its line or lines of symmetry.

    (a)
    (b)
    (c)

2. Write down the order of rotation symmetry of each shape.

    (a)
    (b)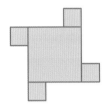
    (c)

3. For each of these figures, state the number of lines of symmetry and the order of rotation symmetry.

    (a)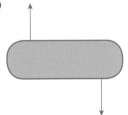
    (b)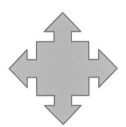
    (c)

4. Which letter or letters from the word SWIFT have
    (a) reflection symmetry only,   **(b)** rotation symmetry only,
    (c) both reflection and rotation symmetry,   **(d)** no symmetry?

5. For each item, if it has reflection symmetry, write down its number of lines of symmetry. If it has rotation symmetry, write down its order of rotation symmetry.

    (a) Photo frame   **(b)** Circular dish   **(c)** Fork

6. Describe the symmetry of these signs.

(a) Peace

(b) Danger

(c) Pharmacy

7. Copy and complete these drawings so that they are symmetrical about the dotted line. State the order of rotation symmetry of each completed figure.

(a)

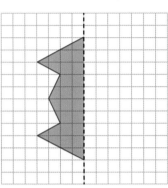

(b)

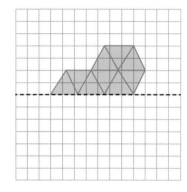

8. Copy and complete this drawing so that it is symmetrical about the dotted line. State whether the completed figure has rotation symmetry.

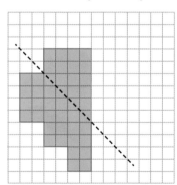

Write in Your Journal

1. If a shape has rotation symmetry of order 3, must it have reflection symmetry?
2. If a shape has 3 lines of symmetry, must it have rotation symmetry of order 3?

Explain your answers to these questions with diagrams.

10 PERIMETER AND AREA OF RECTANGLES SQUARES AND TRIANGLES

WHAT IS IN THIS CHAPTER:

10.1 Perimeter of Squares and Rectangles

10.2 Area of Squares and Rectangles

10.3 Perimeter and Area of Triangles

Sam likes to ride his bike at the local park. Sam wants to find out how far he rides in one lap. The cycle track is a rectangle that is 200m long and 100m wide. He can find out the length of one lap by working out the perimeter of the rectangle.

LET'S LEARN TO

▶ find the perimeter of squares, rectangles and triangles

▶ calculate the area of squares, rectangles and triangles

1. Perimeter and Area

(a) The **perimeter** of a plane figure is the length of its boundary. The unit of perimeter is usually cm or m.

(b) The **area** of a plane figure is the amount of space enclosed by the boundary of the figure. The unit of area is usually cm² (square centimetre) or m² (square metre).

REMARK

A plane figure is a two-dimensional object.

2. Perpendicular Lines

Two lines are perpendicular if they intersect (cross each other) at 90°. An angle that is 90° is also called a right angle.

You mark a right angle with the symbol ∟.

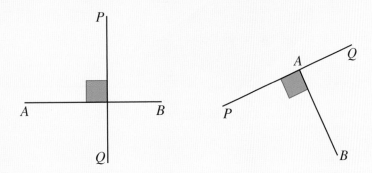

In each diagram, the lines AB and PQ are perpendicular. The symbol $\perp$ shows that two lines are perpendicular. So for both of these diagrams you can write $AB \perp PQ$.

3. Types of Triangles

Triangles can be classified according to the lengths of their sides.

(a) Scalene
(no sides are equal)

(b) Isosceles
(two sides are equal)

(c) Equilateral
(all sides are equal)

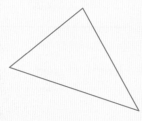

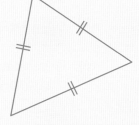

You indicate two or more equal sides on any shape by drawing an equal number of dashes at the centre of those sides.

REMARK

In geometry, when two sides or two line segments are of equal length, you can say the sides or line segments are equal.

10.1 Perimeter of Squares and Rectangles

You are going to measure the length of the outline of a cover of a book and see how different shapes can be made with the same outline.

 CLASS ACTIVITY 1

Objective: To investigate the outlines of different shapes.

1. Measure the length and width of this textbook. Copy and complete the table below.

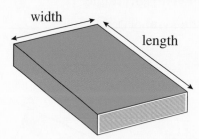

Book length		cm
Book width		cm
Length of outline = length + length + width + width		cm
$2 \times$ length + $2 \times$ width		cm

2. Draw around the outline of the book. Put a drawing pin in each corner of the outline and then take a piece of string and lay it over the outline. Make sure the start and end of the string meet, with no overlap and no gaps. Cut the string so that it is the same length as the length of the outline.

   (a) Make a shape using the string as the outline on a piece of card. Fix the corners of the shape by sticking some drawing pins on the card. Sketch the shape. Make more shapes in this way. What is the relationship between these shapes and the outline of the book?

   (b) Form a square using the string. What is the length of each side of the square?

   (c) Form an equilateral triangle using the string. What is the length of each side of the triangle?

The **perimeter** of a closed figure is the total length of its outline. For a rectangle, the perimeter is **twice the sum of the length and width**.

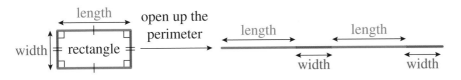

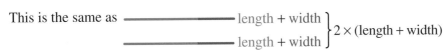

For a rectangle, perimeter = 2 × (length + width).

For a square, perimeter = 4 × length.

Example ① Find the perimeter of each of these figures.

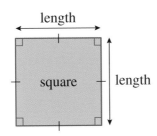

(a) 12 cm

square

(b) 25 cm

rectangle   9 cm

Solution **(a)** Perimeter of the square
= 4 × 12
= 48 cm

(b) Perimeter of the rectangle
= 2 × (25 + 9)
= 2 × 34
= 68 cm

 **DISCUSS**

How else can you work out the perimeter of the rectangle?

Try It! ① Find the perimeter of each of these figures.

(a)   18 cm

7 cm   rectangle

(b) 16 cm

square

Example 2

Given the perimeter, find the unknown length in each of these figures.

(a) Perimeter = 66 cm   (b) Perimeter = 84 cm

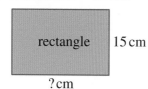

Solution

(a) Draw a bar model to show the perimeter of the rectangle:

Perimeter = 66 cm

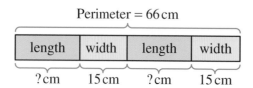

Taking only half of this:

Half of perimeter = 66 ÷ 2 = 33 cm

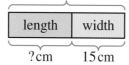

Length + width = 33

Length + 15 = 33

Length = 33 – width

= 33 – 15

= 18 cm

(b) Using a bar model to show the perimeter of the square:

Perimeter = 84 cm

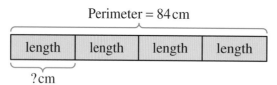

Perimeter = 4 × length

4 × length = 84

Length = 84 ÷ 4

= 21 cm

Try It! 2

Given the perimeter, find the unknown length in each of these figures.

(a) Perimeter = 84 cm   (b) Perimeter = 76 m

Example ❸

A 24 m by 13 m rectangular area on the ground has just been covered with fresh concrete. To prevent people from stepping on the wet concrete, a tape is tied around the four poles standing at the corners. Assuming no overlap, what is the length of tape required?

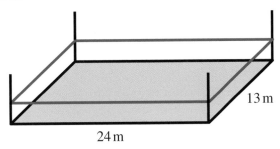

24 m

13 m

Solution

Perimeter of the enclosed ground = 2 × (24 + 13)
$$= 2 \times 37$$
$$= 74 \text{ m}$$

Therefore, 74 m of tape is required.

> **DISCUSS**
>
> What different strategies are there for calculating 2 × 37? Which one do you prefer?

Try It! ❸

A school playground is shaped like a rectangle and measures 50 m by 25 m. A child walks all the way around the outer edge of the playground. Calculate the total distance the child has walked.

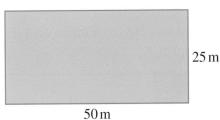

25 m

50 m

PRACTICE 10.1 🧩

⚙ LEVEL 1

1. Find the perimeter of each of these figures. Draw a bar model to explain your reasoning.

(a)

15 cm

7 cm

(b)

 9 m

15 m

(c)

11 cm

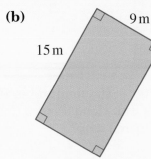

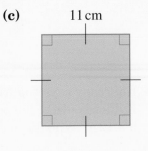

2. Find the length of the unknown side in each of these figures. Draw a bar model to explain your reasoning.

(a)

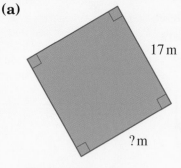

17 m

? m

Perimeter = 64 m

(b)

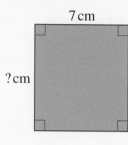

7 cm

? cm

Perimeter = 32 cm

(c)

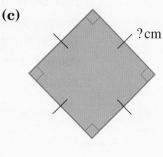

? cm

Perimeter = 68 cm

LEVEL 2

If the question does not have a diagram, it can help you visualise the problem if you draw your own diagram.

3. A rectangular football pitch measures 105 m by 68 m. Work out the perimeter of the football pitch.

4. A rectangular vegetable plot has a perimeter of 80 m and a length of 30 m. Find the width of the plot.

5. A piece of wire is bent into the shape of a square of side length 24 cm. What is the length of the piece of wire?

6. Two square bathroom tiles are placed next to each other and have a perimeter of 96 cm. Find the side length of one bathroom tile.

PROBLEM SOLVING

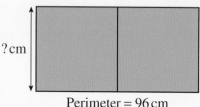

? cm

Perimeter = 96 cm

7. A shopping centre has a square fountain with a statue on a square platform in the middle. The fountain measures 3 m by 3 m and the platform measures 1 m by 1 m.

PROBLEM SOLVING

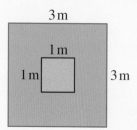

3 m

1 m

1 m

3 m

Kourtney says that the perimeter of the fountain is 16 m.
Kylie says that the perimeter is 8 m. Kendall says that
it's 12 m. Who do you agree with, and why?

Workbook 1A Link
Exercise 10.1

10.2 Area of Squares and Rectangles

The **area** of a plane figure is the amount of space enclosed by the boundary of a figure. Let's recall how the area of a rectangle and the area of a square are calculated.

Look at this rectangle with length 7 cm and width 3 cm.

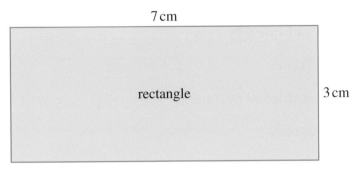

Picture this rectangle as being made up of small 1 cm by 1 cm squares. There are 7 small squares across the length and 3 small squares across the width.

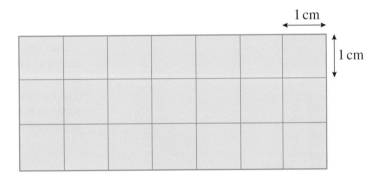

You can now find the area of the whole rectangle by counting the number of small 1 cm by 1 cm squares enclosed by the boundary. There are 21 squares, each with an area of 1 cm². So the area of the whole rectangle is 21 cm².

You may consider the whole rectangle is made up of 3 rows of 7 small 1 cm by 1 cm squares or 7 columns of 3 small 1 cm by 1 cm squares. In other words, the rectangle contains 3 lots of 7 cm² or 7 lots of 3 cm² squares.

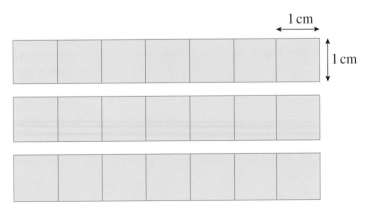

REMARK

The area of a square of side 1 cm is 1 square centimetre, denoted by 1 cm².

The area of a square of side 1 m is 1 square metre, denoted by 1 m².

REMARK

Area is measured in square units such as mm², cm² or m². You can say either 'square centimetres' or 'centimetres squared'. (The same is true for millimetres and metres.)

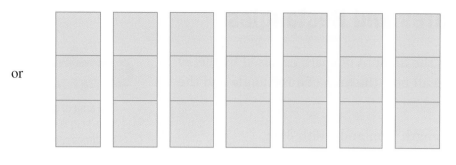

or

REMARK

Use the multiplication table on page 359 to check the value of 3×7.

3 lots of $7\,\text{cm}^2$ is another way of saying 3 multiplied by $7\,\text{cm}^2$,

so the area of the rectangle $= 3 \times 7\,\text{cm}^2 = 21\,\text{cm}^2$.

7 lots of $3\,\text{cm}^2$ is another way of saying 7 multiplied by $3\,\text{cm}^2$,

so the area of the rectangle $= 7 \times 3\,\text{cm}^2 = 21\,\text{cm}^2$.

Notice that the calculations $3 \times 7\,\text{cm}^2$ and $7 \times 3\,\text{cm}^2$ each give the answer $21\,\text{cm}^2$, and you also get this answer from the product $7\,\text{cm} \times 3\,\text{cm}$.

The above result can be generalised by the following formula.

> For a rectangle, area = length × width

REMARK

You can also write this as area of a rectangle = width × length. This is an example of the **commutative** law of multiplication.

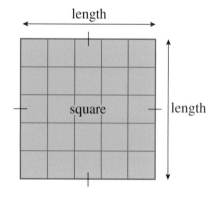

Here the square has sides of length $5\,\text{cm}$. The boundary of the square encloses 5 lots of 5 smaller squares, each with an area of $1\,\text{cm}^2$.

Therefore the area of the square $= 5 \times 5$

$$= 25\,\text{cm}^2$$

> For a square, since the lengths of all the sides are the same,
> area = length × length.

REMARK

Try counting the number of smaller squares in rows, and then again in columns. There are 5 lots of 5, so 25 squares, which is the same result as calculating the number of squares by multiplication.

Objective: To understand the concept of the area of squares and rectangles.

A shopping centre is organising an indoor market.

The area allocated for each stall is a 2 m by 1 m rectangle. The floor plan of the space used for the indoor market is shown below. Every square on the plan represents an actual length of 1 m by 1 m.

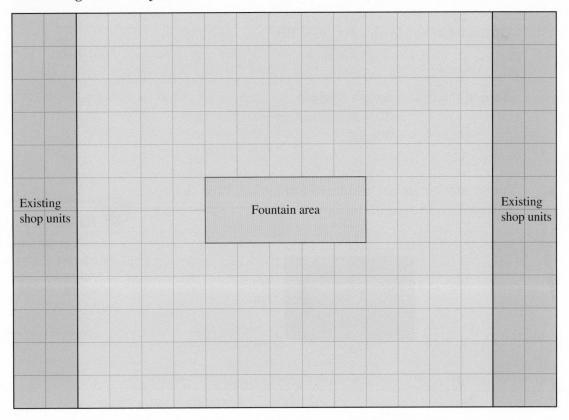

Stalls can only be set up in the grey shaded area around the middle – they can't be placed over the fountain or over the green area, where there are shops already.

There should be a distance of 1 m between the stalls, the fountain area and the existing shops, and stalls must be placed directly over the grey squares (without overlapping the lines). The rental fee for each stall is £50.

1. Imagine you own the shopping centre. Discuss with your classmates how you can place as many stalls as possible so that you can charge the most rent. Copy the diagram and then draw the stalls on it to show your final layout.

2. Repeat Question **1** using all the same rules as before, except the stalls can be any shape of area exactly 5 m².

Note: For an extra challenge, work out how much rent you would receive in each question above.

Example 4

A rectangular school field has a length of 30 m and width of 12 m. Find the perimeter and area of the field.

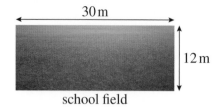

school field

Solution

Perimeter of the field = 2 × (30 + 12)
                       = 2 × 42
                       = 84 m

Area of the field = length × width
                  = 30 × 12
                  = 360 m²

Try It! 4

A rectangular carpet measures 5 m by 3 m. Find the perimeter and area of the carpet.

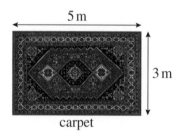

carpet

REMARK

Remember that you can re-draw the carpet with 5 columns and 3 rows, to help you with this question.

Example 5

A square tile has a length of 30 cm. The floor of a room is completely covered with 50 of these tiles. What is the area of the floor?

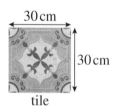

tile

Solution

Area of one tile = length × length
                 = 30 × 30
                 = 900 cm²

Area of 50 tiles = 900 × 50
                 = 45 000 cm²

Therefore, the area of the floor is 45 000 cm².

A tile in the shape of a square has a length of 40 cm.
A wall is covered completely with 100 of these tiles.
What is the area of the wall?

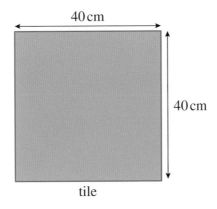

40 cm

40 cm

tile

Example 6

The area of a rectangular card is 132 cm². If the length of the card is 12 cm, what is the width of the card?

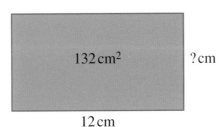

132 cm²   ? cm

12 cm

Solution

Area of card = length × width
$$132 \text{ cm}^2 = 12 \text{ cm} \times \text{width}$$
Width = 132 ÷ 12
= 11 cm

Inverse relationship between multiplication and division.

Try It! 6

The top face of a rectangular box has a width of 8 cm. If the area of the top face is 80 cm², find the length of the face.

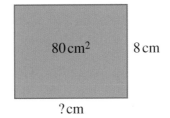

80 cm²   8 cm

? cm

REMARK

Use the division table on page 359 to check the value of 132 ÷ 12.

RECALL

Inverse relationship between multiplication and division:
if
number 1 = number 2 × number 3,
then
number 3 = number 1 ÷ number 2
and
number 2 = number 1 ÷ number 3.

You can represent these relationships in a diagram:

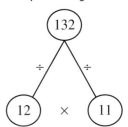

PRACTICE 10.2

LEVEL 1

1. Find the area of each of these figures.

(a)
6 cm
3 cm

(b)
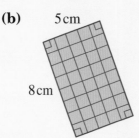
5 cm
8 cm

(c)
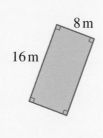
8 m
16 m

(d)
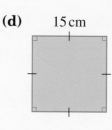
15 cm

2. Find the length of the unknown side in each of these rectangles.

(a)
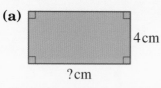
4 cm
? cm
Area = 28 cm²

(b)

6 cm
? cm
Area = 108 cm²

(c)
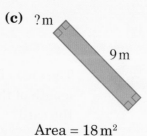
? m
9 m
Area = 18 m²

LEVEL 2

Remember you can draw a diagram if it helps you to visualise the question.

3. The length of a square card is 14 cm. Find the area of the card.

4. A rectangle has length 15 m and you want to find its width. Its area is 75 m². Copy and complete this calculation:

Width = _____ ÷ _____

= _____

5. The rectangular cover of a textbook has an area of 432 cm². Find the length of the cover if the width is 18 cm.

6. A rectangular wall tile is 25 cm by 10 cm. It takes 240 of these tiles to tile a wall. What is the area of the wall?

7. A square plot of land is worth £2000 per square metre. The length of the plot of land is 10 m. Logan thinks the land is worth £20 000, but Jake thinks it's worth £200 000. Which of them do you think is correct, and why?

£
FINANCE

8. A living room is 10 m by 6 m. The cost of carpet is £34 per square metre. What is the cost of carpet for the whole living room?

£
FINANCE

> **Workbook 1A Link**
> Exercise 10.2

10.3 Perimeter and Area of Triangles

A triangle has three sides. The perimeter of a triangle therefore is the sum of the lengths of its three sides.

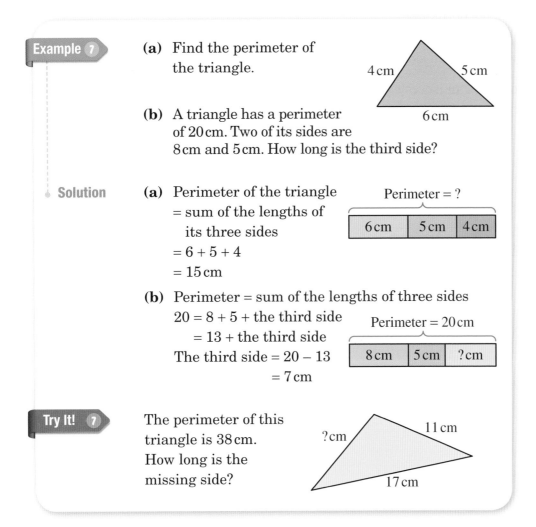

Example 7

(a) Find the perimeter of the triangle.

(b) A triangle has a perimeter of 20 cm. Two of its sides are 8 cm and 5 cm. How long is the third side?

Solution

(a) Perimeter of the triangle
= sum of the lengths of its three sides
= 6 + 5 + 4
= 15 cm

Perimeter = ?

| 6 cm | 5 cm | 4 cm |

(b) Perimeter = sum of the lengths of three sides
20 = 8 + 5 + the third side
= 13 + the third side
The third side = 20 − 13
= 7 cm

Perimeter = 20 cm

| 8 cm | 5 cm | ? cm |

Try It! 7

The perimeter of this triangle is 38 cm. How long is the missing side?

Remember from the start of this chapter that an isosceles triangle has two equal sides. An equilateral triangle has three equal sides.

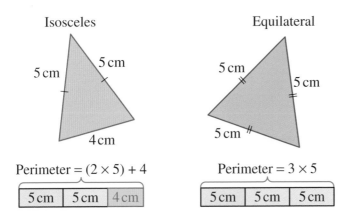

Isosceles

Perimeter = (2 × 5) + 4

| 5 cm | 5 cm | 4 cm |

Equilateral

Perimeter = 3 × 5

| 5 cm | 5 cm | 5 cm |

Example 8

(a) A flag is an isosceles triangle. The side touching the pole is 10 cm long. The other two equal sides are each 15 cm long. What is the perimeter of the flag?

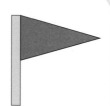

(b) An equilateral triangle has a perimeter of 30 cm. How long is each side?

Solution

(a) The flag is an isosceles triangle, so
Perimeter = (2 × length of one equal side)
            + the length of the third side
         = (2 × 15) + 10
         = 30 + 10
         = 40 cm

(b)

For an equilateral triangle,
        Perimeter = 3 × length of one side
             30 = 3 × length of one side
Length of one side = 30 ÷ 3
                   = 10 cm

Try It! 8

(a) One face of a building is an equilateral triangle of side length 80 m. Find the perimeter of the face.

(b) An isosceles triangle has a perimeter of 36 cm. The unequal side is 10 cm long. How long is each of the two equal sides?

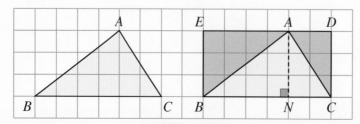

You are now going to find out how the area of a triangle is related to the area of a rectangle.

CLASS ACTIVITY 3

Objective: To explore the area of a triangle.

1. (a) Using a ruler, draw triangle *ABC* on a piece of square grid paper.

   (b) Draw a rectangle *EBCD* around *ABC* as shown. Cut out *EBCD*.

(c) Fold along the line AB. Then fold along the line AC.

 (i) What is the relationship between triangles ABN and BAE?

 (ii) What is the relationship between triangles CAN and CAD?

 (iii) What can you say about the area of triangle ABC and the area of the rectangle $EBCD$? Explain your answer.

2. Draw three more triangles and repeat the steps above. See if you notice the same results when you draw different types of triangles.

3.

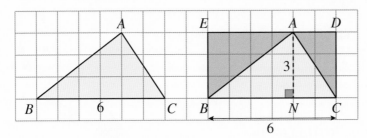

> **REMARK**
>
> Letters can be used to label a diagram so that it is easier to refer to its vertices, sides and angles.

If $\triangle ABC$ has lengths $BC = 6$ cm and $AN = 3$ cm,

(a) Area of $EBCD$ = length × width

$$= \underline{\hspace{1cm}} \times \underline{\hspace{1cm}}$$

$$= \underline{\hspace{1cm}} \text{ cm}^2$$

> **REMARK**
>
> Triangle ABC can be denoted by $\triangle ABC$ (a small triangle symbol and the letters of the vertices).

(b) Area of $\triangle ABC = \frac{1}{2} \times$ area of the rectangle

$$= \frac{1}{2} \times \underline{\hspace{1cm}}$$

$$= \underline{\hspace{1cm}} \text{ cm}^2$$

4.

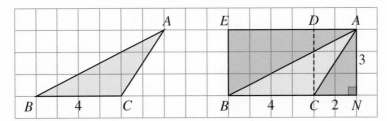

The diagram shows a triangle ABC with $BC = 4$ cm and $AN = 3$ cm. The rectangle $AEBN$ is added to it in order to find the area of the triangle. Copy and complete the working below.

(a) Area of $\triangle ABN = \frac{1}{2} \times$ area of the rectangle $AEBN$

$$= \frac{1}{2} \times BN \times \underline{\hspace{1cm}}$$

$$= \frac{1}{2} \times 6 \times \underline{\hspace{1cm}}$$

$$= \underline{\hspace{1cm}} \text{ cm}^2$$

(b) Area of $\triangle ACN = \dfrac{1}{2} \times$ area of the rectangle _____

$$= \dfrac{1}{2} \times CN \times \text{_____}$$

$$= \dfrac{1}{2} \times 2 \times \text{_____}$$

$$= \text{_____} \text{ cm}^2$$

(c) Area of $\triangle ABC =$ Area of $\triangle ABN - \text{_____}$

$$= \text{_____} - \text{_____}$$

$$= \text{_____} \text{ cm}^2$$

(d) Can you work out the area of $\triangle ABC$ using the lengths of BC and AN directly?

As you discovered in Class Activity 3, the area of a triangle is half the area of the enclosing rectangle. This means you can find the area of a triangle using the formula $\dfrac{1}{2} \times$ length of enclosing rectangle $\times$ width of enclosing rectangle.

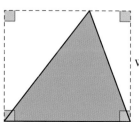

width of rectangle

length of rectangle

You can make a more general formula for the area of a triangle without needing to draw the enclosing rectangle every time. In this picture, the **base** of the triangle is equal to the length of the rectangle and the **perpendicular height** of the triangle is equal to the width of the rectangle.

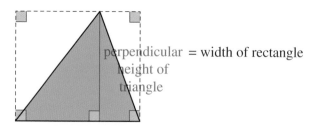

perpendicular = width of rectangle height of triangle

base of triangle = length of rectangle

The perpendicular height of a triangle is the perpendicular drawn from the opposite vertex to the base.

Area of a triangle $= \dfrac{1}{2} \times$ base $\times$ perpendicular height

You can use this formula for any triangle. If the triangle is a right-angled triangle, both the base and the perpendicular height can be sides of the triangle.

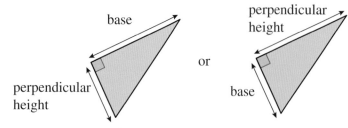

base

perpendicular height

or

perpendicular height

base

For any triangle, the base can be any of the three sides. The perpendicular height can lie inside or outside of the triangle, as long as it is perpendicular to the chosen base.

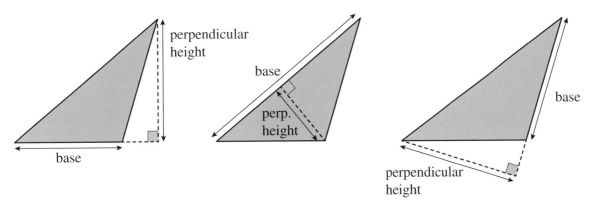

You can now practise identifying a base and the corresponding perpendicular height in different triangles.

CLASS ACTIVITY 4

Objective: To identify the base and the perpendicular height in a triangle.

1. Identify two different possible bases on each triangle and the corresponding perpendicular height to each base.

   (a)

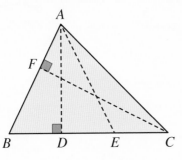

   (b)

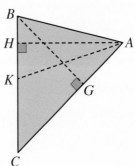

   (c)

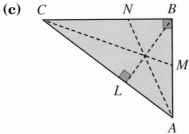

   (d)

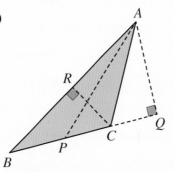

2. Use tracing paper to copy each triangle PQR and draw the perpendicular height to the base PQ.

   (a)

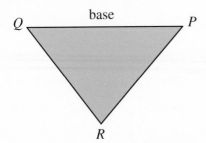

   (b)

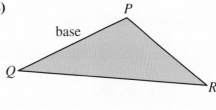

3. For each triangle identify the base corresponding to the perpendicular height *XN*.

(a)

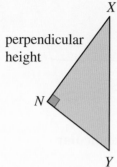

perpendicular height

(b)

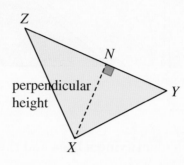

perpendicular height

Example ⑨

Find the area of each of these triangles.

(a)

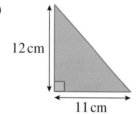

12 cm
11 cm

(b)

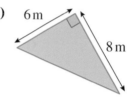

6 m
8 m

Solution

(a) Area of triangle $= \frac{1}{2} \times$ base $\times$ perpendicular height

$$= \frac{1}{2} \times 11 \times 12$$

$$= \frac{1}{2} \times 132$$

$$= 66\,\text{cm}^2$$

(b) Area of triangle $= \frac{1}{2} \times$ base $\times$ perpendicular height

$$= \frac{1}{2} \times 6 \times 8$$

$$= 3 \times 8$$

$$= 24\,\text{m}^2$$

Try It! ⑨

Find the area of each of these triangles.

(a)

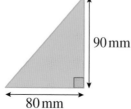

90 mm
80 mm

(b)

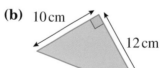

10 cm
12 cm

REMARK

Remember to start by identifying a base and its corresponding perpendicular height.

REMARK

To get the right answer, it doesn't matter if you multiply by a half at the start or at the end. Note that in example **(a)**, you multiply by $\frac{1}{2}$ at the end, but in example **(b)**, you multiply by $\frac{1}{2}$ at the start. Be careful though, you cannot multiply every number by a half:

$$\frac{1}{2} \times 4 \times 8 = 2 \times 8 \quad ✓$$

NOT

$$\frac{1}{2} \times 4 \times 8 = 2 \times 4 \quad ✗$$

Example 10

(a) Raheem says that the area of this triangle is given by $\frac{1}{2} \times 12 \times 8$. Marcus says it's actually $\frac{1}{2} \times 12 \times 10$. Explain who is correct and calculate the area of the triangle.

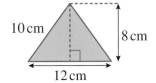

(b) Find the area of $\triangle PQR$.

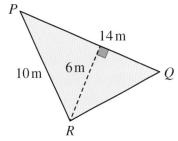

(a) You need to use the base and the perpendicular height to calculate the area of a triangle.

If the base of the triangle is 12 cm, then the perpendicular height must make a right angle with this side. So the perpendicular height is 8 cm, not 10 cm. So Raheem is correct.

$$\text{Area of the triangle} = \frac{1}{2} \times 12 \times 8$$
$$= 48 \, \text{cm}^2$$

(b) Area of the triangle

$$= \frac{1}{2} \times \text{base} \times \text{perpendicular height}$$
$$= \frac{1}{2} \times 14 \times 6$$
$$= 42 \, \text{m}^2$$

(a) Find the area of this triangle.

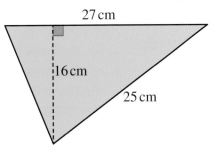

(b) Serena thinks that the area of $\triangle ABC$ is given by $\frac{1}{2} \times 3 \times 7$. Her sister Venus thinks that actually it's given by $\frac{1}{2} \times 5 \times 7$.

Which of the sisters do you think is right? Explain why the other one is wrong.

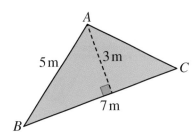

(a) Find the area of this shaded triangle.

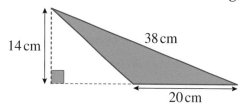

(b) The area of $\triangle ABC$ is $24\,cm^2$. $AC = 6\,cm$. Find the length of AB.

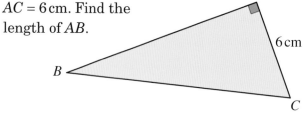

Solution

(a) Area of triangle $= \dfrac{1}{2} \times$ base $\times$ perpendicular height

$\qquad\qquad = \dfrac{1}{2} \times 20 \times 14$

$\qquad\qquad = 140\,cm^2$

(b) Area of $\triangle ABC = \dfrac{1}{2} \times AB \times AC$

$\qquad\qquad 24 = \dfrac{1}{2} \times AB \times 6$

$\qquad\qquad 24 = 3 \times AB$

$\qquad AB = 24 \div 3$

$\qquad\quad\ = 8\,cm$

Try It! ⑪

(a) Find the area of this shaded triangle.

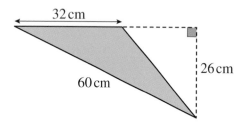

(b) The area of $\triangle PQR$ is $60\,cm^2$. $PR = 8\,cm$. Find the length of QR.

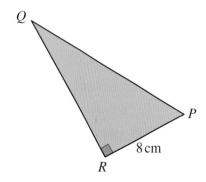

Example 12

$\triangle PQR$ represents a rose garden of area $156 \, \text{m}^2$.
The length of one side of the garden, PR, is $24 \, \text{m}$.
A path runs at a right angle to this side.
What is the length of the path?

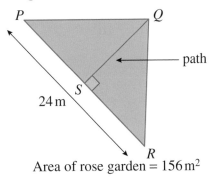

Area of rose garden $= 156 \, \text{m}^2$

Solution

The path makes a right angle to the base at S, so the length of the path is equal to the perpendicular height.

$$\text{Area of rose garden} = \tfrac{1}{2} \times \text{base} \times \text{length of path}$$

$$156 = \tfrac{1}{2} \times 24 \times \text{length of path}$$

$$156 = 12 \times \text{length of path}$$

$$\text{length of path} = 156 \div 12$$

$$\text{length of path} = 13 \, \text{m}$$

The length of the path is $13 \, \text{m}$.

REMARK

You can use the division table on page 359 to check the division calculations.

Try It! 12

The balcony of a flat has an area of paving and an area of fake grass, represented by $\triangle ABC$. The grass has an area of $480 \, \text{m}^2$. Find the unknown length, BC.

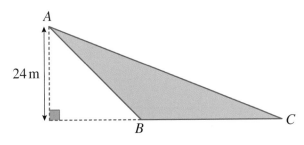

PRACTICE 10.3

LEVEL 1

1. Find the perimeter of each triangle.

   (a)

   15 cm
   8 cm
   17 cm

   (b)
   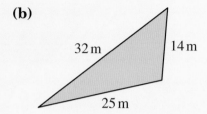

   32 m
   14 m
   25 m

2. Find the area of the rectangle and the shaded triangle in each diagram.

   (a)

   4 cm
   5 cm

   (b)
   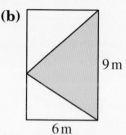

   9 m
   6 m

3. Find the area of each shaded triangle.

   (a)

   6 m
   4 m

   (b)
   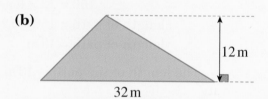

   12 m
   32 m

   (c)

   16 cm
   22 cm

   (d)
   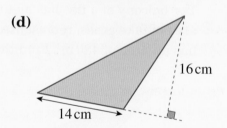

   16 cm
   14 cm

LEVEL 2

4. Find the perimeter and area of each shaded triangle.

   (a)

   50 cm
   A   *D*   *B*
   24 cm
   40 cm   30 cm
   C

   (b)
   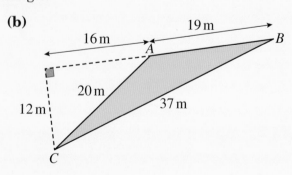

   19 m
   16 m
   A   *B*
   20 m
   12 m   37 m
   C

5. △*XYZ* represents a view of an ice cream cone. Find the perimeter and area of the triangle.

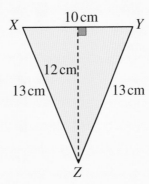

6. A school wants to paint its new logo on the school playground. The logo is made up of a white, a red and a blue triangle as shown in the diagram.

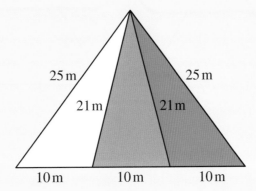

Vina thinks that the logo will need less blue paint than red and white paint, because the blue triangle has the same base but a smaller perimeter than the other two. Hajrah disagrees, and thinks it will need the same amount of paint of each colour. Who do you agree with? Explain your answer.

7. △*ABC* has a base length of 18 cm and an area of 63 cm². Find the perpendicular height of the triangle.

Hint: Draw the triangle first.

8. A triangular advertisement board has an area of 96 m² and a perpendicular height of 6 m. Find the base length of the board.

Hint: Draw the triangle first.

Workbook 1A Link
Exercise 10.3

REVIEW

Perimeter and Area of a Rectangle

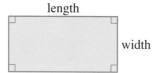

Area of a rectangle
= length × width
Perimeter of a rectangle
= 2 × (length + width)

Perimeter and Area of a Square

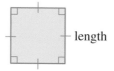

Area of a square
= length × length
Perimeter of a square
= 4 × length

Perimeter and Area

Perimeter and Area of a Triangle

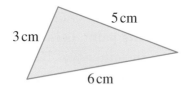

Perimeter of a triangle = sum of the lengths of its three sides

e.g. perimeter of this triangle = 6 + 5 + 3
= 14 cm

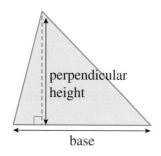

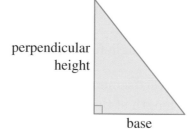

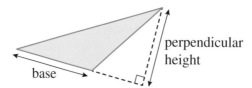

Area of a triangle = $\frac{1}{2}$ × base × perpendicular height

Composite figures are made up of different shapes. The figure below is made up of a rectangle, a square and a triangle.

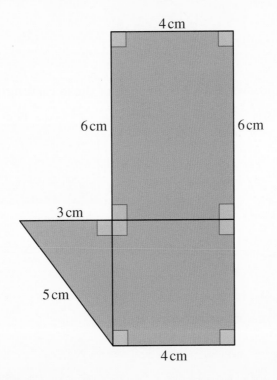

Workbook 1A Link
Problem Solving 10

Find the perimeter and the area of the composite figure.

REVISION EXERCISE 10 🧩🧩

1. Find the perimeter and area of each of these figures.

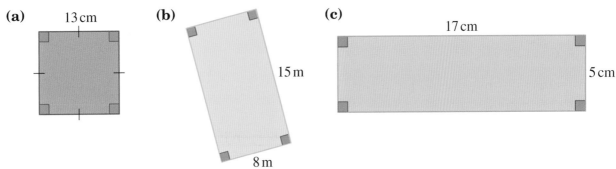

(a) 13 cm

(b) 15 m 8 m

(c) 17 cm 5 cm

2. For each figure, find the length of the unknown side.

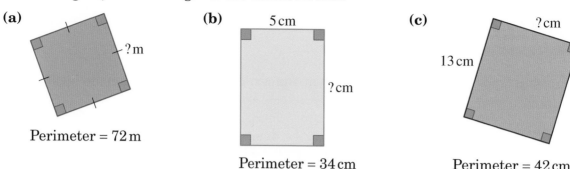

(a) ?m
Perimeter = 72 m

(b) 5 cm
?cm
Perimeter = 34 cm

(c) ?cm
13 cm
Perimeter = 42 cm

3. Find the length of the unknown side, *AB*, in each of these rectangles.

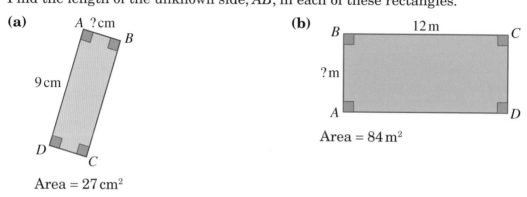

(a) A ?cm
B
9 cm
D
C
Area = 27 cm²

(b) B   12 m   C
?m
A   D
Area = 84 m²

4. Find the perimeter and area of each shaded triangle.

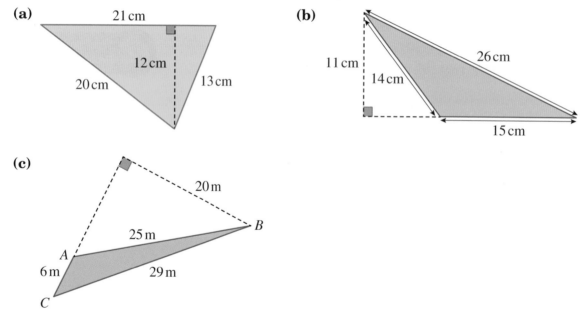

(a) 21 cm
12 cm
20 cm   13 cm

(b) 11 cm   26 cm
14 cm
15 cm

(c) 20 m
25 m   B
A
6 m   29 m
C

5. A rectangular playground has a perimeter of 222 m and a length of 75 m. Find the width of the playground.

6. A triangular banner has an area of 68 m² and a perpendicular height of 8 m. Find the length of the base of the banner.

7. Arrange these shapes in order of their areas from the smallest to the largest.

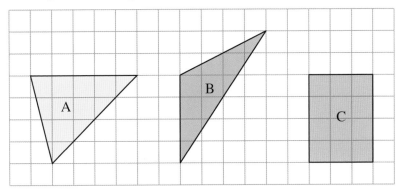

8. Samira has a rectangular garden *ABCD*. The path *BD* splits the garden into two triangles. She wants to know the perimeter of the rectangular garden.

Eyal says that she just needs to measure the perimeter of triangle *ABD* and multiply it by 2. Do you think he's correct, and why?

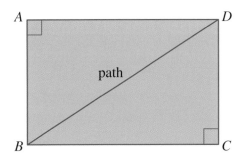

9. The orange shaded area represents a wide path, around a rectangular lawn, *PQRS*. Find the area of the path *ABCD*.

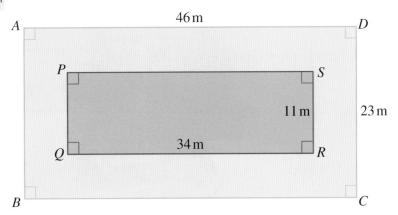

Write in Your Journal

Four square tiles of side 30 cm are arranged into a shape. Each tile must have a side connected with at least one other tile. Draw the shapes that can be formed. Which shape has the smallest perimeter? Can you explain why?

11 VOLUME AND SURFACE AREA OF CUBOIDS, INCLUDING CUBES

WHAT IS IN THIS CHAPTER:

Many rooms and buildings are basically cuboid-shaped. The largest section of the Vehicle Assembly Building at NASA's Kennedy Space Centre is a cuboid.

LET'S LEARN TO

▶ draw nets of cuboids, including cubes

▶ sketch cubes and cuboids

▶ calculate the surface areas of cuboids, including cubes

▶ calculate the volumes of cuboids, including cubes

1. Perimeter and Area of a Square

A square has four sides of equal length and four right angles.

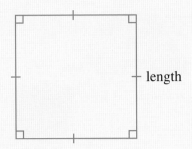
length

Perimeter of a square = 4 × length
Area of a square = length × length

Example   For a square of side length 5 cm,
$$\text{perimeter} = 4 \times 5$$
$$= 20 \, \text{cm},$$
$$\text{area} = 5 \times 5$$
$$= 25 \, \text{cm}^2.$$

2. Perimeter and Area of a Rectangle

A rectangle has two pairs of sides of equal length and four right angles.
The equal sides are opposite each other.

length
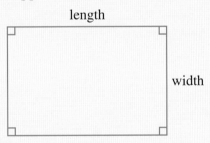
width

Perimeter of a rectangle = 2 × (length + width)
Area of a rectangle = length × width

Example   For a rectangle with length 5 cm and width 3 cm,
$$\text{perimeter} = 2 \times (5 + 3)$$
$$= 2 \times 8$$
$$= 16 \, \text{cm},$$
$$\text{area} = 5 \times 3$$
$$= 15 \, \text{cm}^2.$$

11.1 Nets of Cuboids, including Cubes

There are many three-dimensional solid objects in daily life. These objects occupy space. Three-dimensional is usually written as 3D. Some examples of 3D solid objects are shown.

can

football

chocolate bar

traffic cone

tent

cube puzzle

A **face** of a solid is a flat surface that forms part of the boundary of the solid.

Here are two types of 3D solid objects, both with six faces.

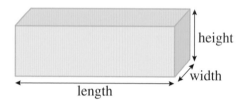

height

width

length

Cuboid

- Each face of a cuboid is a rectangle or a square.

- Opposite faces are identical.

- The dimensions of a cuboid are called the length, width and height.

- The length, width and height of a cuboid may be different to each other.

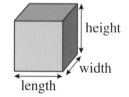

height

width

length

Cube

- Each face of a cube is a square.

- All six faces are identical.

- The length, width and height of a cube have to be equal.

A **net** is a flat, 2D figure that can be folded to form a 3D solid.

Objective: To draw the nets of a cube. You will need a marker
pen, a ruler and thin, square grid card.

REMARK

In this activity, you
could also cut out lots
of identical individual
squares and then tape
them together to form
the nets.

1. Copy the figures shown onto thin, square grid card.
   Cut them out and try to fold them into cubes.

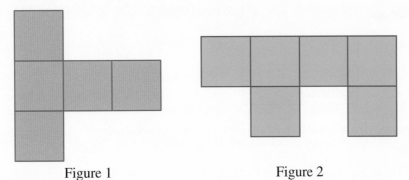

Figure 1   Figure 2

   (a) Are you able to fold Figure 1 into a cube? Why?

   (b) Are you able to fold Figure 2 into a cube? Why?

2. Use the marker pen to draw the figure below.

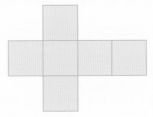

3. Cut out the shape and fold it into a cube.

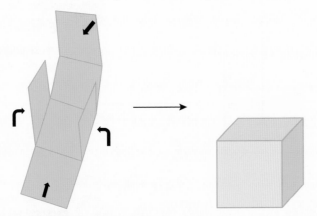

   (a) How many squares are there in the original figure?

   (b) How many faces does the cube have?

4. Try drawing another two different nets of the cube on square grid paper.
   Compare your nets with your classmates. How many different nets
   have you found as a class?

Learn to draw a 3D object, such as a cube or cuboid, on paper.

 **CLASS ACTIVITY 2**

Objective: To draw a cube and a cuboid on paper. You will need square grid paper, a pencil, an eraser and a ruler.

1. Using a ruler, draw a square with side length 4 cm on the paper.

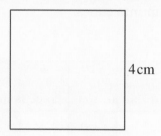

4 cm

2. On the same diagram, draw another identical square overlapping the first square.

1st square

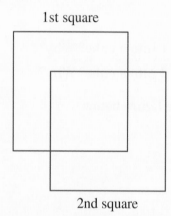

2nd square

3. Draw lines to join the four pairs of corners of the two squares, to form the image of a cube of edges 4 cm.

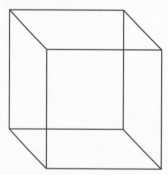

REMARK

You can use dotted lines for edges that are hidden from view.

4. Now, using the same method, draw a cuboid with length 5 cm and height 2 cm.

5. For the cubes and cuboids you've drawn, count the edges and the vertices. Compare your answers with those of your classmates'.

DISCUSS

Brogan says, "A cube has six square faces. I know a square has 4 edges and 4 vertices, so a cube must have 24 edges and 24 vertices." Do you agree?

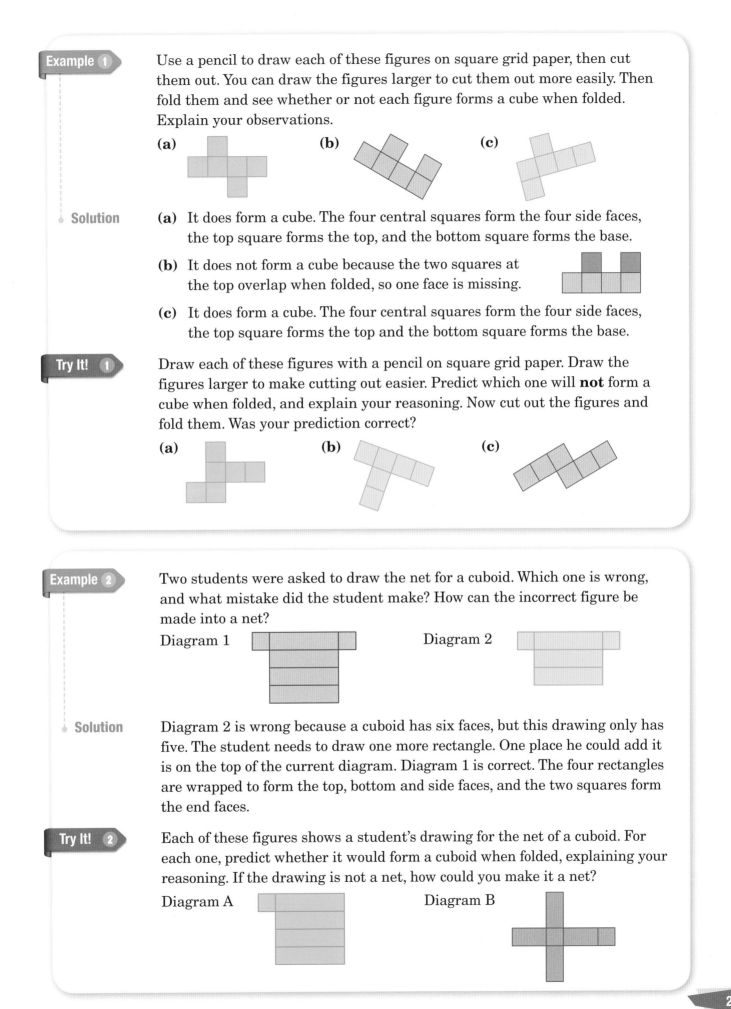

Example 1

Use a pencil to draw each of these figures on square grid paper, then cut them out. You can draw the figures larger to cut them out more easily. Then fold them and see whether or not each figure forms a cube when folded. Explain your observations.

(a)   (b)   (c)

Solution

(a) It does form a cube. The four central squares form the four side faces, the top square forms the top, and the bottom square forms the base.

(b) It does not form a cube because the two squares at the top overlap when folded, so one face is missing.

(c) It does form a cube. The four central squares form the four side faces, the top square forms the top and the bottom square forms the base.

Try It! 1

Draw each of these figures with a pencil on square grid paper. Draw the figures larger to make cutting out easier. Predict which one will **not** form a cube when folded, and explain your reasoning. Now cut out the figures and fold them. Was your prediction correct?

(a)   (b)   (c)

Example 2

Two students were asked to draw the net for a cuboid. Which one is wrong, and what mistake did the student make? How can the incorrect figure be made into a net?

Diagram 1   Diagram 2

Solution

Diagram 2 is wrong because a cuboid has six faces, but this drawing only has five. The student needs to draw one more rectangle. One place he could add it is on the top of the current diagram. Diagram 1 is correct. The four rectangles are wrapped to form the top, bottom and side faces, and the two squares form the end faces.

Try It! 2

Each of these figures shows a student's drawing for the net of a cuboid. For each one, predict whether it would form a cuboid when folded, explaining your reasoning. If the drawing is not a net, how could you make it a net?

Diagram A   Diagram B

PRACTICE 11.1

⚙ LEVEL 1

1. Which of these figures do you think will form a cube when folded? Explain your answers. Now copy and cut out these figures. Try forming a cube from each of the figures to see if you are correct.

   (a)

   (b)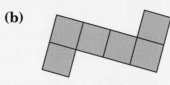

   (c)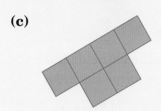

   (d)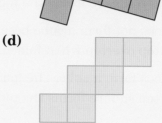

2. Predict which of these figures will not form a cuboid. Explain your answers. Now copy and cut out these figures. Try forming a cuboid from each of the figures to see if your prediction is correct.

   (a)

   (b)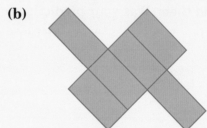

   (c)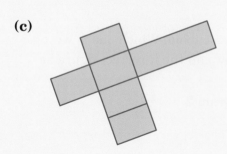

   (d)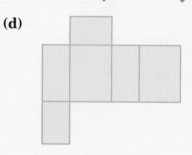

⚙ LEVEL 2

3. On plain paper draw a cube that has edges of length 3 cm.

   📖 OPEN QUESTION

4. On plain paper draw a cuboid in which two of the faces have length 4 cm and width 3 cm.

   📖 OPEN QUESTION

5. On square or plain paper draw two different, accurate nets of a cube with side length 3 cm.

   📖 OPEN QUESTION

6. On square or plain paper draw two different, accurate nets of a cuboid with length 3 cm, width 2 cm and height 4 cm.

   📖 OPEN QUESTION

7. Copy and complete each figure so that it becomes a net of a cuboid.

 (a) 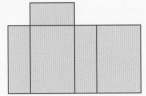 **(b)**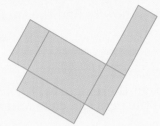

8. Copy each figure and modify one of its rectangles so that it becomes a net of a cuboid.

(a)  **(b)**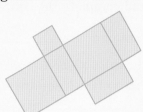

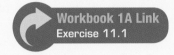

11.2 Surface Area of Cuboids, including Cubes

The **surface area** of a 3D solid is the total area of all the faces of the solid.

 CLASS ACTIVITY 3

Objective: To observe the relationship between the surface area of a solid and its net.

1. Collect some empty cardboard boxes of different shapes and sizes, cardboard inner rolls from kitchen towels or toilet rolls, and some tins of food such as soup.

2. Use a pair of scissors to cut along some edges of a closed box such that the shape formed is in one piece and can lie flat on your desk.

3. Compare the shape you have formed with your classmates' shapes. If two or more of you started with the same box, what is different and what is the same about the shapes you have formed? Do they have the same area?

4. The flat shape you have formed is a net of the box. Explain why this is so.

5. What is the relationship between the area of the net and the surface area of the box?

6. Cut an open box, such as a gift box without its lid, in a similar way.

7. What is the same and what is different about the nets of a closed box and an open box?

8. Cut the paper label of a soup can along a straight line from the top to the bottom. Lie the label flat on your desk. What shape do you get?

From Class Activity 3, you see that different nets of the same 3D solid have the same total area. The total area of any possible net is the surface area of the 3D solid. Now look at how to find the surface area of a cuboid and a cube.

Objective: To use the nets of a cube and a cuboid to find their surface areas.

1. Look at this figure which is made out of six squares. Copy and complete the sentences.

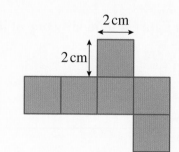

(a) This is the net of a _____.

(b) Calculate the area of each square face of the net. Area of each square face = _____ cm²

(c) Surface area of the cube formed by this net = _____ cm²

2. Look at this figure then copy and complete the sentences.

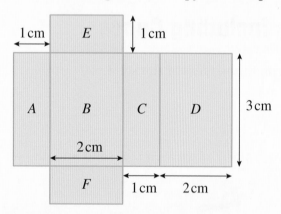

(a) This is the net of a _____.

(b) Calculate the area of each face of the net.

Area of A = _____ cm²

Area of C = _____ cm²

Area of B = _____ cm²

Area of D = _____ cm²

Area of E = _____ cm²

Area of F = _____ cm²

(c) Surface area of the cuboid formed by

this net = _____

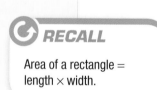

RECALL

Area of a rectangle = length × width.

As you can see from Class Activity 4, you can find the total surface area of a cube or cuboid by finding the area of its net.

 Example 3 Find the surface area of the cube.

 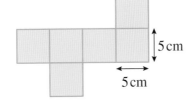

Solution Calculate the area of 1 square face.

Area of 1 face $= 5 \times 5$

$\qquad\qquad = 25\,\text{cm}^2$

There are 6 identical faces on a cube.

$\therefore$ Surface area of the cube $= 6 \times 25$

$\qquad\qquad\qquad\qquad\qquad = 150\,\text{cm}^2$

Try It! 3 A toy-box is shaped like a cube, with sides of length 1 m.

(a) Find the surface area of the toy-box.

(b) The top face of the box is a removable lid. What is the surface area of the toy-box with the lid removed?

 Example 4 Find the surface area of the cuboid.

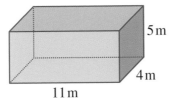

Solution Start by drawing a net of the cuboid.

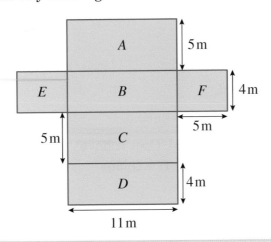

Continued

The cuboid has six rectangular faces. Each rectangular face has the same dimensions and hence the same area as the face opposite it.

Method 1
Areas of rectangles A and $C = 2 \times (11 \times 5)$
$$= 2 \times 55$$
$$= 110\,\text{m}^2$$

Areas of rectangles E and $F = 2 \times (4 \times 5)$
$$= 2 \times 20$$
$$= 40\,\text{m}^2$$

Areas of rectangles B and $D = 2 \times (11 \times 4)$
$$= 2 \times 44$$
$$= 88\,\text{m}^2$$

Surface area of cuboid $= 110 + 40 + 88$
$$= 238\,\text{m}^2$$

Method 2
Areas of rectangles A, B, C and D Think of A, B, C and D as
$= (5 + 4 + 5 + 4) \times 11$ one large rectangle.
$= 18 \times 11$
$= 198\,\text{m}^2$

Areas of rectangles E and $F = 2 \times (4 \times 5)$
$$= 2 \times 20$$
$$= 40\,\text{m}^2$$

Total surface area of cuboid $= 198 + 40$
$$= 238\,\text{m}^2$$

Try It! ④   Here is a cuboid.

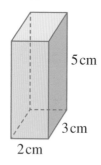

5 cm
3 cm
2 cm

(a) Draw a net of this cuboid.

(b) Work out the surface area of the cuboid.

(c) Draw a second net for the cuboid. Does it have the same surface area as the first? Explain your reasoning.

REMARK

Here's the net again for your reference.

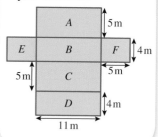

A   5 m
E   B   F   4 m
5 m   C   5 m
D   4 m
11 m

REMARK

From *Method 1*, you can see that the surface area of a cuboid
$= 2 \times$ length $\times$ width
$+ 2 \times$ width $\times$ height
$+ 2 \times$ length $\times$ height.

REMARK

You can use the multiplication table on page 359 to check these calculations.

Example 5

An open glass display case is in the shape of a cube. The case does not have a top. The surface area of the case is 125 cm². Find the area of one face of the display case.

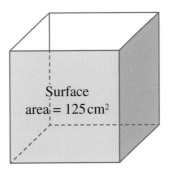

Surface area = 125 cm²

Solution   Draw a net of the display case. Since the top is open, there are only five faces.

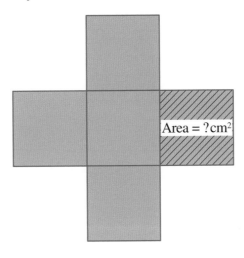

Area = ? cm²

There are five faces, the area of one face = 125 ÷ 5
$$= 25 \text{ cm}^2$$

Try It! 5

A closed gift box is made in the shape of a cube. The surface area of the box, including its lid, is 216 cm².

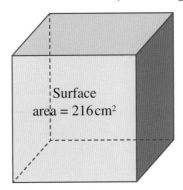

Surface area = 216 cm²

(a) Find the area of one face of the box.

(b) The lid of the box is taken off to open the box. Draw a net of the open box and calculate its surface area.

(c) Compare your net with your classmates' nets and calculations. Do your answers agree?

PRACTICE 11.2

LEVEL 1

1. Find the surface area of each cube. **Hint:** You can start by drawing a net of each cube.

   (a)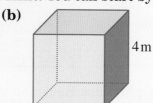
   2 cm

   (b)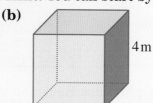
   4 m

   (c)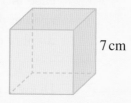
   7 cm

2. Find the surface area of each cuboid. **Hint:** You can start by drawing a net of each cuboid.

   (a)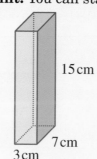
   3 cm   2 cm
   12 cm

   (b)
   15 cm
   7 cm
   3 cm

   (c)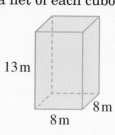
   13 m
   8 m
   8 m

LEVEL 2

3. Given the surface area of each cube, find the area of one face of the cube.

   (a) Surface area = 78 cm²

   ? cm²

   (b) Surface area = 108 m²

   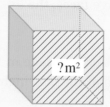
   ? m²

4. A box without a lid is in the shape of a cube. The top of the box is open. The surface area (not including the inside of the box) is 215 cm². Find the area of one face.

   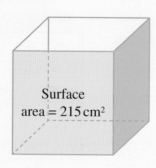
   Surface area = 215 cm²

5. A tray is made out of thin pieces of wood glued together. What is the total area of wood used to make the tray? **Hint:** Start by drawing a net of the tray.

   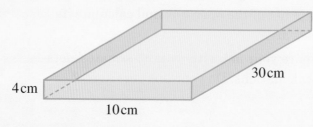
   4 cm
   10 cm
   30 cm

Workbook 1A Link
Exercise 11.2

11.3 Volume of Cuboids, including Cubes

An apple, a water bottle and a cooking pot all take up space in a room, even though they each have very different shapes. The same is true for any solid. The amount of space occupied by a solid is called its **volume**.

Volume = 1 m³

1 cm

Volume = 1 cm³

1 m

DISCUSS

At primary school you will have measured the volume of a container by filling it with water and pouring the water into a measuring cylinder. This tells you the volume inside the container. Will this always be the same as the amount of space that the container occupies?

Just as you can use 1 cm by 1 cm squares to measure the area of a 2D shape, you can also use 1 cm by 1 cm by 1 cm cubes to measure the volume of a 3D solid. The volume of a 1 cm cube is 1 cubic centimetre, denoted by 1 cm³. The volume of a 1 m cube is 1 cubic metre, denoted by 1 m³.

This is an image of a cuboid with dimensions 5 cm by 2 cm by 1 cm.

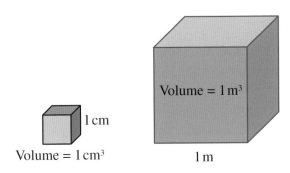

5 cm

1 cm

2 cm

REMARK

The 'dimensions' of a cuboid are its length, width and height.

Divide this whole cuboid into lots of small cubes, each with sides 1 cm × 1 cm × 1 cm. The whole cuboid is 5 cubes long, 2 cubes wide and 1 cube high. Each small cube has volume 1 cm³.

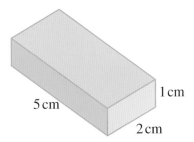

1 cm

1 cm   1 cm

REMARK

A 5 cm by 2 cm by 1 cm cuboid could also be drawn like this:

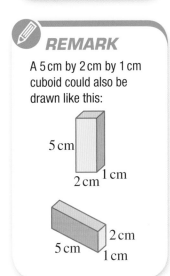

5 cm

2 cm   1 cm

5 cm

2 cm

1 cm

You can now find the volume of the whole cuboid by counting the small 1 cm by 1 cm by 1 cm cubes that are used to make it. There are 10 small cubes, each with a volume of 1 cm³, so the volume of the whole cuboid is 10 cm³.

REMARK

You can make a cuboid model with interlocking cubes.

Consider a cuboid formed by stacking three of the cuboids with dimensions 5 cm by 2 cm by 1 cm, one on top of another. The new cuboid has dimensions 5 cm by 2 cm by 3 cm.

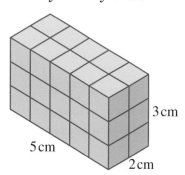

To count the small 1 cm by 1 cm by 1 cm cubes, you can imagine cutting this shape into slices. There are three ways you can slice it – across the length, width or height.

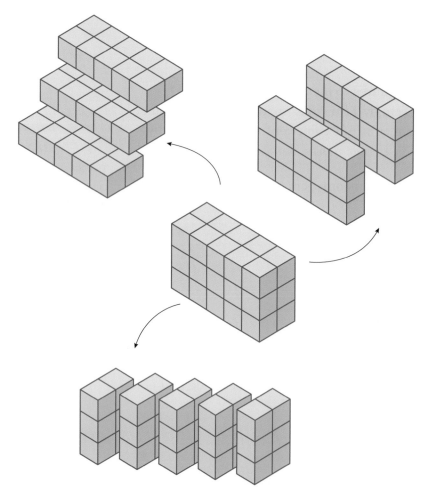

Now count the small cubes:

In the top left, there are three slices with 10 small cubes in each slice, so there are 30 small cubes in total.

In the top right, there are two slices with 15 small cubes in each slice, so there are 30 small cubes in total.

At the bottom, there are five slices with six small cubes in each slice, so there are 30 small cubes in total.

Notice that no matter how you slice the whole cuboid, there is always the same number of small cubes. Each small cube has a volume of $1\,cm^3$. There are always 30 small cubes, and so the volume of the whole cuboid is $30\,cm^3$.

Can you see a quicker way to work out the total number of small cubes and hence the volume of the cuboid?

Example 6

Find the volume of this cuboid with dimensions 6 cm by 3 cm by 2 cm.

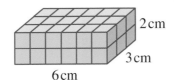

Solution

It's difficult to count the small cubes, as some of them are hidden from view, so cut the cuboid into two slices, where each slice is 1 cm thick:

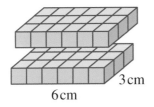

Number of small cubes in one slice = 6×3

Number of small cubes in two slices = $6 \times 3 \times 2$

$= 36$

So the volume of the cuboid = $36\,cm^3$

Try It! 6

A jewellery box is a cuboid with dimensions 4 cm by 5 cm by 3 cm.

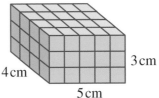

(a) Decide how you want to slice the box into slices that are 1 cm thick. Draw or create the slices using interlocking cubes. Work out the total number of small cubes in each slice, and then the total number of small cubes in all the slices. Compare your answer with your classmates' answers.

(b) Hence find the volume of the box.

(c) Can you see a quicker calculation to work out the total number of small cubes and hence the volume of the box?

From these examples, you can see that

Volume of a cuboid = length × width × height

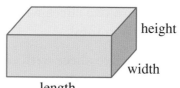

height
width
length

A cube is a cuboid with length = width = height.

Volume of a cube = length × length × length

length

Example 7

A block of ice is in the shape of a cube. Find the volume of the block of ice.

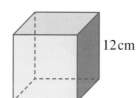

12 cm

Solution

Volume of the ice cube = length × length × length
$$= 12 \times 12 \times 12$$
$$= 144 \times 12$$
$$= 1728 \, cm^3$$

DISCUSS

Is there another way that you can write $12 \times 12 \times 12$?

Try It! 7

A wooden block is in the shape of a cube with length 7 cm. Find the volume of the block.

Example 8

A water tank is in the shape of a cuboid. It is completely filled with water. What is the volume of water in the tank?

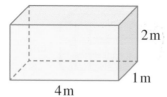

2 m
1 m
4 m

DISCUSS

If the tank has dimensions 4 m by 2 m by 3 m, would it make a difference if you worked out 4×2 and then multiplied by 3, or if you worked out 2×3 and then multiplied by 4? Would it make a difference if you worked out 3×4 and then multiplied by 2?

Solution

Volume of water in the tank = length × width × height
$$= 4 \times 1 \times 2$$
$$= 8 \, m^3$$

Try It! 8

An empty shoe box is in the shape of a cuboid. What is the volume of the shoe box?

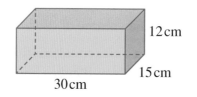

12 cm
15 cm
30 cm

CLASS ACTIVITY 5

Objective: To calculate surface area and volume in real-world situations.

A production engineer designs a corn flakes
box of length 18 cm, width 6 cm and height 25 cm.

1. Calculate the surface area of the box.

2. The cost of the cardboard for the box is 2 pence per 100 cm².

    Work out the cardboard cost of the box. Give your answer
    to the nearest 10 pence.

    There are flaps inside the box so that the sides can be glued together. How
    much do you think this would affect your calculation of the cost of the
    cardboard needed to make the box? Discuss this with your classmates.

3. What is the maximum volume of corn flakes that can be put into the box?

Example 9

A container with a rectangular base area of 28 cm² is filled
with water. If the volume of water in the container is
224 cm³, what is the depth of the water in the container?

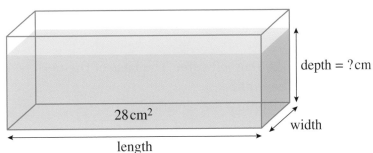

> **RECALL**
>
> Area of a rectangle =
> length × width

Solution

Volume of water = length × width × depth of water
Volume of water = area of base × depth of water
    224 = 28 × depth of water
Depth of water = 224 ÷ 28
        = 8 cm

> **RECALL**
>
> Inverse relationship between
> multiplication and division:
> if
> number 1 = number 2 × number 3,
> number 3 = number 1 ÷ number 2
> and
> number 2 = number 1 ÷ number 3.

Try It! 9

A rectangular tank
of length 4 m is filled
with water. The depth
of the water is 3 m. The
volume of water in
the tank is 24 m³. Find
the width of the tank.

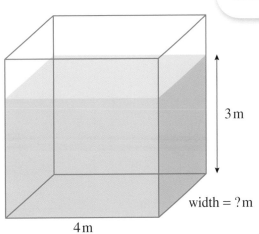

PRACTICE 11.3

LEVEL 1

1. Find the volume of each cube.

   (a)
   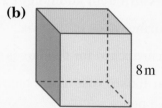
   3 cm

   (b)
   8 m

2. Find the volume of each cuboid.

   (a)
   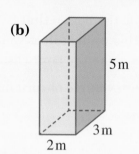
   5 cm
   6 cm
   20 cm

   (b)
   5 m
   3 m
   2 m

3. Which has the greater volume, a cube with side length 11 cm or a cuboid with dimensions 8 cm by 8 cm by 20 cm?

LEVEL 2

4. A rectangular tank is filled with 25 200 cm³ of water. The base of the tank is 40 cm by 30 cm. What is the depth of the water in the tank?
   Hint: Draw a diagram to help you visualise the question.

5. A container is 30 cm long, 20 cm wide and 40 cm high. 4800 cm³ of water is poured into it. Will the water overflow? Explain your answer.

   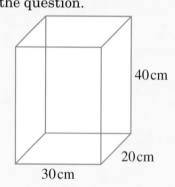
   40 cm
   20 cm
   30 cm

6. A rectangular tank is 4 m deep. When seven cubes filled with water, each of side length 2 m, are emptied into it, it becomes full. What is the base area of the rectangular tank?

   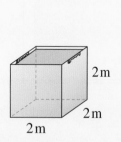
   2 m
   2 m
   2 m

   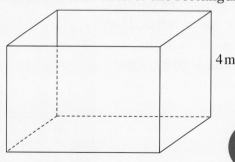
   4 m

   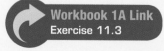
   Workbook 1A Link
   Exercise 11.3

Nets

The net of a 3D solid is a plane figure that can be folded to form the solid.

A solid may have more than one net.

Cube

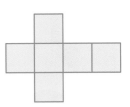

Cuboid

Volume

Volume of a cube
= length × length × length

length

Volume of a cuboid
= length × width × height

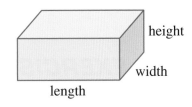

height

width

length

Volume and Surface Area of Cuboids, including Cubes

Surface Area

Surface area of a cube
= 6 × area of one face
= 6 × length × length

length

Surface area of a cuboid
= 2 × length × width + 2 × width × height + 2 × length × height

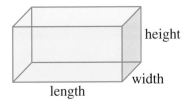

height

width

length

Find the volume and total surface area of each of these solids, which are made up of 1 cm cubes.

(a)

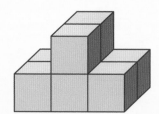

(b)

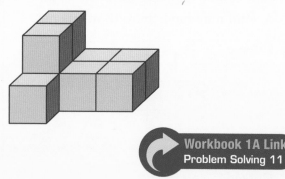

Workbook 1A Link
Problem Solving 11

REVISION EXERCISE 11

1. Predict which of these are nets of cuboids or cubes. Explain why you think so. Now copy each figure and cut it out. See if it can be folded to form a cuboid or a cube and see if your predictions are correct.

(a)

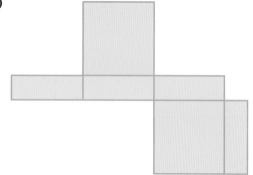

(b)

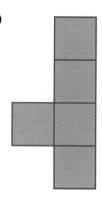

(c)

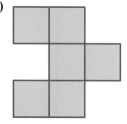

(d)

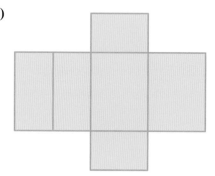

2. Find the total surface area and volume of each of these cubes and cuboids.

(a)
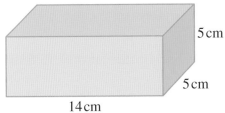
5 cm
5 cm
14 cm

(b)
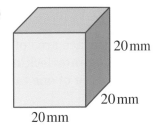
20 mm
20 mm
20 mm

(c)
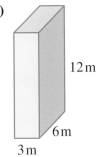
12 m
6 m
3 m

(d)
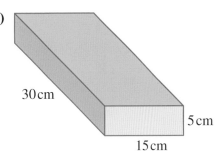
30 cm
5 cm
15 cm

3. Find the total surface area and volume of each of these 3D objects. Ignore the overlap of the lid in (a).

(a)
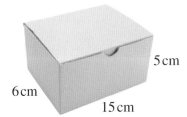
5 cm
6 cm
15 cm

(b)
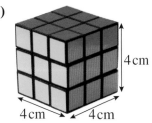
4 cm
4 cm
4 cm

4. If a cube has a total surface area of 1176 cm², what is the area of one square face of the cube?

5. Copy and complete each of these figures so that each forms a net of a cube or a cuboid.

OPEN QUESTION

(a)
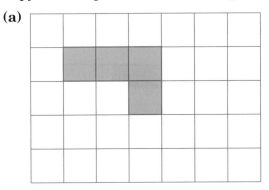

(b)
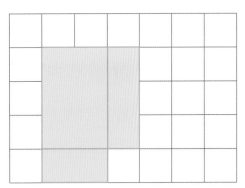

309

6. Draw two different cuboids that each have a volume of 160 cm³. Label the length, width and height of each cuboid clearly. Explain each of your choices.

7. Find the volume and total surface area of each of these solids, which are made up of 1 cm cubes. **Hint:** Build the shapes using interlocking cubes to help you find the volume. To find the surface area, work out the area of one face, and count how many faces you can see on all sides of your shape.

(a)

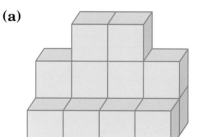

(b)

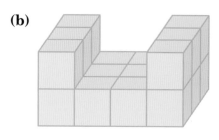

8. You melt some wax of volume 80 cm³. You pour the molten wax into a mould that has a shape of a cuboid with a square base of side length 4 cm.

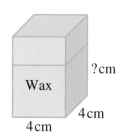

?cm

Wax

4 cm

4 cm

(a) What is the area of the square base of the mould?
(b) Find the height of the wax in the mould.

9. A nursery would like to build a rectangular sandpit that is 9 m long, 6 m wide and 1 m deep in the playground. Sand costs £30 per cubic metre. The budget to spend on sand is £1500. Can enough sand be purchased to fill the sandpit completely?

Write in Your Journal

Josh wants to buy a box to store his collection of comics. Each comic is 20 cm wide and 25 cm long, and a few mm thick. Draw or describe a box that it would be sensible for Josh to buy. What are the dimensions of the box? Explain why you have chosen these dimensions for the box.

12 COLLECTING, ORGANISING AND DISPLAYING DATA

WHAT IS IN THIS CHAPTER:

12.1 Collecting, Classifying and Tabulating Data

12.2 Pictograms, Vertical Line Charts and Bar Charts

12.3 Grouped Data

Find out some data about the students in your class. You could find out how many hours your friends spent listening to music at the weekend, or how many of your year group would like vending machines at school. You can display this information in a way that helps others to interpret the data.

LET'S LEARN TO

- ▶ collect data using different methods
- ▶ classify, organise and tabulate data
- ▶ read and interpret pictograms, vertical line charts and bar charts
- ▶ represent data in pictograms, vertical line charts and bar charts
- ▶ identify the advantages and disadvantages of pictograms, vertical line charts and bar charts
- ▶ understand and interpret grouped data
- ▶ draw a grouped frequency table
- ▶ draw grouped data in a bar chart

1. **Fraction**

   (a) A part of a whole can be represented by a fraction. The shaded part in the diagram represents $\frac{5}{6}$ of the whole shape.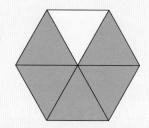

   (b) A fraction can be converted to an equivalent fraction by multiplying or dividing its numerator and denominator by the same non-zero number.

   e.g. $\quad \dfrac{11}{20} = \dfrac{11 \times 5}{20 \times 5}$ $\qquad \dfrac{12}{28} = \dfrac{12 \div 4}{28 \div 4}$

   $\qquad\qquad = \dfrac{55}{100}$ $\qquad\qquad\quad = \dfrac{3}{7}$

2. **Inequalities**

   (a) $a < b$ means a is less than b.

   e.g. $\quad \dfrac{6}{13} < \dfrac{11}{13}$

   When two fractions have the same denominator, the fraction with the smaller numerator is the smaller of the two.

   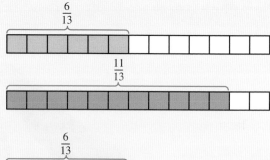

   (b) $p > q$ means p is greater than q.

   e.g. $\quad \dfrac{6}{13} > \dfrac{6}{17}$

   When two fractions have the same numerator, the fraction with the smaller denominator is the greater of the two.

   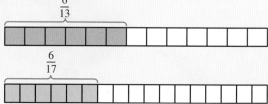

3. **Percentage**

   (a) A percentage is a fraction with 100 as the denominator. $\frac{x}{100}$ is denoted by $x\%$.

   (b) If there are 6 red balls in a basket of 25 balls, the percentage of red balls $= \dfrac{6}{\underset{1}{25}} \times \overset{4}{100}\%$

   $\qquad\qquad\qquad\qquad\qquad\qquad\qquad\qquad\qquad\qquad\qquad\qquad = 24\%$

4. **Ratio**

   (a) A ratio is a way of representing information about two quantities, which are often measured with the same unit.

   The ratio of a to b is written $a : b$.

   (b) If there are 24 apples and 16 oranges, the ratio of the number of apples to the number of oranges

   $= 24 : 16$

   $= 24 \div 8 : 16 \div 8 \qquad$ Divide both parts of the ratio by 8.

   $= 3 : 2$

   Thus, a ratio can be simplified by dividing all of its parts by the same non-zero number. The ratio of the number of apples to the total number of apples and oranges

   $= 24 : (24 + 16)$

   $= 24 : 40$

   $= 3 : 5 \qquad$ Divide both parts of the ratio by 8.

12.1 Collecting, Classifying and Tabulating Data

A Data Collection

Statistics is the collection, classification, tabulation, analysis and interpretation of data. Each individual item of data is also known as a statistic.

On 30 June 2016, the total population of the UK was about 65 648 100. There were about 696 300 babies born in England and Wales in 2016. These are some examples of statistics.

Designing a survey is a part of data collection.

CLASS ACTIVITY 1

Objective: To understand how data is collected through surveys.
Task: Work in pairs to design a simple survey form.

You will need to use word processing software.

1. Design a simple survey. Your survey form should include at least three questions. Some possible topics are:

- favourite movie,
- favourite sport,
- birthday months,

- favourite singer or band,
- number of siblings,
- favourite food and drink.

An example is shown.

Profile Information

1. In which month were you born?

☐ January ☐ February ☐ March ☐ April
☐ May ☐ June ☐ July ☐ August
☐ September ☐ October ☐ November ☐ December

2. What is your zodiac sign?

☐ Aries ☐ Taurus ☐ Gemini ☐ Cancer
☐ Leo ☐ Virgo ☐ Libra ☐ Scorpio
☐ Sagittarius ☐ Capricorn ☐ Aquarius ☐ Pisces

3. How many pupils in your form were at the same primary school as you?

☐ 0–5 ☐ 6–10 ☐ 11–15 ☐ 16–20
☐ More than 20

REMARK

Search the Internet for some free online survey applications or software that can help you create survey forms easily.

2. Compare your survey with another pair. Which questions do you think are most effective? Why?

Conducting surveys is one way to collect data. Data can also be collected through

- existing documents and past records,
- interviews,
- online questionnaires,
- taking measurements or readings using instruments, for example, measuring temperature using a thermometer.

B Classifying and Tabulating Data

When there is too much data, it will be difficult to read and interpret the data. Grouping or classifying the data will make reading the data much simpler.

 CLASS ACTIVITY 2

Objective: To practise classifying and tabulating data.

Task: Work in a pair or small group and record your results using the method described.

You will need a six-sided dice.

1. Predict which number on the dice will show up the highest number of times in 12 rolls. Write down your guess.

2. Copy the table. Roll the dice 12 times. For each roll, mark a stroke '/' (called a **tally**) under the 'Tally' column in the same row as the outcome. To make counting easier, mark every fifth tally with a cross stroke through the previous four. Complete the table as you carry out the activity.

Number rolled	Tally	Frequency
1		
2		
3		
4		
5		
6		

 REMARK

Using a tally, 5 is marked as ////. 6 is marked as //// /. 7 is marked as //// //. How is 13 marked?

The number of times each outcome occurs is called the **frequency** of the outcome. Write down the frequency of each outcome by counting its corresponding tally marks after you have recorded all 12 rolls. The table formed is called a **frequency table**.

Answer the following questions.

(a) Which number appeared most frequently?

(b) Which number appeared least frequently?

(c) Did you make the correct prediction?

DISCUSS

If you rolled the dice 12 times, and you got 4 five times and the other numbers at most twice each, what might you think?

Example 1

Data was collected from a group of 40 students on the number of times they had visited the Museum of Science and Industry in Manchester.

0	4	3	2	1	2	0	1	8	2
1	5	1	1	2	4	1	3	2	1
0	1	3	2	2	1	0	2	7	2
2	0	2	1	2	4	3	1	1	2

(a) Copy and complete the frequency table for the data.

REMARK

Frequency tables can be set out either horizontally, like this one, or vertically, like the one in Class Activity 2.

Number of visits to the Museum of Science and Industry	0	1	2	3	4	5	6	7	8
Tally									
Frequency									

(b) What was the most frequently occurring number of times that students had visited the museum?

(c) How many students had visited the Museum of Science and Industry more than three times?

(d) How many students had visited the Museum of Science and Industry six times or fewer?

Solution **(a)**

Number of visits to the Museum of Science and Industry	0	1	2	3	4	5	6	7	8
Tally	⁙	⁙ ⁙ ⁚	⁙ ⁙ ⁙	////	///	/		/	/
Frequency	5	12	13	4	3	1	0	1	1

DISCUSS

Explain why the answer to part **(b)** is two and not 13.

(b) The highest frequency is 13, so the most frequently occurring number of visits is two.

(c) Number of students who visited more than three times = 3 + 1 + 0 + 1 + 1
= 6

REMARK

More than three times means four times or more.

(d) Number of students who visited six times or fewer = total number of students − number of students who visited more than six times
= 40 − (1 + 1)
= 40 − 2
= 38

DISCUSS

For part **(d)** you could also add up the numbers of students who visited six times or fewer.

Is one of these methods better? Why do you think this is?

Data was collected from a group of 40 students on their scores for a spelling test. The maximum score for the test is 10.

5	4	3	2	8	8	7	7	9	8
8	8	8	8	2	4	7	3	8	7
6	1	3	8	7	7	7	8	7	2
8	8	7	8	7	4	3	7	7	8

(a) Copy and complete the frequency table for this data.

Score	0	1	2	3	4	5	6	7	8	9	10
Tally											
Frequency											

(b) What was the highest score obtained for the test?
(c) What score was obtained by the greatest number of students?
(d) How many students scored fewer than 5 out of 10?
(e) How many students passed the spelling test if a student needed to score more than 5 out of 10 to pass?

REMARK

Fewer than 5 out of 10 means four or fewer.

Example **2**

This data shows the number of watches sold at a shop in a week.

Day	Monday	Tuesday	Wednesday	Thursday	Friday	Saturday	Sunday
Number of watches sold (Frequency)	7	9	15	12	25	22	26

(a) How many watches were sold altogether?
(b) On which day was the highest number of watches sold?
(c) How many more watches were sold on Thursday than on Monday?
(d) What fraction of all the watches sold in the week was sold on Wednesday?

Solution

(a) Total number of watches sold in a week
$$= 7 + 9 + 15 + 12 + 25 + 22 + 26$$
$$= 116$$

(b) The highest number of watches was sold on Sunday.

DISCUSS

Why do you think this day is the most popular for buying watches?

(c) $12 - 7 = 5$

Five more watches were sold on Thursday than on Monday.

(d) Fraction of watches sold on Wednesday
$$= \frac{\text{number of watches sold on Wednesday}}{\text{total number of watches sold in a week}}$$
$$= \frac{15}{116}$$

Try It! 2 This table shows the modes of transport taken by a group of students to travel to school.

Mode of transport	Number of students (Frequency)
Bus	15
Car	6
Train	12
Bicycle	4
Walk	8

(a) How many students were there in the group?

(b) Which mode of transport was used by the highest number of students?

(c) How many more students took a bus than walked to school?

(d) What fraction of students in the group cycled to school?

 DISCUSS

What assumption have you made when answering **(a)**? Do you think this assumption is reasonable?

PRACTICE 12.1

⚙ LEVEL 1

1. Conduct a survey in your class to find out how many siblings each student has. Copy and complete the table and answer the questions.

OPEN QUESTION

Number of siblings	0	1	2	3	4	More than 4
Tally						
Number of students (Frequency)						

(a) How many students were there in your survey?

(b) How many students had three siblings?

(c) How many students had fewer than two siblings?

2. Data was collected about the ages of students in a cheerleading team.

10	14	13	12	15	14	13	13
12	13	11	10	14	15	15	12
12	10	11	14	14	13	12	12

(a) Copy and complete the frequency table to represent the given data.

Age	Tally	Frequency
10		
11		
12		
13		
14		
15		

(b) How many students are there in the cheerleading team?
(c) How many 11-year-old students are there?
(d) Are there more students who are under 11 years old than students who are over 14 years old?

LEVEL 2

3. The table shows the numbers of movies that a surveyed group of people watched in a month.

Number of movies	0	1	2	3	4	5
Number of people (Frequency)	37	42	24	18	8	9

(a) How many people participated in the survey?
(b) How many people watched fewer than three movies in a month?
(c) What fraction of the people watched at least three movies in a month?
Hint: Remember that 'at least three' means three movies or more.

4. The table shows the favourite colours of a group of students.

Favourite colour	Pink	Green	Yellow	Red	Blue
Number of students (Frequency)	14	10	9	17	13

(a) Which colour is the most popular?
(b) How many more students preferred pink to yellow?
(c) What is the fraction of students whose favourite colour is not red?

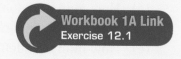

Workbook 1A Link
Exercise 12.1

12.2 Pictograms, Vertical Line Charts and Bar Charts

People can usually grasp information quickly and easily from a picture or a graph. Thus, you often use a statistical graph to display the organised data.

A Pictograms

Pictograms use pictures or symbols to represent data. They make the presentation interesting and attractive.

Number of apples in Ali's orchard

 represents 200 apples

DISCUSS

How many green apples do you think there are in Ali's orchard? What do you think the half apple symbol shows? How many apples are there in total?

Advantages
- It is attractive.
- It is easy to understand.

Disadvantages
- It cannot be drawn easily.
- It is not suitable for large amounts of data.
- It is not easy to read and interpret data values accurately when only a fraction of the picture or symbol is shown.

CLASS ACTIVITY 3

Objective: To create a pictogram from a set of data.

Task: Work in a pair or small group to create a pictogram from the data below. Class 7S are holding a bake sale and Cassie and her friends all bring in cupcakes. Cassie brings in 12 cakes, Oliver bakes 6 cakes, Saskia brings in 15 cakes and Ahmed bakes 9 cakes.

1. Look at the data about the cake sale and decide on a suitable image to use to represent the data. You should also decide what quantity of cakes one whole image represents. Add this information into your key.

2. Using your chosen image, create a pictogram for this data.

3. Compare your pictogram with those of your classmates. Discuss the images you used and the choice you made about what one of your images would represent.

REMARK

The **key** is where you look to find out what quantity one whole image represents in a pictogram.

Example ③ This pictogram shows the number of second-hand cars sold in a week.

Number of second-hand cars sold

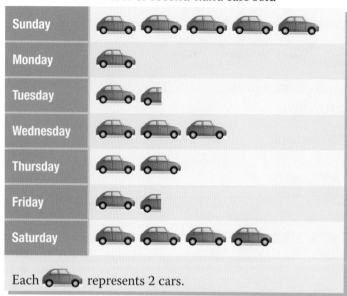

Each represents 2 cars.

(a) How many cars were sold on Tuesday?

(b) What was the total number of cars sold in the week?

(c) On which day were the highest number of cars sold?

(d) On which day was the number of cars sold twice as many as the number sold on Friday?

(e) What fraction of the cars sold in the week was sold on Saturday?

DISCUSS

Are most cars sold during the week or at the weekend? Why do you think this is?

Solution

(a) Since each  represents 2 cars, represents 3 cars.

∴ 3 cars were sold on Tuesday.

(b) There are a total of 18 cars.

∴ the total number of cars sold in the week is $18 \times 2 = 36$.

(c) The highest number of cars were sold on Sunday.

(d) On Friday, 3 cars were sold. Since $2 \times 3 = 6$, the number of cars sold on Wednesday is twice the number sold on Friday.

(e) $\dfrac{\text{Number of cars sold on Saturday}}{\text{Number of cars sold in the week}} = \dfrac{4 \times 2}{36}$

$= \dfrac{8}{36}$

$= \dfrac{8 \div 4}{36 \div 4}$

$= \dfrac{2}{9}$

REMARK

You can check the answers to multiplications like these using the multiplication table on page 359.

This pictogram shows the number of cakes sold by a shop over five days.

Number of cakes sold

Each represents 4 cakes.

(a) How many cakes were sold on Wednesday?

(b) What was the total number of cakes sold over the five days?

(c) On which day was the smallest number of cakes sold?

(d) How many more cakes were sold on Friday than on Tuesday?

(e) What fraction of the cakes sold in the five days were sold on Monday?

DISCUSS

The shop has to close one day next week for cleaning. What day do you recommend? Explain your choice.

Vertical Line Charts

Vertical line charts use lines of different heights on a pair of axes to represent data.

The diagram below is a vertical line chart that shows the favourite sports of a survey of students.

The horizontal axis shows the different categories of sport. There are five categories shown. The vertical axis shows the frequency.

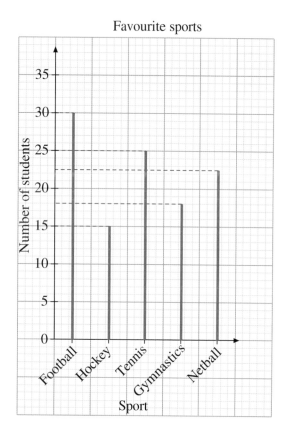

DISCUSS

Write down five things that you know about the data from reading this graph. For example, which sport was the most popular? How many students chose netball as their favourite sport?

In this vertical line chart, the height of each line indicates the number of students choosing the sport represented by that line as their favourite.

Advantages
- Data values can be read accurately.
- Data values can be compared easily.

Disadvantages
- It is not easy to compare each data value with the whole set of data.

Example 4

This vertical line chart shows the number of siblings that a survey of people have.

Numbers of siblings of a survey of people

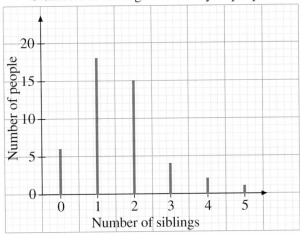

Number of siblings

(a) How many people have no siblings?

(b) How many people have at least one sibling?

(c) What is the total number of people in the survey?

Solution

(a) Number of people with no siblings = 6

(b) Number of people with at least one sibling
   $= 18 + 15 + 4 + 2 + 1$
   $= 40$

(c) Total number of people $= 6 + 18 + 15 + 4 + 2 + 1$
   $= 46$

Try It! 4

This vertical line chart shows the favourite pets in a survey of a group of students.

Favourite pets

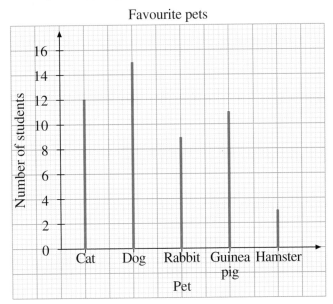

(a) Which pet is the most popular?

(b) How many people like cats or dogs best?

(c) How many people didn't choose a guinea pig?

REMARK

Using a ruler, you can draw horizontal lines from the top of each data line to the vertical axis to help you read the frequency.

DISCUSS

What do you notice about the answers to (a) and (b) and the answer to (c)?

REMARK

Number bonds can help you add up numbers like this more efficiently. Look at page 362 for help with this.

Example **5**

Imogen finds out the shoe sizes of a survey of 29 women and records the results in a frequency table. She also starts to draw a vertical line chart to display the data. Copy and complete the vertical line chart.

DISCUSS

Why might this data be collected? Who would find it useful to know this information?

Shoe size	4	$4\frac{1}{2}$	5	$5\frac{1}{2}$	6
Number of women (Frequency)	5	8	7	6	3

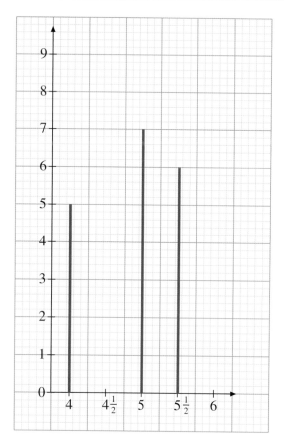

Solution

There are missing vertical lines for the shoe sizes $4\frac{1}{2}$ and 6. You need to draw these lines.

Use the frequency table to find the missing information.

Draw a straight vertical line from the shoe size on the horizontal axis up to the correct frequency height.

Remember to give the vertical line chart a title and label the axes.

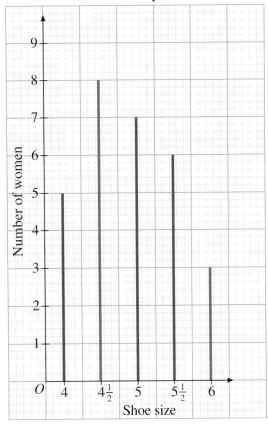

Shoe sizes of a survey of 29 women

Try It! 5 The table shows the number of hours that a surveyed group of students spent on their homework in one week.

Number of hours	Number of students (Frequency)
1	12
2	8
3	9
4	7
5	3

Draw a vertical line chart to represent the data.

 DISCUSS

This was a survey of Year 8 students. Do you think the data from a survey of Year 11 students would look the same?

C Bar Charts

Bar charts can be drawn horizontally or vertically. In the type of bar charts in this section, the bars should be of equal width and the gaps between adjacent bars should be equal. There is a gap between the first bar and the vertical or the horizontal scale.

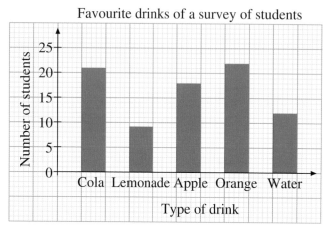

Bar chart with vertical bars

DISCUSS

Can you think of four statements about the data that you can see when you read this bar chart?

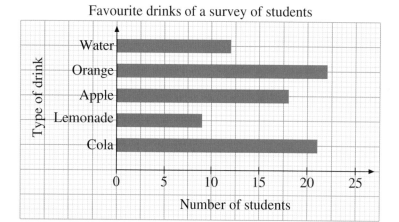

Bar chart with horizontal bars

In a bar chart, the width of each bar is the same while the height (or length) of each bar represents the frequency in each category.

DISCUSS

How does the horizontal bar chart differ from the vertical bar chart? Are the statements you made about the data still correct? Which chart is easier to read?

DISCUSS

If you had a chart without numbers, could you still make statements about the data?

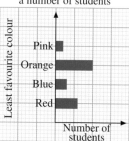

Least favourite colours of a number of students

What can you say about the data in this bar chart?

Advantages

- Data values can be read accurately.
- Data values can be compared easily from the heights (or lengths) of the bars.

Disadvantages

- It is not easy to compare each data value with the whole set of data.

Objective: To create a bar chart using a spreadsheet program.

1. The following table shows the favourite ice cream flavours of a survey of a group of students.

Favourite ice cream flavour	Chocolate	Vanilla	Strawberry	Mango	Mint
Number of students (Frequency)	13	8	9	5	5

   (a) Copy the data into a spreadsheet program.

	A	B	C	D	E	F
1	Favourite ice cream flavour	Chocolate	Vanilla	Strawberry	Mango	Mint
2	Number of students	13	8	9	5	5

   (b) Use the data to create a bar chart.

   Highlight the entire table and then click the Insert menu option →

   Column or Bar Chart → 2D Clustered Column.

   (c) Write down three things that you notice about the presentation of the bar chart created.

   (d) Write down three statements about the data that you can make from the bar chart.

   (e) Change the data in your spreadsheet and see how the bar chart changes.

2. Using the same data, see if you can produce a horizontal bar chart.

   (a) How is the horizontal bar chart different from the original bar chart?

   (b) Do you think one of these charts presents the data better? If so, why?

REMARK

Your spreadsheet program might work slightly differently so you may have to adjust these instructions. If the steps are not easy to work out, your teacher can help you produce a bar chart.

Example 6

This table shows the number of rotten apples found in each box during an inspection.

Number of rotten apples	1	2	3	4	5
Number of boxes (Frequency)	6	10	2	3	4

(a) Draw a bar chart to represent the given data.
(b) How many boxes of apples were inspected?
(c) How many boxes of apples had more than two rotten apples?
(d) What percentage of the boxes of apples inspected had at most two rotten apples?

Solution

(a)

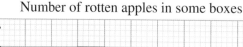
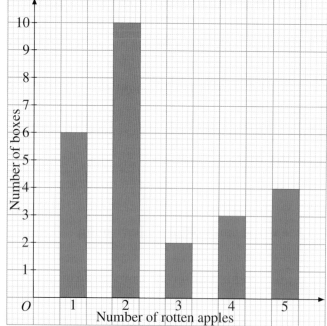

Number of rotten apples in some boxes

(b) Number of boxes inspected = 6 + 10 + 2 + 3 + 4
$$= 25$$

(c) Number of boxes with more than two rotten apples
$$= 2 + 3 + 4$$
$$= 9$$

(d) Number of boxes with at most two rotten apples
$$= 25 - 9$$
$$= 16$$

Percentage of boxes with at most two rotten apples
$$= \frac{16}{25} \times 100\%$$
$$= 64\%$$

RECALL

You can also work out the percentage by changing the denominator to 100:

$$\frac{16}{25} = \frac{16 \times 4}{25 \times 4}$$
$$= \frac{64}{100}$$
$$= 64\%$$

This table shows the types of sport played in a survey of students.

Type of sport	Football	Badminton	Rugby	Tennis	Basketball
Number of students (Frequency)	16	6	2	4	12

(a) Copy and complete the bar chart to represent the given data.

Types of sport played by students in the survey

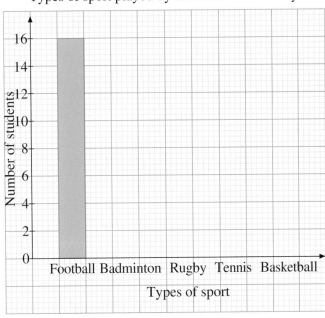

(b) Which sport was the most popular?
(c) What percentage of the students in the survey played football?
(d) What percentage of the students in the survey did not play basketball?

CLASS ACTIVITY 5

Objective: To gather data, draw and compare pictograms, bar charts and vertical line charts.

1. Search in newspapers, online news websites or other media to find an article that includes a set of interesting data.
2. Present the data in a pictogram.
3. Present the data in a vertical line chart.
4. Present the data in a bar chart.
5. Which of the above charts do you think works best for your data and why? Why don't the other charts work as well?
6. Write your own article about your chart to present to your class. Explain what your chart shows.

Example 7

The table shows the sales of cars from three car dealers in a month.

Company	AD	BM	TY
Number of cars sold	15	9	12

The sales manager of AD company represents the data in the bar chart below.

Point out three faults in the chart and redraw the chart.

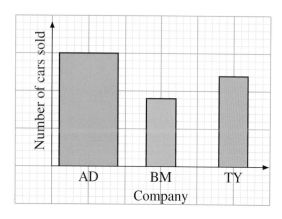

Solution

The three faults in the chart are:
1. The width of the bar for AD company is double that of the bars for the other companies. Comparing the areas of the bars incorrectly gives the impression that the sales of AD are much higher than the sales of the other companies.
2. There is no scale on the vertical axis. This makes it impossible to read the actual sales of these companies from the chart.
3. The chart has no title. This makes it hard to know exactly what the chart is showing.

An improved bar chart is shown below.

Sales of cars in a month

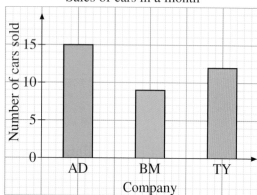

The table shows the number of pets owned by students in a survey.

Number of pets	1	2	3
Number of students	11	18	5

The data is represented in the bar chart below.

Point out three faults in the chart and redraw the chart.

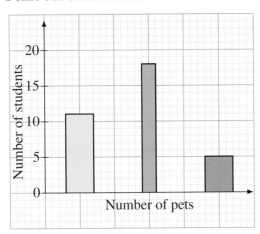

D Compound Bar Charts

A bar chart may have more than one bar for each item. This is called a **compound bar chart**.

Example 8

The horizontal compound bar chart shows the number of students who received awards in the school from 2014 to 2017.

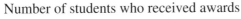

Number of students who received awards

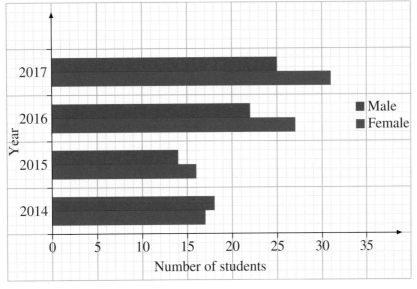

■ Male
■ Female

REMARK

Look carefully at the key in **Example 8**. It tells you that each red bar represents the number of males and each blue bar represents the number of females.

DISCUSS

How do you think this data was collected?

Continued

(a) In which year did the highest number of female students receive awards?

(b) How many students received awards in 2016?

(c) In which year were there more male students than female students receiving awards?

(d) What was the ratio of male to female students receiving awards in 2015? Give your answer in its simplest form.

Solution

(a) Year 2017 had the highest number of female students receiving awards.

(b) Number of students who received awards in 2016
= 22 + 27
= 49

(c) More male students than female students received awards in the year 2014.

(d) In 2015,
number of male students receiving awards = 14,
number of female students receiving awards = 16.
Ratio of these male students to these female students = 14 : 16
= 7 : 8

Try It! **8** The horizontal compound bar chart shows the favourite drinks, from a vending machine, of students in a survey.

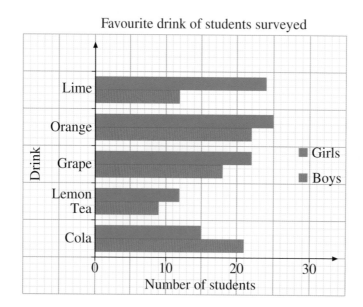

Favourite drink of students surveyed

DISCUSS

Why do you think this data was collected? Who do you think decided to collect it?

(a) How many students were surveyed?

(b) Which drink was liked by more boys than girls?

(c) Which drink was the most popular?

(d) What was the ratio of the number of boys to the number of girls whose favourite drink was grape? Give your answer in its simplest form.

PRACTICE 12.2

⚙ LEVEL 1

1. This pictogram shows the earnings of three stalls at a food fair.

£
FINANCE

Stall	Earnings
A	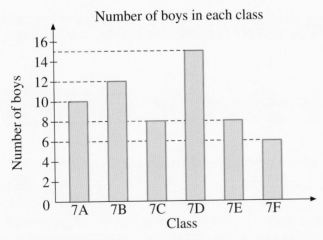
B	
C	

Each 🌰 represents £100.

(a) Work out the earnings of Stall A, Stall B and Stall C.

(b) How much more did Stall A earn than Stall B?

(c) Find the ratio of the earnings of Stall B to the earnings of Stall C in its simplest form.

2. This bar chart shows the number of boys in each class.

Number of boys in each class

[Bar chart: y-axis "Number of boys" from 0 to 16, x-axis "Class" with 7A, 7B, 7C, 7D, 7E, 7F. Bars: 7A = 10, 7B = 12, 7C = 8, 7D = 15, 7E = 8, 7F = 6]

(a) What is the total number of boys in the six classes?

(b) Which class has the highest number of boys?

(c) Which class has the lowest number of boys?

(d) Which two classes have the same number of boys?

(e) Which class has half as many boys as class 7B?

3. The vertical line chart shows the favourite flavours of jelly of a group of 50 people responding to a survey.

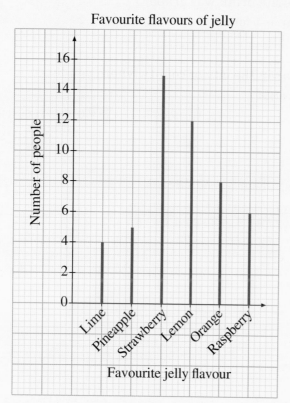

(a) Which is the least popular flavour of jelly from the survey, and what is its frequency?

(b) What percentage of the people surveyed like orange jelly best?

(c) If you add the numbers for the two most popular flavours together, what is that sum as a percentage of the total?

⚙️ LEVEL 2

4. This table shows the number of copies of different types of publication sold in a bookshop.

Types of publication	Newspapers	Novels	Magazines	Comics
Number of copies sold	120	80	145	95

(a) Draw a bar chart to represent the data.

(b) What fraction of all the publications sold are newspapers? Give your answer in its simplest form.

5. This table shows the number of students from a year group who are members of uniformed groups. No student is in more than one group.

Uniformed group	Girl Guides	CCF	Scouts	Red Cross
Number of students	12	14	8	6

(a) Draw a vertical line chart to represent the data.

(b) What fraction of the students who are members of uniformed groups are members of CCF?

(c) There is a total of 100 students in the year group. What is the ratio of the number of students who are not in any uniformed group to the total number of students? Give your answer in its simplest form.

6. Draw a bar chart to show the rainfall in a year in the city or county where you live. Put the months of the year on the horizontal axis.

OPEN
QUESTION

Workbook 1A Link
Exercise 12.2

12.3 Grouped Data

Here are the test scores of 24 students.

65	86	78	93	53	76	80	95
81	72	69	74	49	61	60	58
67	91	65	82	66	75	43	57

If you make a frequency table by counting the frequency of each score, the table would be very large. It is also difficult to analyse. You can group the data into different **classes** to make it more manageable.

Score	Tally	Frequency
40–49	//	2
50–59	///	3
60–69	///// //	7
70–79	/////	5
80–89	////	4
90–99	///	3
	Total	24

In the frequency table, the scores are divided into classes 40–49, 50–59, etc. The classes should be non-overlapping and contain all the data values. The class 40–49 contains all scores from 40 to 49 inclusive, which are 43 and 49. Hence, the frequency for this class is 2.

DISCUSS

What are the scores included in the class '90–99'? Can you tell what the individual scores are by reading from the table?

What is the purpose of including the total frequency in the table?

REMARK

The number of classes in a frequency table is usually between 5 and 10. The classes should have no overlap and should cover all the data.

REMARK

40–49 means 40 to 49, not 40 subtract 49.

335

Example **9**

The frequency table shows the number of messages sent using mobile phones by some people on a single day.

Number of messages	0–4	5–9	10–14	15–19	20–24
Frequency	11	24	32	17	6

(a) How many people sent more than 14 messages on this day?

(b) Draw a bar chart to represent the data.

(c) Find the ratio of the number of people who sent 5 to 9 messages to the number of people who sent 10 to 14 messages. Express the ratio in its simplest form.

Solution

(a) Number of people who sent more than 14 messages
= number of people who sent 15 to 19 messages +
   number of people who sent 20 to 24 messages
= 17 + 6
= 23

(b) The required bar chart is shown.

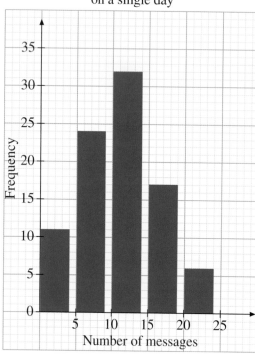

Number of messages sent by people on a single day

(c) The required ratio
= 24 : 32
= 3 : 4   Divide both parts by 8.

 DISCUSS

The number of messages are grouped into equal-sized classes in this example. Classes do not always have to be of equal size. Can you think of an example where it would not be sensible to have equal-sized classes?

 **REMARK**

When you have numerical data you can use a scale like this one.

The frequency table shows the number of emails received by a group of colleagues on a particular day.

Number of emails received	21–40	41–60	61–80	81–100	101–120
Frequency	13	24	19	12	5

(a) How many people received fewer than 61 emails?

(b) Draw a line chart to represent the data.

(c) Find the ratio of the number of people who received from 81 to 100 emails to the number of people who received from 41 to 60 emails. Express your answer in the simplest form.

Example 10

A botanist collected 30 leaves and measured their lengths. The results in cm are:

6.6	12.5	8.9	7.8	5.0	8.1	12.3	9.7	10.0	6.5
11.4	5.8	8.5	7.0	8.4	13.6	9.5	10.1	14.9	5.4
8.5	7.7	6.0	14.8	8.3	7.5	9.3	6.0	7.2	12.9

(a) Copy and complete the frequency table.

Length (x cm)	Tally	Frequency
$5 \leq x < 7$		
$7 \leq x < 9$		
$9 \leq x < 11$		
$11 \leq x < 13$		
$13 \leq x < 15$		
	Total	

(b) Find the percentage of leaves with lengths less than 9 cm.

Solution

(a) In the class '$5 \leq x < 7$', the expression $5 \leq x < 7$ is called a **class interval**.

It means the length x cm is greater than or equal to 5 cm and less than 7 cm.

Hence, it contains the readings 6.6, 5.0, 6.5, 5.8, 5.4, 6.0, 6.0. Therefore, its frequency is 7.

REMARK

The data in this question is expressed as decimals.

DISCUSS

Which class should you put 7.0 in and why?

REMARK

You can use this type of class interval when some of the data values are decimals. You can also have class intervals of the form $5 < x \leq 7$. This means the length, x, is greater than 5 and less than or equal to 7.

You can read the data values one by one and mark the tallies.

After marking, you count the frequency for each class.

Length (x cm)	Tally	Frequency
$5 \le x < 7$	~~||||~~ ||	7
$7 \le x < 9$	~~||||~~ ~~||||~~ |	11
$9 \le x < 11$	~~||||~~	5
$11 \le x < 13$	||||	4
$13 \le x < 15$	|||	3
	Total	30

(b) From the table, total frequency $= 7 + 11 + 5 + 4 + 3$
$= 30$

Number of leaves with lengths less than 9 cm
$= 7 + 11 = 18$

Percentage of leaves with lengths less than 9 cm
$= \frac{18}{\cancel{30}_3} \times \cancel{100}^{10}\% = 60\%$

RECALL

Look back at page 6 in Chapter 1 for a reminder about inequality signs and Chapter 4 to recall using letters to represent numbers.

DISCUSS

How else can you rewrite $\frac{18}{30}$ as a percentage?
Start by reducing $\frac{18}{30}$ to a simpler equivalent fraction.

Try It! 10 A vet recorded the masses of 25 dogs. The results in kg are:

19.0	9.7	11.5	12.0	8.3	13.4	16.8	17.4	24.7
21.4	13.0	6.8	7.5	14.6	17.0	11.7	20.9	26.4
23.2	18.7	28.9	19.1	22.8	18.9	18.5		

(a) Copy and complete the frequency table.

Mass (x kg)	Tally	Frequency
$5 \le x < 10$		
$10 \le x < 15$		
$15 \le x < 20$		
$20 \le x < 25$		
$25 \le x < 30$		
	Total	

(b) Find the percentage of dogs with masses less than 15 kg.

1. The table shows the number of calls received by a company on 70 working days.

Number of calls	10–19	20–29	30–39	40–49	50–59
Frequency	7	12	23	18	10

   (a) On one particular day 22 calls were received. Which group does this belong to?
   (b) On how many days were the number of calls more than 49?
   (c) Find the ratio of the number of days with 30 to 39 calls to the number of days with 40 to 49 calls.
   (d) Draw a bar chart to represent the data.

2. The table shows the time taken to run 400 m by 50 athletes.
   Hint: $48 \leq t < 50$ means that the time taken is more than or equal to 48 seconds, but less than 50 seconds.

Time (t seconds)	Frequency
$48 \leq t < 50$	3
$50 \leq t < 52$	9
$52 \leq t < 54$	16
$54 \leq t < 56$	12
$56 \leq t < 58$	6
$58 \leq t < 60$	4

   (a) Find the number of athletes whose times taken are less than 50 seconds.
   (b) Find the percentage of athletes whose times taken are greater than or equal to 54 seconds.

3. A magazine conducts a survey about the ages of its readers. The results, in years, are:

41	25	34	59	31	43	35	50	31	45
26	28	56	68	39	43	62	37	33	51
29	35	47	53	34	46	64	58	28	53

(a) Copy and complete the frequency table.

Age (years)	Tally	Frequency
20–29		
30–39		
40–49		
50–59		
60–69		
Total		

(b) Find the number of readers whose ages are 50 or above.

(c) Find the percentage of readers who are in their thirties.

4. The volumes in cm^3 of hydrogen produced in 25 repetitions of an experiment are recorded below.

14.3	12.8	16.2	13.6	15.7	10.8	14.9	19.3	17.2
19.6	10.8	15.4	18.2	17.9	21.4	15.0	13.5	14.7
17.6	18.5	12.5	11.7	16.0	15.6	11.4		

(a) Copy and complete the frequency table.

Volume (x cm^3)	Tally	Frequency
$10 \leq x < 12$		
$12 \leq x < 14$		
$14 \leq x < 16$		
$16 \leq x < 18$		
$18 \leq x < 20$		
$20 \leq x < 22$		
Total		

(b) Find the ratio of the frequency of the class '$12 \leq x < 14$' to the frequency of the class '$16 \leq x < 18$'. Give your answer in its simplest form.

(c) Find the percentage of times that the volume produced is not less than $18\,cm^3$.

Workbook 1A Link
Exercise 12.3

Collection of Data

Data can be collected through surveys, online questionnaires, interviews, existing records and taking measurements.

Tallying

You keep track of the counts by tallying.
For example: ~~////~~ / represents a count of six.

Grouping Data

Data can be grouped into class intervals. This is useful when there are many different values. It can make data more manageable.

Data

Pictogram

Advantages
- It is attractive.
- It is easy to understand.

Disadvantages
- It cannot be drawn easily.
- It is not suitable for a large amount of data.
- It is not easy to read and interpret data values accurately when only a fraction of the picture is shown.

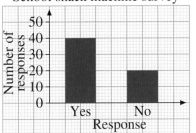

Number of apples in Ali's orchard

Red apples	
Green apples	
Golden apples	

🍎 represents 200 apples

Bar Chart

Advantages
- Data values can be read accurately.
- Data values can be compared easily from the lengths (or heights) of the bars.

Disadvantage
- It is not easy to compare each data value with the whole set of data.

School snack machine survey

Vertical Line Chart

Advantages
- It can be drawn easily.
- Data values can be read accurately.
- Data values can be compared easily from the heights of the lines.

Disadvantages
- It is not easy to compare each data value with the whole set of data.
- It is not visually attractive.

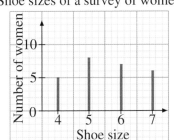

Shoe sizes of a survey of women

CHALLENGE 12 💡

25 people go to a fancy dress party. Two people dress as animals. Three more people dress as celebrities than those that dress as animals. Twice as many people dress as fictional characters than those that dress as animals. The remaining people dress as clowns. Draw a horizontal bar chart or a vertical bar chart that shows the different outfits at the fancy dress party.

> **Workbook 1A Link**
> Problem Solving 12

REVISION EXERCISE 12 ✤✤✤

1. 50 people were interviewed to find out the types of house they lived in.

Type of house	Tally	Number of people (Frequency)
One-bedroom	### ###	10
Two-bedroom		6
Three-bedroom	### ### ### /	
Four-bedroom		11
Five-bedroom	### //	7

(a) Copy and complete the table.

(b) Which type of house was the most common?

(c) What fraction of the people interviewed lived in a two-bedroom house?

2. The frequency table shows the numbers of sit-ups achieved in one minute by 75 students. The data is grouped into classes of equal sizes.

Number of sit-ups	25–27	28–30	31–33			40–42
Frequency	9		24	17	8	2

(a) Copy and complete the table.

(b) Display the data in a line chart.

(c) Which class has one-third the frequency of the class '31–33'?

(d) What fraction of the students achieved more than 33 sit-ups in one minute?

3. This table shows the number of fish in each of six fish tanks.

Tank	Number of fish in tank
A	15
B	14
C	17
D	15
E	10
F	9

(a) Draw a bar chart to represent the given data.
(b) Which tank has the smallest number of fish?
(c) Which tanks have the same number of fish?
(d) What fraction of the total number of fish is in tank B?

4. A toy-box contains a variety of plastic squares, triangles, pentagons and circles. This chart shows the number of different shapes in the toy-box.

Number of shapes in the toy-box

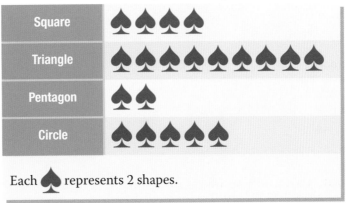

Each ♠ represents 2 shapes.

(a) What is the name for a chart that uses a symbol or picture to represent a certain number of things?
(b) Make a table to show the number of each type of shape in the box.
(c) Find the total number of shapes in the box.
(d) One week later, four plastic squares and two triangles were lost. What fraction of the remaining shapes are circles? Express the fraction in its simplest form.

5. A mushroom grower is interested in the masses of his mushrooms. He weighs 40 of the mushrooms he has picked on one day and the results, in grams, are shown.

20.8	26.0	10.7	16.0	24.7	29.3	24.1	26.4	34.5	23.7
27.0	24.6	16.3	32.5	11.7	18.3	17.4	13.2	21.3	18.5
26.5	23.8	15.4	22.2	27.1	19.0	25.6	23.1	15.9	21.7
32.8	30.9	21.5	28.8	22.8	27.1	31.5	23.9	28.0	32.4

(a) Copy and complete the frequency table. The classes should be of equal size.

Masses of mushrooms (x g)	Tally	Frequency
$10 \leq x < 15$		
$15 \leq x < 20$		
$30 \leq x < 35$		
Total		

(b) Find the ratio of the number of mushrooms, with mass x g, in the class '$15 \leq x < 20$' to the number in the class '$30 \leq x < 35$'.

Write in Your Journal

1. What are the important things to consider when collecting and organising data?
2. What are the advantages and disadvantages of using pictograms and bar charts to present statistical information?

Integrated Examples

Example 1

The diagram shows a triangle ABC with $AB = 5\,\text{cm}$, $BC = 3\,\text{cm}$ and $\angle ABC = 90°$.

(a) Measure $\angle ACB$.

(b) Work out the area of $\triangle ABC$.

(c) Four of $\triangle ABC$ are placed together to form the figure below.

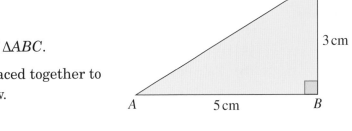

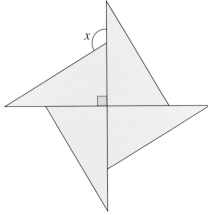

(i) Find the size of $\angle x$. Give the reason for your answer.

(ii) Describe the symmetry of the figure.

Solution

(a) Place a protractor with its centre over C and the zero line along BC.

Reading the outer scale (this starts at zero), $\angle ACB = 59°$.

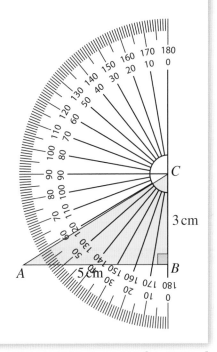

(b) Area of $\triangle ABC$

$= \dfrac{1}{2} \times \text{base} \times \text{perpendicular height}$

$= \dfrac{1}{2} \times AB \times BC$

$= \dfrac{1}{2} \times 5 \times 3$

$= \dfrac{15}{2}$

$= 7\dfrac{1}{2}\,\text{cm}^2$

Continued

(c) (i) $\angle x + \angle 59° = 180°$ (Angles on a straight line add up to 180°.)

$$\angle x = 180° - 59°$$ Using the inverse relationship between addition and subtraction.
$$= 121°$$

REMARK

Here is the bar model for Example 1 part **(c)**.

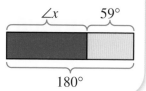

(ii) The figure does not have reflection symmetry. It has rotation symmetry of order 4 about the centre of rotation where the lines cross at right angles.

Try It! ①

ABN is a straight line and $\angle ANC = 90°$.
$AB = 3\,\text{cm}$, $BN = 2\,\text{cm}$ and $CN = 2\,\text{cm}$.

(a) Measure $\angle ABC$.

(b) Calculate the area of $\triangle ABC$.

(c) Four of $\triangle ABC$ are placed together to form the figure below.

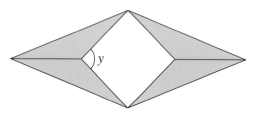

RECALL

Remember that angles at a point add up to 360°.

(i) Find the size of $\angle y$. Give the reason for your answer.
Draw a bar model to explain your reasoning.

(ii) Describe the symmetry of the figure.

Example ②

Oliver measured 18 angles in his bedroom. The results are listed.

36°   127°   58°   320°   132°   97°   41°   296°   198°

315°   263°   24°   228°   60°   115°   143°   15°   324°

(a) Copy and complete the table with Oliver's angles.

Acute angle	36°,
Obtuse angle	
Reflex angle	

(b) Identify pairs of angles from the list that will form angles at a point.

(c) Draw a bar chart to display the number of each different type of angle that Oliver measured.

Solution **(a)**

Acute angle	36°, 58°, 41°, 24°, 60°, 15°
Obtuse angle	127°, 132°, 97°, 115°, 143°
Reflex angle	320°, 296°, 198°, 315°, 263°, 228°, 324°

RECALL

Acute angle $< 90°$,
$90° <$ obtuse angle $< 180°$,
$180° <$ reflex angle $< 360°$.

(b) $36° + 324° = 360°,$
$132° + 228° = 360°,$
and $\quad 97° + 263° = 360°.$
These three pairs of angles {36°, 324°}, {132°, 228°}
and {97°, 263°} form angles at a point.

RECALL

Remember you can partition the numbers to make the addition easier.

REMARK

Look at the last digits of the angles: you want to look for pairs of last digits that add to make 10. Check the number bonds on page 362 to see which numbers add up to 10.

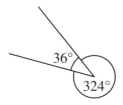

(c)

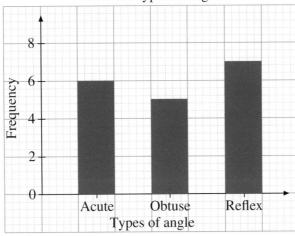

Try It! ② Janice measured 16 angles in a book. The results are listed.

123°   12°   89°   347°   98°   143°   46°   257°
168°   270°   57°   256°   30°   128°   143°   155°

(a) Copy and complete the table for the list of angles.

Acute angle	
Obtuse angle	123°,
Reflex angle	

(b) Identify pairs of angles from the list that will form angles on a straight line.

(c) Draw a vertical line chart to display the number of each different type of angle that Janice measured.

Example 3

A building block is 8 cm long and has square ends with sides that are 3 cm.

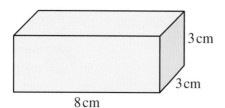

(a) Find the perimeter and area of one

    (i)   square face,

    (ii) rectangular face.

(b) Draw a net of the block.

(c) Find the surface area of the block.

(d) Find the volume of the block.

(e) The pictogram shows the colours of all the building blocks in a kit. Which colour is represented by the greatest number of symbols? How many building blocks of that colour are there?

Colours of building blocks

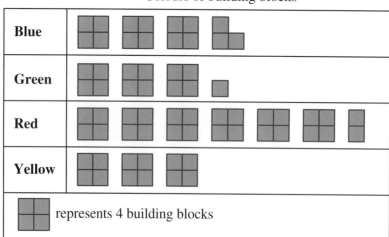

Solution   (a) (i)   Perimeter of a square face = 4 × length

$$= 4 \times 3$$

$$= 12 \text{ cm}$$

Area of a square face = length × length

$$= 3 \times 3$$

$$= 9 \text{ cm}^2$$

    (ii) Perimeter of a rectangular face = 2 × (length + width)

$$= 2 \times (8 + 3)$$

$$= 2 \times 11$$

$$= 22 \text{ cm}$$

$$\text{Area of a rectangular face} = \text{length} \times \text{width}$$
$$= 8 \times 3$$
$$= 24\,\text{cm}^2$$

(b) A net of the block is shown.

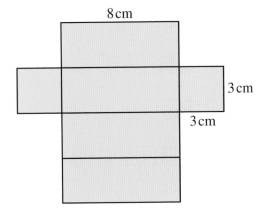

RECALL

You can find the total surface area of a cuboid by finding the area of its net.

DISCUSS

Can you draw a different net? Does your new net have the same area?

(c) There are four identical rectangular faces, and two identical square faces.
$$\text{Surface area of the block} = 4 \times \text{area of the rectangular face}$$
$$+\, 2 \times \text{area of the square face}$$
$$= 4 \times 24 + 2 \times 9$$
$$= 114\,\text{cm}^2$$

REMARK

You can use the multiplication table on page 359 to check these calculations.

(d) Volume of the block = length × width × height
$$= 8 \times 3 \times 3$$
$$= 72\,\text{cm}^3$$

(e) The row representing the red coloured blocks has the greatest number of symbols.
Hence, the greatest number of building blocks are red.
The number of red building blocks = 6 × 4 + 2
$$= 26$$

Try It! 3 A rectangular box is 5 cm long and has square ends with sides that are 2 cm.

(a) Find the perimeter and area of one

    (i) square face,

    (ii) rectangular face.

(b) Draw a net of the box.

(c) Find the surface area of the box.

(d) Find the volume of the box.

Continued

(e) The pictogram shows the sizes of some boxes in a shop. Which size of box is represented by the smallest number of symbols? How many boxes of that size are there?

Sizes of boxes

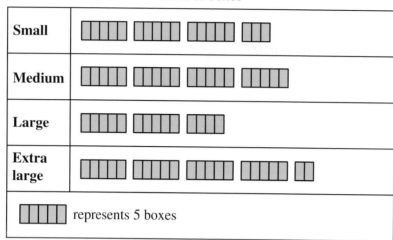

represents 5 boxes

REVIEW EXERCISE 3

1. Measure angles a, b and c and state their types.
   Hint: You can extend the sides of an angle to make the angle easier to measure.

2. *DEF* is a straight line. Find the sizes of angles x, y and z.
   Hint: Use bar models to explain your reasoning.

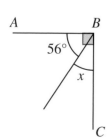

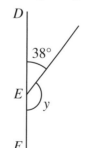

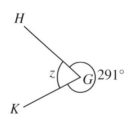

3. Copy the diagrams and draw any lines of symmetry.

(a)

(b)

4. State the order of rotation symmetry about the given centre of rotation of each diagram.

(a)   **(b)**

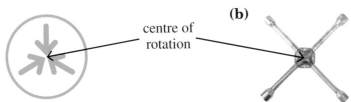

5. (a) Each side of a square is 7 cm. Draw a diagram and find
    (i) the perimeter of the square,
    (ii) the area of the square.
  (b) A rectangular lawn is 8 m by 5 m. Draw a diagram and find
    (i) the perimeter of the lawn,
    (ii) the area of the lawn.

6. (a) Find the area of $\triangle ABC$.

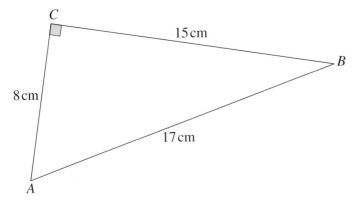

  (b) Find the area of $\triangle PQR$.

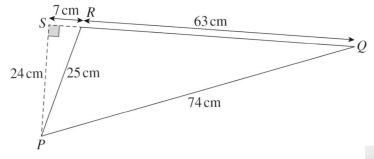

7. Each edge of a wooden cube is 5 cm long.
  (a) Draw a net of the cube.
  (b) Calculate the surface area of the cube.
  (c) Calculate the volume of the cube.

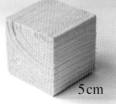

8. An aquarium tank is 60 cm long, 28 cm wide and 50 cm high. You can use a calculator for this question.

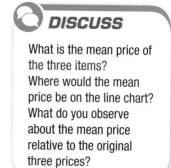
50 cm
28 cm
60 cm

(a) Draw the net of the tank. Remember that the top of the tank is open.

(b) Calculate the surface area of the four walls and the base of the tank.

(c) Calculate the volume of the tank.

OPEN QUESTION (d) Draw another tank that would hold the same volume of water. Explain your answer.

9. The vertical bar chart shows the prices of three items bought by Zoe.

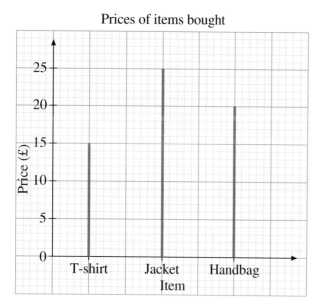

Prices of items bought

Price (£)

25
20
15
10
5
0

T-shirt   Jacket   Handbag
              Item

DISCUSS

What is the mean price of the three items?
Where would the mean price be on the line chart?
What do you observe about the mean price relative to the original three prices?

(a) What is the difference in price between the T-shirt and the handbag?

(b) What is the total price of the three items?

10. The pictogram shows the number of daffodils in four flowerbeds.

Flowerbed A	🌼 🌼 🌼
Flowerbed B	🌼 🌼 🌼 🌼 🌼
Flowerbed C	🌼 🌼 🌼 🌼
Flowerbed D	🌼 🌼 🌼 🌼
🌼 represents 6 daffodils	

(a) Which flowerbed has the greatest number of daffodils?

(b) What is the difference between the number of daffodils in flowerbeds A and D?

11. *ABCD* is a rectangular playground measuring 7 m by 4 m, and *BE* = 3 m. Calculate

    (a) ∠*BAC*, giving the reason for your answer,

    (b) ∠*BEC*, giving the reason for your answer,

    (c) the perimeter of the playground,

    (d) the area of Δ*AEC*.

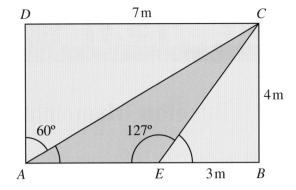

12. The diagram shows two arrows joined to form a double-headed arrow.

    (a) Copy the diagram and draw any lines of symmetry.

    (b) State its order of rotation symmetry, and show where the centre of rotation should be.

    (c) Add two more arrows to your diagram so that its order of rotation symmetry becomes 4.

    (d) Does your diagram still have reflection symmetry?

    (e) Can you add just one arrow to the original diagram so that it has both reflection symmetry and rotation symmetry?

13. The diagram is a net of a cube of edge 7 cm.

    (a) Find the surface area of the cube.

    (b) Find the volume of the cube.

    (c) Which face is opposite to face *A* when the net is made into the cube?

    Hint: To verify your prediction, you could draw the net, cut it out and fold it up.

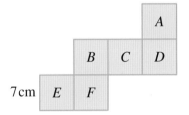

14. The frequency table shows the number of push-ups that some students can do in one minute.

Number of push-ups	Frequency
10–14	12
15–19	19
20–24	32
25–29	11
30–34	6

    (a) What does 10–14 mean in the table?

    (b) Find the total number of students recorded in the table.

    (c) How many students can do more than 29 push-ups in one minute?

    (d) What is the ratio of the number of students who can do 10–14 push-ups to those who can do 20–24 push-ups in one minute? Express your answer in the simplest form.

PROBLEMS IN REAL-WORLD CONTEXTS

A. Rushton Triangular Lodge

Rushton Triangular Lodge is an extraordinary building in Northamptonshire. It was built by Sir Thomas Tresham in 1593. Many things in the Lodge involve the number three. The Lodge has three external walls that are all 33 feet long. Each side has three triangular windows and three triangular points, called 'gables', one above each window. There are three floors and a triangular chimney.

1. The diagram shows the upper floor plan of the Lodge. Explain why the triangle formed by the three external walls is an equilateral triangle.

   Hint: Read the introduction again to help you answer this question.

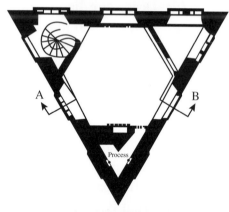

2. The image shows a trefoil window of the Lodge.

   (a) Does the window have reflection symmetry? If so, sketch the window and draw on its lines of symmetry.

   (b) Does the window have rotation symmetry? If so, what is its order of rotation symmetry, and where is the centre of rotation?

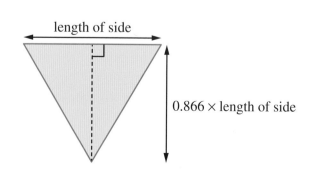

3. **(a)** A French tourist would like to know the length of the external wall, in metres. Note that 1 foot = 12 inches and 1 inch = 2.54 cm. Express the length of the external wall

   (i) in inches,

   (ii) in centimetres, to the nearest 10 cm,

   (iii) in metres, using the result in **(ii)**.

   (b) It is known that the perpendicular height of an equilateral triangle is approximately 0.866 times the length of any of its sides. The triangle shown represents the upper floor of the lodge.

   length of side

   0.866 × length of side

   (i) Using your result from **(a) (ii)**, find the perpendicular height, in centimetres. Give your answer to the nearest 10 cm.

(ii) Convert your result from **(i)** to metres and use it to find a value for the enclosed area of the upper floor. Give your answer in square metres (m²).

(iii) Use your result from **(ii)** to find the total area of the three floors. Round your answer to the nearest 10 square metres.

DISCUSS

What features that you can see on the plan do you ignore when you work out the floor area?

B. Living Room Extension

The diagram shows the floor plan of a house. $AB = 9\,\text{m}$, $BC = 6\,\text{m}$, $CD = 5\,\text{m}$ and $DE = 1\,\text{m}$.

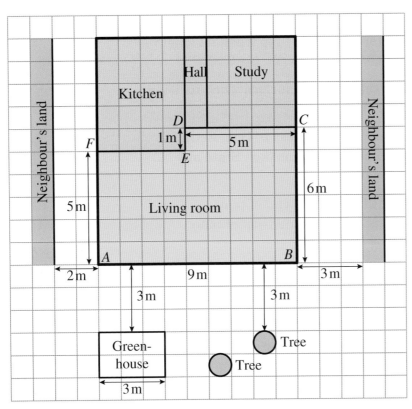

1. Find the perimeter of the living room.

2. Find the area of the living room.

3. Alice wishes to extend the living room by moving a wall outwards. She can move any of the outer walls, but must leave a metre between the wall and her neighbour's land, the greenhouse and any trees. She looks at extending walls AB and DC by 1.5 m to form $AGHDEF$.

   The dotted lines show the extension.

   (a) What would be the area of the new living room?

   (b) (i) What other options could she consider? Describe three more options: which wall will move, and by how much?

   (ii) Calculate the area of the new living room for each option.

   (iii) Which option would create a new living room with the largest area?

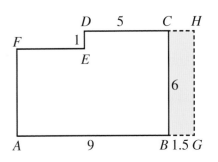

DISCUSS

Remember your problem-solving techniques from the Problem-solving Processes and Heuristics chapter. Which of the Pólya methods you have learnt could you use here?

355

C. Extendable Table

The table top of an extendable table is 147 cm by 95 cm when it is not extended. It becomes 204 cm by 95 cm when it is extended.

1. Find the increase in the perimeter of the table top when its length is increased from 147 cm to 204 cm.

2. Find the increase in the area of the table top surface when its length is increased from 147 cm to 204 cm.

3. The table top is made of solid pine. Its thickness is 4 cm. Estimate the mass of the extended table top in kilograms (kg). State any assumptions you made for your calculation.

    Hint: You should find out what the mass of 1 cm³ of pine is.
    The mass of 1 cm³ of pine is called the 'density' of pine.

D. Carat Gold

Carat is a unit for measuring how pure gold is. Pure gold is 24 carats, denoted by 24k. Therefore, 24k gold means 100% gold. Canadian Maple Leaf gold coins are made from pure gold.

1. South African Krugerrand gold coins are 22 carat gold. This means each one contains 22 parts gold and 2 parts other metals by mass. Find the ratio of the mass of gold to the mass of other metals in a Krugerrand coin. Give your answer in the simplest form.

2. 18 carat gold contains 18 parts of gold and 6 parts other metals by mass. It is mainly used for gold jewellery. The FIFA World Cup Trophy 2018 is also made of 18 carat gold and has a malachite base. Find the percentage of gold in 18 carat gold.

REMARK

When answering each question, you may find it helpful to represent the information using a bar model.

3. 9 carat gold contains 9 parts of gold and 15 parts of other metals. 22 carat gold contains 22 parts gold and 2 parts of other metals. A jeweller has 200 grams of gold. He makes bracelets in either 9k gold or 22k gold and each bracelet weighs 48 grams. How many 9k and 22k bracelets should he make in order to use as much of the 200 g of gold as possible?

DISCUSS

Which of the problem-solving methods you learnt could you use to help you answer this question?

E. Height of a Tree

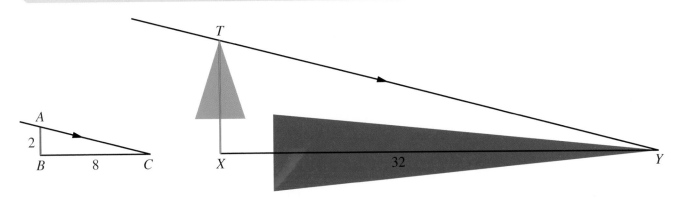

AB is a vertical pole of height 2 m. It casts a shadow BC of length 8 m on the horizontal ground. At the same time, a tree TX casts a shadow XY of length 32 m on the horizontal ground.

1. Measure $\angle ACB$ in the book, which is the angle that the sun ray makes with the horizontal ground.

2. **(a)** Find the fraction $\frac{\text{length of } AB}{\text{length of } BC}$, expressing your answer in its simplest form.

    (b) Find the ratio of the length of AB to the length of BC.

    (c) Express the length of AB as a percentage of the length of BC.

3. It is a useful fact that the angle the sun ray makes with the ground in both of these triangles is the same, meaning that $\angle TYX = \angle ACB$. It is hence known that the fractions $\frac{\text{length of } AB}{\text{length of } BC}$ and $\frac{\text{length of } TX}{\text{length of } XY}$ are equivalent. Use your knowledge of equivalent fractions to find the height of the tree TX.

MATHS

This method is often used to find the height of something that is difficult to measure directly. An example is the spire of a church.

NUMBER HACKS: REFERENCE SHEETS

Addition and Subtraction Within 20

Here's an **addition grid** for pairs of whole numbers with their sum less than or equal to 20. If you want to calculate 5 + 13, for example:

- Find 5 in the top row (with a blue background) and 13 in the first column (with a pink background).
- Follow the 5 down and the 13 across until the column crosses the row. This gives the answer you want: the sum 5 + 13 = 18.

+	1	2	3	4	5	6	7	8	9	10	11	12	13	14	15	16	17	18	19	20
1	2	3	4	5	6	7	8	9	10	11	12	13	14	15	16	17	18	19	20	
2	3	4	5	6	7	8	9	10	11	12	13	14	15	16	17	18	19	20		
3	4	5	6	7	8	9	10	11	12	13	14	15	16	17	18	19	20			
4	5	6	7	8	9	10	11	12	13	14	15	16	17	18	19	20				
5	6	7	8	9	10	11	12	13	14	15	16	17	18	19	20					
6	7	8	9	10	11	12	13	14	15	16	17	18	19	20						
7	8	9	10	11	12	13	14	15	16	17	18	19	20							
8	9	10	11	12	13	14	15	16	17	18	19	20								
9	10	11	12	13	14	15	16	17	18	19	20									
10	11	12	13	14	15	16	17	18	19	20										
11	12	13	14	15	16	17	18	19	20											
12	13	14	15	16	17	18	19	20												
13	14	15	16	17	18	19	20													
14	15	16	17	18	19	20														
15	16	17	18	19	20															
16	17	18	19	20																
17	18	19	20																	
18	19	20																		
19	20																			
20																				

> This bar model represents that 5 + 13 = 18 and also that 13 + 5 = 18.

| 5 | 13 |

18

> **REMARK**
>
> You get the same answer by starting from 13 in the top (blue) row and 5 in the first (pink) column (instead of 5 in the top row and 13 in the first column). This tells you that 5 + 13 = 13 + 5. This is an example of the commutative law of addition.

Here's a **subtraction grid** for subtracting a whole number from 20 or less. If you want to calculate 14 − 8, for example,

- Find 14 in the top row and 8 in the first column.
- Find where the column and row cross each other. This gives the answer you want: the difference 14 − 8 = 6.

> This bar model represents that 14 − 8 = 6 and also that 14 − 6 = 8.

−	20	19	18	17	16	15	14	13	12	11	10	9	8	7	6	5	4	3	2	1
1	19	18	17	16	15	14	13	12	11	10	9	8	7	6	5	4	3	2	1	
2	18	17	16	15	14	13	12	11	10	9	8	7	6	5	4	3	2	1		
3	17	16	15	14	13	12	11	10	9	8	7	6	5	4	3	2	1			
4	16	15	14	13	12	11	10	9	8	7	6	5	4	3	2	1				
5	15	14	13	12	11	10	9	8	7	6	5	4	3	2	1					
6	14	13	12	11	10	9	8	7	6	5	4	3	2	1						
7	13	12	11	10	9	8	7	6	5	4	3	2	1							
8	12	11	10	9	8	7	6	5	4	3	2	1								
9	11	10	9	8	7	6	5	4	3	2	1									
10	10	9	8	7	6	5	4	3	2	1										
11	9	8	7	6	5	4	3	2	1											
12	8	7	6	5	4	3	2	1												
13	7	6	5	4	3	2	1													
14	6	5	4	3	2	1														
15	5	4	3	2	1															
16	4	3	2	1																
17	3	2	1																	
18	2	1																		
19	1																			
20																				

14

| 8 | |

Difference = 6

14

| | 6 |

Difference = 8

> **REMARK**
>
> If you follow down from 8 and across from 14, the column and row don't cross! You will evaluate subtractions such as 8 − 14 in Student Book 2A. Subtraction is usually not commutative: number 1 subtract number 2 is **not** equal to number 2 subtract number 1 (except when both numbers are the same).

Multiplication and Division Tables

The grid below shows a **multiplication table**, from 1×1 to 20×20. You'll find it really helpful in many maths lessons. There are lots of ways in which you can use it – it's not just for working out the answers to multiplication questions.

The next few pages will show you four different uses for the multiplication table.

You learned up to 12×12 at primary school: test yourself to see if you still remember the values.

×	1	2	3	4	5	6	7	8	9	10	11	12	13	14	15	16	17	18	19	20
1	1	2	3	4	5	6	7	8	9	10	11	12	13	14	15	16	17	18	19	20
2	2	4	6	8	10	12	14	16	18	20	22	24	26	28	30	32	34	36	38	40
3	3	6	9	12	15	18	21	24	27	30	33	36	39	42	45	48	51	54	57	60
4	4	8	12	16	20	24	28	32	36	40	44	48	52	56	60	64	68	72	76	80
5	5	10	15	20	25	30	35	40	45	50	55	60	65	70	75	80	85	90	95	100
6	6	12	18	24	30	36	42	48	54	60	66	72	78	84	90	96	102	108	114	120
7	7	14	21	28	35	42	49	56	63	70	77	84	91	98	105	112	119	126	133	140
8	8	16	24	32	40	48	56	64	72	80	88	96	104	112	120	128	136	144	152	160
9	9	18	27	36	45	54	63	72	81	90	99	108	117	126	135	144	153	162	171	180
10	10	20	30	40	50	60	70	80	90	100	110	120	130	140	150	160	170	180	190	200
11	11	22	33	44	55	66	77	88	99	110	121	132	143	154	165	176	187	198	209	220
12	12	24	36	48	60	72	84	96	108	120	132	144	156	168	180	192	204	216	228	240
13	13	26	39	52	65	78	91	104	117	130	143	156	169	182	195	208	221	234	247	260
14	14	28	42	56	70	84	98	112	126	140	154	168	182	196	210	224	238	252	266	280
15	15	30	45	60	75	90	105	120	135	150	165	180	195	210	225	240	255	270	285	300
16	16	32	48	64	80	96	112	128	144	160	176	192	208	224	240	256	272	288	304	320
17	17	34	51	68	85	102	119	136	153	170	187	204	221	238	255	272	289	306	323	340
18	18	36	54	72	90	108	126	144	162	180	198	216	234	252	270	288	306	324	342	360
19	19	38	57	76	95	114	133	152	171	190	209	228	247	266	285	304	323	342	361	380
20	20	40	60	80	100	120	140	160	180	200	220	240	260	280	300	320	340	360	380	400

1 To Multiply Two Numbers

Say you need to find the answer to 9×7.

- Find 9 in the top row and 7 in the first column.
- Then follow the 9 down and the 7 across until the column crosses the row, and that's the answer you want: the product $9 \times 7 = 63$.

Because of the commutative law of multiplication, you expect $9 \times 7 = 7 \times 9$. So you must get the same product by starting from 7 in the top row and 9 in the first column. See if you can find the value of the product 7×9 in the table.

×	1	2	3	4	5	6	7	8	9	10	11	12	13	14	15	16	17	18	19	20
1	1	2	3	4	5	6	7	8	9	10	11	12	13	14	15	16	17	18	19	20
2	2	4	6	8	10	12	14	16	18	20	22	24	26	28	30	32	34	36	38	40
3	3	6	9	12	15	18	21	24	27	30	33	36	39	42	45	48	51	54	57	60
4	4	8	12	16	20	24	28	32	36	40	44	48	52	56	60	64	68	72	76	80
5	5	10	15	20	25	30	35	40	45	50	55	60	65	70	75	80	85	90	95	100
6	6	12	18	24	30	36	42	48	54	60	66	72	78	84	90	96	102	108	114	120
7	7	14	21	28	35	42	49	56	63	70	77	84	91	98	105	112	119	126	133	140
8	8	16	24	32	40	48	56	64	72	80	88	96	104	112	120	128	136	144	152	160
9	9	18	27	36	45	54	63	72	81	90	99	108	117	126	135	144	153	162	171	180
10	10	20	30	40	50	60	70	80	90	100	110	120	130	140	150	160	170	180	190	200
11	11	22	33	44	55	66	77	88	99	110	121	132	143	154	165	176	187	198	209	220
12	12	24	36	48	60	72	84	96	108	120	132	144	156	168	180	192	204	216	228	240
13	13	26	39	52	65	78	91	104	117	130	143	156	169	182	195	208	221	234	247	260
14	14	28	42	56	70	84	98	112	126	140	154	168	182	196	210	224	238	252	266	280
15	15	30	45	60	75	90	105	120	135	150	165	180	195	210	225	240	255	270	285	300
16	16	32	48	64	80	96	112	128	144	160	176	192	208	224	240	256	272	288	304	320
17	17	34	51	68	85	102	119	136	153	170	187	204	221	238	255	272	289	306	323	340
18	18	36	54	72	90	108	126	144	162	180	198	216	234	252	270	288	306	324	342	360
19	19	38	57	76	95	114	133	152	171	190	209	228	247	266	285	304	323	342	361	380
20	20	40	60	80	100	120	140	160	180	200	220	240	260	280	300	320	340	360	380	400

2 To Divide Two Numbers

Because $9 \times 7 = 63$, you can also say that $63 \div 7 = 9$ and $63 \div 9 = 7$.

So you can use the multiplication table to divide two numbers – surprisingly!

For example, to find the answer to $270 \div 15$:

- Find the divisor 15 in the first column and read across until you find the dividend 270.
- Read up to the top row and you get the quotient $270 \div 15 = 18$.

See if you can use this method to check that $270 \div 18 = 15$.

A division might have a remainder. If you can't find the number you're looking for, instead find the **largest** number that's **less than** the number you're looking for.

RECALL

This is the inverse relationship between multiplication and division.

For example, to work out $110 \div 13$:

- Find the divisor 13 in the first column and read across, looking for the dividend 110.
- There's no 110, but 104 is the largest number that's less than 110, so stop at 104 and read up to the top row. This gives you the quotient 8.
- To work out the remainder, subtract the number where you stopped in the table from the dividend in the original calculation. In this example, $110 - 104 = 6$, so the remainder is 6.
- The final answer to $110 \div 13 = 8$ remainder 6.

3 Equivalent Fractions

Look at the **rows** that start with 3 and 5. You can think of the numbers in these two rows as the numerator and denominator of fractions: $\frac{3}{5}$ .... , $\frac{36}{60}$, ... , $\frac{48}{80}$, ... etc.

3	3	6	9	12	15	18	21	24	27	30	33	36	39	42	45	48	51	54	57	60
5	5	10	15	20	25	30	35	40	45	50	55	60	65	70	75	80	85	90	95	100

These fractions are all **equivalent** and they can all be simplified to $\frac{3}{5}$. This is because you multiply the numerator 3 and the denominator 5 by the **same** whole number to turn $\frac{3}{5}$ into any other fraction created by these two rows.

For example, $\frac{3}{5} = \frac{3 \times 4}{5 \times 4} = \frac{12}{20}$

You can work out equivalent fractions by selecting any two rows. Look at, for example, the rows starting 4 and 5. How many equivalent fractions can you write down?

×	1	2	3	4	5	6	7	8	9	10	11	12	13	14	15	16	17	18	19	20
1	1	2	3	4	5	6	7	8	9	10	11	12	13	14	15					
2	2	4	6	8	10	12	14	16	18	20	22	24	26	28	30					
3	3	6	9	12	15	18	21	24	27	30	33	36	39	42	45	48	51	54	57	60
4	4	8	12	16	20	24	28	32	36	40	44	48	52	56	60	64	68	72	76	80
5	5	10	15	20	25	30	35	40	45	50	55	60	65	70	75	80	85	90	95	100

This tells you that $\frac{64}{80} = \frac{60}{75} = \ldots = \frac{4}{5}$.

4 Equivalent Ratios

Look at the **columns** that start with 3 and 5. You can think of each pair of numbers as a ratio. The table shows you that the ratio $15 : 25$ is **equivalent** to $3 : 5$, and to $6 : 10$, and to $12 : 20$, ... and so on. This is because to turn $3 : 5$ into another of the ratios created by these two columns, you multiply both numbers in the ratio by the **same** number. For example, $3 : 5 = 3 \times 4 : 5 \times 4 = 12 : 20$.

×	1	2	3	4	5
1	1	2	3	4	5
2	2	4	6	8	10
3	3	6	9	12	15
4	4	8	12	16	20
5	5	10	15	20	25
6	6	12	18	24	30
7	7	14	21	28	35

This also tells you that $3 : 5 = 6 : 10 = 9 : 15 = \ldots$

Number Bonds to 10

Knowing off-by-heart Number Bonds to 10 is really useful, because these simple facts help you work out lots of different calculations quickly and easily. Look at the number line from 0 to 10 and see how it can be split into eleven different Number Bonds:

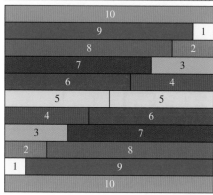

10	+	0	=	10
9	+	1	=	10
8	+	2	=	10
7	+	3	=	10
6	+	4	=	10
5	+	5	=	10
4	+	6	=	10
3	+	7	=	10
2	+	8	=	10
1	+	9	=	10
0	+	10	=	10

If you know these number pairs that add up to 10, when you spot them in an addition question you can say the answer right away: "What do you add to **23** to get 30? You add **7**."

REMARK

3 + 7 = 10.
So 23 + 7
= 20 and 3 + 7
= 20 and 10
= 30

The pattern of the Number Bonds to 10 is the same for the Number Bonds to 100, and to 1000. For example, if you know that 4 + 6 = 10, then you also know that 40 + 60 = 100, and that 400 + 600 = 1000.

Say, for example, you want to calculate 76 + 34.

This is the same as: 7 tens and 6 ones plus 3 tens and 4 ones.
In total you have: 7 tens and 3 tens = 10 tens = 1 hundred
              plus   6 ones and 4 ones = 10 ones = 1 ten

So 76 + 34 = 100 + 10 = 110

	Hundreds	Tens	Ones
76		10 10 10 10 10 10 10	1 1 1 1 1 1
34		10 10 10	1 1 1 1
76 + 34	100	10	

The pattern with decimals is exactly the same. Zoom in on the number line between 0 and 1:

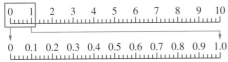

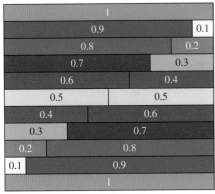

1	+	0	=	1
0.9	+	0.1	=	1
0.8	+	0.2	=	1
0.7	+	0.3	=	1
0.6	+	0.4	=	1
0.5	+	0.5	=	1
0.4	+	0.6	=	1
0.3	+	0.7	=	1
0.2	+	0.8	=	1
0.1	+	0.9	=	1
0	+	1	=	1

For example, if you know that 2 + 8 = 10, then you also know that 0.2 + 0.8 = 1. You could zoom in even further, and know that 0.02 + 0.08 = 0.1, and so on.

The pattern with percentages is also the same:

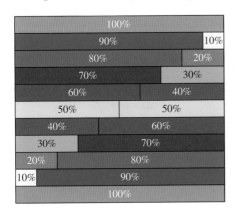

100%	+	0%	=	100%
90%	+	10%	=	100%
80%	+	20%	=	100%
70%	+	30%	=	100%
60%	+	40%	=	100%
50%	+	50%	=	100%
40%	+	60%	=	100%
30%	+	70%	=	100%
20%	+	80%	=	100%
10%	+	90%	=	100%
0%	+	100%	=	100%

Say, for example, you want to calculate 90% of 400.

Instead, you can calculate 10% of 400, which is 40 because 400 ÷ 10 = 40.

The picture above reminds you that 90% + 10% = 100%, which is the same as 100% − 10% = 90%.

So 90% of 400 = 100% of 400 − 10% of 400
$$= 400 − 40$$
$$= 360$$

DISCUSS

What other strategies can you use to work out 90% of 400? What strategy would you use to work out 75% of 400?

Recall the inverse relationship between addition and subtraction: if number 1 + number 2 = sum, then sum − number 1 = number 2

ANSWERS

Fully-worked solutions for this book are available in Teacher Guide 1A.

Chapter 1   Adding and Subtracting Whole Numbers

Try It!

1. (a) $2 \times 10\,000 + 8 \times 1000 + 5 \times 10 + 4 \times 1$
   (b) thousands
   (c) 8000

2. (a) 6, 6000   (b) 8, 8

3. (a) <   (b) >

4. 1040

5. 3981

6. 555 g

7. 6177

8. (a) 32   (b) 49

9. £178

10. 55 m

11. (a) 102   (b) 780

12. (a) 5   (b) 185

13. (a) 92   (b) 611
    (c) 5963

14. (a) 601   (b) 128

15. 26 cm

Practice 1.1

1. (a) $3 \times 1000 + 2 \times 10 + 8 \times 1$
   (b) $3 \times 1000 + 2 \times 100 + 8 \times 10$
   (c) $3 \times 10\,000 + 2 \times 1000 + 8 \times 100$
   (d) $3 \times 10\,000 + 2 \times 10 + 8 \times 1$

2. (a) 30   (b) 3
   (c) 30 000   (d) 3000

3. 7004

4. (a) 8416, 6   (b) 61 999, 60 000

5. (a) >   (b) <
   (c) <   (d) <

6. (a) 30 007 and 30 070
   (b) 30 007, 30 907 and 30 070
   (c) 38 970, 38 030 and 38 709
   (d) 38 970 and 38 709

7. (a) $7 \times 10\,000 + 7 \times 1000$
   (b) 70 000

8. (a) 2   (b) 20 000

9. Ben, Karim, Isaac

10. e.g. 80 020

Practice 1.2

1. (a) 812   (b) 1012
   (c) 1012   (d) 1012

2. (a) 1513   (b) 2213
   (c) 3189   (d) 68 733

3. (a) 92   (b) 275
   (c) 907   (d) 1161

4. 831 g

5. 614 ml

6. £7200

7. (a) 251 cm   (b) 490 cm

8. (a) e.g. 4800, 4088   (b) e.g. 8000, 888
   (c) e.g. 8800, 88

9. (a) Student A: no regrouping, Student B: aligning digits
   (b) 20 000

10. $3547 + 2689 = 6236$

Practice 1.3

1. (a) 49   (b) 649
   (c) 449   (d) 449

2. (a) 224   (b) 144
   (c) 2212   (d) 23 758

3. (a) 37   (b) 211
   (c) 170   (d) 465

4. (a) 53   (b) 278
   (c) 2444   (d) 18 426

5. 39

6. 87 cm

7. (a) 700 km   (b) 8 km

8. (a) £371   (b) £29

9. (a) Student A: no regrouping, Student B: aligning digits
   (b) 77 648

10. e.g. 1000, 2500

Practice 1.4

1. (a) 80   (b) 83
   (c) 127   (d) 172

2. (a) 34   (b) 75
   (c) 435   (d) 493

3. (a) 631   (b) 122
   (c) 553   (d) 20

4. (a) 601   (b) 641
   (c) 2224   (d) 2184

5. (a) 140   (b) 50
   (c) 195   (d) 41

6. (a) 29   (b) 29
   (c) 655   (d) 136

7. 300 ml

8. The number '24' at the intersection of R4 and C3 is wrong; it should be '23'.

9. (a) B
   (b) D
   (c) C
   (d) A

10. Student's calculations

Challenge 1

0603

Revision Exercise 1

1. (a) $3 \times 10\,000 + 9 \times 100 + 4 \times 10 + 7 \times 1$
   (b) 3, which is 30 000

2. (a) ones   (b) 400

3. (a) $<$ (b) $<$

4. (a) 3024   (b) 62 127
   (c) 5647   (d) 84 204

5. (a) 170   (b) 704
   (c) 712   (d) 675

6. (a) Shop Budget   (b) £36

7. 4119

8. 3660 kJ

9. 14 431

10. Top to bottom, left to right: 212, 213, 216, 215, 214, 217, 218

Chapter 2   Multiplying and Dividing Whole Numbers

Try It!

1. (a) 148   (b) 548

2. 34 974

3. (a) 3055
   (b) (i) 235
       (ii) 2820
       (iii) 3055

4. (a) 13 359   (b) 13 359

5. 768

6. £3600

7. (a) 196   (b) 512

8. (a) 24   (b) 16 r 2

9. (a) 178 r 0   (b) 629 r 2

10. (a) 26   (b) 330

11. 120

12. 11, 2 ml

13. (a) 470   (b) 6800

14. (a) 608   (b) 32

15. (a) 1085   (b) 2960
   (c) 2150

16. (a) 771   (b) 5706
   (c) 18 870

17. (a) 79   (b) 24

18. 1584

19. 1, 2, 3, 6, 9 and 18

20. (a) 1 and 5   (b) 5

21. 7, 14, 21, 28, 35 and 42

22. (a) 3, 6, 9, 12, 15, 18, 21, 24, 27 and 30
      9, 18, 27, 36, 45, 54, 63, 72, 81 and 90
   (b) 9, 18 and 27
   (c) 9

23. 17 and 19

24. $2 \times 3 \times 3 \times 5$

Practice 2.1

1. (a) $3 \times 28 = 84$
   (b) $4 \times 47 = 188$
   (c) $51 + 51 + 51 + 51 + 51 = 5 \times 51$
   (d) $79 + 79 + 79 = 3 \times 79$

2. (a) (i) 106   (ii) 212
       (iii) 654   (iv) 1090
   (b) 4×53 has a value twice as large as 53×2.

3. (a) (i) 4824   (ii) 48 024
       (iii) 2350   (iv) 11 750
   (b) 235×50 has a value five times as large as 235×10.

4. (a) (i) 336   (ii) 357
       (iii) 10 777   (iv) 15 425
   (b) 21×17 has a value 21 units higher than 16×21.
   (c) 830×13 would be 13 units higher than 829×13. that is, 10 790

5. (a) 100   (b) 225
   (c) 216   (d) 729

6. £126

7. 52 years

8. £561

9. 5980 ml

10. 504

Practice 2.2

1. (a) (i) 25   (ii) 15
     (iii) 128   (iv) 112
  (b) 3696 ÷ 7 is greater because 3696 is being divided into fewer equal parts.

2. (a) 12   (b) 112
  (c) 11   (d) 31

3. (a) 14 r 2   (b) 150 r 5
  (c) 12 r 3   (d) 58 r 0

4. (a) 17   (b) 182
  (c) 18   (d) 65

5. 64

6. (a) 325   (b) 79   (c) 3250

7. 54 cm

8. (a) 54   (b) 3

9. (a) 8   (b) £2480

10. 3, 8, 4

Practice 2.3

1. (a) 780   (b) 2900
  (c) 180   (d) 236

2. (a) 43   (b) 620
  (c) 520   (d) 1896

3. (a) 660   (b) 24
  (c) 5112   (d) 19

4. (a) 92   (b) 125
  (c) 1675   (d) 5350

5. (a) 18 520   (b) 8382
  (c) 34   (d) 6630

6. (a) 117   (b) 2520
  (c) 86 625   (d) 15

7. £6615

8. £637

9. £5850

10. Student's own answer

Practice 2.4

1. (a) 1, 2, 5 and 10
  (b) 1, 3, 9 and 27
  (c) 1, 2, 3, 4, 6, 9, 12, 18 and 36
  (d) 1, 2, 4, 5, 8, 10, 20 and 40

2. (a) 3, 6, 9, 12, 15 and 18
  (b) 10, 20, 30, 40, 50 and 60
  (c) 11, 22, 33, 44, 55 and 66
  (d) 20, 40, 60, 80, 100 and 120

3. (a) Not prime   (b) Prime
  (c) Prime   (d) Prime

4. 31, it is prime

5. (a) The factors of 10 are 1, 2, 5, 10.
     The factors of 15 are 1, 3, 5, 15.
  (b) 1 and 5   (c) 5

6. (a) 4, 8, 12, 16, 20, 24, 28, 32, 36 and 40
     6, 12, 18, 24, 30, 36, 42, 48, 54 and 60
  (b) 12, 24 and 36   (c) 12

7. (a) $2 \times 3 \times 7$ (b) $3 \times 5 \times 7$
  (c) $2 \times 2 \times 2 \times 3$ (d) $3 \times 3 \times 11$

8. 60 cm

9. (a) 42, 96 and 135
  (b) For each multiple of 3 in part (a) the sum of its digits is a multiple of 3. This works for any multiple of 3.

Challenge 2

The two whole numbers 63 and 82 give the greatest possible product 5166.

Revision Exercise 2

1. (a) 1410   (b) 2926
  (c) 2754   (d) 6045

2. (a) 374   (b) 1600
  (c) 5304   (d) 5966

3. (a) (i) 258
     (ii) 369
  (b) 37

4. (a) 134 r 0   (b) 429 r 2
  (c) 51 r 1   (d) 106 r 20

5. (a) 1670   (b) 48
  (c) 63 125   (d) 36 427

6. (a) 1, 2, 3, 4, 6, 9, 12, 18 and 36
     1, 3, 5, 9, 15 and 45
  (b) 1, 3 and 9   (c) 9

7. (a) 10, 20, 30, 40, 50, 60, 70, 80, 90 and 100
     15, 30, 45, 60, 75, 90, 105, 120, 135 and 150
  (b) 30, 60 and 90
  (c) 30   (d) 2, 3 and 5

8. 180

9. 32

10. £1810

Chapter 3   Calculation
Try It!

1. (a) 1830 ml   (b) 1800 ml

2. £15 000

3. (a) 150   (b) 70
  (c) 24 300   (d) 6

4. (a) 200   (b) 180

5. Under-estimate

6. Not reasonable

7. **(a)** 60   **(b)** 8

8. **(a)** 316   **(b)** 26

9. **(a)** 67   **(b)** 21

10. **(a)** 204   **(b)** 12

11. **(a)** 85   **(b)** 5

12. 9

13. 45

14. 9 miles

15. **(a)** 41   **(b)** 546 875
    (c) 46

16. **(a)** 5, 2   **(b)** 39, 5

17. 82

18. £1782

Practice 3.1

1. **(a)** A: 1380

2. **(a) (i)** 930   **(ii)** 450
   (b) (i) 1690   **(ii)** 3930

3. **(a) (i)** 400   **(ii)** 400
   (b) (i) 2500   **(ii)** 36 300

4. **(a) (i)** 5000   **(ii)** 10 000
   (iii) 27 000   **(iv)** 63 000

   (b) (i) 30 000   **(ii)** 10 000
   (iii) 840 000   **(iv)** 100 000

5. B, C and D (4750, 4825 and 4775) round to 4800, to the nearest 100.

6. 410 ml

7. 1300 m

8. £10 000

9. **(a)** £118 192
   (b) £120 000
   (c) The value obtained in **(b)** is closer to the value in **(a)** than it is to this answer.

10. **(a)** e.g. 37 500, 37 602 and 37 914
    (b) e.g. 38 499, 38 456 and 38 098

Practice 3.2

1. Student C (80 + 290) is correct.

2. **(a)** 80   **(b)** 520
   (c) 1200   **(d)** 10

3. **(a)** 1000   **(b)** 6900
   (c) 910 000   **(d)** 6

4. **(a)** 70   **(b)** 40
   (c) 380   **(d)** 120

5. **(a)** 0   **(b)** 8900
   (c) 3900   **(d)** 1700

6. Calculation B (1150 − 755)

7. Over-estimate

8. Over-estimate

9. **(a) (i)** 18 000   **(ii)** 17 500
   (b) Both totals in part (a) have been over-estimated. If you first rounded each number to the nearest hundred before adding, you get a closer estimate to the actual total.

10. Emma

Practice 3.3

1. **(a)** 27   **(b)** 4
   (c) 26   **(d)** 76

2. **(a)** $8 \times (3 + 2) \times 9$ **(b)** $160 \div (40 - 32) \div 8$
   (c) $84 \div 12 - 6 \times 2$ **(d)** $(81 + 15) \div 3 \times 4$

3. Calculation A: $2 \times 6 - 2$

4. **(a)** 50   **(b)** 40
   (c) 84   **(d)** 68

5. **(a)** 16   **(b)** 88
   (c) 2   **(d)** 240

6. **(a)** 105   **(b)** 27
   (c) 45   **(d)** 27
   (e) 57   **(f)** 41
   (g) 3   **(h)** 9

7. **(a)** 260   **(b)** 98
   (c) 125   **(d)** 3

8. **(a)** 86, 86   **(b)** 163, 257
   (c) 18, 18   **(d)** 1, 4

9. 35 cm³

10. 464 ml

Practice 3.4

1. **(a)** 3634   **(b)** 42 228
   (c) 52 472   **(d)** 405
   (e) 203 401   **(f)** 103 823

2. **(a)** 64 r 3   **(b)** 191 r 5
   (c) 256 r 0   **(d)** 84 r 223

3. **(a)** 7135   **(b)** 1305
   (c) 4571   **(d)** 4168

4. **(a)** 369 138   **(b)** 56
   (c) 148   **(d)** 9464

5. £1140

6. 690

7. 199 cm

8. 5

9. 49 minutes

Challenge 3

(a) 1
(b) 6460

Revision Exercise 3

1. (a) 330 (b) 3100
    (c) 10000 (d) 50000

2. 61734, 61659 and 61650

3. (a) 2000 (b) 8700
    (c) 29300 (d) 377

4. (a) 221 (b) 66
    (c) 520 (d) 83

5. (a) 4443 (b) 4315
    (c) 13917 (d) 749

6. (a) 1359 grams (b) 1400 grams

7. (a) $99\,m^2$ (b) $100\,m^2$

8. (a) 238 (b) 240

9. 15 cm

10. 442 grams

Chapter 4   Use of Letters

Try It!

1. (a) Sum of 4 and p, add p to 4, 4 plus p, p more than 4
    (b) Subtract 8 from q, take away 8 from q, q minus 8, 8 less than q
    (c) Product of r and 13, multiply r by 13, r times 13, r groups of 13
    (d) Quotient of 20 divided by s, divide 20 by s, s divided into 20

2. (a) 69 marks (b) 96 marks
    (c) $(p + 7)$ marks

3. (a) 50 mm (b) 74 mm
    (c) $2d$ mm

4. (a) £150 (b) £50
    (c) £$\left(\dfrac{750}{W}\right)$

5. (a) 11 (b) 17

6. (a) 30 (b) 3

7. (a) 54 (b) 30

Practice 4.1

1. (a) 'Add 9 to a' or 'a plus 9'
    (b) 'Subtract b from 10' or '10 minus b'
    (c) 'Multiply 8 by c' or '8 times c'
    (d) 'Divide d by 12' or '12 divided into d'

2. $m + 7$

3. $36 - p$

4. $4q$

5. $\dfrac{W}{2}$

6. (a) 10 (b) 15
    (c) $7 + n$

7. (a) 171 cm (b) 179 cm
    (c) $(h - 5)$ cm

8. (a) 30 (b) 54
    (c) $6p$

9. (a) 9 apples (b) 5 apples
    (c) $\dfrac{90}{M}$ apples

10. One student is absent on that day.

Practice 4.2

1. (a) 11 (b) 15

2. (a) 8 (b) 1

3. (a) 20 (b) 55

4. (a) 4 (b) 7

5. (a) 19 years (b) 23 years
    (c) 11 years old

6. (a) 75 cm (b) 92 cm

7. (a) 28 (b) 63

8. (a) 24 cm (b) 15 cm
    (c) 12 parts

9. (a) $53\,cm^3$ (b) $18\,cm^3$

10. e.g. $x + 4$

Challenge 4

(a) (i) 20
    (ii) $500 - 30n$
(b) Not enough sheets of paper to print 18 booklets.

Revision Exercise 4

1. (a) 490 ml (b) 520 ml
    (c) $(240 + x)$ ml

2. (a) 4 (b) 17
    (c) $a - 9$

3. (a) £8000 (b) £9400
    (c) £$4y$

4. (a) 24 grams (b) 65 grams
    (c) $\dfrac{m}{5}$ grams

5. (a) 68 (b) 95

6. (a) 2 (b) 9

7. (a) 21 (b) 42

8. (a) 2 (b) 5

9. (a) 68 °C (b) 13 °C

10. (a) £13 (b) No

Try It!

1. (a) 506   (b) 615
   (c) 109 is a prime number.

2. (a) (i) 530
        (ii) 600
   (b) 450
   (c) No

3. (a) hundreds   (b) 40 000
   (c) (i) $43\,285 - 2x$
        (ii) 42 685

Review Exercise 1

1. (a) £($2 \times 10\,000 + 3 \times 1000 + 8 \times 10 + 5 \times 1$)
   (b) 3000
   (c) £23 100

2. (a) (i) 8055
        (ii) 8830
   (b) 8055

3. (a) 517   (b) 1331

4. (a) (i) 150   (ii) 750   (iii) 900
   (b) 1472

5. (a) £478   (b) Increases by £2

6. (a) 827   (b) 56

7. (a) 6, 12, 18, 24, 30, 36, 42, 48, 54, 60
   (b) 9, 18, 27, 36, 45, 54, 63, 72, 81, 90
   (c) 18
   (d) 30

8. (a) 331   (b) 200
   (c) 6435

9. (a) 205   (b) 890
   (c) 95

10. (a) 24   (b) 72
    (c) $8n$

11. (a) 41   (b) 43
    (c) 5
    (d) (i) $28 + a < 6b - 23$ (ii) $6b - 23 > \dfrac{150}{c}$

12. (a) (i) 16
         (ii) 25
         (iii) 36
    (b) $4^2 + 1$ and $6^2 + 1$ are prime numbers.
    (c) 4

13. (a) 171   (b) 7
    (c) £513

14. (a) £($128 + x$)
    (b) (i) £198
         (ii) £163

15. (a) $4y$ watts
    (b) (i) 1300 watts
         (ii) 975 watts

16. (a) £($15 - 4n$)
    (b) £7
    (c) Cost of ticket must be positive.

Chapter 5   Understanding Fractions

Try It!

1. Student's diagram

2. $\dfrac{2}{11}$

3. (a) Student's diagram
   (b) $\dfrac{6}{13}$

4. (a) Student's diagram
   (b) $\dfrac{4}{9}$

5. (a) Student's diagram
   (b) $\dfrac{5}{8}$

6. $\dfrac{5}{12}$

7. (a) $\dfrac{49}{60}$
   (b) $\dfrac{5}{24}$

8. (a) 2
   (b) $1\dfrac{1}{3}$

9. (a) $\dfrac{11}{6}$
   (b) $\dfrac{39}{8}$

10. Student's diagram

11. $1\dfrac{2}{3}$ m

12. (a) $\dfrac{2}{8}, \dfrac{3}{12}, \dfrac{4}{16}, \dfrac{5}{20}, \dfrac{6}{24}$
    (b) $\dfrac{4}{6}, \dfrac{6}{9}, \dfrac{8}{12}, \dfrac{10}{15}, \dfrac{12}{18}$

13. (a) 8   (b) 65
    (c) 2   (d) 11

14. (a) 1   (b) 4

15. (a) $\dfrac{6}{7}$ (b) $\dfrac{7}{8}$

16. (a) Equivalent   (b) Not equivalent
    (c) Equivalent

17. $\dfrac{5}{9}$

18. $\dfrac{2}{7}$

19. $4\dfrac{5}{6}$

20. 18 kg

21. 70

22. 40 minutes

Practice 5.1

1. (a) $\dfrac{1}{2}$ (b) $\dfrac{2}{5}$

   (c) $\dfrac{7}{15}$

2. Student's diagrams

3. Student's diagram

4. (a) $\dfrac{3}{7}$

   (b) $\dfrac{1}{3}$

5. (a) Diagram is not divided into equal parts. So, what is shaded is not $\dfrac{1}{5}$ of the whole diagram.

   (b) Diagram is divided into 5 equal parts of which one is shaded. The shaded portion is $\dfrac{1}{5}$ of the whole diagram.

6. (a) Student's diagram

   (b) The number line is not divided into equal intervals/parts. So, the total length of two parts on her number line does not represent $\dfrac{2}{6}$.

7. (a) $\dfrac{2}{3}$ (b) $\dfrac{3}{5}$

8. (a) $\dfrac{43}{60}$ (b) $\dfrac{19}{60}$

   (c) $\dfrac{11}{24}$

9. $\dfrac{1}{8}$

10. (a) Student's diagrams

    (b) Student's diagrams

Practice 5.2

1. (a) $\dfrac{3}{4},\dfrac{2}{9},\dfrac{4}{6}$ (b) $\dfrac{7}{3},\dfrac{4}{4},\dfrac{9}{7}$

   (c) $3\dfrac{1}{5},5\dfrac{2}{9}$

2. (a) (i) $2\dfrac{7}{8}$ (ii) $3\dfrac{5}{9}$ (b) $1\dfrac{4}{6}$

3. (a) $2\dfrac{3}{5}$ (b) $1\dfrac{5}{8}$

   (c) 2 (d) $2\dfrac{2}{7}$

4. (a) $\dfrac{10}{7}$ (b) $\dfrac{11}{5}$

   (c) $\dfrac{31}{8}$ (d) $\dfrac{47}{10}$

5. (a) 10 (b) 21 (c) 8

6. Student's diagrams

7. $2\dfrac{5}{6}$

8. 4

9. Student's diagrams

Practice 5.3

1. (a) $\dfrac{6}{30}$ (b) $\dfrac{8}{48}$

   (c) $\dfrac{2}{5}$

2. (a) $\dfrac{4}{10},\dfrac{6}{15},\dfrac{8}{20},\dfrac{10}{25},\dfrac{12}{30}$ (b) $\dfrac{8}{14},\dfrac{12}{21},\dfrac{16}{28},\dfrac{20}{35},\dfrac{24}{42}$

   (c) $\dfrac{6}{10},\dfrac{3}{5},\dfrac{24}{40},\dfrac{36}{60},\dfrac{48}{80}$

3. (a) $\dfrac{3}{10}$ (b) $\dfrac{1}{10}$

   (c) $\dfrac{1}{4}$ (d) $\dfrac{3}{11}$

   (e) $\dfrac{3}{4}$ (f) $\dfrac{2}{5}$

   (g) $\dfrac{1}{3}$ (h) $\dfrac{4}{5}$

4. $\dfrac{28}{35}$

5. (a) 70 (b) 27

   (c) 48 (d) 3

   (e) 54 (f) 11

6. (a) Not equivalent   (b) Equivalent

   (c) Equivalent   (d) Not equivalent

   (e) Equivalent   (f) Equivalent

7. Siti and Jane have the same amount of rice because $\dfrac{6}{8}$ and $\dfrac{9}{12}$ are equivalent fractions.

8. (a) 2 (b) 30

Practice 5.4

1. (a) $\dfrac{7}{9}>\dfrac{5}{9}$ (b) $\dfrac{3}{7}<\dfrac{3}{5}$

2. (a) $\dfrac{1}{5}>\dfrac{1}{8}$ (b) $\dfrac{2}{3}>\dfrac{2}{5}$

   (c) $\dfrac{3}{7}<\dfrac{3}{4}$ (d) $\dfrac{19}{100}>\dfrac{19}{1000}$

3. (a) $\dfrac{3}{6}$ (b) $\dfrac{2}{10}$

   (c) $\dfrac{2}{11}$ (d) $\dfrac{9}{15}$

4. (a) $1\dfrac{2}{9}$ (b) $\dfrac{16}{5}$

5. $\dfrac{5}{9},\dfrac{5}{7},\dfrac{5}{4}$

6. $1\dfrac{3}{7},\dfrac{5}{7},\dfrac{3}{7}$

7. $\dfrac{5}{8},\dfrac{5}{7},\dfrac{13}{7}$

8. $\dfrac{21}{8}>\dfrac{19}{8}$ so the mast is longer than the pole.

9. Student's answer

Practice 5.5

1. (a) 3 fish   (b) 6 fish

2. (a) 3 beads   (b) 12 beads

3. (a) 8 kg   (b) £48

   (c) 144 ml   (d) 320 m

4. £9

5. 25

6. (a) 45 minutes   (b) 4 hours

7. (a) 15   (b) 35

8. 28

9. $\dfrac{11}{18} > \dfrac{5}{9}$ so choose $\dfrac{11}{18}$ to get more apples.

Challenge 5

$\dfrac{15}{24}$

Revision Exercise 5

1. (a) $\dfrac{3}{4}$ (b) $\dfrac{1}{6}$

    (c) $\dfrac{7}{10}$ (d) $\dfrac{7}{15}$

2. $\dfrac{3}{9}$

3. $\dfrac{5}{2} = 2\dfrac{1}{2}$

4. $3\dfrac{1}{4}$

5. (a) $3\dfrac{2}{3}$ (b) $3\dfrac{3}{4}$

    (c) 3   (d) $4\dfrac{2}{7}$

6. (a) $\dfrac{5}{3}$ (b) $\dfrac{13}{5}$

    (c) $\dfrac{23}{6}$ (d) $\dfrac{33}{8}$

7. (a) 8   (b) 15

8. (a) $\dfrac{1}{20}$ (b) $\dfrac{19}{100}$

9. (a) $\dfrac{4}{5}$ (b) $\dfrac{1}{6}$

    (c) $\dfrac{9}{10}$ (d) $\dfrac{1}{4}$

10. (a) £12   (b) 45 cm

    (c) 8 grams   (d) 140 minutes

11. (a) 44 ml   (b) 88 ml

12. (a) $\dfrac{3}{5} < \dfrac{3}{4}$ so Dan is faster.

    (b) 36 minutes

Chapter 6   Tenths, Hundredths and Thousandths

Try It!

1. (a) $5 \times 1 + 9 \times \dfrac{1}{100} + 3 \times \dfrac{1}{1000}$

    (b) Student's answer

2. (a) $\dfrac{4}{10}$ (b) $\dfrac{4}{100}$

3. £8.64

4. Melon C

5. Gloria

6. (a) $\dfrac{2}{5}$ (b) $\dfrac{7}{250}$

7. (a) $71\dfrac{1}{4}$ (b) $7\dfrac{1}{8}$

8. (a) 0.6   (b) 0.22

9. (a) 2.16   (b) 16.045

10. (a) 396   (b) 396.5

     (c) 3965

11. (a) £14   (b) £1400

12. Frances

13. (a) 0.521   (b) 0.521

     (c) 8.521

14. Gillian

15. (a) 3.5 litres   (b) 0.35 litres

16. (a) 0.375 litres   (b) 4200 g

17. (a) (i) 1500 mm   (b) 24 minutes

       (ii) 1.50 m

     (c) 2.3p

18. 61%

19. (a) 10%   (b) 40%

     (c) 36%

20. (a) $\dfrac{3}{10}$ (b) $\dfrac{7}{20}$

     (c) $\dfrac{17}{25}$

21. (a) 67%   (b) 4%

     (c) 40%

22. (a) 0.47   (b) 0.6

     (c) 0.06

23. (a) 20   (b) 70%

24. 24 kg

25. £2275

Practice 6.1

1. (a) $1 \times 10 + 2 \times 1 + 3 \times \dfrac{1}{10}$

      Twelve and three tenths

    (b) $9 \times 1 + 3 \times \dfrac{1}{10} + 4 \times \dfrac{1}{100}$

      Nine, three tenths and four hundredths

    (c) $9 \times 1 + 3 \times \dfrac{1}{100} + 4 \times \dfrac{1}{1000}$

      Nine, three hundredths and four thousandths

    (d) $9 \times \dfrac{1}{10} + 3 \times \dfrac{1}{100} + 4 \times \dfrac{1}{1000}$

      Nine tenths, three hundredths and four thousandths

2. (a) 1.47   (b) 0.147

    (c) 30.508   (d) 3.581

3. (a) $\dfrac{5}{10}$ (b) $\dfrac{5}{100}$

    (c) 5 ones   (d) $\dfrac{5}{1000}$

4. (a) <   (b) <

    (c) <   (d) >

5. (a) 0.273   (b) 3.50

    (c) 16.91   (d) 1.698

6. Shop B

7. Alice

8. (a) (i) 3   (b) Diamond A
    (ii) 2

9. 7, 8 and 9

10. e.g. 0.31, 0.374, 0.4, 0.409, 0.49, 0.499

Practice 6.2

1. (a) $\frac{3}{10}$ (b) $\frac{4}{5}$

    (c) $\frac{3}{25}$ (d) $\frac{2}{25}$

2. (a) $3\frac{1}{2}$ (b) $3\frac{3}{5}$

    (c) $4\frac{8}{25}$ (d) $5\frac{3}{50}$

3. (a) 0.5   (b) 0.6
    (c) 0.45   (d) 0.08

4. (a) 1.25   (b) 2.8
    (c) 3.05   (d) 4.28

5. (a) Student's diagram   (b) They are the same.
    (c) Student's answer

6. (a) $\frac{1}{250}$ (b) $\frac{1}{8}$

7. (a) $2\frac{2}{125}$ (b) $2\frac{53}{500}$

8. (a) 0.625   (b) 0.024

9. (a) 5.165   (b) 6.018

10. Crab

Practice 6.3

1. (a) 248   (b) 24.8
    (c) 23.6   (d) 2300.6
    (e) 93 800   (f) 9380

2. (a) 4.19   (b) 4.019
    (c) 9.081   (d) 90.81
    (e) 53.904   (f) 5.394

3. 0.0375×100

4. (a) 2.67 m   (b) 3600 ml
    (c) 1.59 kg   (d) 300p
    (e) 15 minutes   (f) 4800 m

5. (a) £49.50   (b) £495

6. 20.3×10

7. No, when you multiply a decimal number by 10, each digit moves one place left.

8. (a) (i) 2.37 kg   (b) 3
    (ii) 0.237 kg

9. (a) 36 000 m   (b) 24 minutes
    (c) 1500 m

Practice 6.4

1. (a) 68%   (b) No

2. 64%

3. (a) 30%   (b) 25%
    (c) 60%   (d) 68%

4. (a) $\frac{4}{5}$ (b) $\frac{12}{25}$

    (c) $\frac{2}{25}$ (d) $\frac{9}{20}$

5. (a) 9%   (b) 90%
    (c) 21%   (d) 56%

6. (a) 0.4   (b) 0.04
    (c) 0.38   (d) 0.59

7. 0.88, $\frac{22}{25}$, 88%

    0.04, 4%, $\frac{8}{200}$

    0.4, $\frac{2}{5}$, 40%

    0.3, 30%, $\frac{6}{20}$

8. (a) $\frac{29}{50}$ (b) 58%

9. (a) 56%   (b) 44%

Practice 6.5

1. (a) 8 kg   (b) 36 cm
    (c) 12 days   (d) £52

2. (a) 20 km   (b) 81 ml
    (c) 24 kg   (d) 208 m²

3. The same

4. £1120

5. 21 litres

6. (a) 30 kg   (b) 20 kg

7. Shop B

8. (a) 54   (b) 198

9. Samira's bar model

Challenge 6

42%

Revision Exercise 6

1. (a) $2 \times 10 + 9 \times 1 + 5 \times \frac{1}{10} + 7 \times \frac{1}{100}$
    (b) tenths
    (c) Stick insect B

2. (a) $\frac{21}{25}$ (b) $1\frac{1}{4}$

    (c) $3\frac{2}{25}$

3. (a) 0.32   (b) 3.5
    (c) 4.06

4. Student's table

5. (a) 381.6   (b) 5893
    (c) 0.968   (d) 0.674
    (e) 530.1   (f) 9.065

6. (a) 936 cm   (b) 36 minutes
    (c) 6.503 kg   (d) 0.287 litres

7. (a) 120 grams   (b) 280 grams

8. (a) 500   (b) 1500

9. (a) 15%   (b) No

10. Option B

Chapter 7   Introduction to Ratio

Try It!

1. (a) Student's bar model
   (b) 4:1
   (c) 1:4

2. (a) Student's bar model
   (b) 7:6
   (c) 6:4
   (d) 4:17

3. (a) Student's bar model
   (b) Yes
   (c) No

4. (a) 4:3
   (b) The ratio 3 : 7 is the ratio of the length of the red ribbon to the total length of the red and blue ribbons.

5. (a) $\frac{9}{2}$ (b) $\frac{9}{11}$

6. (a) 3:14   (b) 3:11

7. (a) $\frac{3}{5}$ (b) 450 ml

8. (a) 7:4   (b) 112 g

9. (a) e.g. 5:20, 6:24   (b) e.g. 6:3, 2:1

10. (a) 1:4   (b) 6:13
    (c) 2:1   (d) 13:8

11. (a) 5:3   (b) 240 g

Practice 7.1

1. 3:2

2. 1:3

3. 2:5

4. 4:3

5. 3:2

6. (a) 2:5   (b) 3:8
   (c) 5:3   (d) 8:5

7. (a) 2:3   (b) 3:2
   (c) 3:10

8. (a) Yes   (b) No

9. (a) The ratio 7:4 is the ratio of the number of female contestants to the number of male contestants.
   (b) The ratio 11:4 is the ratio of the total number of contestants to the number of male contestants.

10. Student's own answer

Practice 7.2

1. (a) $\frac{1}{3}$ (b) $\frac{2}{5}$
   (c) $\frac{7}{4}$ (d) $\frac{11}{6}$

2. (a) 1:2   (b) 3:10
   (c) 12:5   (d) 15:8

3. (a) 2:3
   (b) (i) 5:4   (ii) No

4. 7:2

5. 54 cm

6. 150 m²

7. (a) Student's bar model
   (b) $\frac{8}{3}$ (c) £56

8. (a) 7:5   (b) 10

9. (a) 9:4   (b) £980

Practice 7.3

1. (a) e.g. 6:10   (b) e.g. 12:9
   (c) e.g. 6:9   (d) e.g. 140:80

2. (a) 1:2   (b) 5:7
   (c) 3:1   (d) 9:8

3. (a) Equivalent   (b) Not equivalent
   (c) Equivalent   (d) Equivalent
   (e) Equivalent   (f) Equivalent

4. 3:9

5. 24:19

6. (a) (i) 1:4
       (ii) 1:16
       (iii) 1:4
   (b) The ratios in (a)(i) and (a)(iii) are qual.

7. (a) 7:8   (b) 80

8. (a) 6:11   (b) £51

9. Yes

Challenge 7

7:9

Revision Exercise 7

1. (a) 5:4   (b) 4:9

2. (a) 1:2   (b) 2:3
   (c) 1:2

3. (a) $\frac{4}{3}$ (b) $\frac{5}{8}$

4. (a) 9:40   (b) 1:4
   (c) 2:3   (d) 5:3

5. (a) 1:3   (b) 3:4
   (c) 11:9   (d) 5:3

6.   **(a)** Equivalent   **(b)** Equivalent
    (c) Not equivalent   **(d)** Equivalent

7.   **(a)** 9:20   **(b)** 4:3

8.   **(a)** $\dfrac{16}{7}$ **(b)** 48 grams

9.   **(a)** 9:11   **(b)** 9:2
    (c) £120

10. **(a)** 30 m²   **(b)** 8 m²
    (c) 4:15

Integrated Examples and Review Exercise 2

Try It!

1.   **(a)** $\dfrac{2}{5}$ **(b)** 40%
    (c) 60%   **(d)** 2:3

2.   **(a)** $9\times\dfrac{1}{10}+1\times\dfrac{1}{100}+8\times\dfrac{1}{1000}$ **(b)** **(i)** $\dfrac{1}{100}$
                                          (ii) 10
    (c) 918 grams   **(d)** 2:3

3.   **(a)** Q is smaller.   **(b)** 31%
    (c) 124 grams

Review Exercise 2

1.   **(a)** $\dfrac{2}{5}$ **(b)** 0.4
    (c) 40%

2.   **(a)** £21   **(b)** 66 kg

3.   **(a)** $\dfrac{4}{9}>\dfrac{2}{9}$, so Jane gets the greater prize.
    (b) £4800

4.   **(a)** $1\dfrac{4}{5}=\dfrac{9}{5}$, $1\dfrac{2}{7}=\dfrac{9}{7}$
    (b) $\dfrac{1}{5}>\dfrac{1}{7}$, so cake A is heavier.

5.   **(a)** $2\times10+5\times1+3\times\dfrac{1}{10}+7\times\dfrac{1}{100}$
    (b) 7 hundredths
    (c) 25.34 < 25.37, so Annabel is faster.

6.   **(a)** $\dfrac{19}{25}$ **(b)** 3%
    (c) 3.65   **(d)** 0.49

7.   **(a)** 250 g   **(b)** 1.39 litres
    (c) £4.65   **(d)** 3650 cm

8.   **(a)** 2:3   **(b)** £10

9.   **(a)** 3:2   **(b)** 2:3
    (c) 2:5

10. **(a)** 80   **(b)** 63 cm

11. **(a)** Student's diagram
    (b) $2\dfrac{1}{4}$ is to the right of 1.3 on the number line, so $2\dfrac{1}{4}>1.3$.
    (c) $\dfrac{13}{10}$
    (d) The possible ways are $1.3=\dfrac{2}{5}+\dfrac{9}{10}=\dfrac{1}{2}+\dfrac{4}{5}=\dfrac{3}{5}+\dfrac{7}{10}$

12. **(a)** £100   **(b)** £45
    (c) 20:9

13. **(a)** 24 cm   **(b)** 45 cm
    (c) 8:15

14. **(a)** 3:2   **(b)** 60%
    (c) 36

15. **(a)** 27   **(b)** 141 kg

Chapter 8   Measures and Angles

Try It!

1.   70°

2.   100°

3.   240°

4.   Student's diagram

5. $\angle a$ is reflex, $\angle b$ is obtuse, $\angle c$ is a right angle, $\angle d$ is acute

6.   38°

7.   65°

8.   317°

9.   **(a)** 180°   **(b)** 4

Practice 8.1

1.   **(a)** 23°   **(b)** 198°
    (c) 324°   **(d)** 158°

2.   Student's diagrams

3. $\angle a=80°$, $\angle b=100°$, $\angle c=77°$, $\angle d=136°$, $\angle e=149°$, $\angle f=80°$

4.   Student's diagrams

Practice 8.2

1.

Size of angle	Type of angle
36°	acute
72°	acute
95°	obtuse
107°	obtuse
182°	reflex
242°	reflex

2.   Robert is not correct.

3.   Student's diagrams

4.   Student's angles

Practice 8.3

1.   **(a)** 60°   **(b)** 26°

2.   **(a)** 124°   **(b)** 63°

3. (a) 258° (b) 53°

4. 3

5. 45°

6. 102°

7. 231°

8. 60° or 80°

Challenge 8

(a) (i) 360°
    (ii) 150°

(b) 6°

Revision Exercise 8

1. (a) 124° (b) 44°
    (c) 141° (d) 270°

2. Student's diagrams

3. (a) Reflex (b) Acute
    (c) Reflex (d) Obtuse

4. (a) 33° (b) 105°
    (c) 37° (d) 165°

5. (a) True
    (b) False
    (c) False

6. Not enough information

7. 330°

8. (a) 140° (b) 41°

9. 225°, 270° and 315°

Chapter 9   Symmetry

Fully-worked solutions for this book are available in Teacher Guide 1A.

Try It!

1. (a) 5 (b) 6

2. (a) 2 (b) 0
    (c) 8

3. Student's diagrams. Shape **(a)** has no other lines of symmetry. Shape **(b)** has 1 more line of symmetry.

4. (a) 4 (b) No rotation symmetry
    (c) 3 (d) 8

5. (a) Number of lines of symmetry = 6
    Order of rotation symmetry = 6
    (b) Number of lines of symmetry = 0
    Order of rotation symmetry = 2
    (c) Number of lines of symmetry = 1
    No rotation symmetry

Practice 9.1

1. (a) Student's diagram
    Number of lines of symmetry = 1

(b) Student's diagram
    Number of lines of symmetry = 2

(c) Student's diagram
    Number of lines of symmetry = 5

2. (a) Student's diagram
    Number of lines of symmetry = 2
    (b) Student's diagram
    Number of lines of symmetry = 1
    (c) Student's diagram
    Number of lines of symmetry = 2

3. 16

4. (a) 1 (b) 4
    (c) 0

5. (a) Student's diagram
    Number of lines of symmetry = 1
    (b) Student's diagram
    Number of lines of symmetry = 1
    (c) Student's diagram
    Number of lines of symmetry = 8

6. e.g. **BEE, HEX, HOB, COB, BED, MUM, TUT**

7. 8310

8. Student's diagrams

9. Student's diagrams

10. Student's diagrams. **(d)** is not possible.

Practice 9.2

1. (a) 4 (b) 2
    (c) No rotation symmetry

2. (a) 2 (b) 2
    (c) 5

3. (a) Number of lines of symmetry = 2
    Order of rotation symmetry = 2
    (b) Number of lines of symmetry = 4
    Order of rotation symmetry = 4
    (c) Number of lines of symmetry = 4
    Order of rotation symmetry = 4

4. (a) No rotation symmetry (b) 2
    (c) 2

5. (a) Number of lines of symmetry = 0
    Order of rotation symmetry = 3
    (b) Number of lines of symmetry = 0
    Order of rotation symmetry = 2
    (c) Number of lines of symmetry = 3
    Order of rotation symmetry = 3

6. (a) Student's diagram
    (b) ii (c) Student's diagrams

7. Student's shapes

8. Student's shapes

Challenge 9

Student's diagrams

Revision Exercise 9

1. Student's diagrams

2. (a) 2   (b) 4   (c) 3

3. (a) Number of lines of symmetry = 0
      Order of rotation symmetry = 2
   (b) Number of lines of symmetry = 4
      Order of rotation symmetry = 4
   (c) Number of lines of symmetry = 4
      Order of rotation symmetry = 4

4. (a) W, T   (b) S
   (c) I   (d) F

5. (a) Number of lines of symmetry = 2
      Order of rotation symmetry = 2
   (b) Number of lines of symmetry = 8
      Order of rotation symmetry = 8
   (c) Number of lines of symmetry = 1
      No rotation symmetry

6. (a) Number of lines of symmetry = 1
      No rotation symmetry
   (b) Number of lines of symmetry = 1
      No rotation symmetry
   (c) Number of lines of symmetry = 4
      Order of rotation symmetry = 4

7. (a) Student's diagram
      Order of rotation symmetry = 2
   (b) Student's diagram
      Order of rotation symmetry = 3

8. Student's diagram
   No rotation symmetry

Chapter 10 Perimeter and Area of Rectangles, Squares and Triangles

Try It!

1. (a) 50 cm   (b) 64 cm
2. (a) 30 cm   (b) 19 m
3. 150 m
4. 16 m, 15 m^2
5. 160 000 cm^2
6. 10 cm
7. 10 cm
8. (a) 240 m   (b) 13 cm
9. (a) 3600 mm^2 (b) 60 cm^2
10. (a) 216 cm^2 (b) Serena
11. (a) 416 cm^2 (b) 15 cm
12. 40 m

Practice 10.1

1. (a) 44 cm   (b) 48 m
   (c) 44 cm

2. (a) 15 cm   (b) 9 cm
   (c) 17 cm
3. 346 m
4. 10 m
5. 96 cm
6. 16 cm
7. Kendall

Practice 10.2

1. (a) 18 cm^2 (b) 40 m^2
   (c) 128 m^2 (d) 225 cm^2
2. (a) 7 cm   (b) 18 cm
   (c) 2 m
3. 196 cm^2
4. 75 ÷ 15 = 5 m
5. 24 cm
6. 60 000 cm^2
7. Jake
8. £2040

Practice 10.3

1. (a) 40 cm   (b) 71 m
2. (a) 20 cm^2, 10 cm^2 (b) 54 m^2, 27 m^2
3. (a) 12 m^2 (b) 192 m^2
   (c) 176 cm^2 (d) 112 cm^2
4. (a) 120 cm, 600 cm^2 (b) 76 m, 114 m^2
5. 36 cm, 60 cm^2
6. Hajrah
7. 7 cm
8. 32 m

Challenge 10

32 cm, 46 cm^2

Revision Exercise 10

1. (a) 52 cm   (b) 46 m
   (c) 44 cm
2. (a) 18 m   (b) 12 cm
   (c) 8 cm
3. (a) 3 cm   (b) 7 m
4. (a) 54 cm, 126 cm^2 (b) 55 cm, 82.5 cm^2
   (c) 60 m, 60 m^2
5. 36 m
6. 17 m
7. B, A, C
8. No
9. 684 m^2

Chapter 11 Volume and Surface Area of Cuboids, Including Cubes

Fully-worked solutions for this book are available in Teacher Guide 1A.

Try It!

1. **(b)** will not form a cube when folded.

2. Diagram A is not a net. Diagram B is a net.

3. **(a)** $6\,m^2$ **(b)** $5\,m^2$

4. **(a)** Student's diagram
   (b) $62\,cm^2$
   (c) Yes

5. **(a)** $36\,cm^2$
   (b) $180\,cm^2$
   (c) Student's answer

6. **(a)** Student's diagram
   (b) $60\,cm^3$
   (c) You can multiply the three dimensions (length, width and height) together to get the same result.

7. $343\,cm^3$

8. $5400\,cm^3$

9. $2\,m$

Practice 11.1

1. **(a)** No **(b)** Yes
   (c) No **(d)** Yes

2. **(a)** Yes **(b)** No
   (c) No **(d)** Yes

3-8. Student's diagrams

Practice 11.2

1. **(a)** $24\,cm^2$ **(b)** $96\,m^2$
   (c) $294\,cm^2$

2. **(a)** $132\,cm^2$ **(b)** $342\,cm^2$
   (c) $544\,m^2$

3. **(a)** $13\,cm^2$ **(b)** $18\,m^2$

4. $43\,cm^2$

5. $620\,cm^2$

Practice 11.3

1. **(a)** $27\,cm^3$ **(b)** $512\,m^3$

2. **(a)** $600\,cm^3$ **(b)** $30\,m^3$

3. The cube has the greater volume.

4. $21\,cm$

5. No

6. $14\,m^2$

Challenge 11

(a) $8\,cm^3$, $28\,cm^2$
(b) $9\,cm^3$, $32\,cm^2$

Revision Exercise 11

1. **(a)** Yes **(b)** No
   (c) No **(d)** No

2. **(a)** $330\,cm^2$, $350\,cm^3$ **(b)** $2400\,cm^2$, $8000\,cm^3$
   (c) $252\,cm^2$, $216\,cm^3$ **(d)** $1350\,cm^2$, $2250\,cm^3$

3. **(a)** $390\,cm^2$, $450\,cm^3$ **(b)** $96\,cm^2$, $64\,cm^3$

4. $196\,cm^2$

5. Student's diagrams

6. Student's diagram

7. **(a)** $14\,cm^3$, $44\,cm^2$ **(b)** $18\,cm^3$, $54\,cm^2$

8. **(a)** $16\,cm^2$ **(b)** $5\,cm$

9. No

Chapter 12 Collecting, Organising and Displaying Data

Fully-worked solutions for this book are available in Teacher Guide 1A.

Try It!

1. **(a)** Student's frequency table
   (b) 9 **(c)** 8
   (d) 11 **(e)** 28

2. **(a)** 45 **(b)** Bus
   (c) 7 **(d)** $\frac{4}{45}$

3. **(a)** 15 **(b)** 54
   (c) Tuesday **(d)** 11
   (e) $\frac{2}{9}$

4. **(a)** Dogs **(b)** 27
   (c) 39

5. Student's diagram

6. **(a)** Student's diagram **(b)** Football
   (c) 40% **(d)** 70%

7. Student's diagram

8. **(a)** 180 **(b)** Cola
   (c) Orange **(d)** 9:11

9. **(a)** 37 **(b)** Student's diagram
   (c) 1:2

10. **(a)** Student's frequency table
    (b) 40%

Practice 12.1

1. Student's own answers

2. **(a)** Student's frequency table
   (b) 24
   (c) 2
   (d) No, there are 3 students in each category.

3. (a) 138   (b) 103

    (c) $\dfrac{35}{138}$

4. (a) Red   (b) 5

    (c) $\dfrac{46}{63}$

Practice 12.2

1. (a) Stall A £550, stall B £300, stall C £475

    (b) £250

    (c) 12:19

2. (a) 59   (b) Class 7D

    (c) Class 7F   (d) Classes 7C and 7E

    (e) Class 7F

3. (a) Lime, 4   (b) 16%

    (c) 54%

4. (a) Student's diagram   (b) $\dfrac{3}{11}$

5. (a) Student's diagram   (b) $\dfrac{7}{20}$

    (c) 3:5

6. Student's diagram

Practice 12.3

1. (a) 20–29   (b) 10

    (c) 23:18   (d) Student's diagram

2. (a) 3   (b) 44%

3. (a) Student's frequency table

    (b) 10

    (c) 30%

4. (a) Student's frequency table

    (b) 4:5

    (c) 20%

Challenge 12

Student's diagram

Revision Exercise 12

1. (a) Student's frequency table

    (b) Three-bedroom houses

    (c) $\dfrac{3}{25}$

2. (a) Student's frequency table

    (b) Student's diagram

    (c) 37–39

    (d) $\dfrac{9}{25}$

3. (a) Student's diagram   (b) Tank F

    (c) Tanks A and D   (d) $\dfrac{7}{40}$

4. (a) Pictogram   (b) Student's frequency table

    (c) 40   (d) $\dfrac{5}{17}$

5. (a) Student's frequency table

    (b) 4:3

Integrated Examples and Review Exercise 3
Try It!

1. (a) 135°   (b) $3\,cm^2$

    (c) (i) 90°

       (ii) The figure has two lines of symmetry. Thus, it has line symmetry. It has rotation symmetry of order 2.

2. (a) Acute angles: 12°, 89°, 46°, 57°, 30°

       Obtuse angles: 123°, 98°, 143°, 168°, 128°, 143°, 155°

       Reflex angles: 347°, 257°, 270°, 256°

    (b) 12° and 168°, 57° and 123°

    (c) Student's diagram

3. (a) (i) 8 cm, $4\,cm^2$

       (ii) 14 cm, $10\,cm^2$

    (b) Student's diagram

    (c) $48\,cm^2$

    (d) $20\,cm^3$

    (e) The Large size has the smallest number of boxes, 14.

Review Exercise 3

1. $\angle a = 82°$(acute), $\angle b = 324°$(reflex), $\angle c = 123°$(obtuse)

2. $\angle x = 34°$, $\angle y = 142°$, $\angle z = 69°$

3. Student's diagrams

4. (a) 3   (b) 4

5. (a) (i) 28 cm

       (ii) $49\,cm^2$

    (b) (i) 26 m

       (ii) $40\,m^2$

6. (a) $60\,cm^2$ (b) $756\,cm^2$

7. (a) Student's diagram   (b) $150\,cm^2$

    (c) $125\,cm^3$

8. (a) Student's diagram   (b) $10\,480\,cm^2$

    (c) $84\,000\,cm^3$

    (d) Student's diagram and explanation

9. (a) £5   (b) £60

10. (a) Flowerbed B   (b) 4

11. (a) 30°   (b) 53°

    (c) 22 m   (d) $8\,m^2$

12. (a) Student's diagram   (b) 2

    (c) Student's diagram   (d) Student's own answer

    (e) No

13. (a) $294\,cm^2$ (b) $343\,cm^3$

    (c) F

14. (a) 10, 11, 12, 13 and 14 push-ups

    (b) 80

    (c) 6

    (d) 3:8

Problems in Real-world Contexts

A. **1.** Since each external wall is 33 feet long, all three walls are equal length. Hence, the walls form an equilateral triangle.

    2. **(a)** Reflection symmetry. Number of lines of symmetry = 3

       (b) Rotation symmetry of order 3

    3. **(a)** **(i)** 396 inches

           (ii) 1010 cm

           (iii) 10.10 m

       (b) **(i)** 870 cm

           (ii) 43.935 m^2

           (iii) 130 m^2

B. **1.** 30 m

    2. 50 m^2

3. **(a)** 59 m^2

    (b) **(i)** Student's answer

       (ii) Student's answer

      (iii) Student's answer

C. **1.** 114 cm

    2. 5415 cm^2

    3. 38.76 kg

D. **1.** 11 : 1

    2. 75%

    3. Two 22k bracelets and six 9k bracelets

E. **1.** 15°

    2. **(a)** $\frac{1}{4}$

       (b) 1 : 4

       (c) 25%

    3. 8 m